MAR 17 1995

CLARK PUBLIC LIBRARY

DISCARD

883
Hom   Homer.
              The Iliad

CLARK PUBLIC LIBRARY
303 WESTFIELD AVENUE
CLARK, NJ 07066
908-388-5999

HOMER

THE ILIAD

HOMER

THE ILIAD

*Translated and with an Introduction
by* MICHAEL RECK

IconEditions
An Imprint of HarperCollins*Publishers*

THE ILIAD. Copyright © 1994 by the Estate of Michael Reck. All rights reserved.
Printed in the United States of America. No part of this book may be used or
reproduced in any manner whatsoever without written permission except in the
case of brief quotations embodied in critical articles and reviews. For information
address HarperCollins Publishers, Inc., 10 East 53rd Street, New York, NY 10022.

HarperCollins books may be purchased for educational, business, or sales promo-
tional use. For information, please write: Special Markets Department, Harper-
Collins Publishers, Inc., 10 East 53rd Street, New York, NY 10022.

FIRST EDITION

Designed by C. Linda Dingler
Map by Paul Pugliese

Library of Congress Cataloging-in-Publication Data

Homer.
  [Iliad. English]
  The Iliad / Homer : translated and with an introduction by Michael Reck. —
1st ed.
    p. cm.
  ISBN 0-06-430398-5
  1. Epic poetry, Greek—Translations into English. 2. Achilles (Greek mythol-
ogy)—Poetry. 3. Trojan War—Poetry. I. Reck, Michael. II. Title.
PA4025.A2R37 1994
883'.01—dc20   94-7340

94 95 96 97 98 ❖/RRD 10 9 8 7 6 5 4 3 2 1

Contents

The Iliad

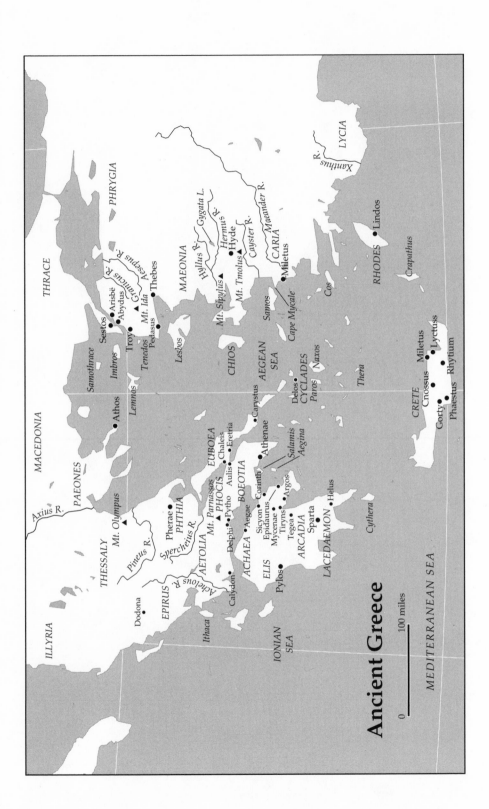

Ancient Greece

ILLYRIA

MACEDONIA

THRACE

PHRYGIA

PAEONES

Axius R.

Mt. Olympus ▲

THESSALY

Pineus R.

Spercheius R.

PHTHIA

Pherae ●

EPIRUS

Dodona ●

Ithaca

IONIAN SEA

Achelous R.

AETOLIA

Calydon ●

Mt. Parnassos ▲

PHOCIS

Delphi ● Pytho

Aegae

ACHAEA

ELIS

Pylos ●

Sicyon ●

Corinth ●

Epidaurus ●

Mycenae ●

Tiryns ●

Tegea ●

ARCADIA

Sparta ●

LACEDAEMON

Helus ●

EUBOEA

Chaleis ●

Eretria ●

Aulis ●

BOEOTIA

Athenae ●

Salamis

Aegina

Argos ●

Cythera

Samothrace

Imbros

Lemnos

Athos ●

Sestos ●

Abydus ●

Arisbē ●

Cranicus R.

Aesepus R.

Troy ●

Tenedos

Mt. Ida ▲

Pedasus ●

Thebes ●

Lesbos

CHIOS

Carystus ●

Deros ●

CYCLADES

Paros Naxos

Thera

AEGEAN SEA

MAEONIA

Hyllus R.

Gygata L.

Hermus R.

Hyde ●

Mt. Sipylus ▲

Mt. Tmolus ▲

Cayster R.

Maander R.

CARIA

Miletus ●

Samos

Cape Mycale

Cos

LYCIA

Xanthus R.

RHODES ● Lindos

Crapathus

CRETE

Miletus ●

Cnossus ●

Lyctuss ●

Gotty ●

Phaestus ●

Rhytium ●

MEDITERRANEAN SEA

0   100 miles

INTRODUCTION

Homer the Singer

The Oral Tradition

Spoken or chanted recitation carried Homer deep into the consciousness of the early Greeks. Ardent talkers ever, a people of open-air conversation, discussion, and debate—and of peripatetic philosophy—they derived their literature from the human voice. Papyrus scrolls were cumbrous to keep and costly to copy, so until at least the fourth century B.C., literature was normally *heard*, not read.

The original epic performers had actually sung or chanted to their own accompaniment on the lyre, adapting material from a vast traditional stock to create a new poem for each performance. Like Demodocus, blind bard at the Phaeacian court in the *Odyssey*, these ancient Greek jongleurs must have sung brief lays impromptu. But toward the end of the seventh century B.C., when literacy was already making inroads on the oral tradition, a staff began to be carried instead of a lyre, while the performers became mere reciters and ceased to sing.

These professional reciters, the "rhapsodes," brought the Homeric poems from city to city, competing for prizes at the great festivals. A red-figure amphora of about 490 B.C. depicts one of them, robed and holding a staff, which he may have thumped on the ground for emphasis while reciting. And Plato's dialogue *Ion* describes a rhapsode at a fourth-century festival: he stands on a dais richly clad, wears a golden wreath, declaims to an audience of twenty thousand, knows Homer by heart, weeps as he recites sad passages. Ion's performance was "rhapsodical" indeed, his histrionic declamation a sign the tradition was declining.

Not until our own century was it demonstrated how the *Iliad* and the *Odyssey* were actually made. Harvard professor Milman Parry (1902–1935), in his brilliant Sorbonne dissertation, proved that Homeric poetry's decorative epithets were created to fit the meter, and he showed that this whole system of set phrases is so complex that it could hardly have been created by a single man. Parry then went into the field to observe and record Yugoslavian folk singers, the *guslari*, and from their performance he drew analogies with Homeric practice. The *guslari* composed at the moment of recitation, "stitching together" phrases, verses, and themes from the oral tradition. This was what the ancient Greek bards had done, Parry concluded—and indeed the Greek word *rhapsodos* means literally "stitcher of songs."

An accomplished "song stitcher" had to learn his trade by practice, imitating and copying his masters before he could do his own songs. Hence Homer's renowned objectivity: the singer was expressing not himself but the material at hand, approaching his task as a craftsman who aims at doing a job well. The Greeks called the Muses daughters of Zeus and Memory—and the epic muse Calliope must have been an especially favored daughter, because a capacious memory was the tool of the singer's trade. Part of Homer's own superiority to the other bards may simply have been that his memory was better than theirs, so he had more metric phrases and epic themes for his inspired synthesizing. Such a memory-bound art lives not in the artist but in the tradition: the "individual talent" *becomes* the tradition.

This tradition lives in the air, not on the printed page, and sound is its very medium—as was noted by Parry, who found in Homer "a poetry controlled by patterns of sound to a degree far beyond that with which we are familiar," and by Ezra Pound, who wrote that the *Odyssey* had taught him "melodic invention." Homeric sound creates maximum impact and vivacity by cunningly reflecting the poetry's feeling and action. Re-creating Homer's medium—vivid, fluid sound—is the challenge of the translator.

Homer in History

Since Homeric epic was a coral-reef accumulation through countless generations, it must be immeasurably ancient. The Mycenean scholar T. B. L. Webster thinks that a silver vase of ca. 1600 B.C. illustrates "a very old story about a siege of a city by the sea," later attached to the Trojan tale. Two objects mentioned in the *Iliad*, the boar's-tusk helmet of Book 10 and Aias' shield, may be traced as far back as the fifteenth century. By 1210 B.C., when Homeric "Troy" was taken—Schliemann and his successors have shown it was on a hill four miles inland from the Dardanelles—itinerant bards would already have been making epic lays from a stock of themes and metric phrases. The battle at Troy was incorporated into this tradition of sung heroic poetry and began its long way through the centuries, one bard learning from another.

The fall of Troy came near the end of the Mycenean period, and in some respects Homer describes that brilliant Mycenean civilization accurately, though he composed long afterward: he knew where its urban centers were, and the poems' bronze armor and weapons, palaces and chariot warfare, reflect Mycenean reality. The tradition had told Homer this much. But the society depicted in the Homeric poems is a far later one—and in attempting to re-create that lost world of the Mycenean palaces, the *Iliad* far understates their wealth, as if such grandeur were inconceivable in the poet's own impoverished age.

The Trojan War was merely one aspect of a troubled time, with Mycenean civilization crumbling and all the eastern Mediterranean in turmoil. About 1200 B.C., the Hittite empire in central Anatolia collapsed, while the ancient kingdom of Egypt suffered mass piratical raids. Finally, with the sacking of Mycenae around 1100, the thousand-year Mycenean empire came to an end. In Greece this general destruction of the old order is loosely called "the Dorian invasion," a gradual hostile infiltration by a Greek-speaking people from the northwest. The process is poorly understood, and not all authorities follow Greek legend in attributing Mycenae's downfall exclusively to the Dorians—fratricidal warfare and climatic deterioration have also been blamed.

But the Dorians are historical, their existence shown by the fact that a West Greek dialect spread itself over the Peloponnesus during this period. Mycenean civilization was simply decapitated—the great palaces destroyed, their complex bureaucracy made defunct, the Mycenean syllabary alphabet forgotten—and life thereafter must have been primitive indeed. The conquerors introduced no new material characteristics whatsoever, and living standards sank to a very low level. Almost no architectural remains of this time may be found, for people lived in the plainest mud-brick huts.

As the only urban center to resist the Dorian onslaught, Athens became the preeminent Greek city. With most of Greece under barbarian domination, the Athenians could regard themselves as the heirs of the Mycenean past, and here the epic of Troy would have been sung on—doubtless as individual lays rather than poems anything like the length of our present *Iliad* and *Odyssey*. And here, with the native population swollen by refugees from the Dorians, a special language of oral epic developed, a blend from many dialects.

In these uneasy years, Athens produced a new form of ceramics, so-called geometric pottery, an artistic attempt to create order out of chaos in a Greek world overwhelmed by barbarians. With its figures in silhouette reduced to their minimal formal elements, geometric pottery is "an art stripped down to essentials just as life was stripped down to essentials with the collapse of the Mycenean palaces" (Webster). Our own *Iliad* text has astonishing symmetrical and parallel structures, traces of the geometrically ordered view of the universe that dominated those formative years in the epic tradition.

The Trojan War must have first been sung there on the Greek mainland: the Homeric gods live on Greek Olympus, the chief Greek heroes are from the mainland, and the *Odyssey* says that all the surviving leaders of the expedition went home after the war at Troy. None of the few meager Greek colonies in Asia Minor could be maintained after Mycenae fell. But as Dorian pressure increased, an outward movement across the Aegean began again, refugees funneled through Athens, forming its nucleus, and by the tenth century B.C., new Greek settlements had been founded along the Anatolian coast and on offshore islands such as Chios. These new colonizers of Asia Minor would have brought their epic with them. The songs of Troy—looking back to a great past when Mycenae had conquered Knossos and dominated the eastern Mediterranean—must have provided a heartening retrospect for poor Greek settlers among hostile natives.

Early Greek epic followed a pattern of oral traditions in many parts of the world. Originally made for recitation before kings and aristocrats, as the *Iliad*'s love of genealogies shows, the epic gradually became available to the whole people. Marketplace and tavern replaced the court as typical venue for epic performance, though values remained firmly pro-aristocratic—note, for example, the harsh treatment of the obstreperous commoner Thersites in *Iliad* 2.

These early epic songs were probably still short lays like Demodocus'. Such massive production as our Homeric epics would have required a venue of another kind, where bards could hold forth for days—and this became possible only in the new eastern colonies during the late ninth century or later. About that time, the Pan-Ionian Festival was established at Mykale, on a peninsula opposite Samos, to promote the political unity of these new Greek settlements in Asia Minor. Here and at the Delia on the island of Delos, epic singers competed with each other, at least informally. In the milieu of these early festivals many scholars seek "Homer."

But is there any Homer to seek? He is the shadowiest of literary figures, far more mysterious than even Shakespeare. We may even ask if he existed at all—or could "Homer" be merely, as Giambattista Vico surmised, a collective name for the creation of many generations of poets? The ancients themselves had no doubt of Homer's reality. They provided him with a number of biographies, largely or wholly ficti-tious, and almost any ancient epic was ascribed to him until Aristotle reduced the number to the *Iliad,* the *Odyssey,* and a burlesque epic poem called the *Margites.* Homer was believed to have been blind, like the *Odyssey's* Demodocus, his name interpreted (falsely, it seems) as meaning *"ho mē orōn,"* the unseeing one.

Homeric epic, blending dialects and objects from different periods, is doubtless a product of gradual evolution, the work of many bards—yet much argues for the assumption that the ancients were right and Homer did indeed exist. The poems show compelling signs of a single powerful creative genius: shrewd narrative strategy and use of fore-shadowing, psychological depths in characterization, the unparalleled clarity and brilliance of the verse itself. Moreover, the *Iliad* and the *Odyssey* have an inextricable unity of style and diction, while the system of formulas is consistent in the two epics. Both show an artistic and moral plan. Of course, the Homeric poems are composite works, as Parry showed—but for Homer, "composition" meant putting together composite parts, masterfully.

The author of our *Iliad* and the *Odyssey* almost certainly lived in Asia Minor. His poems are mainly in Ionic, the Greek dialect of the southern Asia Minor coast and some of the nearby islands, while the extended similes, so typically Homeric, are also of Ionian provenance and linguistically later than the rest of the poems. Homer's geographi-cal knowledge is precise and detailed concerning the Anatolian coast, vague concerning the Greek mainland, wild and woolly concerning Odysseus' home island of Ithaca, off to the west. Seven places in Asia Minor and its offshore islands disputed the honor of being Homer's birthplace in antiquity, the island of Chios having the best claim—mainly because (from at least the sixth century B.C.) it had a guild of singers, the Homerids, dedicated to preserving and reciting Homer's poems.

But were both poems made by the same mind? With rare excep-tions, antiquity thought they were, while some modern scholars have found that linguistic and literary differences between the two poems are so great they cannot have been by the same bard. Again, the ancients were probably right. Tone and vocabulary in the two poems are indeed different, but no more different than their subject matter.

Both depend heavily on a poetic tradition, in themes as well as language. The two poems are actually less different than, say, "early" and "late" Yeats. The unknown author of "On the Sublime" wrote in the first century A.D. that the *Iliad* was a work of Homer's youth, the *Odyssey* of his old age—and this is a reasonable assumption.

The Homeric poems' composite nature makes their dating difficult. Though certain linguistic features (contraction of verbs, the "digamma" sound) predate 900 B.C., much of the formulaic expression was created later than that time. Using the criterion of objects mentioned in the poems, it appears that nothing like our present *Iliad* existed until the 700s—the fact that Dorians and Athenians are virtually unmentioned merely showing the severe conservatism that ruled the choice of material. By the early 600s, echoes of Iliadic themes are found in pottery, painting, and literature. On the whole, it seems best to fix the final composition of the *Iliad* in the mid or late 700s B.C., the *Odyssey* a generation or so later.

Homer's century was then the eighth, and his epic reflects that age of restless exploration and change—sea voyages, overseas settlements, decline of the old monarchies, development of city-states. Schadewaldt shrewdly supposes that Homer was reinterpreting traditional heroic material in the light of his century's new awareness of psychological ambiguities. The eighth century also brought new consciousness of a Hellenic identity: the Olympic Games were established in 776 B.C., bringing Greeks together in athletic competition, while the Trojan War attracted more and more interest as an all-Greek enterprise, new cults being founded associated with Homeric figures—Helen, Agamemnon, Menelaus, and Odysseus.

Especially in the eastern settlements, audiences would have responded to the *Iliad*'s theme of a joint Hellenic expedition against an Asian enemy, and in fact the Pan-Ionian Festival aimed at strengthening the eastern colonists' sense of being Greek amid hostile Asian peoples. As refugees driven from their mainland homes by the Dorians, these eastern Greeks would have felt close to the *Odyssey*, that "epic of the displaced person" (Steiner). An era of overseas colonization would have welcomed the *Odyssey*'s theme of seafaring, perhaps even encouraged its creation.

But by far the most revolutionary of all the eighth century's innovations was the adaptation of the Phoenician alphabet to Greek. Among so many murky Homeric questions, one of the most debated is the relation between Homer and the new alphabet. How and when did a written Homeric text come into existence—and did writing help in its composition?

The Text Itself

After Parry's work, there can be no doubt whatsoever that Homer's style is oral. "At every point Homer's art presupposes recitation," C. M. Bowra noted justly. Yet the fact that Homer and the introduction of Greek writing were both in the mid eighth century encourages speculation as to whether writing had a role in the poems' composition.

Some scholars believe it did not. Albert Lord's field studies in Yugoslavia showed that writing corrupts the oral poet's style by making him use less formulary material, become more "literary." And because the Homeric poems so strictly adhere to the formula system that characterizes the oral style (usually a single phrase for each metrical need), Lord considers that writing could have played no part in the poems' composition. He does believe they were transcribed at the time they were composed, perhaps to Homer's dictation. Technical difficulties might argue against even this: eighth-century writing materials were quite possibly only leather (papyrus came to Greece at a later date), inadequate to large-scale works such as Homer's. In fact, only sketchy accounts of history survive from this time.

Yet the remarkable coincidence in time between Homer and the advent of the Greek alphabet strengthens the supposition that writing did assist Homer in composition, or that the poems were transcribed in his lifetime. Moreover, the *Iliad* and the *Odyssey* are unique in oral poetry—artistically more complex and almost unparalleled in length—which might indicate that their composition was somehow aided by writing. Lord may actually have been wrong in drawing analogies between contemporary Yugoslavian oral poetry and the early Greek situation, when there was no written culture that could influence an oral poet who decided to write his works down.

Oral improvisation would then account for the Homeric poems' development *before* they were set down in writing rather than for the poems as we have them now. Müller ingeniously supposes that writing was at first specialized, used to "create and record" the great epics of the Greek people long before it could be applied to other forms of extended discourse. If so, an eighth-century recording of Homer would be entirely possible.

Performance of the Homeric poems at those early Ionian festivals may even have *required* writing. Webster correctly surmises that the Homeric poems' artistic unity "compels us to assume continuous recital." However, a human voice does not have the strength to do this. In Yugoslavia, for example, Parry observed that the bards could usually chant twenty minutes at a stretch, and one performance even lasted over two hours—but nothing like the three days of steady recitation required to recite the entire *Iliad* at a festival. So Homer could not have sung it all himself. A team of reciters must have been needed, and a written text would have stabilized and coordinated their performance.

However the Homeric poems were first put down in writing, the oral tradition's age-long agglomeration must have come to an end by about 700 B.C., for the poems are virtually silent concerning anything datable after that time. The text's subsequent history is complex and speculative—and awe-inspiring in the tenacity with which men have clung to these great cultural treasures through the ages.

In the sixth century B.C., the Athenian tyrant Pisistratus or his son Hipparchus imported the Homeric poems to Attica, presumably from Asia Minor, and commanded that they be recited at the Pan-Athenaic Festival. One early source says that Hipparchus compelled the recitation of the poems "in due order." Scholars generally agree that this Athenian sponsorship gave only a superficial Attic coloring to the text. There was no conscious modernization, no discernible tinkering with the text. The Pisistrateans could not have done that even if they had wished to, the poems were already so well known, so greatly revered.

Yet in subsequent centuries—with countless copyists transmitting papyrus-roll texts and rhapsodes prone to histrionic exaggeration keeping up the oral tradition—the Homeric poems' vast popularity did not insure them against change. The epics tended to accumulate additional lines, as seen on early papyri that have survived in the Egyptian sands. At last, in the third and second centuries B.C., the Alexandrian scholars Zenodotus, Aristophanes of Byzantium, and Aristarchus rigorously excluded these additions, to establish a text that is more or less what we have now, and subsequent papyri very much resemble our present-day text.

Thereafter a gap of a millennium in the manuscript record, and an everlasting debt to medieval monks for copying and preserving the Homeric poems through all these centuries. Venetus A, an *Iliad* text from the tenth century A.D., is the earliest complete manuscript and the best one. Its publication in 1788 marks the beginning of modern Homeric scholarship and readership.

Homer's Vision

William Butler Yeats, a lifelong lover of Homer, wanted his own verse "cold and passionate as the dawn." Homer views the events of war in just this way—coldly because he sees battle and death as plain facts of life and knows that fate is inescapable, passionately because he feels for the grand gestures of heroism and for men's suffering in war. Macleod's comment is profound: "What war represents for Homer is humanity under duress and in the face of death; and so to enjoy or appreciate the *Iliad* is to understand and feel for human suffering."

The *Iliad* is first and foremost about heroism. Facing danger bravely, steadfastness and devotion to the task, loyalty to friends— these elements of the "heroic code" powerfully evoked in the *Iliad* are part of any life lived decently. So the *Iliad* intimately concerns even those of us who have never seen a battlefield and never want to. We feel the exhilaration of the heroic life in images like this:

> As a skilled equestrian harnesses up
> a team of four superlative horses
> to drive them thundering toward a city
> along a straight highway, while passersby
> stare amazed as he leaps unerringly
> from horse to horse and they gallop onward—
> thus giant Aias moved from deck to deck
> with mighty strides, voice rising to the sky
> as he roared horribly for his warriors
> to save their ships.
>
> (15.679–688)

Paradoxically enough, battle itself seems to interest the chronicler of the Trojan War rather little. Details of combat are described only briefly, skill in arms or strategy are hardly considered. Duels generally end in the death of one of the participants, and wounds are ignored—

not a palliation of war's horrors but simply an elimination of super-fluities, Griffin notes acutely. What does concern Homer is heroism: how a man faces death.

The *Iliad* sees the end of life as unmitigated disaster. There is no consolation or reward for the dead, the afterlife being only a shadow existence—worth less than the most miserable day among the living, Achilles declares when he meets Odysseus in Hades. The horror and pathos of death are stressed, as when Achilles drags Hector's body behind his chariot after the duel that culminates the *Iliad:*

> Hector was dragged in a dust cloud, his dark
> hair streaming wildly, his head—once so fair—
> smeared with dust, now Zeus had abandoned him
> to humiliation in his own homeland.
>
> (22.401–404)

In the light of death's overwhelming catastrophe, battle glory becomes an "insubstantial pageant." This awareness brings no complaint, as when Achilles says:

> In battle a man wins cattle and sheep,
> and in trade he gets cauldrons and horses,
> but once a man has breathed out his soul
> neither trade nor battle will win it back.
>
> (9.406–409)

Such stark, clear-eyed realism is quintessentially the *Iliad*'s. Thoreau, who kept the *Iliad* on his table at Walden, wrote as a man steeped in the text: "Be it life or death, we crave only reality. If we are really dying, let us hear the rattle in our throats and feel cold in the extremities; if we are alive, let us go about our business."

In scene after scene, force is shown as momentarily victorious but ultimately futile. And with the poem's last book, the circle of violence and vengeance is finally broken: Achilles courteously receives Priam, father of his greatest enemy, and they weep together, each for his own loss—Achilles for Patroclus, Priam for Hector. "We hear you, old man, were once happy too," says Achilles, quietly drawing himself into the picture of general suffering.

This moving encounter of Achilles and Priam brings a note of forgiveness and compassion. It may well have been Homer's creation out of his inherited heroic material. In his mouth, a tale of Greek victory becomes a moral exploration of war, with no villains, no "cause," no thesis. Since both sides suffer, both are viewed with sympathy and both have their heroes and exploits. The tale is told so dispassionately that even its omnipresent pathos is subdued, immanent in the nature of things presented with such direct vision.

Achilles' evolution from unbridled wrath against Agamemnon to forgiveness, from savage fury against the Trojans to compassionate reception of Priam, gives the *Iliad* its moral axis. At the conclusion of the poem, with "tragedy wrought to the uttermost," he emerges grander than ever, but morally, not militarily. He has accepted fate—as Hector too accepts fate in deciding to face Achilles and in the end, despite momentary fear and ignominious flight, dies grandly.

Military glory is mere illusion for another reason: warriors are really pawns of the gods, utterly subject to fate. Even the culminating combat brings Achilles no glory— Athena has played the decisive role in his victory over Hector. Yet this overwhelming power of fate and the gods does not mean that the *Iliad*'s characters *feel* helpless. The poem is actually rich in gusto and enjoyment of physical existence, and fate is not felt as an oppressing force—in the manner of, say, Thomas Hardy. Men know that fate rules all, but the uncertainty as to what its decrees actually are, and when and how they will be fulfilled, gives leeway for free action.

Neither is the gods' power felt as crushing. For all their vast superiority to men, the Olympians belong to no different realm of being. Men are often compared to gods, and gods have human form, being simply more powerful than men as well as ageless and immortal. There are no monstrous Olympians—the vaguely defined "Old Hundred Hands" being far in the past—and the miraculous element is kept within strict bounds. The Olympians can be merely an external expression of men's feeling, a kind of metaphor, and their actions in the world usually symbolically correspond to what was motivated by purely human circumstances. This makes almost everything in Homer visible and adds to the impact of the verse.

These rather this-worldly gods are, however, by no means a merely decorative or playfully literary convention. The Olympians' intervention on earth gives men's activities heightened significance in terms of the divine, and at the same time humbles them, showing mortals helpless before the gods' power—as Achilles recognizes at the end of the Iliad:

> The gods have spun this fate for wretched men:
> to live in pain, while they themselves have none.
>
> (24.525–526)

The gods are central to the meaning of mortal existence—its grandeur as well as its degradation.

Yet Homer's Olympians—often trivial, frivolous, and petty—can hardly form a moral pattern for men. They are sometimes portrayed humorously, even satirically, in a way we may find hard to understand. Of course, laughter and high seriousness are not necessarily mutually exclusive, as witness English "metaphysical poetry" or Zen Buddhism. And the Homeric gods' very amorality is an indication of their awe-inspiring power—they need give no account to men by any standards of earthly morality. They are as amoral as nature itself.

Herodotus believed Homer and Hesiod had defined the Greek gods—and one of Homer's innovations, influenced by divine society in Near Eastern religion, may have been to put the gods in a pantheon on Mount Olympus. This idea was foreign to later Greek belief, which continued to emphasize local religious cults in crude forms quite unlike Homer's sophisticated Olympian society. Homeric Olympus is a cosmos of bickering and banter, intrigue and maneuvering for power—but with no fatal consequences, hence carefree and light-hearted. From the gods' exalted eminence, little is really serious.

Homer's Artless Art

Because of its oral nature, the *Iliad* moves with marvelous speed—"like the wind," as Mozart said of his *Haffner* Symphony. After all, if the story had not been straightforward and immediately accessible, a listening crowd would merely have wandered off. Ezra Pound wrote me when I was just beginning my translation, putting his pincers on the essence of Homeric style: "Nobody will care a damn about the metre if there is FLOW."

The *Iliad*'s FLOW comes from its translucent simplicity—events are clearly ordered, with syntax paratactical—without connectives—subordinate clauses relatively rare. This plainness, so necessary in the oral style, gives the poem its kinetic energy. Alexander Pope excellently summarized the matter when he wrote of Virgil: "Nature and Homer were, he found, the same." Homer's stylistic starkness, with frequent descriptions of elemental things of nature, does make his great effects seem natural phenomena themselves.

These evocations of elemental nature, usually found in the similes, well deserve the epithet "sublime," applied to Homer by readers over two millennia. Such breathtaking moments—James Joyce called them "epiphanies"—are often pictures of natural energy, as when Thetis "leapt hawklike from snowy Olympus" (18.615), but they may also be images of tranquillity, evoking nature's awesome vastness, like the still mist in 5.522–526 or the stars in 8.555–559. Here we remember that many Olympians were nature gods and Zeus ruled the sky. The world is divine.

Homer's sublimity can appear in humble minutiae too, such as that renowned comparison of the Trojan elders to "crickets that sit on some tree / where they pour their lily-like voices forth" (3.151–152), or the warriors battling for Sarpedon's armor:

> They swarmed all about his body like flies
> which buzz and murmur through a farmer's pens
> in springtime, when milk overflows the pails. . . .
>   (16.641–643)

This evocation of utter tranquillity amid maximum violence is a favorite ironic jolt of Homeric style, found also in Achilles' pursuit of Hector past the washing basins "where the Trojan women / went to wash their very finest clothing / in peacetime, before the Achaeans came" (22.154-156) and in another grand picture of nature:

> As a star rises among stars at night—
> Hesperus, loveliest in the heavens—
> so shone the pointed spear that Achilles
> brandished in his right hand for Hector's doom
> as he scanned him seeking a place to stab.
>   (22.317–321)

Such moments as these are indeed "sublime," with that overwhelming impact which made Emily Dickinson, in the presence of the greatest poetry, feel she was being scalped. Their power lies in their particulars.

"The truth is concrete," Bertolt Brecht observed, and the *Iliad*'s tale is told truthfully in a Brechtian sense, its concrete particulars often unobtrusively representing more than themselves. Consider—a few examples among a myriad— Poseidon's feet, the sea beasts, and the dry axle in 13.17–31, and the wolves' slender tongues in 16.155–167. Homer chooses his particulars so well that the story appears to tell itself.

This skillful handling of detail is essential to Homer's "emotional writing in the dispassionate style," as Griffin calls it, and defines an impersonality that makes his art seem artless. "Many-minded Homer" (Yeats's phrase) feels for much because he keeps emotional distance from all, so even his most poignant scenes are not sentimental or moralizing. Yeats, who "Cast a cold eye / On life, on death," and Flaubert, with his *"sobriété dans la pathétique et la précision du détail,"* were Homer's epigones in this respect. But he has no equals.

The *Iliad*'s objective attitude reflects a profound perception of war's futility. Both sides are sacrificed to that futility, so the two are treated impartially—as in the stunning last lines of Book 4, where

> so many Trojans and Danaans that day
> lay facedown in dust by one another.

With biting irony, the onetime opponents are shown "facedown in dust," this concrete particular expressing all the indignity of their inglorious end and the degradation of war itself.

Irony, undercutting all heroic deeds, is at the heart of Homer's art. The whole epic itself is built on an irony: Achilles' appeal to Zeus is granted, but unbeknownst to him, this will cost the life of his dearest friend, Patroclus. At the very end, Achilles realizes that the gods' purposes are inscrutable and kindly receives Priam, seeing for the first time how things really are. His dispassion means compassion, and the poem leaves him doomed but undeluded. The gap between reality and what Achilles thinks is true has finally been bridged, the terrible ironic tension resolved.

Concerning This Translation

After Milman Parry's work in the 1920s and 1930s—a watershed in epic studies—we can be sure that the Homeric poems were made for speaking. Parry went into the Montenegrin mountains, recorded large amounts of contemporary folk poetry, and by showing similarities to Homer, demonstrated beyond doubt that Homer composed in an oral style. Hence my new translation of the *Iliad* for the spoken voice.

"The Word as spoken or sung" (Harry Levin's phrase) is in fact the medium of our own time as it was of Homer's. We too live in an oral and aural age—vide McLuhan—and ever since Whitman, the swing of spoken language has buoyed up much of our poetry. If each age needs its own translations, those for our time should be speakable.

Homeric meter—based on syllable length and not stress, with rules of substitution unknown to our language—cannot be re-created in English. Therefore I have chosen the form that seemed best for rendering Homer's metrical tautness: a ten-syllable roughly iambic line. I translate almost line for line, often word for word, treating only the epithets freely. These I add or omit at will for reasons of metric, as the Homeric singers themselves did.

My reader should, in the mind's ear, hear a voice chanting or declaiming, "the song firm and well given" (Pound, Canto 52). The translation may be read aloud, with proper pauses at the end of lines and an emphasis on rhythm—or even intoned out of doors, as was the original. Melody is all.

I have tried to re-create that breathtaking speed which Matthew Arnold called a characteristic of Homer's style. W. F. Jackson Knight wrote truly that the best translations of Homer are the simplest, which do not clog the story by extraordinary or archaic words. To be sure, the *Iliad*'s Greek was a conglomerate never actually spoken as such, but this poetic language was so familiar to its audience that it could not block the poem's flow. The Homeric epics were formed when all language was talk, and they are alive with real speech.

Pound defined literature as "news that stays news." So the *Iliad* stays fresh as dawn for us today. My translation is for readers who wish to enjoy Homer as his contemporaries heard him.

HOMER

THE ILIAD

Book One: The Rage

The Greeks—called Achaeans, Argives, or Danaans—have been besieging Troy for nine years. Their commander, Agamemnon, Atreus' son, seizes the lady Briseis, captive of his best warrior, Achilles.

Sing, Goddess, Achilles' maniac rage:
ruinous thing! it roused a thousand sorrows
and hurled many souls of mighty warriors
to Hades, made their bodies food for dogs
and carrion birds—as Zeus's will foredoomed—
from the time relentless strife came between
Atreus' son, a king, and brave Achilles.

   Which immortal brought about that quarrel?
None but Apollo—he sent pestilence
to ravage the Achaeans: indignant   10
Agamemnon had spurned his priest Chryses,
who came to those high-beaked ships on the beach
with a vast ransom for his daughter, held
the wreaths of archer Apollo upraised
on a golden staff and implored them all,
especially their two distinguished lords:
"Atreus' sons and you other Achaeans,
may the gods on Olympus grant that you
sack Priam's city and return safe home,
but take the ransom, release my dear child,   20
respect Apollo's unspeakable power."

   And all the other warriors roared hurrah
for reverencing the priest, taking ransom,
but Atreus' son Agamemnon was not

pleased a bit, sent him scathingly away:
"Now see here, you old man, let me never
catch you hanging around our ships again,
or the god's staff and wreaths may not save you.
I won't free that girl, she will stay with me
till old age takes her in Argos, my home,   30
working the loom and lying in my bed.
Don't vex me—go away while you still can."

   That aged priest was frightened and obeyed,
slipped silently off by the booming sea,
and after he had gone some distance, prayed
fervently to far-worker Apollo:
"O Silverbow who stands over Chrysë
and holy Cilla, who rules Tenedos,
god of pestilence, remember how I
honored you with delightful offerings   40
of bulls and goats, so fulfill my appeal:
let them pay for my tears with your arrows."

   Phoebus Apollo granted his prayer,
strode from tall Olympus in a fury,
quiver and bow slung over his shoulders,
and the arrows clattered upon his back
as that god advanced. He came like the night.
Not far from the ships he knelt down and shot
with a dreadful crash of his silver bow:
first ravaged the mules, next those agile hounds,   50
and the warriors themselves felt his weapons
sting—and pyres for the dead burned everywhere.

   Nine days long the god's arrows swept their camp,
then Achilles summoned an assembly
on the inspiration of queen Hera,
who pitied her people as they perished.
After those Danaans had come together
Achilles rose among them and declared:
"Atreus' son, now we may be driven off
and sail for home, if we survive at all,   60
with war and plague both devastating us.

But let's ask a soothsayer or a priest
or some interpreter of sacred dreams
who can tell us why that god is angry,
if we failed in vows or in sacrifice,
and he may take offerings of lambs or goats
to save our people from his pestilence."

After he had spoken, he sat. And up
rose Calchas, most distinguished diviner,
who knew all past and present and future   70
and had guided the Danaan ships to Troy
by his prophecy, gift of Apollo.
Then he addressed them with these measured words:
"Very well, Achilles—you wish to know
why archer Apollo is indignant,
so I shall tell you. But first you must swear
to defend me with your words and your deeds,
because what I say will infuriate
a man who rules our people mightily.
An angry king can crush a commoner—   80
though he swallows his rage that very day,
he won't give up his grudge till he gets me.
Consider it well: can you keep me safe?"

And swiftfooted Achilles answered him:
"Courage, dear fellow—tell us what you know.
I swear by Apollo, whom you invoke
when you declare your oracles to us,
no one, while I live and see on this earth,
will lay heavy hands on you by our ships—
no one here, not even Agamemnon,   90
who boasts he is far better than us all."

That wise diviner took heart and declared:
"It's no matter of vows or sacrifice
but only the priest that Agamemnon
slighted when he wouldn't free his daughter—
therefore the god has ravaged us, and will.
Our Danaans cannot be out of danger
till that girl is returned to her father

unransomed and holy sacrifice sent
to Chrysë. Then Apollo might relent."   100

 After he had spoken, he sat. And up
rose Atreus' son mighty Agamemnon,
fuming: his dark heart was drenched with anger
and his eyes glittered like flickery flame.
Glaring fiercely at Calchas, he bellowed:
"Not a single pleasant word for me, eh?
Yes, you love to prophesy trouble, won't
say anything good or make it happen.
So now you'd like to persuade our people
Apollo has afflicted us because   110
I decline to ransom Chryses' daughter
and would rather keep her for my own home.
Well, I prefer her to Clytemnestra,
my own wedded wife—she's just as pretty
and not inferior in intelligence.
I shall give her back if it's better so—
a prince must see to his people's welfare—
though I must have some replacement: I can't be
the only one here without some booty,
and all of you see I'm letting her go."   120

 Then Peleus' son Achilles answered:
"Glorious Agamemnon, greedy man,
what replacement can possibly be given?
We made no depot of common treasure—
all we captured has been distributed,
and taking that back would not be proper.
Return her, as the god commands, and you
shall have three or four times more after Zeus
allows us to sack that city of Troy."

 Glorious Agamemnon roared in reply: 130
"You may be good at battle, Achilles,
but you can't put anything past me!
So you may keep your plunder, why should I
go without? You'd like me to give up mine?
Our people can grant me another prize

that suits my mind, a gift equal to yours—
if not, I'll go myself and take something
of yours or of Aias or Odysseus.
The person I come to will not be glad.
But we can consider all this later—   140
now let's set a ship on the rippling sea
with a crew of sturdy rowers, oxen
for sacrifice, and Chryses' fair daughter
herself. And we'll choose a canny captain—
Aias or Idomeneus or Odysseus
or even you, terrible Achilles—
to appease the anger of Apollo."

And nimble Achilles shouted, scowling:
"Ah, you unscrupulous shifty scoundrel,
why did our people obey your commands   150
and travel so far to fight your battles?
No Trojan spearmen had ever harmed me
before I came here to enter combat—
neither stolen my cattle and horses
nor plundered my harvests back in Phthia,
since a good deal lies between our peoples,
shadowy mountains and the booming sea.
But we all followed you here, you swindler,
to get revenge for you and your brother—
and little gratitude we've had for it.   160
This time you threaten to take the lady
I won in war, a gift from our people.
I never have booty like yours when we
sack some prosperous Trojan citadel,
though almost all the desperate fighting
falls to my hands. If spoils are ever split,
yours is far more, while I bring some trinket
back to the ships when I weary of war.
Now I'll take my people home to Phthia—
I don't believe we can stay around here   170
making you wealthy after this insult!"

   Atreus' son Agamemnon answered him:
"Well, go, if you want to! You won't hear me
begging you to stay! I've many others
who will honor me—most of all, wise Zeus.
I hate you more than any of our lords,
you're so fond of quarrels and war and strife.
Though you may be strong, a god gave you that.
Go on home with your ships and your people,
rule over your Myrmidons, I don't care,   180
be angry all you wish. But listen here:
since Apollo has claimed Chryses' daughter,
a ship shall be sent with my own comrades
to return her, while I take your lady,
lovely Briseis—I'll come for her myself
so you know who's mightier and no one
will ever try to rival me again."

   Now Achilles stayed in a fury, torn
by indecision as he considered
whether to take that sharp sword by his side   190
and cut Agamemnon down on the spot
or hold his temper and control himself.
But as he stood there wrestling with his thoughts
and drawing his great sword, Athena came
from heaven at the behest of Hera,
who loved both warriors and watched over them.
She seized Achilles' blond hair from behind,
invisible to everyone but him.
That son of Peleus turned amazed and knew
Athena, her eyes flashed so terribly,   200
and addressed her in agitated words:
"Why have you come again, daughter of Zeus?
To witness Agamemnon's insolence?
Well, you'll see what will happen very soon:
this barefaced arrogance will cost his life."

   The goddess green-eyed Athena replied:
"I came to calm you—if you obey me—
from heaven at the behest of Hera,
who loves you both and watches over you.

So control your temper, don't draw your sword,   210
but scold him as much as your heart desires,
and let me assure you, my dear fellow:
some day you'll receive splendid recompense
for this insult. Calm down, do as I say."

   And Peleus' son swift Achilles answered:
"Very well, goddess, I know it's better
to hold my temper as you two command,
for the gods help mortals who do their will."

   His huge hand stayed still on the silver hilt,
then he slipped that weapon back, obeying   220
Athena's instructions—and off she raced
to rejoin the gods in Zeus's palace.

   But Achilles remained in a fury
and roared his rage at lord Agamemnon:
"You big drunkard, you fainthearted swindler,
you don't dare battle beside our people
or go with the commanders on ambush—
for that sort of thing gives you the shivers!
You'd rather stay back in our camp instead
and plunder anyone who disobeys.   230
Ruthless king, you rule over nobodies,
or this would be your last slight, Atreus' son.
Now I swear and declare a mighty oath
by this speaker's staff, which never again
will grow green branches since someone hacked it
from its stump in the mountains, stripped away
its leaves and bark, and now our Achaeans
solemnly hold it to proclaim justice
in Zeus's name—by this same staff I swear
someday your men will long for Achilles,   240
every one of them, while you stand helpless
to stop that fierce Hector from murdering
many. Then you'll eat your heart out with grief
you insulted your most glorious warrior."

   After Peleus' son had said this, he flung
the gold-studded staff to the ground and sat.
Agamemnon stood there furious. But up
rose Nestor, most eloquent orator,
whose speech flowed sweet as honey from his tongue.
He'd already seen two generations   250
pass away, people born and bred with him
back in Phthia, and now he ruled the third.
Then he addressed them with these measured words:
"What a disaster for our Achaeans!
How Priam and his haughty progeny
and all his people will be delighted
when they hear you two have been quarreling,
our wisest, our best on the battlefield!
But listen here: you're both younger than me,
and warriors more powerful than you   260
have been my companions, heeded my words.
I've never seen such people, never will—
men like Peirithous and fiery Dryas,
Caenius, Exadius, Polyphemus,
and illustrious Theseus, the gods' own peer,
mightiest men who ever walked on earth,
mighty men who fought mighty enemies,
mountain centaurs, and massacred many.
Warriors like these were my comrades in arms
after I came to them at their summons.   270
I battled beside them as an equal,
and no one on earth is a match for them,
but they were careful to heed my advice.
So you two should also respect my words.
Your majesty, don't take away that girl,
let her stay with the lord who won her first.
And you, Peleus' son, must respect a king—
remember it's no common distinction
to be a monarch glorified by Zeus.
You're powerful indeed, a goddess' son,   280
but he ranks higher because he rules more.
And you, Agamemnon, keep your temper,

don't be indignant with prince Achilles,
our people's bulwark in bitter battle."

   Atreus' son Agamemnon answered him:
"What you say is entirely correct, sir,
but this man wants to be above us all,
lord it over all, domineer us all,
and there's one person here won't knuckle under.
Even if the gods made him our mightiest,   290
does that give him an excuse to abuse—?"

   But illustrious Achilles cut him off:
"They'd call me a coward, good for nothing,
if I yielded to everything you say.
You can order them around, but not me—
I'll never obey your orders again.
Now let me tell you this, and I mean it:
I won't lift a hand to defend the girl,
since you're only taking back what you gave—
but you will not grab any other thing   300
I keep as my own beside my beaked ship.
Come try it if you wish, and you shall see
dark blood will be dripping about my spear."

   When this rough exchange of words was finished,
those two rose and dismissed the assembly.
Agile Achilles returned to his camp
with Patroclus and his other comrades,
while Atreus' son ordered a swift ship launched
with a crew of twenty rowers, oxen
for sacrifice, and Chryses' fair daughter   310
herself—and Odysseus went as captain.

   So they set sail on the watery ways
while Atreus' son commanded solemn rites
to wash their defilement into the brine,
then offered Apollo a sacrifice
of bulls and goats beside the restless sea:
its odor swirled to heaven with the smoke.

Thus they were busied—but Agamemnon
didn't forget his threat to Achilles,
called Talthybius and Eurybates,   320
his estimable heralds, and told them:
"I want you to visit Achilles' camp
and take her away, his lovely Briseis.
If he should decline, I shall come myself
with many warriors—much the worse for him."

So he sent them off with this harsh command.
They went uneasily by the restless sea
till they reached those Myrmidon ships and tents.
Beside his ship they found prince Achilles
seated—and he was not glad to see them.   330
In terror and awe of that commander
they stood without saying a word, but he
knew just what was on their minds and declared:
"Heralds, I wish you a very good day.
Come, I don't blame you but Agamemnon,
who has sent you for this lady Briseis.
Very well then, bring her out, Patroclus,
and let them have her. But they're witnesses
before the blessed gods and all mortals
and before their cruel master, if ever   340
I'm needed to stave off some disaster
from our armies. That man has lost his mind,
he can't consider reasonably how
to save our people in their greatest need."

Patroclus did as his friend had ordered,
brought that rosy-cheeked Briseis from the tent
and handed her over—so they returned
with the unwilling girl. But Achilles
left his people, walked down the beach, weeping,
gazed over the wine-dark waters and prayed   350
to his divine mother with hands upraised:
"Ah, Mother, since my life will be so short,
at least I might have been given honor
by thunderlord Zeus—but now I have none.

Our commander, mighty Agamemnon,
has played me false, made off with my lady."

   His illustrious mother heard him from where
she sat in the deeps by her ancient sire,
and rose from the murky sea like a mist,
seated herself before him as he wept,   360
and stroked him with her fingers, murmuring:
"My child, why these tears? Have you some trouble?
Speak up, tell me, don't keep it a secret."

   Achilles groaned heavily and replied:
"You know all things, so why should I say it?
We sacked Eëtion's sacred city Thebes,
brought all the battle booty back with us here,
and when it was split, that son of Atreus
took Chryses' incomparable daughter.
Her father, priest to mighty Apollo,   370
approached the Achaean ships on the beach
with a vast ransom for his daughter, held
the wreaths of archer Apollo upraised
on a golden staff, and implored them all,
especially their two distinguished lords.
And all the other warriors roared hurrah
for reverencing the priest, taking ransom,
but Atreus' son Agamemnon was not
pleased a bit, sent him scathingly away.
The priest went back furious—and Apollo   380
granted his prayer, for he loved him dearly,
and bombarded the Achaeans, so they
died in droves, as the god's bitter arrows
ravaged our camp. A canny diviner
told us what was troubling the Far Shooter,
and I advised them to appease that god,
which made Agamemnon most indignant.
He stood threatening me, and now he did it—
sent a ship to return the priest's daughter
to Chrysë, with presents for Apollo,   390
and the heralds have just taken away
the lady Briseis, my battle booty.

But help me, help your son, if you're able:
go to Olympus, entreat Zeus by all
you ever said or did to make him glad.
You often boasted in my father's home
that you alone among the immortals
had saved our Zeus from a shameful defeat
when the other Olympians trussed him up—
Poseidon, Athena, and queen Hera.   400
You came, great goddess, and loosened his bonds
with help from that hundred-handed monster
the gods call Briareus and mortals
Aegaeon, his father Poseidon's peer.
Yes, he took his seat by thunderlord Zeus,
and the blessed gods abandoned their plan.
Remind him of this now, kneel before him
and beg him to help those Trojan armies
till they pen our people by the ships' sterns
with awful slaughter. Then they'll love their king,   410
and Atreus' son Agamemnon may learn
he was mad to insult his best warrior."

    Silverfoot Thetis answered him, weeping:
"My dear child, why did I ever rear you?
If only you were spared this misery
by the ships, since your life will be so brief:
you're doomed to an early death and endless
sorrow—and I gave you birth for all this.
All right, I shall take your message to Zeus
at his palace on snowy Olympus   420
while you wait here by your seafaring ships
and rage if you wish, but stay out of war.
Only yesterday king Zeus went away
to feast in Ethiopia with all the gods—
but after twelve days, when he comes again,
I'll fall at his feet in supplication,
and I expect our appeal will succeed."

    Then she departed and left Achilles
angrily brooding over the lady
armed force had taken, while shrewd Odysseus   430

came to Chrysë with those gifts for the god.
After they put inside the deep harbor
they furled their sails and stowed them in the hold,
brought the mast to the crutch by its forestays
and quickly rowed the ship to its moorings,
dropped anchor stones, and fastened the hawsers—
and out stepped the men onto the sea beach
and out came the cattle for Apollo
and out came Chryses' delightful daughter.
Shrewd Odysseus led her to the altar   440
and placed her in her father's arms, saying:
"Chryses, king Agamemnon has sent me
to return your girl and make sacrifice
so we may appease that powerful god
who has brought such sorrows on our people."

    And the aged priest joyfully embraced
his own dear child. Then they brought their oxen
to the altar of archer Apollo,
washed their hands and took sacred barley grains.
And Chryses prayed aloud with hands upraised: 450
"O Silverbow who stands over Chrysë
and holy Cilla, who rules Tenedos,
just as you heeded my prayer before
and ravaged their armies to honor me,
fulfill my supplication once again:
save the Danaans from that disgusting plague."

    Phoebus Apollo granted his prayer.
After they prayed and sprinkled barley grains,
they slit the oxen's throats and flayed the hides,
carved up the shanks and covered them in fat,   460
a double layer dressed with raw meat pieces.
These the priest cooked on sticks and poured red wine
for the gods, as young men stood by with their forks.
When Apollo's offering, the shanks, was done,
they carved up all the rest and spitted it,
roasted it well, and slipped it from the spits.
When the work was finished, their meal prepared,
they feasted of that abundant banquet.

And when they had dined to their hearts' content,
young men brought bowls brimful of mellow wine,   470
made libations, and everyone was served.
So all day long those Achaean warriors
chanted charming hymns to appease the god
who fells from afar. He heard and was glad.

  As the sun descended and darkness came
they lay down to sleep by the ship's moorings,
and just as dawn's rosy fingers appeared
they set sail for the great Achaean camp
with a fair wind from archer Apollo.
Having raised the mast, they spread their white sails;   480
wind filled the mainsail, and the murky deep
swashed and surged on the prow as they hurried
over those waves on their watery way.
Thus they came to the great Achaean camp
and immediately dragged that high-beaked ship
onto the beach, put long props beneath it,
then scattered here and there among the tents.

  But he stayed raging beside his swift ships,
Peleus' magnificent son Achilles—
went neither to the people's assemblies   490
nor into that terrible battle but
sat eating his heart out, longing for war.

  At the twelfth dawn after their departure
those everlasting gods came trooping back
from their feast. Thetis hadn't forgotten
her son's appeal, so she rose from the waves
and unto Olympus at break of day.
She found thunderlord Zeus seated apart
on steep Olympus' very highest peak,
then knelt before him and embraced his knees   500
with her left hand, chucked his chin with the right,
and implored that lordly son of Cronos:
"Ah, father Zeus, if ever I pleased you
by my words or deeds, fulfill my prayer:
honor my son, who is doomed to perish

so very soon. Mighty Agamemnon
has played him false, made off with his lady.
Avenge him, majestic Olympian Zeus:
let the Trojans triumph, till those Argives
reward my son with some rich recompense."   510

But thunderlord Zeus sat there in silence,
whereupon lovely Thetis hugged his knees
even closer, implored him once more:
"Nod to me as a sign that you promise,
or refuse—it's your royal privilege—
so I may know how much you despise me."

Very much vexed, cloudgathering Zeus answered:
"Oh my, what trouble you'll get me into
with Hera—she will scold me even more.
Even now she's telling the other gods   520
I favor the Trojan side in battle.
Away with you now, or you may be seen
by Hera, and let me think it over.
All right, all right, I shall—and bow my head,
for among the gods this is the surest
pledge: once I have bowed, my word's never false,
never recalled, and never unfulfilled."

Thus Cronos' son spoke, and bowed his dark brows—
and those ambrosial locks shook forward on
his godly head, as great Olympus quaked.   530

After they settled things between them, she
leapt from bright Olympus into the sea,
while Zeus returned home. All the immortals
rose from their seats before their father—none
dared remain, but each god ran to greet him.
So he sat on his throne. Yet queen Hera
hadn't failed to notice his conference
with silverfoot Thetis, nymph of the sea,
and spoke most cuttingly to Cronos' son:
"And what are you up to now, you rascal?   540
You always like to work behind my back

in that sneaky way of yours—you'll never
tell me honestly what you really think."

Then the father of gods and men replied:
"Hera, don't spy into everything of mine—
you might be surprised, although you're my wife.
Whatever is proper for you to learn
you shall, before any gods or mortals—
but when I desire to make my own plans,
do not, if you please, inquire into that."   550

And gentle-eyed queen Hera answered him:
"You dreadful fellow, what a thing to say!
I never once pried into your affairs
but let you do exactly as you wish.
And now I'm afraid that you may be fooled
by silverfoot Thetis, nymph of the sea,
who came this morning to kneel before you—
and I believe you agreed Achilles
will have your blessing, while many perish."

Whereupon cloudgathering Zeus replied: 560
"My love, you exercise your mind too much.
You may be sure this talk will only serve
to estrange us further—the worse for you.
And even if it's true, such is my will.
So sit down quiet and be a good wife,
for none of the gods could help you if I
should choose to beat some sense into you."

Then gentle-eyed queen Hera was frightened
and held her temper and sat down silent,
while the gods were vexed in Zeus's palace.   570
And artisan Hephaestus spoke up first
to console his mother, white-armed Hera:
"Oh, this is terrible, a disaster,
you two quarreling because of mortals
and making such a fuss. Our glorious feasts
will not be joyful with this contention.
I should think my mother might be wiser
and treat mighty Zeus affectionately,

so he won't scold her and ruin our feasts.
Why, what if that Lightning Lord took a mind   580
to bowl us over? He very well could.
Be kindly to the Olympian, mother,
and soon he'll be gracious again, I'm sure."

Up he leapt, took the double-handled cup,
and laid it in her lovely hands, saying:
"Endure your tribulations, Mother dear.
I should hate to see you being beaten
and me entirely unable to help,
the Olympian's such a tough opponent.
Remember when I tried to save you last?   590
He grabbed my foot, flung me out of heaven,
and all day long I fell, till at sunset
down I came in Lemnos, little life left,
where the Sintian people took care of me."

The goddess white-armed Hera smiled at this
and, smiling, received the cup from her son.
Next he dipped sweet nectar out of the bowl
and poured it for the others, left to right.
So heady laughter rose among the gods
as they watched Hephaestus puffing about.   600

Then all day long till the sun descended
they feasted of that abundant banquet,
with Apollo plucking his splendid lyre
and the Muses trilling their melodies.

But after the sun's brilliant light had set,
each god retired to sleep in his palace,
since each had his home that lame Hephaestus
had fashioned for him with consummate skill—
and Lightning Lord Zeus went up to the bed
where he lay when slumber overcame him   610
and slept beside Hera the golden-throned.

Book Two: The Warriors and the Ships

Agamemnon tests his armies by urging them to sail home.
List of warriors and ships at Troy.

Now the other gods and mortal warriors
slumbered all night, but sweet sleep escaped Zeus,
who was planning how to give Achilles
distinction and make many Danaans die.
Finally he decided it was best
to send Atreus' son a deceitful dream,
so his words flew out as he summoned one:
"Hurry off to the ships, Deceitful Dream!
And after you reach Agamemnon's camp
deliver the following instructions: 10
he must prepare his armies for battle
as soon as he can, because that city's
ripe for the taking, now our immortals
have all been won over by queen Hera,
and the Trojans will have hosts of troubles."

So the Dream hurried off on this errand.
It quickly came down to the Danaan ships
and found king Agamemnon in his tent,
drenched in a dripping ambrosial slumber.
There it took the shape of aged Nestor,   20
Agamemnon's favorite counselor,
and bent over his bed to address him:
"You're sleeping, son of illustrious Atreus!
Responsible chiefs shouldn't sleep all night
with problems to solve, people to protect.
But listen! I'm a messenger from Zeus,

who worries for you though he's far away.
You must prepare your armies for battle
as soon as you can, because that city's
ripe for the taking, now our immortals   30
have all been won over by queen Hera,
and the Trojans will have hosts of troubles
from Zeus. Keep this in mind, don't forget it
when honey-dripping sleep abandons you."

   Then it scurried away and left him there
pondering things which would never happen:
he thought he'd take the city that same day—
fool! he little knew what Zeus really planned,
to bring more desperate devastation
on Trojans and Danaans in bitter war.   40
The god's voice ringing in his ears, he woke,
sat straight up, tied his tunic about him,
and over his shoulders he flung a cloak,
bound elegant sandals about his feet,
slung on his back a silver-studded sword,
then seized his imperishable scepter
and went his way along the lines of ships.

   Now Dawn had ascended high Olympus,
proclaiming day for all the immortals
as Agamemnon ordered his heralds   50
to summon an Achaean assembly—
so the people came running at their call.
But first he held a council of the lords
by the ship of that Pylian king Nestor
and proclaimed a devious plan to them:
"My friends, as I slept, a divine dream came
through the ambrosial night, quite like Nestor
in form and height and handsome appearance.
It stood over my head and said to me:
'You're sleeping, son of illustrious Atreus!   60
Responsible chiefs shouldn't sleep all night
with problems to solve, people to protect.
But listen! I'm a messenger from Zeus,
who worries for you though he's far away.

You must prepare your armies for battle
as soon as you can, because that city's
ripe for the taking, now our immortals
have all been won over by queen Hera,
and the Trojans will have hosts of troubles
from Zeus. Keep this in mind.' Whereupon it   70
fluttered away, as sweet sleep released me.
So let's see if our men will do battle.
But first I'll determine their sentiments
by urging them to escape in their ships
while you stand by and try to restrain them."

   After he had spoken, he sat. And up
rose Nestor, sovereign of sandy Pylos,
to address them with these well-measured words:
"My heroic friends and fellow warriors,
if another man had told us this dream   80
we might call it a lie and ignore it,
but it appeared to our mightiest lord.
So let's see if our men will do battle."

   Then he strode away from their assembly,
and all those commanders rose and obeyed
aged Nestor. The people hurried out
like a swarm of murmurous honeybees
that endlessly pour from their combs and caves
to cluster above the flowers in spring,
some over one flower, some another: 90
thus swarms of warriors hurried from their ships
that lay in lines along the sandy beach
toward the meeting place—and among them blazed
swift Rumor, sent by Zeus to rouse their rage.
Terrible turmoil! Earth groaned under them
as they sat; the din was huge: nine heralds
tried to keep order, bellowed for silence
so the words of their leaders might be heard.
Finally all were made to take their seats
in silence. Then king Agamemnon rose   100
holding a scepter made by Hephaestus
for the thunderlord son of Cronos, Zeus,

who presented it to cunning Hermes,
and that god had given it to Pelops,
who ceded it to illustrious Atreus;
Thyestes received it at his decease
and left it to lordly Agamemnon
as ruler of Argos and many isles.
Leaning on this scepter, he addressed them:
"Friends, Danaan warriors, servants of Ares: 110
Cronos' son Zeus made a great fool of me—
that cruel god! He bowed his head to promise
we should sack their city, return safe home—
but it seems he tricked us; now he decrees
we'll go back disgraced after many die.
Ah, this must be what pleases mighty Zeus,
who has toppled towers in many towns
and will topple more, such is his power.
And what a shameful name we'll leave behind
when such a distinguished army as ours   120
stays stalemated here battling uselessly
against fewer men, with no end in sight!
Yes, if all we Trojans and Achaeans
swore oaths of truce for counting the people
who have their homes in that splendid city
and our contingents made up groups of ten
which each took a Trojan to pour its wine,
many of us would have no wine pourer,
we're so superior in numbers to those
Trojans of the town. But it's their allies,   130
spear-slinging warriors from many cities,
they are the ones who frustrate our efforts
to plunder that prosperous capital.
Nine long years we've waited here already,
and our ships are rotten, their rigging's slack,
while our poor children and wives, we suppose,
sit in our palaces waiting, and yet
the job we came for still hasn't been done.
But every man here should do as I say:
let's set sail for our beloved homeland,   140
because I know we'll never take that town."

Whereupon a mighty excitement stirred
in the crowd, who knew nothing of his plan.
And they rose like waves on the Icarian
Sea, when a blustery southeaster blows
tumultuously from father Zeus's clouds.
And as a west wind sweeps the deep wheat fields
to bend its ears with a boisterous blast,
that army began to move, ran roaring
for the ships, while dust from under their feet   150
whirled skyward and they called one another
to seize those ships, drag them into the sea,
then cleared the runways—and their homesick cries
reached heaven as they knocked the ships' props out.

   They would have returned, even against fate,
but Hera saw them and called Athena:
"Dear me, energetic daughter of Zeus,
will our Achaeans really be fleeing
over the sea's broad back to their homelands
and leave Priam's people their pride and joy,   160
Argive Helen, for whose sake so many
have perished here very far from their homes?
But you hurry down among those warriors
and restrain them with reasonable words—
don't in any case let them launch their ships!"

   That goddess green-eyed Athena obeyed,
darted down from the peaks of Olympus
and quickly came to the Achaean fleet,
where she found magnificent Odysseus
standing. He hadn't laid hands on his ship   170
and seemed quite paralyzed in his sorrow.
Green-eyed Athena approached him and shrieked:
"Ho, you ingenious son of Laertes,
letting your people fall head over heels
to scramble onto those ships and escape
and leave Priam's people their pride and joy,
Argive Helen, for whose sake so many
have perished here very far from their homes.
You must hurry out among those warriors

and restrain them with reasonable words—   180
don't in any case let them launch their ships!"

   Odysseus recognized the goddess' voice,
so he rushed away—and, running off, flung
his cloak to the herald Eurybates.
First he approached great Agamemnon, took
that imperishable scepter from him
and hurried along those ships on the beach.

   Whenever he met an Achaean lord
he planted himself before him and said:
"My dear friend, isn't it wrong to panic?   190
You sit right down and keep your people still.
Agamemnon may want to try us out,
but a hard reckoning will come later.
And didn't we hear him proclaim his plan?
If he becomes angry, we'll regret it.
They are haughty men, these kings who command
with honors from Cronos' son glorious Zeus."

   But when he saw a commoner shouting
he whacked him with the scepter and declared:
"Come now, fellow, sit still here and listen   200
to your betters, you coward and shirker,
useless in combat or concocting plans.
Every Achaean can't be a leader—
many lords mean trouble. We need one lord,
one king, ruling by divine right from Zeus,
who grants him laws and scepter to command."

   Thus Odysseus ranged among them—and they
came back to the meeting place from their ships,
bellowing as when the sea waves' breakers
batter the beach in an endless thunder.   210

   Then everyone else sat in good order,
and only Thersites chattered away.
He loved to use all the wild words he knew,
cursing the leaders for no good reason,
whatever would make the Achaeans laugh.

He was the ugliest man there at Troy:
bandy-legged, lame in one foot, with shoulders
hunched over his chest—and above all this,
a pointed head with some scraggly hair.
Achilles and Odysseus hated him   220
since he scolded them most of all, but now
he shrieked at their leader—and the people
listened in indignation as he howled
long and loud against lord Agamemnon:
"Ah, Atreus' son, what more could you desire?
Your tents are full of bronze and those women
you grab for yourself when your battalions
have sacked some city and you get the best.
Or is it gold you want—some Trojan chief
hauling a pile here to ransom his son,   230
my prisoner or another Achaean's—
or you'd like a tender girl to sleep with
and keep for yourself? No, it isn't right
a leader should give us so much trouble!
Weak sisters, cowards, women more than men,
let's take our ships home and leave this fellow
to chew on his booty—then he may learn
if we were any help to him or not.
Now he cheated Achilles, his better,
played him false, made off with his lady.   240
Yes, he's really a meek one—if he weren't,
it would be your last insult, Atreus' son."

    Thus Agamemnon got a tongue-lashing
from Thersites—but Odysseus strode up
and reprimanded him, scowling fiercely:
"Well, Thersites, you've a quick tongue, all right,
but now I think you had better be quiet.
For me you're the lowest of all our men
who came here to Ilios with Atreus' sons,
so just stop slandering our commanders   250
with all this nonsense about going home.
We still don't know what the outcome will be—
we may very well return successful.

And now it's Atreus' son Agamemnon
you're yelling at, for receiving so many
gifts from our people—an insolent speech.
Well, let me assure you, my dear fellow:
when I find you playing the fool again,
may they chop off my head that very day
and call Telemachus my son no more   260
if I don't grab you and tear off your clothes—
your cloak, your robe, all that covers your crotch—
and send you whimpering back to the ships
with some sharp whacks to remember it by!"

So Odysseus struck him with the scepter—
and he doubled up and blubbered fat tears
as a bloody welt rose over his back
from that golden scepter, then sat, afraid,
in helpless pain, and wiped a tear away.
Despite their worries, the Achaeans laughed,   270
and one would catch his neighbor's eye and say:
"Hey, Odysseus has done a lot of good
with his plans and leadership in battle,
but this time's really better than ever:
he made that blabbermouth shut his trap
and now I expect he'll never again
yammer against our glorious commanders."

Next up rose city-sacking Odysseus
with the scepter—and by him Athena,
disguised as a herald, called for silence   280
so those Danaans, back to the very last,
could hear his advice and take it to heart.
He addressed them with these well-measured words:
"Atreus' son, my lord, it seems our people
wish to shame you more than any mortal
by not fulfilling the promise they made
that day they set sail from grassy Argos:
they wouldn't return till Troy was taken.
But now they're more like babies or widows
weeping and wailing they want to go home.   290
Well, there's cause enough for discouragement.

A sailor who stays one month from his wife
on the seaborne fleet knows what trouble means
when winter tempests toss the choppy seas,
while for us nine solid years have gone by
and still we're here, so I blame nobody
for being impatient. Yet what a disgrace
to return empty-handed in the end!
Then stand fast, friends! stay awhile till we learn
if Calchas prophesied the truth or not.   300
We know one thing for sure, and all of you
who remain alive are my witnesses.
It seems like only yesterday our ships
gathered at Aulis for the trip to Troy
and at those altars round a sacred spring
we made our offerings to the immortals
beneath a plane tree where the water flowed.
Then a great omen came: a blood-red snake,
awful, brought to the light by Zeus himself,
slithered out and darted to the plane tree,   310
where a nest of innocent sparrow chicks
cowered under the leaves on the top bough—
eight little ones, with their mother the ninth.
The snake ate them as they peeped piteously
and the mother fluttered about and wailed,
next coiled itself and caught her, screaming, too.
After it had eaten all nine sparrows
it was translated by its creator,
Cronos' lordly son, who changed it to stone
as we stood amazed at what had happened.   320
A horrid portent! but immediately
aged Calchas began to prophesy:
'Now why are you silent, my Achaeans?
Wise Zeus has shown us a mighty omen,
slow to come, slow fulfilled, but most glorious:
just as the serpent devoured nine sparrows—
eight little ones, with their mother the ninth—
we'll battle at Ilios that many years,
but in the tenth their capital will fall.'
He said all this, and now it's happening.   330

Well, stay here, my people, stay right here till
we plunder their city, as Zeus has planned!"

   And the Danaans bellowed hurrah—those ships
echoed horribly with roars of warriors
applauding ingenious Odysseus' words.
Next veteran Nestor rose and declared:
"Here we're babbling away like silly boys
ignorant of battle enterprises.
But what's become of our oaths and our vows?
Well, to the bonfire with our strategy,   340
our wine offerings, our trusty handclasps!
Our wrangling's worthless, and it hasn't helped
for all the long years we've been in Ilios.
Atreus' son, keep your purpose steadfast
and lead us through that relentless struggle,
and to hell with the rest, those one or two
who stand apart with their conspiracies
to clear out before we know whether Zeus
was lying when he promised us or not!
I tell you, majestic Zeus did bless us   350
that day we boarded our seafaring ships
with death and destruction for the Trojans—
flashed lightning on our right, a splendid sign—
so nobody here be hurrying home
till he takes a Trojan lady to bed,
the reward of his struggles for Helen.
If any man's so eager to return
just let him lay a hand on his black ship
and he'll perish today before us all.
Plan well, my lord, hear others' suggestions   360
and don't neglect my own worthwhile advice.
Divide our men by clans, Agamemnon,
so cousin aids cousin and clan aids clan.
If our Achaeans obey you in this,
you can determine which men are cowards
and which are brave, when each clan fights alone—
and in case we fail, we'll know whether our
own cowardice or the gods have caused it."

Atreus' son Agamemnon answered him:
"Indeed, sir, you've shown us the way again.   370
By Zeus and Athena and Apollo,
I wish we had ten counselors like you—
then Priam's prosperous citadel soon
would fall before the force of our armies.
But Cronos' son Zeus has given me grief,
mixed me all up in useless contention.
I quarreled with Achilles for that girl
and I got angry first, but if ever
we come to agreement again, I swear
those Trojans will never escape their doom.   380
Now take your meals so we can start combat.
Sharpen your spears, put your shields in order,
let your thundering horses have fodder,
look to your chariots, and think of battle,
and that strenuous struggle will rage all day.
We'll have no rest, even for a moment,
till falling night parts the warriors' fury.
Sweat will drench chests about leather shield straps,
arms that fling spears become weary with weight,
sweat drench horses tugging at their chariots.   390
And if I see anyone here hang back
beside our high-beaked ships on the beach,
that man will be devoured by dogs and birds."

And the Achaeans cheered wildly, like waves
on some high headland when south winds hurl them
against a crag that the billows batter
ceaselessly from one side or another.
So they rose and scattered among the ships,
kindled bonfires and prepared their dinners,
then each of them sacrificed for a god,   400
praying to escape death and war's damage.
Mighty Agamemnon offered a bull—
a fattened five-year-old—to Cronos' son,
as trusty lieutenants stood at his side:
Nestor first of all, then Idomeneus,
both Aiantes and the son of Tydeus,

with ingenious Odysseus as the sixth.
And Menelaus came uninvited,
having guessed what his brother was about.
They stood beside that bull, took sacred barley,   410
and Agamemnon intoned a prayer:
"Most glorious great Zeus who lives in ether,
may the sun never set and darkness come
till I send Priam's palace crashing down
blackened with soot, and the fire sears his gates,
while my sword slashes through Hector's tunic
and all about him many of his men
are toppled into dust and bite the earth."

But Cronos' son Zeus was implacable:
took sacrifice, yet sent him more sorrows.   420
After they prayed and sprinkled barley grains
they slit the victim's throat, then flayed its hide,
carved up the shanks and covered them in fat,
a double layer dressed with raw meat pieces.
So they burned these over a fire of sticks
and cooked the inner parts on wooden spits.
When that god's offering, the shanks, was done
they carved up all the rest and spitted it,
roasted it well, and slipped it from the spits.
When the work was finished, their meal prepared,   430
they feasted off that abundant banquet.
After they had eaten and drunk their fill
aged Gerenian Nestor addressed them:
"Our distinguished leader Agamemnon,
it's high time for us to stop postponing
the work that god has given us to do.
So order our estimable heralds
to summon the people among their ships
while we hurry through the camp together
and make them eager for bitter battle."   440

Atreus' son Agamemnon assented,
commanded his clear-voiced heralds to call
the Achaean contingents to combat—
and the people assembled at their cries.

That son of Atreus and his captains ran
to marshal their men, as Athena came
holding the immortal storm-shield aegis
from which a hundred golden tassels hung—
each one worth a hundred sturdy cattle—
and rushed resplendently through those armies   450
so every Achaean felt his heart stirred
for the crash of implacable combat.
Then war became sweeter than returning
in the ships to their beloved homelands.

    As ravenous flames make a forest blaze
on a mountaintop, where the glare gleams far,
the glitter of their marvelous armor
flashed dazzling through the sky up to heaven.

    They were like those numerous flocks of birds
on the Asian meadow round Caÿstrius,   460
wild geese and herons and preening-necked swans
who wheel about proud of their powerful wings
while their clanging cries make the fields resound:
such hordes of warriors poured from ships and tents
onto the great Scamandrian plain—and earth
rang dreadfully under those armies' tread.
They stood on the flowery Scamandrian fields
countless as leaves and flowers in their season.

    As the myriad hordes of murmurous flies
that swarm through a farmer's stables and pens   470
in springtime, when milk overflows the pails,
so many Achaeans faced those Trojans
raging to devastate the enemy.

    As goatherds easily separate flocks
that mingle together in the pasture,
the Achaean chiefs marshaled their people—
among them illustrious Agamemnon,
with head and eyes like thunderhurling Zeus,
waist like fierce Ares, chest like Poseidon.
As a bull stands out from a herd of cows,   480
superb and distinguished among them all,

so Zeus made Atreus' son Agamemnon
preeminent among hosts of warriors.

  Now tell me, Olympian Muses, since you
are goddesses and present everywhere,
while we hear mere rumors and know nothing,
who were the Achaean lords and leaders.
Though I had ten tongues and as many mouths,
a tireless voice and a heart made of brass,
I couldn't name and number every one   490
if the Olympian Muses, Zeus's brood,
did not call to my mind who they all were.
Then these were the commanders and their ships.

  The Boeotians were led by Peneleos,
Arcesilaus, Leitus, and Clonius,
and they came from Hyria, rocky Aulis,
Scolus, and mountainy Eteonus,
Thespeia, Graea, broad Mycalessus,
from Harma, Eilesium, and Erythrae,
held Eleon, Hylë, and Peteon,   500
Ocalea and the Medeian fortress,
Copae, Eutresis, dove-haunted Thisbe,
owned Cornoeia and grassy Haliartus,
lived in lovely Plataea and Glisas,
garrisoned the Hypotheban fortress
and held Onchestus, grove of Poseidon,
owned grape-clustered Arnë and Mideia
with Nisa and Anthedon by the sea.
They brought fifty seafaring ships, on each
a hundred and twenty tough Boeotians.   510

  Those from Aspledon and Orchomenus,
led by Ascalaphus and Ialmenus—
sons of Ares, conceived in Actor's halls
to Astyochë, when that mighty war god
crept into the chamber of his lady—
came with a fleet of thirty high-beaked ships.

The Phocians were led by Ephitus' sons
intrepid Schedius and Epistrophus—
and they held Crisa and rocky Pytho,
Daulis, Cyparissus, and Panopeus,   520
Hyampolis too and Anemoreia
and the eddying streams of Cephisus
with Lilaea where that river rises,
and forty black ships accompanied them.
So those lords marshaled Phocian battalions,
who armed themselves to the Boeotians' left.

The Locrians followed Oileus' son Aias,
less massive than Telamonian Aias—
a short man who'd brought no armor with him
but had no peer in managing the spear—   530
and they owned Cynus, Opus, Calliarus,
Bessa, Scarphë, and lovely Augeiae,
Tarphë and Thronium on the Boagrius.
And with them came forty seafaring ships
of the Locrians, whose home faced Euboea.

Fiery Abantes came from Euboea,
Calchis, Eretria, Histiaea,
Carinthus by the sea and steep Dios—
men with homes in Carystus and Styra
whose serried battalions were commanded   540
by Calchedon's son proud Elephenor.
And with him many a long-haired warrior
stretched spears toward the enemy, determined
to shatter the armor about their chests—
and forty black ships accompanied him.

And those who owned that citadel Athens,
realm of Erechtheus whom Athena reared
when the fertile fields had given him birth—
she set him up in her own rich temple,
where he took sacrifice of bulls and rams   550
from the young Athenians in due season—
were led by Peteos' son Menestheus,
a man with no peer on the face of earth

marshaling horses and armored warriors
except for glorious Nestor, his senior.
And a fleet of fifty ships had brought them.

Great Aias brought twelve ships from Salamis,
beached them by the Athenian battalions.

Then those who owned Argos and walled Tiryns,
Hermionë and Asinë round the gulf,   560
Troezen and vine-rich Epidaurus,
Achaeans from Aegina and Mases,
were led by intrepid Diomedes
with Capaneus' son prince Sthenelus
and incomparable Euryalus,
godlike grandson of gallant Talaus,
though Diomedes had supreme command—
and a fleet of forty ships came with him.

Those from that tough citadel Mycenae,
wealthy Corinth, and sturdy Cleonae,   570
Orneia and lovely Araethyrae
and Adrastus' capital, Sicyon,
from Hyperesia and Gonoessa,
Pellenë and the land round Aegium
along the seacoast and in Helicë,
brought a hundred ships under Atreus' son
Agamemnon, with far the most and the best
spearmen. He stood there in brilliant armor,
a splendid spectacle among them all
for his rank and the numbers of his men.   580

And those who held rugged Lacedaemon,
Pharis, Sparta, and dove-haunted Messë,
spearmen from Bryseiae and Augeiae,
from Amyclas and Helus by the sea,
from Laas and the land round Oetylus,
brought sixty ships under Menelaus,
Agamemnon's brother. So they formed ranks
as great Menelaus strode here and there
urging them forward, most furious to win
the reward of his struggles for Helen.   590

Those from Pylos and lovely Arenë,
from Aipy and Thryum, Alpheius' ford,
from Cyparisseis, Amphigeneia,
Pteleus and Dorium, where the Muses
met Thamyris and ended his singing
as he returned from Eurytus' palace—
he boasted he'd defeat them easily
if they competed with him in singing,
so they were furious, took away his sight,
made him forget his marvelous music—   600
were led by veteran Gerenian Nestor,
and ninety seafaring ships made their fleet.

Arcadians from under Mount Cyllene
by Aepytus' tomb, keen for close combat—
men from Pheneus, wool-rich Orchomenus,
Rhipë, Stratia, and windy Enispë,
who held Tegea and Mantinea
and Stymphalus and pleasant Parrhasia—
were led by Arcaeus' son Agapenor
with sixty swift ships that carried a horde   610
of Arcadian spearmen raging for war.
Atreus' son king Agamemnon himself
gave them ships to cross the wine-dark waters,
they knew so little of seafarers' lore.

Then those from Buprasium and famed Elis
between Hyrminë and far Myrsinus,
fair Olesium and the Olenian peak,
were under four commanders, each with ten
swift ships carrying many Epeians,
some under Amphimacus and Thalpus,   620
one Cteatus' and one Eurytus' son,
while formidable Diores led some
and some followed godlike Polyneixes,
Agasthenes' son in Augeias' line.

But men from Dulichium and those holy
Echinean isles that lay facing Elis
were led by indomitable Meges,

son of Zeus's well-beloved Phyleus,
who fled from his father's wrath to Elis—
and a fleet of forty ships came with them. 630

And Odysseus led the Cephallenians
from Ithaca and wooded Neritus,
Crocyleia and rugged Aegilips,
from delightful Samos and Zacynthus
and the mainland that lay facing those isles.
Their commander was canny Odysseus,
and a dozen red-prowed ships came with him.

But Thoas led the Aetolian warriors
from Pleuron, Olenus, and Pylenë,
Calchis by the sea and steep Calydon, 640
because gallant Oeneus' sons were no more,
Oeneus no more, blond Meleager dead—
so Thoas commanded the Aetolians,
and they came with a fleet of forty ships.

And lord Idomeneus led the Cretans,
warriors of Gortys and sturdy Knossos,
Lyctus, Miletus, chalk-rich Lycastus,
those bustling cities Phaestus and Rhytium,
and others from the hundred towns of Crete
commanded by noble Idomeneus 650
with Meriones, peer of dreadful Ares.
And a fleet of eighty ships had brought them.

Tall, brave Tlepolemus, Heracles' son,
brought nine ships from Rhodes with haughty Rhodians
who lived on that island in three cities,
Lindus, Ialysus, chalk-bright Cameirus.
Their warriors were led by Tlepolemus,
Astyocheia's son by Heracles,
who made her prisoner at Ephyrë
when he sacked so many rich citadels. 660
After Tlepolemus grew to manhood
he murdered his father's own dear uncle,
that aged veteran Licymnius, then
built ships immediately, summoned his men,

and fled, being threatened by those other
sons and grandsons of stalwart Heracles.
After much suffering, he came to Rhodes,
where his people founded three cities, loved
by that ruler of gods and mortals, Zeus,
who showered fabulous riches on them.   670

And Nireus led three vessels from Symë—
Nireus, son of Aglaia and Charops,
Nireus, handsomest among the Danaans
except for Peleus' magnificent son.
Yet he was a weakling and no leader.

Those men from Nisyrus and Crapathus,
glimmering Cos and the Calydnian isles,
were led by Pheidippus and Antiphus,
king Thessalus' sons in Heracles' line,
and thirty swift ships accompanied them.   680

And those whose home was Pelasgian Argos—
men from Alopë, Alos, and Trachis,
Phthia and Hellas of handsome women,
known as Myrmidons, Hellenes, Achaeans—
brought fifty ships led by prince Achilles,
but they weren't thinking of infamous war
since they had no lord to order their ranks,
now Achilles stayed sulking by the ships
in a fury over tender Briseis,
his booty in that desperate struggle   690
for Lyrnessus and the Theban bastion
when he slew Mynes and Epistrophus,
king Evenus' sons in Selepus' line.
So he lay brooding, though soon he would rise.

Those from Phylacë, flowery Pyrasus,
Demeter's grove, and pastoral Iton,
sea-washed Antron and grassy Pteleos,
were led by fiery Protesilaus
while he still lived, but dark earth held him now,
his wife left desolate in Phylacë,   700
his home half built—a Dardanian slew him

as he led his warriors ashore at Troy.
Thus they longed for their lord, though they had one,
since they were commanded by Podarces,
son of that rich sheep rancher Iphlicus
and brother to great Protesilaus
but a younger warrior, hardly the peer
of his firstborn brother. So his people
weren't lordless, though they longed for the glorious
lord they lost. And forty ships came with them.   710

   Those from Pherae by the Boibean lake,
from Boibë and Glaphyrae and Ialcus,
brought eleven ships with Admetus' son
Eumelus, borne by that dazzling lady
Alcestis, loveliest of Pelias' daughters.

   And men from Methonë and Thaumacis,
Meliboeia and rugged Olizon,
led by that keen archer Philoctetus,
brought seven ships, on each fifty rowers
expert at bending the bow in battle.   720
But their commander lay in agony
on the isle of Lemnos, where they left him
with an awful bite from a water snake.
He lay there in pain—but soon his people
would well remember the leader they lost.
Thus they longed for their lord, though they had one:
Medon, a natural son of Oileus,
borne by Rhenë to that city sacker.

   And men from Tricca and steep Ithomë
who held Eurytus' city, Oechalia,   730
were led by Asclepius' sons those healers
glorious Podaleirus and Machaon—
and thirty black ships accompanied them.

   From Ormenius, the Hypereian spring,
Asterium, and Titanus' snowy peaks,
spearmen were led by prince Eurypylus,
and a fleet of forty ships came with him.

Then those from Argissa and Gyrtonë,
Orthë and shimmering Oloösson,
were commanded by proud Polypoetes,   740
Perithous' son and a grandson of Zeus
conceived by charming Hippodameia
when his father defeated the centaurs,
drove them from Pelium to the Aethices—
and their lieutenant was lord Leonteus,
Coronus' son in the line of Caenus—
and a fleet of forty ships came with them.

Gouneus brought twenty-two ships from Cyphus
with the Enienes and the Peraebians,
who resided in wintry Dodona   750
and tilled the fields beside Titaressus,
which pours lovely streams in the Peneius
yet will not join the silver Peneius,
flows over those currents like olive oil,
since it is a branch of the dreadful Styx.

Intrepid Prothous led the Magnetes
who lived by Peneius and by Pelion
with its forest of quivering foliage.
And a fleet of forty ships came with him.

These were the Danaan lords and commanders.   760
Now tell me, O Muse, which were best of all
those warriors and horses with Atreus' sons.

Far the best horses were Admetus' mares,
with his son as charioteer, swift as birds,
like in color and age, just matched in height—
silverbow Apollo had raised those mares,
conveyers of Ares' dread and dismay.
Far the best warrior was giant Aias,
strongest man there except for Achilles,
whose horses were also far superior.   770
But he stayed back beside his high-beaked ships,
in a towering rage at Agamemnon
Atreus' son—and on the beach his people
practiced archery and tossed the discus

while their horses munched clover and parsley
not far away from the glorious chariots
that lay well covered in their masters' tents
as the men themselves wandered here and there,
longing for their lord, but stayed clear of war.

Then they marched out like land-devouring fire.   780
Earth groaned under them as when thunderlord
Zeus devastates the land of Typhoeus,
where that volcano monster has his bed—
thus the earth groaned hugely beneath their feet
while they came hurrying over the plain.

But windfoot Iris ran to the Trojans,
taking a terrible message from Zeus.
She found them assembled at Priam's gates,
all together, young men as well as old.
So Iris scurried up to them and spoke   790
in the form of Priam's son Polites,
who maintained a lookout for his people
from a post on Aesyetes' funeral mound
to see when the Achaeans left their ships.
Taking his shape and voice, Iris shouted:
"Old Priam, your words run on forever
as if it were peacetime. But this is war!
Yes, I've done lots of fighting in my time,
but I never saw an army so large—
as numerous as the leaves or the sands—   800
and they march straight toward us over our plain!
Very well, Hector, this is your duty:
here in our city are all our allies,
who babble languages of different lands,
so let each lord command his own people
and marshal their ranks and lead them to war."

Hector knew the goddess' voice as she spoke,
dismissed the meeting, and they rushed to arms.
The gates were flung open, and out they poured
on foot and on chariot, with a great roar.   810

Now before the city lies a steep hill
far out on the plain, where it stands alone—
mortals call it Brambly Hill, and the gods
the barrow of nimblefoot Myrinë.
There those Trojans and their allies gathered.

The Trojan command was held by Hector,
Priam's brave son, with far the most and best
armored warriors, furious to wield keen spears.

Those Dardanians were under Aeneas,
son of Anchises and Aphrodite,   820
conceived to a mortal on Mount Ida—
and his lieutenants were Antenor's sons
Acamas and gallant Archelochus.

And Zeleians from the Idaean plains,
rich men who drink Aesepus' dark waters,
Trojan clans, were led by Lycaon's son
Pandarus, whom Apollo gave the bow.

Those from Apaesus and Adresteia
who ruled Pityeia and steep Tereia
were led by brave Adrastus and Amphius,   830
sons of Percotian Merops, most skillful
fortune-teller, who often begged his boys
to stay out of war—but they wouldn't hear,
for the fates of dark death had led them on.

Those who came from Percotë and Practius,
Sestus, Abydus, and famed Arisbë,
were led by Hyrcatus' son lord Asius—
redoubtable Asius from Arisbë,
whose huge tawny horses brought him to Troy.

And Hippothous captained the Pelasgi,   840
who lived in Larissa of thick, rich soil,
with Hippothous and Pylaeus as lords,
two sons of Lethus in Teutamus' line.

Acamas and Peirous led their Thracians
from lands by the swift-flowing Hellespont.

And Ciconians were under Euphemus
son of Zeus's beloved Troezenus.

But Pyraechmes had brought his Paeonians
from far-off Amydon beside the wide
Axius, whose streams are loveliest on earth.   850

From the Enetian fields where she-mules run
Pylaemenes led those Paphlagonians,
Cytorian lords who lived round Sesamon
and kept palaces on the Parthenius
at Cromna, Aegialus, Erythini.

And Halizonians were brought by Odius
from far Alybë, with its silver mines.

Mysians followed the seer Ennomus—
but his prophecy didn't stave off fate:
he perished at the hands of Peleus' son   860
in the river, where many Trojans died.

Phorcys and Ascanius led the Phrygians
from far Ascania, raging for combat.

The Maeonians with Telaemenes' sons
Mesthles and Antiphus, born of a nymph,
came from their farms under snowy Tmolus.

But Nastes had brought the babbling Carians
from Miletus and leafy Mount Phthires,
Maeander's streams, and Mycalë's summits.
Their lords were Amphimachus and Nastes,   870
Nastes and Amphimachus, Nomion's sons,
and Nastes fought wearing gold like a girl—
fool! that gold didn't help to save his life:
he perished at the hands of Peleus' son
in the river, and Achilles got the gold.

Sarpedon and Glaucus led Lycian hordes
from lands by the distant Scamander's streams.

Book Three: The Duel

The Greek prince Menelaus and the Trojan Paris (Alexander) meet in single combat. Aphrodite saves Paris.

After the captains had marshaled their ranks
those Trojans marched out clamorous as birds,
like cranes that clamor under the heavens
when they flee from winter's torrential rains
and, crying wildly, fly toward Oceanus,
bringing death and fate for the Pygmy men
and foully battle them at early dawn—
but the Achaeans marched out silently,
planning how to help their fellow warriors.

As the South Wind covers mountains in mist,   10
a curse for shepherds, camouflage for thieves,
and men see only a stone's throw ahead,
so the clouds of dust whirled up from their feet
when they hurried over the Trojan plain.

After those armies came near each other,
prince Paris pranced out before his people,
on his back a leopardskin and a bow
and his sword. Brandishing two bronze-tipped spears,
he challenged any Achaean leader
to meet him man-to-man in awful war.   20

When Atreus' son Menelaus spied him
striding out mightily before them all
he was glad as a hungry lion who finds
a great carcass of some stag or wild goat
and greedily enjoys a hearty meal

though hunters surround him with their quick hounds—
so Menelaus was glad to see Paris
because he expected revenge at last
and leapt from his chariot in full armor.

But when godlike Paris saw Menelaus   30
appearing among the foremost, his heart
sank, and he slunk back among his comrades.
As a man retreats when he sees a snake
in a mountain valley and starts to shake,
then hurries away, his cheeks deadly pale:
thus that godlike Alexander shrank back
among his men, for fear of Atreus' son.

But Hector saw him and cried bitterly:
"Damn you, Paris, pretty boy, girl crazy,
I only wish you had never been born—   40
and very much better it would have been
than to let you shame our people today!
What a laugh for those Achaeans, who'll say
we chose you as our champion for your face,
though you haven't any courage at all.
Was this how you were when you took your friends
and sailed a fleet on the turbulent sea
to carry off that delightful lady,
a princess of their spear-slinging people
but a plague on your father and city,   50
joy to our enemies, and your disgrace?
So brave Menelaus is too much for you?
You'd learn what sort of warrior you deceived—
useless your lyre or Aphrodite's gifts,
your hair and face, when you lie in the dust.
If we weren't so soft, we'd have hung you up
long ago for the evil you have done."

And that godlike Alexander answered:
"Hector, I know your reproaches are just—
yes, your heart's as firm as a sturdy ax   60
a workman mightily drives through a beam
to hew a hull with his masterful skill:

so steadfast is your will. But don't blame me
for the gifts of golden Aphrodite—
no man can reject the gods' glorious gifts
granted freely to mortals in their grace.
Now if you'd like me to enter combat,
ask the Trojans and Achaeans to sit
while in the middle Menelaus and I
battle for Helen with all her treasures.   70
The person who proves himself superior
may take that princess and her possessions
while the others solemnly swear friendship
so we may live in peace and they return
to Achaea, land of lovely ladies."

   Hector was delighted to hear these words
and strode out to keep his battalions back
with spear held at the middle—and all sat.
But the enemy still showered arrows
and jagged stones at illustrious Hector,   80
till Agamemnon roared to his armies:
"Hold your fire, my men, don't shoot, Achaeans!
It seems great Hector has something to say."

   When they heard their commander's words, they stood
still—and between those armies Hector cried:
"You Trojan and Achaean spearmen, hear
the words of Paris, who has caused this war:
he would request all the rest of you here
to lay your glorious armor on the ground
while in the middle he and Menelaus   90
battle for Helen with all her treasures.
The person who proves himself superior
may take that princess and her possessions
while the others solemnly swear friendship."

   A hush of awe fell over those warriors
till Atreus' son brave Menelaus cried:
"Well, hear me too! my grudge is the greatest,
but now I hope to end this contention
which has brought such horrors on our peoples

because of the quarrel Paris began.   100
Whichever one of us is doomed to die
will do so, while the others can go home.
Bring two lambs—a white ram and a black ewe,
for Earth and for Sun—with a third for Zeus,
then call king Priam to solemnly swear
himself: his sons are so proud and reckless
they might do something wild to spoil the oaths.
Young men are fickle, unstable in mind,
but an experienced lord can calculate
how all may have maximum advantage."   110

  Then the Trojans and Achaeans rejoiced,
for they thought that wretched war had ended.
And they dismounted, aligned their chariots,
took their armor off and laid it on earth
so little space remained between each piece.
Next mighty Hector sent two messengers
to bring lambs from the town and call Priam,
while Agamemnon dispatched Talthybius
with orders to fetch a lamb from his ships—
and he did as that king had commanded.   120

  Now Iris brought white-armed Helen the news,
taking the shape of her sister-in-law,
wife to Antenor's son Helicaon:
Laodicë, Priam's loveliest daughter.
She found Helen in the palace, weaving
an immense purple cloth that depicted
struggles of those Trojans and Achaeans,
all they had suffered in war for her sake.
So Iris scurried up to her and cried:
"My love, come see what incredible things   130
those people are doing down on the plain!
They wanted to tear each other apart,
simply furious for this terrible war,
but now they're leaning on shields and standing
silent, and their spears are stuck in the earth.
Alexander and brave Menelaus

will battle in the middle man-to-man,
and the winner will call you his dear wife."

The goddess' words drenched her heart with longing
for home and parents and former husband.   140
She veiled herself in silvery linen
and rushed from her palace weeping hot tears,
accompanied by two faithful handmaids—
Aithrë, Pittheus' daughter, and Clymenë—
and quickly they came to the Scaean Gates.

There they found Priam, Panthous, Thymoetes,
Lampus, Clytius, and lord Hicetaon,
with wise Ucalegon and Antenor,
counselors seated at the Scaean Gates.
Too old for battle they were, but in words   150
superb, like crickets that sit on some tree
where they pour their lily-like voices forth—
thus those elders sat on the city wall.
When they saw lovely Helen coming near
they said in a flurry of murmured words:
"No wonder the Trojans and Achaeans
have suffered so long for that lady's sake—
she's marvelously like a goddess to see.
Yet let her go home, go home on the ships,
or she'll ruin us and our children too."   160

But king Priam summoned Helen to him:
"Now come, dear child, sit beside me so you
may see your people and former husband.
You aren't to blame but the eternal gods
who brought this miserable war on us.
Tell me the name of that huge Achaean
standing so magnificent over there.
They have others even a head taller,
but I've never seen a man so handsome,
so regal—he must be one of their chiefs."   170

That enchanting Helen said in reply:
"My honored lord, I shall do as you say.
Ah, if only I'd chosen death instead

when I followed your son and abandoned
my home and friends and beloved daughter!
But I didn't—and so I have sorrows.
Very well, let me answer your question:
that man is Atreus' son Agamemnon,
a glorious lord and powerful warrior,
my husband's brother, if it was no dream."   180

    And the old man cried in admiration:
"Lucky son of Atreus, blessed by heaven
with so many young warriors to command!
Once I visited vine-laden Phrygia
and saw their armies of Phrygian horsemen,
people of Otreus and godlike Mygdon,
camping along the river Sangarius.
And I fought beside them as an ally
that day the dangerous Amazons came—
yet even they had fewer men than yours!"   190

    Next the old king saw Odysseus and asked:
"Now tell me, dear child, who can this man be,
shorter by a head than Agamemnon
but wider in the midriff and shoulders?
His armor lies on the bountiful earth
while he marches through the ranks like a ram—
yes, he seems more like some great fleecy ram
moving through an enormous flock of ewes."

    And Zeus's daughter Helen answered him:
"That's wily Odysseus, Laertes' son,   200
reared on the rugged isle of Ithaca,
a man of deception and clever plans."

    Whereupon wise Antenor addressed her:
"Lady, you've spoken a true word indeed.
Odysseus once came with Menelaus
to negotiate with us for your return
and I entertained them in my own home,
so I know their looks and sagacious plans.
When they walked among us in assembly
Menelaus was head and shoulders taller,   210

but, seated, Odysseus was more lordly.
And when they began spinning speech and plans
Menelaus spoke with much fluency
in a resonant tone: few words that went
straight to the point, though he was the younger.
And when that shrewd Odysseus rose to speak
he kept his eyes riveted on the ground,
didn't flail about a bit with his staff,
just held it stiff, like some stupid fellow.
He seemed very rude, all right—a real fool.   220
But when that mighty voice rolled from his chest
and words poured like snow on a winter day,
no mortal being was Odysseus' peer,
and his appearance no longer seemed strange."

   Aged Priam saw Aias next, and inquired:
"Now who is this huge warrior over there
rising head and shoulders above the rest?"

   And enchanting long-robed Helen answered:
"He's giant Aias, bulwark in battle,
and that godlike man is Idomeneus,   230
surrounded by his Cretan commanders.
Menelaus often entertained him
at our home when he came over from Crete.
Now I can see the other Achaeans,
men I know well and can tell their names,
yet two leaders appear to be missing:
Castor and Polydeuces the boxer,
my own half-brothers, sons of my mother.
Either they stayed home in Lacedaemon
or else came here on their seafaring ships   240
but now have no heart to enter battle
for fear of hearing me so vilely cursed."

   But already earth, reviver of life,
held them in Lacedaemon, their homeland.

   Meanwhile the heralds carried offerings
through the city—two lambs and joyful wine
in goatskins—as clarion-voiced Idaeus

brought a glittering bowl with golden cups,
approached that aged Priam, and declared:
"Laomedon's lordly son, you're summoned   250
to drive your chariot down onto the plain
and swear solemn oaths among those warriors.
Alexander and brave Menelaus
will fight for that lady with their long spears:
the winner takes her and all her treasures,
while the others solemnly swear friendship
so we may live in peace and they return
to Achaea, land of lovely ladies."

And the old king shuddered, ordered his men
to quickly harness a team of horses.   260
Now he mounted his chariot, seized the reins,
Antenor leapt up beside him, and they
galloped through the Scaean Gates to the plain.

After they arrived at the battlefield
those two stepped down on the bountiful earth
and strode to that space between the armies.
Agamemnon stood up immediately
with ingenious Odysseus, as heralds
brought the offerings, mixed wine in a bowl,
and poured water over the leaders' hands.   270
Next that son of Atreus drew the dagger
which always hung by his giant scabbard,
cut fleece from the head of each lamb, and then
distributed it among the leaders.
And Atreus' son intoned with hands upraised:
"Most glorious great Zeus who rules from Ida
and you, Sun, who see and hear everything,
you rivers, you Earth, and you Lords of Hell
that take awful vengeance on oath breakers,
be my witnesses and keep these pledges: 280
if Alexander kills blond Menelaus
he may take Helen with all her treasures,
while we sail home on our seafaring ships—
but should Menelaus slay Alexander,
Helen and her treasures shall be given back

and we must have some worthy recompense
to be remembered forever after.
If Priam and his spear-slinging people
refuse to pay it after Paris is dead
I'll stay and fight for our indemnity   290
till I bring this war to a horrible end."

So he cut the lambs' throats with the cruel blade
and laid them down on the ground gasping out
their tender lives, a limpness in their limbs.
Next they dipped wine from the mixing tureen,
made libation with prayer to the gods.
And one or another warrior would say:
"Most glorious great Zeus and you other gods,
may any men who dare to break our oaths
have their brains dashed to the earth like this wine   300
and their sons' too; may their wives become slaves."

But Cronos' son declined to fulfill it.
And Dardanian Priam addressed them next:
"Hear me, all you Trojans and Achaeans!
Now I shall return inside our city
because I cannot bear to stay and see
my beloved son battling Menelaus.
Zeus and the other gods know already
which of those two is doomed to perish."

Next godlike Priam gathered up the lambs,   310
and he mounted his chariot, seized the reins,
Antenor leapt up beside him, and they
galloped back into the city of Troy.
When Priam's son Hector and Odysseus
had measured out the ground for that combat,
they took lots and shook them in a helmet
to determine which spearman would hurl first.
So all the people prayed with hands upraised,
and one or another warrior would say:
"Most glorious great Zeus who rules from Ida,   320
may the ones to blame for this contention

perish and enter the house of Hades,
while we others solemnly swear friendship."

   Now illustrious Hector shook the helmet,
peering warily about—and out leapt
Paris' lot. Those warriors sat down in ranks,
each by his horses and inlaid armor,
while Paris, husband of lovely Helen,
donned his formidable battle attire:
strapped on his legs magnificent shinguards   330
so handsomely adorned with silver bands
and over his chest that sturdy breastplate
his brother Lycaon had given him,
slung on his back a silver-studded sword
and afterward his redoubtable shield,
set on his head a colossal helmet
whose horsehair crest bobbed horribly above,
and grasped a glorious spear that fit his palm.
Meanwhile brave Menelaus did the same.

   After both men were ready for battle   340
they strode to the space between those armies
with most ferocious glares—the sight amazed
those assembled Trojans and Achaeans.
They stood face-to-face in the measured space,
furiously brandishing their brilliant spears.
And gallant Alexander hurled the first:
his weapon hit Menelaus' trim shield,
whose leather deflected the spearpoint. Next
that incomparable son of Atreus
stormed forward with a prayer to father Zeus: 350
"Grant vengeance, Zeus, on that man who wronged me,
Alexander: let him die at my hands
so forever after men may shudder
to wrong the host who welcomes them kindly."

   Then he poised his ashwood spear and hurled it,
and that weapon hit Alexander's shield
so its spearpoint sheared through its shimmering
surface, through the glorious breastplate itself,

and tore straight through his tunic at the waist—
but he leaned aside to escape black fate.   360
Menelaus drew a silver-studded sword,
brought it crashing down on Paris' helmet,
and it split into three or four pieces—
so he gazed toward broad heaven and declaimed:
"Ah, father Zeus, the cruelest god is you!
The moment I was sure of my revenge
my sword shattered, my magnificent spear's
entirely useless, missed him when I threw."

   Next he sprang at Paris, seized his helmet,
and dragged him off, whirling him by its crest   370
till his soft throat was choked by that handsome
embroidered strap fastened under the chin.
Menelaus would have won vast glory,
but golden Aphrodite was watching
and quickly snapped that oxhide strap in two
so his strong hand held an empty helmet—
and he swung it around, sent it spinning
among his comrades, who gathered it up,
and leapt back again, furious to kill him
with another spear. But Aphrodite   380
hid Paris in mist, wafted him away
and set him down in his scented bedroom,
then went to summon Helen: she found her
on the high wall amid her attendants.
That goddess plucked her finely perfumed robe
and spoke in the shape of an ancient dame
who had labored back in Lacedaemon
carding her fine wool, a dear companion.
In this woman's shape, Aphrodite cried:
"Follow me, lady! Paris wants you home.   390
He waits in your room on his handsome bed,
and a fine sight too, not as if he'd come
from war but like a man going to dance
or just sitting down as the dance is done."

And Helen felt her heart leap inside her.
But when she saw the goddess' charming neck
and delightful bosom and brilliant eyes
she was amazed, and her words fluttered out:
"Uncanny creature, why try to fool me?
So this time you would lead me somewhere else   400
in Phrygia, maybe, or in Maeonia,
and give me to another man you love,
since Menelaus has defeated Paris
and plans to take poor wretched me back home—
that's why you came to deceive me again.
Well, go yourself, be a goddess no more,
abandon Olympus for good this time,
serve that man always, watch over him till
he makes you his wife or even his slave!
But I should be ashamed to share his bed: 410
the Trojan women would all reproach me,
and I've many, many griefs already."

   Golden Aphrodite cried in a rage:
"Ha, little fool, don't provoke me, or I
may hate you as much as I love you now—
I'd make more trouble between those warriors,
and you might come to some horrible end."

   These words frightened Zeus's daughter Helen,
who wrapped herself in a bright robe and went
silent and unseen behind the goddess.   420

   When they came to Paris' splendid palace
Helen's maids left her, returned to their work,
as that dazzling lady entered her room.
Laughter-loving Aphrodite took a chair,
placed it in front of Paris for Helen—
so that daughter of Zeus seated herself
but averted her eyes and scolded him:
"You're back! I only wish you had been slain
by that mighty man my former husband!
You boasted you'd defeat him easily—   430
you were so much stronger and more clever.

All right then, challenge brave Menelaus
to meet you in combat again . . . ah, don't,
I implore you—that blond Menelaus,
if you go out against him so very
recklessly, might take your life with his spear."

That illustrious Alexander answered:
"No need to be reproaching me, lady.
Now Athena has aided Menelaus,
but I'll win next time: gods are with us too.   440
Come, my dear, let me hold you in my arms.
I've never desired you quite so wildly—
not even that day I snatched you away
from Lacedaemon with my ships and we
lay together on the isle Cranaë—
as I do adore and desire you now."

He strode to the bed—and his wife followed.

Thus they lay together on their fine bed
while Menelaus stalked through those armies
like a wild beast, seeking Alexander.   450
But none of the Trojans and their allies
could have shown him to brave Menelaus
though none would have hidden him out of love,
because every man hated him like death.
And Atreus' son Agamemnon shouted:
"Trojans and Dardanians and your allies,
you can see brave Menelaus has won,
so return Helen with all her treasures
and let us have some worthy recompense
to be remembered forever after."   460

Then the Achaean warriors roared hurrah.

Book Four: The Oaths Violated

*Athena tricks the Trojans into breaking the truce, so battle
begins again.*

M eanwhile the gods were seated around Zeus
on that golden floor, as glorious Hebe
poured out nectar, and with their golden cups
they toasted one another, watching Troy.
Then mighty Zeus tried to needle Hera,
addressing her in this sarcastic vein:
"Well, two goddesses help Menelaus—
green-eyed Athena and Argive Hera.
But they sit aside and enjoy the sight
while laughter-loving Aphrodite stays   10
always beside that man to protect him,
and now she saved him from sure destruction.
So it seems brave Menelaus has won
and we must consider what should be done—
shall heartbreaking battle begin once more
or may we make peace between their armies?
If this would perhaps find favor with all,
Priam's prosperous city might survive
and Menelaus could have Argive Helen."

   Great groans rose from Hera and Athena,   20
who sat side by side devising troubles
for the Trojans. Athena held her tongue
though father Zeus made her simply furious,
while Hera couldn't keep quiet and cried:
"You horrible man, what a thing to say!
You'd make my tribulations all in vain—
my sweat and struggles, my horses weary

as I roused armies against king Priam?
Well, we other gods will never approve!"

Very much vexed, majestic Zeus answered: 30
"You strange being, have Priam and his sons
done you so much wrong you'll rage forever
till you devastate their delightful town?
If you went inside the gates and high walls
to gobble up that Priam and his sons
and all the rest, you might be satisfied.
Do as you wish—we won't let this quarrel
make more controversy between us two—
but let me tell you this, and I mean it:
if ever I want to sack a city   40
where your favorite mortals happen to live,
don't try to restrain my indignation,
since this time I'm letting you have your way.
Yes, of all the cities that mortal men
have built beneath the sun and starry skies,
the nearest to my heart was holy Troy,
with Priam and his spear-slinging people.
My altar there never lacked splendid feasts
with offerings and libations, as is right."

Then gentle-eyed queen Hera answered him: 50
"Three cities on earth are dearest to me:
Argos, Sparta, and spacious Mycenae.
Destroy these whenever you take a mind,
I won't lift a finger in their defense.
And if I were foolish enough to try,
I couldn't, your power is so immense.
But I must have some say in matters too—
I'm also a god, we've the same parents,
and I am Cronos' most honored daughter,
being both oldest and your wedded wife   60
while you are lord of all the immortals.
So why don't we each give way just a bit,
I to you, you to me—and the other
gods will follow. Tell green-eyed Athena
she should hurry down on the battlefield

to make the Trojan warriors break their oaths
and devastate those boasting Danaans now."

So the father of gods and men obeyed,
immediately told green-eyed Athena:
"Now you hurry down on the battlefield   70
to make the Trojan warriors break their oaths
and devastate those boasting Danaans now."

This was all green-eyed Athena needed,
and she darted down from Olympus' peaks
like a star sent by Cronos' cunning son
as an omen for sailors or warriors,
brilliant, leaving a gleaming trail behind—
thus Pallas Athena plunged to the earth
and leapt among their ranks. Amazement seized
those assembled Trojans and Achaeans,   80
then one would catch his neighbor's eye and say
"This may mean miserable war once more,
or peace may be made between our peoples
by Zeus, who decides the luck of battle."

Thus those armored warriors were conversing
while Athena entered the Trojan hosts
disguised as Antenor's son Laodocus,
in search of Pandarus, their godlike lord.
At last she found that excellent archer,
surrounded by crowds of his followers   90
from the lands by Aesepus' rippling streams.
Athena murmured to him from nearby:
"Lycaon's wily son, will you hear me?
If you were to aim at Menelaus
our Trojans would be extremely grateful,
and Alexander more than anyone.
You'd surely have magnificent presents
if he saw Atreus' son Menelaus
laid low and stretched on the funeral pyre.
Come now, try your luck with Menelaus   100
and promise the archer god Apollo

a glorious sacrifice of firstborn lambs
when you return to sacred Zeleia."

    So Athena persuaded him—the fool!
He quickly took his polished bow, the horns
of a wild ibex he himself had shot
in ambush as it emerged from a cave,
pierced its chest, and it fell down a crevass—
and those fine horns, four feet long from the head,
were fitted together by a craftsman   110
who smoothed them, set a golden tip on top.
Pandarus strung this bow and put it down
carefully, while his men screened him with shields
so the Danaans wouldn't leap to their feet
till Atreus' son Menelaus was slain.
Next he opened his quiver and took out
a brand-new arrow laden with dark pain,
speedily fitted it onto the string,
and promised the archer god Apollo
a glorious sacrifice of firstborn lambs   120
when he returned to sacred Zeleia.
He placed its notches on his ox-gut string,
drew the string to his chest, head to the bow,
and after he'd bent it into a round
that mighty bow clanged, its string sang, and then
his keen-cutting arrow sped through the air.

    Now, Menelaus, you weren't forgotten
by the gods, and most of all Athena,
who stood by you, deflected that arrow,
brushed it away as a tender mother   130
sweeps a horsefly from her sleeping baby,
and led it to where the gold belt buckles
met at the overlap of the breastplate.
Into that glorious belt the arrow bore,
through its elaborate ornament and
on through the intricate breastplate itself
and his girdle, barrier against weapons,
his last protection—even this gave way—

but merely grazed the side of his body
so murky blood came spurting from the wound.   140

   As Maeonian dames stain ivory scarlet,
making a cheekpiece for royal horses,
and a king keeps it in his treasure room,
his coursers' glory, pride of his drivers,
though many warriors implore him for it:
thus, Menelaus, blood stained your great thighs
and your shins with their fine ankles beneath.

   Noble Agamemnon shuddered to see
murky blood spurting from that open wound—
and Menelaus himself shuddered too,   150
but when he saw the barb outside his flesh
he felt vastly relieved and took courage.
Then lord Agamemnon groaned heavily
and, holding Menelaus' hand, intoned:
"Brother, it seems I doomed you by swearing
you'd battle before us as our champion,
since the Trojans have trampled holy oaths.
But this can't nullify their promises,
their wine offerings and trusty handclasps!
The Olympian sees that oaths are fulfilled   160
sooner or later, and they'll pay the price
with their wives and children and their own heads.
Yes, I know one thing in my heart and soul:
someday we'll make an end to that city
with Priam and his spear-slinging people,
while Cronos' son on a heavenly throne
shakes his dark aegis over the Trojans
in indignation at their treachery.
Ah, what anguish for me, Menelaus,
if you die and leave this life—then I'd   170
return to Argos in complete disgrace
since our people would think only of home.
They would leave the Trojans their pride and joy,
Argive Helen, while your bones rot in earth
here in Ilios, your work unfinished.
And one of those haughty Trojans may roar

as he leaps upon your funeral mound:
'A fine revenge king Agamemnon had!
After leading his hosts of warriors here
he sailed back home empty-handed at last   180
and left illustrious Menelaus behind.'
May my grave gape for me that very day!"

  But Menelaus reassured him, saying:
"Take heart, man, don't agitate our people.
The wound's skin-deep only—my gold buckles
deflected that arrow, and beneath them
my sturdy girdle stayed to protect me."

  Atreus' son Agamemnon answered him:
"I hope so, beloved brother, but now
we need a healer who can probe the wound   190
and spread soothing salves to relieve the pain."

  Then he summoned his herald Talthybius:
"Ho there, fellow, run for a physician!
Call the son of Asclepius, Machaon,
tell him to come examine Menelaus,
struck down by some cunning Trojan archer—
glory for him but grief for our people!"

  He did as his master had commanded:
made his way through their bristling battalions
in search of Machaon—and finally   200
spied him with those formidable warriors
he'd brought from Trica, pasture of horses.
So the herald rushed up to him and cried:
"Asclepius' son, Agamemnon calls you
to come examine our Menelaus,
struck down by some cunning Trojan archer—
glory for him but grief for our people!"

  Machaon's heart leapt when he heard these words,
and they hurried together through the camp.
When they came to where Menelaus lay   210
wounded, the commanders gathered round him
in a circle, that godlike man strode up

and quickly excised the awful arrow
so its barbs broke backward on his armor,
then loosened his bright belt and beneath it
the sturdy girdle, bulwark in battle.
And when Machaon discovered that wound
he sucked out the blood and spread soothing salves
Cheiron had once given to his father.

    As they bustled about Menelaus   220
the Trojan phalanx began to advance,
and again the Achaeans formed their ranks.

    Then you wouldn't have seen Agamemnon
drowsy or cowering back from combat
but eager to gain more renown of war.
He left his horses and glorious chariot
with Eurymedon, an attendant squire—
who held those beasts just off the battlefield
according to their master's instructions
in case he wearied marshaling his men—   230
and rushed among those battalions on foot.
Wherever he saw them keen for combat
he roared a harangue of exhortation:
"Keep your courage high, my fine Achaeans!
Cronos' son Zeus is no helper of liars—
those Trojans who have broken holy oaths
will feed the vultures with their tender flesh
as we take their wives and children away
after we sack their prosperous city!"

    But wherever he saw them hanging back   240
he scolded those laggards ferociously:
"For shame, Achaeans can't battle back here!
You stand around dazed like so many fawns
all tired out from a long run on the plain,
who stay stock-still in blank stupidity—
I say you stand that helplessly today.
You're waiting till the enemy comes near
our ships' sterns on the beach, so you learn
if majestic Zeus will rescue you *then*?"

Thus that commander moved through his armies—   250
and, as he went, came to the Cretan hordes
advancing after lord Idomeneus,
who hurried before them brave as a boar
while fiery Meriones roused the laggards.
Great Agamemnon rejoiced at that sight
and addressed him in agitated words:
"Idomeneus, you're distinguished in war
and in accomplishing other jobs too
and at banquets when our Danaan people
mix a festive bowl to honor the best.   260
After our commanders have had their share
your cup stands brimful of mellow red wine
like mine, to drink whenever you desire.
So keep up your courage, my dear fellow!"

That Cretan leader Idomeneus cried:
"Yes, of course I'll follow you, Atreus' son,
as I promised so solemnly before.
Better be urging our other warriors
to enter war, now oaths have been broken
and endless troubles will dog those Trojans   270
because they violated holy oaths."

Pleased with this answer, Atreus' son ran on
and came to the two Aiantes, who stood
arming themselves amid swarms of warriors.
Like clouds some goatkeeper sees from a cliff
sweep over the deep when a west wind roars,
and blacker than pitch they seem from afar,
bringing a mighty storm—and he shudders
at the sight, drives his flock into a cave:
thus those Aiantes and their followers   280
moved into combat in thick battalions
darkly bristling with armor and spears.
Great Agamemnon rejoiced at that sight
and addressed them in agitated words:
"You two tough-minded Danaan commanders,
no need for more encouragement from me—
your men are eager enough already.

By Zeus and Athena and Apollo,
I wish all our people had your mettle—
then Priam's prosperous citadel soon   290
would fall before the force of our armies."

    So he left them there and hurried forward,
found that resonant orator Nestor
urging his Pylian people to advance
with Pelagon, Alastor, and Chromius,
imperious Haemon and sturdy Bias.
The mounted spearmen were marshaled in front,
with many brave foot soldiers to the rear
and laggards put in the middle so they
were forced to enter battle with the rest.   300
First of all he ordered his charioteers
to keep a tight rein on their fine horses:
"No daredevil drivers needed, my men—
don't battle alone before the others.
No skulking back either: move straight ahead,
and when an enemy chariot comes near,
off with your spear—that's the best way, I say,
it's how our ancestors ages before
won their magnificent triumphs in war!"

    Thus Neleus' veteran son addressed them.   310
Great Agamemnon rejoiced at that sight
and addressed him in elevated words:
"Sir, I only wish your arms were as firm
as your own indomitable valor.
But you're awfully old—ah, if only
one of our young men had your years instead!"

    And aged Gerenian Nestor answered:
"Yes, Atreus' son, I'd like to be the same
as the day I brought Ereuthalion down.
But the gods don't grant men all things at once: 320
then I was young, now age has taken me.
I'll stay by my people with wise advice—
this is the duty of veteran warriors—

and leave spear slinging to youngsters with more
bounce in their legs, stamina in battle."

    Pleased with this answer, Atreus' son ran on.
Next he found Peteos' son Menestheus
amid the throngs of Athenian spearmen,
while canny Odysseus stood not far off
where the dense Cephallenian battalions   330
waited, since they hadn't heard the war cry
and those Trojan and Achaean columns
had just begun to move—so they remained
till others of their companions advanced
to engage the enemy in combat.
Great Agamemnon was vexed at that sight
and addressed them in agitated words:
"Ha, you illustrious son of Peteos,
and you over there, you cunning rascal,
what's your excuse for cowering to the rear?   340
I want you among our very foremost
ready to enter relentless combat.
You aren't so slow to answer my summons
when our people celebrate a banquet—
there you're delighted to gobble up meat
and swig our delectable wine all day,
but now you'd be glad if ten regiments
struggled between you and the enemy."

    Odysseus scowled terribly and declared:
"Atreus' son, what a lot of gibberish!   350
Do you really believe we're skulking back
now bitter battle has only begun?
Well, you'll see very soon—if you care to—
Telemachus' father standing fearless
among the foremost. You're talking nonsense."

    But Atreus' son king Agamemnon smiled
and, knowing he was angry, apologized:
"Ah, you ingenious son of Laertes,
no need to be scolding you overmuch.
I know very well how faithful you are,   360

and we see eye to eye in everything.
See here, dear friend, I'll make things good later,
so forgive me if I spoke too harshly."

Then he left them there and hurried ahead,
found Tydeus' son dauntless Diomedes
standing off the battlefield and watching,
his squire Sthenelus mounted beside him.
Great Agamemnon was vexed at that sight
and addressed him in agitated words:
"Damn it, you son of turbulent Tydeus,   370
just waiting back here and gaping all day?
Old Tydeus wouldn't have cowered this way,
he always battled far before the rest,
or so I hear from people who saw him—
I never did, but they call him the best.
Once he visited our home in Mycenae
with Polyneices, gathering recruits
for a siege of the sacred Theban walls,
implored our warrior lords for assistance—
and they were extremely eager to help,   380
but Zeus changed their minds with evil omens.
Thus that embassy departed, and when
they reached the reed-rimmed river Asopus
his comrades sent Tydeus to negotiate.
He entered Thebes and found the Cadmeians
feasting in mighty Eteocles' home,
and our Tydeus wasn't a bit afraid
though alone among many enemies,
challenged them in the games and won each time
easily, with Athena aiding him.   390
This made the Cadmeians most indignant,
and as he returned they set an ambush
with fifty warriors under the command
of Maeon the bloody, bold with his spear,
and that ruthless ruffian Polyphontes.
But Tydeus brought them to an awful end,
killed every Cadmeian except for one,
Maeon, whom he spared obeying omens.

Tydeus was that kind of man, but his son's
worse in battle and better in babble."   400

  Tydeus' son Diomedes said nothing
out of reverence for his commander,
while magnificent Sthenelus answered:
"Agamemnon, it's all a pack of lies!
Our fathers were far inferior to us!
We took Thebes and its seven city gates
with fewer men against a stronger wall
because Zeus helped us by sending omens,
while our fathers failed and paid with their lives.
No, you can't even call them our equals!"   410

  Diomedes scowled at him and declared:
"Hold your tongue, dear fellow, and listen here—
it's no disgrace that great Agamemnon
should rally our people to resistance:
more honor and glory for him if we
devastate those Trojans and take their town,
but if we lose, he'll suffer the most.
Now we should be thinking of furious war!"

  So he leapt from his chariot fully armed,
and that bronze rang horribly as he moved   420
among the troops. Brave men shook to hear it.

  As wave after wave roll straight toward the beach
a day the whistling west wind whips them on—
they crest far out on the waters and then
roar against the shore, but where headlands are
rise towering and spit their salt spray out:
thus rank after rank the Achaeans marched
into that battle, each group commanded
by its own captain. You'd never have thought
a man of them could speak, they moved so still   430
in awe of those leaders—and their armor
flashed dazzling about them as they advanced.
Yet the Trojans were like those countless ewes
who wait to be milked in some rich man's court
and ceaselessly bleat when they hear their lambs—

so clamorous and uproarious were they all,
since their contingents had no common speech
but babbled languages of many lands.
With them went Ares, with their opponents
Athena and Rout and raging Discord,   440
bloodthirsty Ares' sister and comrade
who rises just a bit at first but soon
has her head in heaven, her feet on earth.
Now she stirred up strife between those armies
and raced among them, making groans grow great.

    They came together at the battle place
with a crash of shields and spears and armored
warriors' fury: studded buckler battered
studded buckler, a dreadful din arose.
Together were screams and triumphant shrieks   450
of slain and slayers, earth was drenched in blood.
Loud as when winter torrents hurtle down
from their mountain springs to merge sheer currents
in a mighty gorge where valleys converge,
and far off on some hill a shepherd hears—
such was the roar as those men met in war.

    Antilochus' spear killed the first Trojan
among the foremost, brave Echepolus,
hurtled through his horsehair-crested helmet
into the forehead, so that bronze weapon   460
pierced the bone—then darkness covered his eyes
and he toppled to earth like a wall.
Thus he lay sprawled out till his foot was seized
by Calchedon's son proud Elephenor,
who lugged him off, very eager to win
his bright armor—but only a moment:
Agenor observed Elphenor and jabbed
a giant spear where the shield left him bare
as he bent, and he reeled and fell to earth.
So the soul left his corpse, while over it   470
ghastly work went on: opposing warriors
hurled themselves on one another like wolves.

Next Telamonian Aias flung a spear
at lusty Simoeisius, whose mother
had borne him by the Simois as she came
down from Mount Ida tending her sheep herds,
so they gave him that name—but his parents
had little joy in rearing him, so brief
his life became, cut short by Aias' spear.
As he strode with the foremost, that weapon   480
sheared through his shoulder by the right nipple
and he fell to earth like some poplar
which flourishes on the marshy meadow,
trunk long and smooth, rich foliage above,
till a craftsman takes his ax and hacks it
down—a wheel rim for some handsome chariot—
and it lies drying on a riverbank:
thus Anthemion's son Simoeisius lay
when Aias had slain him. Now Antiphus
hurled at giant Telamonian Aias   490
but missed, hit Odysseus' comrade Leucas
on the groin as he dragged that body off,
so he let it fall, toppled over it.
Furious for his friend's murder, Odysseus
strode to battle in his brilliant armor
and stood before the Trojans, poised a spear,
his eyes darting round—and every man shrank
as it flew through the air: no miss, it hit
Priam's natural son Democoön,
who'd come from his stud farm in Abydus.   500
Straight on its course, that dangerous weapon
bore into his temple; its bronze point sheared
through the head—then darkness covered his eyes
and his armor boomed as he crashed to earth.
Now Hector and his foremost men gave way
while the Danaans bellowed, dragged off the corpse,
and moved on forward. But Apollo saw
from his lookout on Pergamus and howled:
"Rough-riding Trojan warriors, hold your ground!
Those Danaans don't have flesh of iron or stone   510
a well-aimed weapon cannot penetrate.

Remember their illustrious Achilles
isn't with them but sulking by the ships."

Thus that awful god roared, but the Danaans
were backed by Zeus's daughter Athena,
who hurried among them spurring them on.

The next man trapped by fate was Diores,
his right ankle shattered as a jagged
boulder thrown by formidable Peiros,
Thracian commander who came from Aenus,   520
savagely shattered those ankle tendons
and the bone—so he fell back in the dust
stretching both hands to his dear companions,
gasping his life away. Mighty Peiros
stabbed him by the navel, his bowels burst out
onto the ground, and darkness veiled his eyes.

As Peiros leapt back, Thoas hurled a spear
which lodged beside his nipple, pierced the lung—
then he hurried to extract that weapon
from the fallen warrior, drew a keen sword   530
and stabbed him on the navel, took his life.
But Peiros' fine armor fell to his friends:
topknotted Thracians with enormous spears,
who battered that great, that strong, that lordly
Thoas, staggering back to his own men.
So those two lay side by side in the dust—
the Thracians' leader and the Epeians'—
and many others lay dead around them.

Then no man there might have mocked at that war,
and if any combatant stayed unscathed   540
Pallas Athena was holding his hand
to shield him from those showers of weapons—
so many Trojans and Danaans that day
lay facedown in dust by one another.

Book Five: Diomedes' Prowess

*Diomedes dominates the battlefield, wounds Aphrodite and
Ares, who rush back to Olympus.*

Then Pallas Athena gave Diomedes
courage and fury, made him the foremost
so he might win a magnificent name.
From his shield and helmet she lit a flame
like that autumn star which glitters brightest
after it bathes in rippling Oceanus—
she lit this flame on his head and shoulders
and sent him to where most warriors were massed.

   One of those Trojans was wealthy Dares,
priest to Hephaestus—and he had two sons,   10
glorious warriors, Idaeus and Phegeus.
These two thundered toward prince Diomedes
in their chariot, while he advanced on foot.
After they came very near each other
Phegeus flung his formidable spear first,
but it hurtled over Diomedes'
left shoulder—then that son of Tydeus hurled
with very deadly aim and hit his chest
between the nipples, toppled him to earth.
Idaeus leapt from their splendid chariot   20
too terrified to protect his brother—
and now he'd never have escaped his doom
but Hephaestus saved him, hid him in night
so the old priest wouldn't be completely
bereaved. Diomedes seized their horses,
ordered his comrades to take them away.

But when the Trojans saw Dares' two sons,
one running in terror, one lying dead,
they stood aghast—and green-eyed Athena
clutched fiery Ares by the hand and cried: 30
"Ares, Ares, you bloodthirsty ruffian,
let's leave these people to battle alone,
and father Zeus will decide the winner.
He'll be awfully angry if we stay."

Now she led fiery Ares from battle,
seated him on the banks of Scamander,
and those Trojans fled. Each Achaean lord
brought a warrior down: first Agamemnon
slew Halizonian Podius as he wheeled
his chariot round to escape, drove a spear   40
between his shoulders and it pierced his chest—
and his armor boomed as he crashed to earth.

Idomeneus killed Borus' son Phaestus,
who'd come from his farm in fertile Tarnë:
as he turned to escape, that Cretan chief
thrust a spear through his right shoulder, he fell
thundering, and dreadful darkness took him.

Those Cretans tore off his armor—and next
glorious Scamandrius, most skillful hunter,
fell before Menelaus' raging spear.   50
Divine Artemis herself had taught him
to kill all beasts of the mountain forests—
but now he wasn't helped by that goddess
or his famous finesse in archery:
Atreus' son fiery Menelaus drove
a spear between his shoulders as he fled
in terror; it hurtled through to his chest
and his armor clanged as he fell facefirst.

Next Meriones slew canny Phereclus,
a man of legendary craftsmanship—   60
Athena loved him so extravagantly.
He'd built those swift ships for Alexander,
trouble for the Trojans and for himself

since he knew much but not the gods' omens.
Illustrious Meriones pursued him, thrust
a spear into his right buttock and straight
to the bladder beneath the bone—and he
fell moaning to his knees as death took him.

   Then Phyleus' son Meges killed Pedasus,
bastard born, though Theano had reared him   70
very tenderly as one of her own:
from very close before him, Meges hurled
a spear that pierced to the nape of his neck;
the metal severed his tongue at the root
and he fell in the dust, biting cold bronze.

   Next Eurypylus slaughtered Hypsenor,
sole son of Scamander's priest Dolopion,
whom all the people worshiped like a god—
Euaemon's mighty son Eurypylus
ran after him as he fled in terror,   80
drove a sword through his shoulder so the arm
fell bloody to earth, and over his eyes
surged dark death and irresistible fate.

   Thus their strenuous work of war went on—
and you'd never have known which of those hordes
was Diomedes', he raged so wildly:
stormed over the plain like some winterborne
torrent that tears the riverbanks away
and won't be held by those enormous dikes
or the stout walls of flourishing vineyards   90
as it roars on, driven by Zeus's rains,
and many fine fields are devastated—
thus he shattered the Trojan battalions,
no match for his might, despite their numbers.

   But when that son of Lycaon saw him
driving the Trojans in frenzied retreat
he took careful aim with a pliant bow
and shot a terrible arrow that bore
into the armor on his right shoulder
so murky blood oozed over his breastplate.   100

Then Lycaon's son Pandarus bellowed:
"Stand steadfast, you rough-riding Trojans—now
I hit the finest Achaean, and he
won't last much longer if it really was
archer Apollo who sent me to war!"

Yet that quick arrow hadn't brought him down,
so he reeled back to his chariot and called
Capaneus' son intrepid Sthenelus:
"Hop down here, my dear friend, and help me take
this terrible arrow from my shoulder."   110

Then Sthenelus leapt to the earth and drew
the arrow through his shimmering armor
so its barbs wouldn't bend—and dark blood surged
from his tunic. Then Diomedes prayed:
"Hear me, daughter of Zeus, unwearied one!
Remember how you stood by my father
in carnage of combat—now help me too.
Just give me a chance to bring down this man
who shot at me so treacherously and
boasted I wouldn't be long for this world."   120

Pallas Athena heeded his appeal,
threw marvelous lightness over his limbs,
and, standing by him, murmured in his ear:
"Be afraid of nothing, Diomedes,
now I've given you that dauntless courage
your formidable father always had.
And see how I swept the mist from your eyes
so you may tell warriors from immortals.
Don't dare do battle with any other
of the blessed gods you encounter here   130
except for her: if Aphrodite comes,
let her have a taste of your mighty spear."

With this, green-eyed Athena departed,
and Tydeus' son returned to the front ranks.
Though he'd been ferocious before, now he
was three times more, like some lordly lion
a shepherd who watches the woolly sheep

has wounded as he leaps into the fold,
which makes him so desperate there's no defense
from that hurt beast slinking through the stables   140
till those terrified sheep are strewn in heaps
and he leaps raging over the high wall—
thus Diomedes ravaged the Trojans.

   Next he slew Astynous and Hypeiron,
one with a spearcast above the nipple
and one with a sword that tore his shoulder
from the back. He left their bodies lying, then
hurried after Abas and Polydius,
sons of the dream reader Eurydamas,
who hadn't read their dreams when they left home,   150
so dauntless Diomedes slaughtered them both.
Now he fell upon Xanthus and Thoön,
lusty sons of Phaenops, who was aging
and had no other sons to be his heirs,
but Diomedes took their lives, dispatched
both of them, so their father had only
grief remaining—never welcomed them home,
and the next of kin divided his lands.

   Then Diomedes caught two sons of Priam,
Echemnon and Chromius, in one chariot.   160
As a lion leaps among cattle to snap
the neck of some grazing cow or heifer,
thus Tydeus' son sent them toppling to earth
without more ado, took their fine armor,
while his men drove their horses to the ships.

   But when Aeneas observed Diomedes
he hurried among all the flying spears
in search of Pandarus, master archer.
At last he found that son of Lycaon
and, standing near him, murmured in his ear: 170
"Say, Pandarus, where are your arrows
and your fame? You've no peer as a bowman
in Ilios or your homeland of Lycia.
Very well, pray to Zeus and take a shot

at that man who's been such a dreadful plague,
murdered these many fine warriors of ours—
or he may be some god infuriated
because we neglected a sacrifice."

Lycaon's son Pandarus answered him:
"Ah, Aeneas, our canny counselor,   180
he looks very like prince Diomedes—
so I'd guess from his shield and his helmet
and his horses, though he may be a god.
If he is Diomedes, as I believe,
at least he has help from some immortal
who stands beside him invisible and
deflected my arrow as it landed.
Yes, already I tried a shot at him,
which hurtled through his breastplate so it seemed
my bow had sent him down to Hades, but   190
it hadn't. He must be an angry god.
I brought no chariots with me when I came
though my father has eleven at home—
the finest there are, kept in perfect shape,
and for each a team of speedy horses
wait browsing on barley and fresh-cut rye.
The day I was about to leave for Troy
my father insisted I should take them,
said to ride behind those powerful beasts
and lead the Trojans in bitter battle.   200
But I foolishly refused to do it
since I was afraid they would lack fodder,
and they'd never suffered hunger before.
So I left them there, came to Troy on foot
trusting my bow—little use it has been.
I tried a shot at two of their leaders,
Tydeus' and Atreus' sons, hit both men
so they bled, but only made them angrier.
Ah, a miserable day it was for me
when I took this bow from its peg and came   210
here to Ilios for the sake of Hector!
Yet if I ever return home and see

my wife and lands and sumptuous palace,
you can chop off my head that very day
if I don't break this bow in smithereens
and burn it up for all the good it's done."

That magnificent Aeneas replied:
"No need for talk, man—things won't be better
till we take a gleaming chariot and drive
to see if he's proof against our spears too.   220
Just hop up here beside me so you see
how those horses of Tros go galloping
over the plain in pursuit or retreat
and bring us back safely if glorious Zeus
grants victory to Tydeus' son again.
You handle the whip and shimmering reins
while I dismount to meet him in combat,
or you take care of battle while I drive."

Lycaon's son Pandarus answered him:
"Hold the reins yourself, my dear Aeneas—   230
better they have their usual charioteer
if we need to beat a speedy retreat.
Unless they hear your voice they may run wild
and rear against the reins in terror, then
Tydeus' indomitable son would come
to slaughter us both and take our horses.
No, drive your own chariot yourself, while I
batter him back with my great ashwood spear."

And he too leapt on the gleaming chariot,
drove it thunderously toward Diomedes,   240
whose squire Sthenelus saw them approaching
and anxiously called to his commander:
"Oh my, Diomedes, look over there:
two very dangerous Trojan warriors
are driving toward us—one a fine archer,
Lycaon's son Pandarus, the other
lordly Aeneas, who claims as parents
Anchises and golden Aphrodite.

Let's get on our chariot—we're surely doomed
if we stay here with the foremost warriors."   250

  Diomedes scowled at him and declared:
"Nonsense, my boy, I won't consider it—
cowering from combat is not my way;
I'll stay steadfast and sturdy as ever.
And I've no need for a chariot either—
Pallas Athena protects me from fear.
I assure you, those warriors' swift horses
won't be bringing both of them back alive.
And let me tell you another thing too:
if our Athena grants me the glory   260
of slaying them both, leave our horses here
with their reins tied tight to the chariot rail,
then seize Aeneas' magnificent steeds
and drive them back among our Achaeans—
they're from the stock that Zeus granted Tros
as payment for his son Ganymedes,
so no better team runs under the sun.
Lord Anchises stole a strain from that breed
by mating his mares to them secretly,
and six fine colts were born at his palace.   270
Four he kept to rear in his own stables
but gave the other two to Aeneas.
If only those splendid beasts could be ours!"

  As Diomedes conversed with his squire
that enemy chariot came very near.
Pandarus bellowed to Diomedes:
"Turbulent tough-minded son of Tydeus,
it seems my arrow didn't bring you down,
so let's see if this spear will do the job!"

  Then he poised his ashwood spear and hurled it—   280
and straight through that intricately carved shield
his weapon slashed and lodged in the breastplate.
And Lycaon's son Pandarus bellowed:
"Ha, that shot caught your belly, so you won't
last long, while I have a mighty triumph!"

But Diomedes answered unperturbed:
"A clear miss, idiot—and now I'm sure
you won't be escaping till one of you
has glutted murderous Ares with his blood."

Now he hurled a sharp spear, and Athena   290
sent it hurtling onto Pandarus' nose,
through his white teeth, cut his tongue at the root,
and it came out at the base of the chin—
then he pitched from that chariot, his brilliant
armor booming, and those swift-hooved horses
reared up, as life and strength abandoned him.

But lordly Aeneas leapt to the ground
so the Danaans wouldn't despoil that corpse,
bestrode it like an arrogant lion,
shield and dangerous spear held before him,   300
ready to slay any man who came near,
roaring horribly. Diomedes seized
a huge boulder, too much for two warriors
as men are now, but he held it with ease.
He raised this boulder, brought it crashing down
on Aeneas' hip just at the pelvis
so its joint was shattered, the muscles crushed
with a gaping wound. And that commander
tumbled to his knees and leaned on the earth
with a heavy hand, as night took his eyes.   310

Now Aeneas would have perished, but he
was seen by his mother, who conceived him
to Anchises in the Dardanian fields—
golden Aphrodite embraced her son,
enfolded him in her shimmering robe,
invincible shield, so no Achaean
could send a bronze spear hurtling in his breast.

Thus she carried her dear son from battle.
But prince Sthenelus had not forgotten
the instructions his master had given,   320
left his nimble-hooved horses at the rear
with their reins tied tight to the chariot rail

then seized Aeneas' magnificent steeds
and drove them back among the Achaeans,
where he begged Deipylus, his dearest friend
and a playmate in the days of their youth,
to take them from the battlefield. Next he
leapt on his chariot and seized the bright reins
and went to find dauntless Diomedes,
who was rushing after Aphrodite   330
since he well knew she was a weak one, none
of those gods who lord it over combat,
no Athena, no plundering Enyo.
When he found Aphrodite in the crowd
Diomedes lunged out desperately,
and his sharp spear ripped the delicate skin
on her wrist above the palm, tore the flesh
through her ambrosial robe the Graces wove—
and from it poured that immortal ichor
which flows in the veins of the blessed gods,   340
for they eat no bread nor drink gleaming wine,
so they are bloodless and called immortals.
Now she shrieked and dropped her beloved son,
but archer Apollo gathered him up,
covered him in clouds, so no Achaean
could send a bronze spear hurtling in his breast.

  And Diomedes bellowed after her:
"Keep away from combat, daughter of Zeus!
Isn't it enough you fool weak women?
If you ever return, I think you'll learn   350
to shudder at the very sound of war!"

  Quite frantic with pain, she scurried away
till windfoot Iris led her to safety,
much distressed, her fine skin stained with the wound.
She found Ares sitting apart from war,
spear and horses suspended on a cloud—
and fell on her knees, implored her brother
to let her use his sturdy gold-trimmed steeds:
"Save me, dear brother! lend me your horses
so I may drive to our home Olympus.   360

I've been badly wounded by a mortal,
Tydeus' son, who would challenge even Zeus."

   And Ares acceded to her appeal.
Then she mounted the chariot in anguish
while Iris climbed beside her, took the reins
and lashed those horses—so away they flew.
Soon they reached the gods' home, steep Olympus,
where windfoot Iris reined the horses in,
freed them and gave them ambrosial fodder.
Aphrodite fell before her mother   370
Dionë, who gathered her in her arms
and stroked her with her fingers, murmuring:
"Now, now, my dear, which god has treated you
so unkindly, as if you'd been naughty."

   Laughter-loving Aphrodite replied:
"That arrogant Diomedes did it—
stabbed me because I tried to save my son,
Aeneas, my favorite among mortals.
Oh, it's not a war of men anymore—
these Achaeans will attack even gods."   380

   Then delightful Dionë answered her:
"Be brave, my darling, take it patiently.
Many of us Olympians have suffered
from mortal men when we were quarreling—
even Ares, after Aloeus' sons
Otus and Ephialtes left him trussed up
and he lay thirteen months in that bronze jar.
That would have been the end of our Ares,
but their stepmother Eriboea
told Hermes the Helper, who released him   390
just in time, when he was almost done for.
And Hera suffered too when Heracles
hit her right breast with a three-barbed arrow—
why, the pain was simply intolerable—
and this very same man, a son of Zeus,
shot a keen-cutting arrow at Hades
as he stood among the dead in Pylos.

He went to Zeus's Olympian palace
simply racked with pain, that arrow had made
such a horrid wound on his stout shoulder,   400
and there Paeëon applied soothing salves
to heal him, for he was not born to die.
But that hothead Heracles went too far
when he shot his arrows at Olympians.
And now Athena sicced this one on you—
fool! Diomedes doesn't seem to know
men who contend with gods have no long life,
no children come babbling about their knees
to welcome them back from the battlefield.
Despite his might, he'd better consider   410
someone stronger than you may attack him,
so Aegialeia, Adrastus' daughter
and delightful wife of Diomedes,
will wake her household with lamentations
for her dear husband, best of the Danaans."

And she wiped ichor from her daughter's wrist,
so that wound was healed, the awful pains eased.
But Hera and Athena were watching
and tried to provoke Zeus Thunderhurler.
First the goddess green-eyed Athena cried: 420
"Father Zeus, will my words make you angry?
It seems Aphrodite has been urging
some Argive girl to go with her Trojans,
and as she caressed and beseeched her, scratched
her delicate hand on a golden brooch."

The father of gods and men smiled at this,
summoned golden Aphrodite, and said:
"Child, don't busy yourself about battle.
Care for the lovely affairs of marriage,
leave such things to Ares and Athena."   430

Thus the immortal gods were conversing
as Diomedes leapt on Aeneas—
he knew Apollo protected that lord
but stayed unafraid, still relentless to

slay brave Aeneas and take his armor.
Three times Diomedes wildly attacked,
three times great Apollo battered him back.
As he came storming forward the fourth time
Phoebus Apollo bellowed horribly:
"Get away from here, Tydeus' son, don't try   440
striving against immortals—you're only
a miserable man who walks on the earth."

   And great Diomedes fell back a bit,
avoiding the anger of Apollo.
Then that Far Shooter wafted Aeneas
to his temple at holy Pergamus,
where Leto and Artemis healed his wound,
glorified him in the sanctuary.
And Phoebus made a phantom in the form
of Aeneas, wearing the same armor—   450
and over it those opposing warriors
battered at one another's oxhide shields
and elegant bucklers of brilliant bronze.

   Next far-shooting Phoebus Apollo called:
"Ares, Ares, you bloodthirsty ruffian,
won't you intervene to beat back that man
Tydeus' son, who would challenge even Zeus?
He wounded Aphrodite on the wrist
and then went after me like a maniac."

   So Apollo sat on Pergamon's peak   460
while fiery Ares entered the Trojans,
taking the shape of Thracian Acamas,
and bellowed through those assembled armies:
"You sons of Zeus's beloved Priam,
how long will we let the Achaeans win?
Till they battle about our city gates?
Now they've slain a warrior great as Hector,
our able leader Aeneas, but we
can save our comrade's body at the least!"

His words gave a surge of strength to them all,   470
and the Lycian leader Sarpedon roared:
"Hector, what's become of your bravery?
You said you could hold that city alone,
with only your relatives to help you,
but now I can't see any one of them—
they skulk back like dogs before a lion
while your good allies do all the fighting.
I'm one of their lords from a distant land—
yes, it's far to Lycia by Xanthus' streams,
where I left my wife and my baby boy,   480
a splendid fortune and envious neighbors—
and now I've encouraged my Lycian hordes
to enter battle, though we've nothing here
those Danaans might be taking as booty,
while you can't even rally your own men
to fight in defense of their families.
Ah, you'll all be like fishes in a net
when your enemies get their hands on you
and plunder your prosperous capital!
You should worry about this night and day   490
and beg the lords of your glorious allies
to stand steadfast, then no one would blame you."

Sarpedon's words stung Hector to the quick.
He leapt from his chariot in full armor
and hurried among them waving two spears,
urging them to finally make a stand.
Thus they rallied and faced the enemy,
who came forward steadily, unafraid.
As wind sweeps chaff over a threshing floor
when grain is winnowed, and blond Demeter   500
separates chaff while the angry wind blasts
pile it high in white heaps: so those Danaans
grew all white with the dust that their horses
battered to the brazen sky as they dashed
back and forth, their drivers lashing them on.
Every man moved straight ahead, while Ares
veiled the war with night to help the Trojans

and raged everywhere himself, obeying
golden-sword Apollo, who had told him
to enter combat, because Athena,   510
the Danaans' best helper, had departed.
Next Apollo himself sent Aeneas
from the temple, put fury in his heart,
and he joined his companions, who rejoiced
to see him appear before them unscathed
and undaunted. But they asked no questions,
they were so full of the work Apollo,
deadly Ares, and restless Strife had made.

On the other side, the Achaean lords
encouraged their men to stand firm, though they   520
needed no urging: faced the enemy
steadfast as mists that the son of Cronos
sets over mountaintops in still weather,
motionless, when the North Wind and other
winds are asleep, so those shadowy clouds
remain unscattered by the whistling blasts—
thus those Achaean spearmen held their ground.
Agamemnon strode among them, roaring:
"Be men, my friends, remember your courage!
Don't shame yourselves before your companions!   530
Men with self-respect have a chance to live,
but cowards come to a miserable end!"

Next he hurled his spear, hit one of the first,
Aeneas' companion Deïcoön,
honored by the Trojans like Priam's sons
since he always fought among the foremost:
Agamemnon's spear landed on his shield,
which gave way, and that weapon hurtled through,
straight through his girdle and into his groin,
and his armor boomed as he crashed to earth.   540

Then Aeneas slew two Achaean chiefs,
Diocles' sons Crethon and Orsilochus,
whose father lived in Pherae with much wealth
and boasted his descent from the river

Alphaeus, which flows through those Pylian fields
and begat Orsilochus' grandfather,
progenitor of haughty Diocles,
who in turn became father of twin sons,
illustrious Orsilochus and Crethon.
After attaining manhood, they took ships　　　　　　　550
and followed the Danaans to grassy Troy
so the sons of Atreus might have revenge—
but met their own destruction in that land.
They were like two lions of the mountaintop
reared by their dam in a tangly forest,
who prey on the herds of cattle and sheep,
a plague for all people, till they themselves
are brought to earth by a hunter's weapon:
thus Aeneas slaughtered those two brothers,
who toppled like two towering fir trees.　　　　　　　560

　Menelaus pitied them as they fell
and strode out in all his brilliant armor
brandishing a sharp spear, as Ares planned
so Aeneas might make an end of him.
But prince Antilochus saw him advance
and came running, afraid if he was slain
all their enterprise would be abandoned,
since no one could claim Helen—and they stood
ready to battle it out with their spears
as Antilochus reached his companion.　　　　　　　570
Despite his strength, Aeneas didn't stay
when he saw those two standing side by side,
so they dragged both dead bodies to the rear,
placed that luckless pair in their comrades' arms,
and returned to war among the foremost.

　Now they slew Pylaemenes, Ares' peer
and lord of the noble Paphlagonians:
as he stood in a chariot, Menelaus
struck his collarbone with a spearcast; next
Antilochus hurled a stone at his squire　　　　　　　580
Mydon, who was turning round to retreat,
struck him square on the elbow, so his hands

let the ivory-trimmed reins slip to the dust,
then drove a sword deep into his temple,
and, gasping, he toppled from the chariot
headfirst in the dust up to his shoulders.
Thus he lay awhile in that deep sandbed
till his own horses kicked him to the dust
as gallant Antilochus drove them off.

But lord Hector observed those two and charged   590
bellowing, as his battalions followed
mightily, led by Ares and Enyo,
who carried with her confusion of war
while Ares wielded an enormous spear,
running now before Hector, now after.

And Diomedes shuddered at the sight.
As a wanderer crossing a great plain
stops dumbfounded before a swift river,
sees it seething with foam and moves away:
thus that son of Tydeus gave ground and roared: 600
"Friends, remember how we admired Hector
for strength and dexterity with the spear,
but that's because some god stood at his side
as Ares helps him now in mortal shape.
So let's retreat without turning our backs—
better keep our distance before the gods."

Then the Trojans moved in to close combat
as Hector slew two warriors, Anchialus
and Menesthles, riding in one chariot.
Giant Aias pitied them as they fell,   610
ran very near and hurled a mighty spear,
which struck prince Amphius, a man of much wealth
who owned vast wheat fields in Paesus—but fate
brought him to fight for Priam and his sons:
so that formidable spearcast landed
over the belt, rammed into his belly,
and he fell thunderously. Huge Aias
rushed to plunder that corpse, as the Trojans
rained spears at him—and his shield caught many—

and, with his heel on Amphius' body, wrenched   620
the weapon out but could get no armor,
such clouds of missiles showered all around,
and he greatly feared the Trojan phalanx,
many intrepid fully armed warriors
who battered that great, that strong, that lordly
Aias, staggering back to his own men.

   Thus their strenuous work of war went on.
Next resistless fate sent Tlepolemus,
Heracles' heroic son, toward Sarpedon.
After they came very near each other,   630
one a son, one a grandson of wise Zeus,
Tlepolemus called his adversary:
"You cunning Lycian leader Sarpedon,
why skulk back as if you'd never seen war?
It must be a lie you are Zeus's son;
you're nothing like those spear-slinging people
born from thunderlord Zeus in days before—
far different from lionheart Heracles,
my own father, a marvel at battle.
He once came here for Laomedon's mares   640
bringing only six ships and a few warriors,
who plundered Troy with no trouble at all,
but you don't have the strength to be a lord.
No matter how mighty you are, I'm sure
you won't assist the Trojans anymore
after my spear sends you down to Hades."

   That Lycian lord Sarpedon answered him:
"Tlepolemus, your father sacked Ilios
because of Laomedon's foolishness
when he scolded the one who helped him well   650
and refused those mares he had promised him.
But you'll be meeting your own death and fate
this very day, so I have more glory
and Hades the famous horseman your soul."

   Then Tlepolemus poised his ashwood spear—
and the two weapons leapt from their hands

simultaneously: Sarpedon's hit him
square on the neck, and that agonizing
spear sheared through, as darkness covered his eyes,
while Tlepolemus' hurtled through the air,　　　　　　660
struck gallant Sarpedon on the left thigh,
and grazed the bone—but his father saved him.

　His comrades brought him from the battlefield
terribly troubled by that ashwood spear
dragging from his thigh—though no one noticed
or thought to remove it so he might stand,
they had such a struggle to defend him.

　On the other side, the Achaeans brought
Tlepolemus' corpse from the battlefield—
and Odysseus watched them in a fury,　　　　　　670
pondering deeply if he should pursue
Zeus's magnificent son Sarpedon
or rob many more Lycians of their lives.
Yet wily Odysseus wasn't fated
to vanquish that son of Zeus with his spear,
so Athena sent him toward the Lycians:
he slew Chromius, Alastor, Coeranus,
Alcandrus, Halius, and prince Prytanis,
and would have made an end of even more,
but flashing-helmeted Hector saw him　　　　　　680
and strode out in all his brilliant armor,
terror for the Achaeans. Sarpedon
rejoiced to see him and gasped piteously:
"Ah, Priam's son, don't abandon me here!
Take me away to Troy, then let me die
there in your capital, since I'll never
return to my beloved home alive,
a delight for my wife and baby boy."

　But Hector made no answer, hurried by,
raging to devastate the enemy　　　　　　690
and take the lives of many fine warriors.
So Sarpedon's followers stretched him out
under an oak of aegis-bearing Zeus,

and his trusty companion Pelagon
eased the ashwood spear from his wounded thigh—
and his eyes misted, he fainted away.
But the breath of the North Wind revived him
after they had given him up for dead.

   Then, under Ares' and Hector's attack,
those Achaeans did not bolt for the ships,   700
nor could they hold their ground but retreated
steadily when they heard Ares was there.

   And who was the first, who last to be slain
by Priam's son Hector and iron Ares?
Teuthras first, next rough-riding Orestes,
Trechus the Aetolian, Oenomaus,
Helenus and bright-armored Oresbius,
a man from Hyle by Lake Cephisus
with vast estates, and around him other
Boeotians lived on their fertile farmlands.   710

   But when white-armed Hera saw the Trojans
ravaging those Achaeans in battle
her words came pouring out to Athena:
"Dear me, energetic daughter of Zeus,
what about our promise to Menelaus
he would sack that city, return safe home?
He won't, if fiery Ares has his way.
Now we should be thinking of furious war!"

   The goddess green-eyed Athena obeyed.
So those prancing horses were harnessed by   720
Cronos' daughter stately Hera herself,
as lovely Hebe attached eight-spoked wheels
to the splendid chariot's iron axle—
rims imperishable gold and on them
finely formed tires of bronze, a wondrous sight,
and silver hubs spun round on either side—
while the body was woven of plaited gold
and silver-trimmed bands, two rails running round.
The chariot pole was of silver, fastened
to an incomparable golden yoke   730

with golden breast straps—and stately Hera,
raging for battle, harnessed her horses.

  Meanwhile Athena, lord Zeus's daughter,
let her shimmering soft robe slither down
onto the floor of her father's palace,
donned the tunic of Zeus Thunderhurler,
and armed herself for miserable war.
Over her shoulders she slung the aegis—
that terrible storm-cloud shield crowned by Rout
with Courage, Strife, and blood-chilling Onslaught   740
and the horrid repellent Gorgon face,
portent of thunderlord Zeus's power—
took a two-horned four-pronged helmet of gold,
adorned with spearmen from a hundred towns.
She stepped on the brilliant chariot, holding
her huge, stout, heavy spear that devastates
warriors who anger great Zeus's daughter.
Now Hera flicked the horses with her whip,
and open groaned those gates kept by the Hours,
who watch over heaven and Olympus   750
and can split the thick clouds or keep them shut.
So they drove their team through the gleaming gates
and found thunderlord Zeus seated apart
on steep Olympus' very highest peak.
There white-armed Hera reined the horses in
and addressed powerful Zeus, Cronos' son:
"Father Zeus, aren't you angry when Ares
destroys so many Achaean warriors
wantonly, brutally, making me sad
but not Aphrodite and Apollo,   760
who egg that awful madman on?
Papa Zeus, would you be furious if I
bowled him over and chased him from battle?"

  Whereupon cloudgathering Zeus replied:
"Come now, better leave him to Athena—
she's always been his bitterest enemy."

And white-armed Hera did as he had said:
whipped the horses up, and away they flew
there between earth and the starry heavens.
As far as a man can see through the haze   770
when he sits high above the wine-dark sea
those snorting horses traveled at one leap.
But when they came to the land of Ilios,
where Simois and Scamander join their streams,
stately Hera reined her horses in,
freed them from their yokes, and hid them in mist
while Simois gave them ambrosia to graze.

Thus they went their way like two timid doves,
furious to aid the Achaean warriors.
And when they came to where the most and best   780
were massed about mighty Diomedes
in a thick throng, like man-eating lions
or fierce wild boars, most terrible in force,
that goddess white-armed Hera stood and roared
with the semblance of brass-throated Stentor,
whose voice is as loud as fifty others:
"Shame and disgrace, pretty-faced Achaeans!
While Achilles still came out to battle,
those Trojans stayed cowering in their town,
they were so afraid of his giant spear—   790
but now they battle right beside the ships!"

Her words gave a surge of strength to them all.
Then green-eyed Athena neared Diomedes,
found him beside his horses and chariot
cooling the wound from Pandarus' arrow,
since the sweat distressed him under the strap
of his great curved shield and his arm was numb,
so he lifted that strap, wiped off the blood.
And seizing the yoke of his team, she cried:
"Tydeus' son isn't much like his father,   800
who was small in stature but a warrior!
Yes, even when I told him not to fight
or make a show of strength, that time he came
alone among the Cadmeians in Thebes—

I ordered him to feast with them in peace,
but haughty and arrogant as ever,
he challenged the young men to games and won
quite easily, since I stood at his side.
So now I protect you as I did him
and want you to enter battle again—   810
but perhaps all this effort has tired you?
Or are you terrified? Well then, you're no
son of our fiery turbulent Tydeus."

    And that dauntless Diomedes replied:
"Yes, daughter of Zeus, I know who you are,
so let me explain what I have in mind.
I'm neither afraid nor hesitating
but merely remember your instructions
to avoid combat with the blessed gods
except for her: if Aphrodite came,   820
let her have a taste of my mighty spear.
Therefore I've retreated and ordered all
our people to assemble round me here
now Ares is lording it over war."

    And that goddess green-eyed Athena cried:
"Tydeus' son Diomedes, my dear man,
do not fear Ares or any other
immortals, I'll stay so close beside you.
Drive your glorious horses straight toward Ares
and run him through! You're a match for Ares,   830
that crook, that lunatic, that renegade
who was just promising Hera and me
to back our Achaean armies, but see
what that double-crosser did to us now!"

    Then she yanked Sthenelus from the chariot
and he scrambled to get out of the way—
so up beside prince Diomedes she
leapt in a frenzy, and the axle groaned
under a dread goddess and a hero.
Pallas Athena seized the whip and reins,   840
drove his glorious horses straight toward Ares,

who was just stripping the brilliant armor
from enormous Aitolian Periphas.
And as they approached, Athena put on
Hades' cap, so Ares wouldn't see her.

　But when Ares observed Diomedes
he dropped monstrous Periphas on the spot
where he'd struck him down and taken his life
and lumbered straight for that son of Tydeus.
After they came very near each other   850
Ares lunged over Diomedes' reins
with a bronze-tipped spear, raging to slay him,
but green-eyed Athena deflected it,
sent it spinning from his powerful hand.
whereupon dauntless Diomedes thrust
mightily, and Athena drove that spear
into Ares' groin beneath the girdle.
There the fine flesh was gashed most bitterly,
and he withdrew his spear as Ares roared
like nine thousand or ten thousand warriors   860
locked in relentless fury of combat—
and all those Trojans and Achaeans shook
with fear to hear fierce Ares' frenzied cries.

　As a dark rainstorm gathers in the sky
when whistling winds come after some hot day,
so Diomedes saw iron Ares
sailing among the clouds to high heaven.
Soon he reached the gods' home, steep Olympus,
and sat before Zeus, utterly wretched,
showed him that immortal blood pouring forth   870
and blubbered out as well as he could:
"Father Zeus, doesn't this make you angry?
We gods always do the most horrible
things to each other when we help mortals.
Now we all hate you for being the father
of that ruinous, maniac female.
Every other god here on Olympus
is your obedient and faithful servant
except for her—she does what she wishes,

that bitch, simply because she's your daughter!   880
Now she even sicced this swaggering man
Tydeus' son Diomedes on the gods:
he wounded Aphrodite on the wrist
and then went after me like a lunatic.
I got out of there quick—if I hadn't
I'd still be lying among those corpses
or crippled forever by his damned spear."

    Thunderlord Zeus glowered at him and said:
"Don't sit whining around me, you turncoat!
I hate you more than any Olympian,   890
you're so fond of quarrels and war and strife,
as willful and stubborn as your mother
Hera—I have trouble enough with her—
and she's to blame for your suffering now.
Very well, I'll put an end to your pain—
you are, to be sure, my very own son—
but if another god were your father
I'd have thrown you from heaven long ago!"

    And he called his physician Paeëon,
who applied soothing herbs and medicines   900
to heal him, for he was not born to die.
As fig juice makes white milk coagulate
and it quickly curdles when it is stirred,
Paeëon healed Ares so speedily.
And after Hebe had bathed and dressed him
he sat down by Zeus in all his glory.

    And back to Zeus's palace came those two,
green-eyed Athena and Argive Hera,
after they made Ares stop his slaughter.

Book Six: Hector and Andromache

Hector enters Troy to order offerings for Athena, meets his
wife Andromache and their baby boy.

Thus the gods abandoned that battlefield,
and the awful struggle surged back and forth
as they hurled bright spears at one another
between the streams of Xanthus and Simois.

Now giant Aias, Achaean bulwark,
made the first breach in a Trojan phalanx
by stabbing a captain of the Thracians,
Eussorus' intrepid son Acamas:
that great spear sheared through his crested helmet
and onto his forehead, its bronze-tipped point   10
pierced the bone, then darkness covered his eyes.

And prince Diomedes brought down Axylus,
Teuthras' son from the city Arisbe,
a wealthy man beloved by his neighbors
for his freehanded hospitality.
But none of those neighbors stood with him now
to ward off death: Diomedes struck down
both himself and his driver Calesius—
so together they sank beneath the earth.

And Euryalus slew Ophialtus,   20
then pursued Aesepus and Pedasus
borne by the sea nymph Abarbarea
to Beucalion, Laomedon's eldest son,
though his immortal mother was unwed:
one afternoon as he was tending sheep

he lay with that nymph, and she bore twin sons.
But now Euryalus slaughtered them both,
tore the glorious armor from their shoulders.

   Next Polypoetes slew Astyalus,
while Odysseus' terrible spear toppled   30
Pidytes and Teucer killed Areton.
Ablerus fell to Antilochus' spear,
and Agamemnon dispatched Elatus
who lived by the banks of Satnioeis,
Leitus slaughtered Phylacus as he fled,
and Eurypylus laid Melanthius low.

   But fierce Menelaus took Adrestus
alive: his horses panicked as their hooves
caught on a tamarisk branch, that yoke pole
broke, and they galloped away toward the town,   40
where the others were madly retreating,
and their master tumbled from the chariot
facefirst in the dust. Then beside him stood
Atreus' son Menelaus with a spear.
Adrestus clasped his knees and implored him:
"Spare me, Atreus' son, take a great ransom!
My wealthy father has many treasures:
gold and bronze and splendid tools of iron.
You'd have an incomparable ransom
if he heard I was alive at your ships!"   50

   Thus Adrestus beseeched Menelaus,
who would have commanded his trusty squire
to take him captive, but Agamemnon
came running up and scolded his brother:
"Listen here, fellow, why take such trouble
with those Trojans? Were they so kind to you
in your own home? Let none of them escape,
not even a boy in his mother's womb—
we'll kill them down to the very last man,
let their bodies lie unmourned, unburied."   60

These words persuaded lord Menelaus,
so he shoved glorious Adrestus away,
then his brother stabbed him straight through the side.
Backward he fell, and great Agamemnon
tore the spear out with a foot on his chest.

Now aged Nestor called to his people:
"Friends, Danaan warriors, servants of Ares,
no man stay behind gathering booty
so he can bring the biggest share back home;
after our enemies are slain we'll take   70
the armor from their bodies on the plain!"

His words stirred the heart of every warrior.
And then they would have sent those Trojan hordes
streaming helplessly into their city,
but the soothsayer Priam's son Helenus
approached his two commanders and declared:
"Hector and Aeneas, you have the job
of commanding our men, since you're finest
in strategy as well as in combat—
so go among our armies, hold them back   80
before the city gates, or they may fall
in their women's arms and disgrace us all.
And after you rally our battalions
we'll make a last stand against the Danaans,
tired though we are—it's sheer necessity!
Meanwhile you enter the city, Hector,
have our mother summon the old women
to Athena's shrine in the citadel.
And after she opens the temple doors
she should take a robe, the largest and best   90
among her treasures, her favorite one,
and lay it before Athena's statue,
promising her a glorious sacrifice
of twelve yearling heifers if she'll pity
our town and wives and innocent children
and save holy Ilios from Tydeus' son,
that terrible troublemaker in war
who wreaks such havoc among our people.

Even Achilles, son of a goddess,
was not as formidable—this warrior   100
fights so wildly no man can withstand him."

    Gallant Hector did as his brother said:
leapt down from his chariot in full armor
and hurried among them waving two spears,
urging them to finally make a stand.
Thus they rallied and faced the enemy,
who soon gave ground, and the slaughter ended,
for they thought some immortal god had come
from starry heaven to help the Trojans.
He bellowed among his massed battalions: 110
"You haughty Trojans and our famed allies!
Be men, my friends, remember your courage
while I enter the town and admonish
our wives and the elders of our city
to implore the gods and make sacrifice."

    Flashing-helmeted Hector strode away,
that tough leather shield slung over his back,
knocking on neck and ankles as he went.

    Now Glaucus drove toward the son of Tydeus
between those armies, furious for combat.   120
After they came very near each other
dauntless Diomedes bellowed out first:
"Which mortal man are you, my fine fellow?
I've never seen you in combat before,
but here you stand far in front of them all
so coolly awaiting my great spear's sweep.
I've already made many parents weep!
Yet if you're a god come down from heaven
I will not do battle with Olympians.
Even Dryas' son mighty Lycurgus   130
did not last long when he defied the gods
and drove mad Dionysus' worshipers
over holy Mount Nysa, so they all
threw away their wands with fierce Lycurgus
lashing them on—and Dionysus fled

into the sea, where Thetis received him,
that warrior had given him such a scare.
Then the easy-living gods were furious,
and Zeus struck Lycurgus blind and his life
was short, for the immortals hated him. 140
That's why I won't battle against the gods.
If you are a man like the rest of us
come on, and I'll make a quick end of you."

And Hippolochus' son Glaucus answered:
"Dauntless Diomedes, why ask who I am?
Men are like the generations of leaves:
wind spins them to the ground, but the forest
brings new ones forth again when springtime comes—
thus men's generations are born and die.
But if you wish I'll tell you my lineage, 150
though many men know it well already.
In Argos' heart lies the town Ephyrë,
where that sly personage Sisyphus lived,
and he became the father of Glaucus,
whose son was illustrious Bellerophon,
strikingly handsome, a man's man indeed.
King Proetus took a great dislike to him
and exiled him from the land of Argos,
a royal prerogative, since the queen
lusted for the love of Bellerophon 160
and would have seduced him but could never
persuade that honorable gentleman,
so she went to the king and told a lie:
'Proetus, kill Bellerophon or yourself—
that nasty fellow has tried to rape me.'
He was deeply indignant to hear this
but shrank from taking Bellerophon's life
and sent him to Lycia with fatal signs,
many and deadly, engraved on tablets:
orders for the murder of the bearer. 170
Bellerophon went, under the gods' care,
and when he reached Lycia by the Xanthus
that land's ruler was most hospitable,

roasted nine oxen, feasted him nine days.
But after the dawn of the tenth day came
the Lycian ruler asked for those tablets
sent by king Proetus, his daughter's husband—
and when he had read this fatal message
commanded him to slay the Chimaera,
fabulous beast with face of a lion,   180
a serpentine tail, goat in the midriff,
huffing and puffing most horrible flames.
He killed her, following the gods' omens.
Next he matched his might with the Solymni—
mightiest struggle of his life, he said—
and massacred those Amazons the last.
Then the Lycian ruler hatched one more plot
as he returned, chose the fiercest warriors
to ambush him—but none of them came back:
Bellerophon brought all to an awful end.   190
Now the monarch recognized his power
and kept him there and gave him his daughter
with half of his own royal distinctions,
while the Lycians granted him an estate,
a splendid tract of orchards and farmland.
Bellerophon's wife bore him three children—
Isander, Hippolochus, and dazzling
Laodameia, who lay beside Zeus
and conceived magnificent Sarpedon—
but when he too became hated by all   200
the immortal gods, he wandered alone
eating his heart out, avoiding people,
while Ares slaughtered his son Isander
in combat with the Solymni and then
Artemis killed his daughter in a rage.
Gallant Hippolochus was my father,
and when I left for Ilios he told me
to always be the bravest and the best
and never disgrace my family, noblest
in all Ephyrë and the Lycian lands.   210
This is my lineage, and I'm proud of it!"

Glaucus' words pleased dauntless Diomedes,
who stuck his spear in the bountiful earth
and called amiably to that commander:
"Then our families are bound in friendship!
Your Bellerophon once stayed twenty days
as guest with my grandfather Oeneus,
and they exchanged fine gifts of amity:
Oeneus gave a belt stained bright crimson
and Bellerophon a golden goblet,   220
which I left behind when I came to Troy.
But I don't remember noble Tydeus,
I was so young when he fell before Thebes.
Now be my guest when you visit Argos,
while I'll be yours in the land of Lycia.
And we can avoid each other in war—
there are many Trojans and their allies
to be my victims if a god helps me,
many Achaeans for you to attack.
Then let's trade armor, and people will know   230
we are proud of our families' friendship."

Whereupon they leapt down from their chariots,
clasped each other's hands, and swore amity.
But Glaucus must have been out of his mind—
traded his armor for Diomedes',
gold for bronze, hundred oxen's worth for nine!

After Hector came to the Scaean Gates
the Trojan wives and daughters crowded round,
asking for their sons and brothers and friends
and husbands. He told them only to pray,   240
although he had dreadful news for many.

After he arrived at Priam's palace
with its polished colonnades—and inside,
fifty apartments all of polished stone
one by another, where the glorious sons
of Priam slept beside their wedded wives;
and opposite these, within the courtyard,
twelve more apartments all of polished stone,

one by another, where the sons-in-law
of Priam slept beside their modest wives—   250
there his gracious mother ran to greet him
leading Laodicë, her loveliest daughter.
Then she clasped him by the hand and murmured:
"Why have you left the battlefield, my boy?
Ah, those Danaans must be pressing us hard
and therefore you came back inside our walls
to implore great Zeus from the citadel.
Very well, but wait till I bring you wine
so you may pour libations to the gods
and then enjoy a bit of it yourself.   260
Wine does a warrior good when he's wearied
as you are now after so much battle."

   And flashing-helmeted Hector answered:
"Bring me no wine, my beloved mother—
I might be drunk and forget about war.
With unwashed hands I can't make libations
and pray to that mighty son of Cronos,
all bloody and dirty as I am now.
But you hurry to Athena's temple
with the aged ladies of our city—   270
and take a robe, the largest and best
among your treasures and your favorite,
to lay before great Athena's statue,
promising her a glorious sacrifice
of twelve yearling heifers if she'll pity
our town and wives and innocent children
and save holy Ilios from Tydeus' son,
that terrible troublemaker in war.
So you hurry to Athena's temple
while I go looking for Alexander   280
and see if he'll come—damn him anyway:
Zeus the Olympian has made him a plague
on our Trojans and Priam and his sons.
If I saw that man go down to Hades
my heart would be a good deal easier!"

Then she went inside and called her servants,
who ran to gather the aged ladies.
And she herself entered the fragrant vaults
where she kept robes woven by those women
gallant Alexander had brought with him   290
from Sidon as he sailed across the sea
carrying graceful Helen back to Troy.
There Hector's mother Hecabe chose one—
her largest and most splendidly adorned,
which shone like a star and lay below all—
then went her way among the old women.

When they came to the citadel temple
those doors were thrown open by Theano,
wife of the Trojan elder Antenor
and priestess before august Athena.   300
They raised their hands and wailed to the goddess,
then Theano took the robe and placed it
on the knees of great Athena's statue
and prayed to that daughter of mighty Zeus:
"Guardian Athena, our glorious goddess,
break Diomedes' spear, send him tumbling
facefirst in the dust by the Scaean Gates,
and we'll offer you twelve yearling heifers,
never used in the fields, if you pity
our town and wives and innocent children."   310
But Pallas Athena denied her prayer.

And while they implored that daughter of Zeus
Hector entered Alexander's palace,
a stately edifice built for himself
by the finest craftsmen in all Ilios,
who made courtyard, halls, and spacious chambers
beside the other homes of Priam's sons—
there Hector strode through the door carrying
a sixteen-foot spear, and before him blazed
its razor-sharp edge with a golden ring.   320

He found Paris polishing his weapons,
that shield and breastplate, fingering his bow,
while Helen sat by her servant women

to supervise their superb handiwork.
When Hector saw him, he cried bitterly:
"You strange man, don't sit around sulking
while our people perish outside the wall—
and you're the reason relentless combat
surrounds our city. If another man
cowered back like this you'd be indignant.   330
Up with you, then, before our city burns!"

   And that godlike Alexander answered:
"Hector, your reproaches are quite proper,
but allow me to explain the matter.
No, I haven't abandoned our people;
I stayed behind because I felt so sad.
Just as you arrived, my wife was saying
I should return to battle, and I shall,
for the fortunes of war are changeable.
You wait here while I put my armor on,   340
or go ahead and I'll overtake you."

   Flashing-helmeted Hector was silent,
but Helen addressed her husband's brother:
"Ah, Hector, I'm a mischief-making bitch.
I only wish the day I was born
some whirlwind had come and carried me off
to the mountains or the resounding sea,
where I'd have died before it all happened.
Yet since the gods have ordained these sorrows,
I wish I were wife to someone better,   350
who could feel his people's anger and scorn!
This man is weak in the head and always
will be—and I think he'll pay for it too.
But do come in, take a seat on this chair,
Hector. You've suffered more than anyone
for me and for the folly of Paris,
two people Zeus has brought an awful doom
as a song for men forever after."

   And flashing-helmeted Hector answered:
"I cannot be seated, my dear Helen.   360

Now I must hurry back there to relieve
our Trojans, who need me enormously.
You be sure this fellow's quick about it,
so he overtakes me in the city.
But first I must go home for one more look
at my servants and wife and baby boy,
since I don't know if I'll ever return
or fall before those Achaeans today."

Flashing-helmeted Hector strode away
and quickly came to his sumptuous palace.   370
But white-armed Andromache wasn't there—
she had taken her child and a handmaid
to weep and wail upon the city wall.
When Hector couldn't find his peerless wife
he stood at the threshold and demanded:
"Now tell me correctly, you servant girls,
which way has my wife Andromache gone?
To my sisters or to my brothers' wives
or Athena's temple, where the other
women implore that terrible goddess?"   380

And a trusty housekeeper answered him:
"Hector, if you wish to know, I'll tell you:
not to your sisters or your brothers' wives
or Athena's temple, where the other
women implore that terrible goddess,
but to the Scaean Gates, because she heard
our armies are being beaten badly.
So she hurried out to the city wall
like a madwoman, with her nurse and child."

Then Priam's son Hector went from his home   390
along those stately streets the way he came.
And as he arrived at the Scaean Gates,
through which he soon would return to battle,
his lovely wife came running to meet him:
Andromache, daughter of Eëtion
who ruled the Cilicians in Trojan Thebes
under the wooded slopes of Mount Placus

and gave her in marriage to great Hector.
She hurried toward him followed by a nurse
carrying the tender innocent child,   400
Hector's dear son, beautiful as a star,
called Scamandrius by Hector but by some
the Lordling, for his father guarded Troy.
Hector smiled and gazed at his boy, silent,
while Andromache stood weeping by him
and clasped him by the hand as she murmured:
"Dearest man, your courage will ruin you.
You don't pity your child or poor me, soon
a widow, after those Danaan warriors
have brought you to the ground. Then I'd better   410
go down to my own grave, since there will be
no comfort left me if you're dead, nothing
but grief. I have no father or mother—
fiery Achilles murdered my father
as he sacked our Cilician capital,
high-gated Thebes, but though he had slain him
refrained from taking his brilliant armor
and burned his body with highest honors,
while around his towering burial mound
elm trees were planted by the mountain nymphs.   420
And those seven brothers who lived with me
were all sent down to Hades that same day—
agile Achilles slaughtered every one
as they guarded our people's cattle herds,
but my mother, queen in the land of Thebes,
was carried off with the other booty,
freed for an incalculable ransom
and slain by Artemis in her own home.
Ah, Hector, you're my father and mother
and my brother and my lusty husband,   430
so pity me, stay here in the city,
don't widow your wife and orphan your child!
Station your people by the wild fig tree,
a place our wall's the most vulnerable:
three times already they attacked us there
with the Aiantes and Idomeneus

and Atreus' sons and prince Diomedes—
some diviner advised it, I suppose,
or they may have discovered it themselves."

Flashing-helmeted Hector answered her: 440
"Very true, dear lady—but I should be
ashamed to face the Trojans and their wives
if I stayed cowering back from combat.
That's not my way—I have learned to be brave
and always battle among the foremost
for my father's glory and for my own.
Now I know one thing in my heart and soul:
someday disaster will take our city
with Priam and his spear-slinging people—
though I'm not so worried for the Trojans   450
or even my mother or king Priam
or my brothers, those many brave warriors
battered to the dust by their enemies,
as for you, when some armored Achaean
leads you weeping away to slavery.
You'll work someone else's loom in Argos
or carry water in Hypereia
most miserably, under a stern master—
and someone may say as he sees you weep:
'That lady was wife to Hector, the best   460
of those Trojans who fought before their town.'
And then you'll be racked with anguish again
for lack of a man like me to save you.
But I'd rather have the earth cover me
than hear your cries as they drag you away."

And illustrious Hector reached for his boy,
who shrank howling to the nurse's bosom,
his father's appearance frightened him so,
gazed uneasily at the brazen helmet
whose horsehair crest bobbed horribly on top.   470
His father and mother laughed at that sight,
while mighty Hector removed his helmet
and laid it all glittering on the ground.
So he kissed his dear son and fondled him,

then prayed to Zeus and to the other gods:
"Zeus and you others, may this boy of mine
be such a distinguished leader as me,
may he rule Ilios with the same courage,
may they say: 'He's far better than his sire,'
when he brings bloody booty back from war,   480
and may this make his mother's heart be glad."

   Now great Hector gave his beloved wife
her child—and she pressed that boy to her breast,
smiling through tears. Her husband pitied her
and stroked her with her fingers, murmuring:
"Strange lady, don't trouble yourself too much.
Unless it's my fate, I shall not be slain—
and no man on earth, brave or cowardly,
ever escapes death, once he has been born.
So hurry on home to your household tasks,   490
your spinning and loom, let your servants do
their daily duties, and leave war to men
and to me, more than anyone in Troy."

   Then Priam's son Hector took his crested
helmet—and his beloved wife went home,
looking back often, weeping bitter tears.
Quickly she came to that sumptuous palace
of man-slaying Hector, found her many
servants, and all lamented together.
Thus they mourned for Hector while he still lived,   500
because it seemed he would never return
safe from the enemy's depredations.

   Before long Paris too left his palace:
dressed himself in magnificent armor
and hurried nimbly through Priam's city.
As a mighty stallion stuffed with barley
breaks his rope and gallops over the plain
where he loves to bathe in a rippling stream—
exultantly throws his head up, the mane
floats over his shoulders, and he prances   510
to a place where the mares usually graze:

thus Priam's son Paris went striding forth
in armor all a-glitter like the sun,
laughing, and his swift feet carried him on.
He found lord Hector about to return
from where he had lingered beside his wife,
and that godlike prince Alexander cried:
"Sorry to have kept you waiting, brother—
I didn't come quick as you commanded."

  Flashing-helmeted Hector answered him: 520
"You strange fellow, no one in his right mind
can scorn you in battle—you're brave enough,
only carefree and irresponsible,
so I'm sorry to hear you being cursed
by our Trojans for the trouble you caused.
Very well, let's go! We'll make all this good
when Zeus lets us thank the eternal gods,
pouring libations for our deliverance
after we've driven the Danaans from Troy."

Book Seven: The Truce

Single combat between Hector and Aias. Greeks and Trojans hold a truce to bury the dead.

So Hector hurried through the city gates
before his brother Alexander, both
furious to enter relentless combat.
As some god may concede anxious sailors
a breeze, when they weary beating the sea
with their polished oars and can move no more,
so those two seemed to the anxious Trojans.

Now the first of them slew Areithous' son
Menestheus, born of that club-swinging lord
and gentle princess Phylomedusa,   10
while Hector's sharp spear pierced Eioneus' neck
under his helmet, and he toppled down.
Whereupon that Lycian leader Glaucus
hurled at incomparable Iphinous
as he was climbing on his chariot, pierced
his shoulder, and he tumbled to the ground.

But when green-eyed Athena observed them
ravaging Achaeans' ranks in battle
she darted down from the Olympian peaks
toward holy Troy, while Apollo hurried   20
to meet her from the peaks of Pergamon.
They came together by the great oak tree,
and that archer Phoebus Apollo called:
"Daughter of Zeus, why are you scurrying
so arrogantly down from Olympus?
Want to give your Achaeans victory?

When the Trojans perish you've no pity.
But if you deign to hear my suggestion
we can end this dreadful devastation
for today—and afterward they may take   30
Ilios, since it seems you two goddesses
are quite determined to destroy that town."

  The goddess green-eyed Athena replied:
"An excellent plan indeed, Apollo,
and this was precisely why I came.
But how do you propose to stop the war?"

  And Apollo the archer answered her:
"First we'll fill Hector with relentless rage
till he challenges one of their leaders
to meet him man-to-man in awful war.   40
The Achaean warriors won't dare refuse,
and someone will appear as their champion."

  That goddess green-eyed Athena obeyed.
Then Helenus, Priam's son, shrewd seer,
divined what the immortals had devised,
approached great Hector and murmured to him:
"Hector, you canny Trojan commander,
will you hear the advice of your brother?
Ask the Trojans and Achaeans to sit
while you challenge a Danaan commander   50
to meet you man-to-man in awful war.
It's not yet time for you to meet your fate—
a voice from the gods has assured me that."

  Hector was delighted to hear these words
and strode out to keep his battalions back
with a spear held at the middle. All sat,
and Agamemnon seated the Danaans.
Meanwhile Athena and prince Apollo
perched on a lofty oak of father Zeus
in the semblance of two hook-beaked vultures   60
rejoicing at that sight: thick battalions
a-bristle with shields and helmets and spears.
As ripples spread when a west wind rises

and the boundless deep grows dark beneath it,
those opposing warriors sat on the plain.
Now Hector stood between them and shouted:
"Listen to me, Trojans and Achaeans,
I have an important message for all:
Zeus Thunderhurler has thwarted our oaths,
and now he'll bring sorrows for both armies   70
till you plunder our prosperous city
or die yourselves by these seafaring ships.
The finest Achaeans are with you here,
so if one of them dares contend with me
let him battle Hector as your champion.
May Zeus be witness to my proposal:
if his slashing spear makes an end of me
he will take my armor back to the ships
but return my body so our people
can burn it with proper ceremony;   80
while if I kill him, with Apollo's help,
I'll bring his armor into the city
and hang it in Phoebus Apollo's shrine
but return his corpse so the Achaeans
may make a towering funeral mound
and bury it by the wide Hellespont.
Then someday people will say as they sail
their swift ships over the wine-dark waters:
'This is the grave of an ancient spearman
slain by Hector as he raged in battle.'   90
And my glorious name will never perish."

    A hush of awe fell over those warriors,
ashamed to refuse, afraid to accept.
At last Atreus' son Menelaus rose
and, deeply troubled, bellowed scornfully:
"Big-mouthed Achaeans, women more than men,
what a disgrace for our people today
if no one can be found to meet Hector!
Well, sit there and rot, the whole lot of you,
a timid bunch, no bravery at all!   100

I'll do your fighting, and the blessed gods
will grant victory to the man they choose."

   And he threw his shimmering armor on.
Then, Menelaus, your doom would have come
at Hector's hands, he was so much stronger,
but the other lords leapt up and seized you.
Atreus' son king Agamemnon himself
caught your right hand and restrained you, saying:
"Don't do such a foolish thing, Menelaus!
Your grudge is greatest, but you mustn't try   110
to take on such a powerful warrior,
fiery Hector, a terror for many.
Even Achilles, far your superior,
shudders to meet him on the battlefield.
You sit down here among your followers
and let another man represent us.
No matter how brave that person may be,
he'll be happy if he escapes alive
from the fury of horrible combat."

   These words persuaded Menelaus—   120
so his squires came running out and gladly
took the glorious armor from his shoulders.
Next Nestor rose to harangue those armies:
"What a catastrophe for our people
and sorrow, sorrow for old Peleus,
that Myrmidon monarch and orator
who questioned me in his home and rejoiced
as I told him our leaders' ancestry.
If he knew how we were cowering now
he would raise his hands and implore the gods   130
to take his soul away into Hades.
O Zeus and Athena and Apollo,
if only I were youthful as the day
we Pylians met those Arcadians in war
beneath the towering walls of Pheia.
Their leader was godlike Ereuthalion,
who wore the armor of king Areithous,
valiant Areithous, renowned far and wide

as the forcible wielder of a mace,
since he didn't use a spear or a bow   140
but broke battalions with an iron bludgeon.
Lycurgus killed him by a stratagem:
forced him to fight in a narrow pathway
where that club was useless, pierced his middle
with a spear thrust—and he toppled backward—
then took the armor he'd had from Ares,
wore it later in heartbreaking battle.
When Lycurgus reached the ripeness of age
he gave it to his squire Ereuthalion,
who drove out and challenged all our champions,   150
but the others trembled and were afraid.
I was the only one who dared meet him,
though I was the youngest warrior present.
And Athena granted me victory:
tallest, most tremendous man I ever
brought to earth, all a-sprawl there before me.
Yes, if I were just as young and strong today
fiery Hector would have his opponent.
But now not a one of our commanders
dares to meet Hector as our champion."   160

   Thus aged Nestor rebuked them—and nine
men rose: king Agamemnon first of all,
next Tydeus' son dauntless Diomedes
and those two formidable Aiantes,
with Idomeneus and his companion
Meriones, peer of bloodthirsty Ares,
then Euaemon's son prince Eurypylus,
followed by Thoas and shrewd Odysseus,
each one of them keen to meet great Hector.
Veteran Nestor addressed them again: 170
"Now let's draw lots to decide who shall go.
He'll be a blessing for all our people
and blessed himself if he escapes alive
from the fury of horrible combat."

So each leader marked his lot with a sign
and tossed it in Agamemnon's helmet.
Next all the people prayed with hands upraised—
a man would gaze toward the heavens and say:
"Father Zeus, choose Aias or Tydeus' son
or our king of rich Mycenae himself."   180

Then Gerenian Nestor shook the helmet,
and out leapt the lot that most had hoped for—
Aias'—and a herald carried it round
left to right, showed it to all those leaders,
and every man denied that it was his.
But after he had come to the warrior
who'd marked it and thrown it in, huge Aias,
that distinguished captain held out his hand
and recognized it with a joyful start.
So he hurled it to the ground and shouted: 190
"That lot is mine, and I'm delighted,
since I'll surely win out over Hector.
And while I put on my battle attire
pray to our thunderlord son of Cronos
silently, so the Trojans cannot hear,
or out aloud—we needn't keep secrets.
Not a man on earth can make me retreat
by force or by cunning—we're no greenhorns,
we warriors born and bred in Salamis."

And all made prayer to the Thunderlord—   200
a man would gaze toward the heavens and say:
"Most glorious great Zeus who rules from Ida,
let Telamonian Aias win the day,
or if Hector is your favorite too
grant both those combatants equal chances."

So Aias donned his shimmering armor.
When the bronze had covered all his body
he rushed to battle like monstrous Ares
as he goes among armies Zeus sends forth
into the carnage of heartbreaking war—   210
thus that Argive bulwark, giant Aias,

lumbered out with an awful smile, his feet
eating the ground up, and brandished his spear.
All of his people rejoiced at the sight
while every Trojan began to tremble,
and even Hector's heart was hammering,
but now he couldn't consider retreat
because he himself had made the challenge.
Aias came near him with his wall-like shield,
handsome handiwork of Hylian Tychius,   220
most skillful leatherworker in the world,
who made him a shield of seven tough hides
and an eighth bronze layer for a surface.
Holding that shield before him, huge Aias
strode into action and bellowed his boast:
"Priam's son Hector, now you'll learn firsthand
what sort of leaders the Achaeans have
even without lionhearted Achilles!
He's staying beside his Myrmidon ships
in a terrible rage at Agamemnon,   230
but we still have men who can manage you,
and many of them. You throw your spear first."

   Flashing-helmeted Hector answered him:
"Magnificent Telamonian Aias,
don't try to scare me like a little boy
or some weak woman innocent of war.
I've learned some things about combat, I guess—
see how I handle this tough oxhide shield:
left parry, right parry, deft and with might!
I batter my way though the battle swirl   240
and dance the jig of battle pretty well.
My spear won't be hitting you on the sly
but straightaway, as I do it today!"

   Then he poised his ashwood weapon, hurled it
at Aias' colossal shield, those seven
oxhide layers with a metal surface,
and it hurtled through six of those layers
but lodged in the last. Next giant Aias
flung his own far-shadowing spear, and it

hit the ponderous shield of Priam's son   250
so its point hurtled through the shimmering
surface, through that glorious breastplate itself,
and tore straight through the tunic at his waist—
but he leaned aside to escape black fate.
Now each of them took out a second spear,
and they fell to it like a pair of lions
or fierce wild boars, most terrible in force.
First Hector stabbed at giant Aias' shield,
which blunted his spearpoint, deflected it,
then Aias lunged furiously and pierced   260
his opponent's shield, sent him reeling off
with a neck wound that flooded murky blood.
But flashing-helmeted Hector didn't
concede the battle, staggered back and seized
a jagged black stone that lay on the plain
and smashed it at Aias' colossal shield
square in the middle, so the bright bronze boomed.
Next Aias seized a far larger boulder,
swung it around, hurled with measureless might,
so that rock like a millstone battered in   270
Hector's shield, beat down his knees, and he fell
crushed under it—though Apollo raised him.
Then they'd have battled it out with their swords,
but two trusty heralds came running up,
one from the Danaans, one from the Trojans—
clarion-voiced Talthybius and Idaeus—
and held their staffs between those opponents
as the canny herald Idaeus cried:
"Better end your duel for today, dear sons.
We know well enough that Zeus loves you both,   280
and nobody here will doubt your prowess.
Now night is near, we can call off combat!"

   Giant Telamonian Aias replied:
"Well, Hector should say it first, Idaeus,
since he was the one who made the challenge—
I'll do whatever he considers best."

And flashing-helmeted Hector answered:
"Aias, a god gave you wits and power,
an enormous stature, and spear finesse,
so we'll end single combat for today,   290
and later we can fight until heaven
gives victory to one man or the other.
Now night is near, we can call off combat
and those Achaean armies will rejoice,
especially your kinsmen and comrades,
while the men and women of the Trojans
celebrate throughout our metropolis
and thank the immortals in their temples.
Then we'll exchange magnificent presents,
so the people of both armies may say: 300
'Those two warriors met in deadly combat
but afterward parted in amity.'"

Hector gave him a silver-studded sword
with its scabbard and elaborate strap
and received a crimson belt in exchange.
Thus they parted, one toward the Achaeans,
the other toward those Trojans, who rejoiced
to see their Hector returning alive
and unscathed from Aias' horrible might!
They brought him away, amazed he was safe,   310
while, opposite, those Argives led Aias
to mighty Agamemnon in triumph.

When they came to the camp of Atreus' son
he ordered a bull, a fat five-year-old,
slaughtered in honor of thunderlord Zeus.
So they flayed it well, cut the limbs apart,
carved the meat with care and slipped it on spits,
and laid it on the crackling flames to roast.
After all was done, their dinner prepared,
they feasted of that abundant banquet,   320
with Aias receiving the choicest cuts
from Atreus' son mighty Agamemnon.
After they had eaten and drunk their fill,
that veteran whose plans were always best,

Nestor, began weaving the web of speech.
He addressed them with these well-measured words:
"Atreus' son and you other Danaan lords,
we've lost such hosts of illustrious warriors
whose dark blood was spilled about Scamander
while their souls sank to the house of Hades, 330
so at daybreak we should declare a truce
and assemble to collect the corpses
with oxen and mules. We can cremate all
in our Achaean camp and bring the bones
back to their children when we return home.
Over their pyre we'll heap a funeral mound
as a common tomb and, right beside it,
build a great wall to protect our people,
with a set of tight-fitting entrance gates
where our chariots can thunder out to war. 340
Then we'll dig a dangerous moat outside
to bar the way for chariots and warriors
in case the enemy presses us hard."

All those Achaean leaders roared hurrah.
But the Trojans also held a meeting,
a terrible tumultuous one before
great Priam's gates. Antenor spoke the first:
"Trojans and Dardanians and our allies,
only one course remains open for us:
we must return Helen and her treasures 350
to Atreus' sons. We broke our holy oaths,
and I've no hope of anything worthwhile
unless we bring this war to a quick end."

After he had spoken, he sat. Then up
rose Paris, husband of lovely Helen,
and addressed them in agitated words:
"Antenor, this doesn't please me a bit—
I'd expected something better from you!
But if you really mean all this nonsense
you must be completely out of your mind. 360
Well, listen to me, equestrian Trojans,
let me say it straight: I won't give her back

though those treasures I brought here from Argos
will all be returned, together with more."

   After he had spoken, he sat. Then up
rose aged king Priam, wise as the gods,
and addressed them with these well-measured words:
"Trojans and Dardanians and our allies,
I have an important message for all:
after you take your dinners this evening   370
stay wide awake and watchful, every man.
Then at daybreak Idaeus will go out
to tell Agamemnon and Menelaus
the words of Paris, who has caused this war.
He'll also present our people's appeal
for a truce so we may burn the bodies,
and later we can battle till heaven
gives victory to one side or the other."

   And they gladly obeyed their king's commands:
had dinner with their companies and then   380
Idaeus hurried to the ships at dawn.
He found those Achaeans in assembly
by the stern of king Agamemnon's ship
and, standing in the middle, addressed them:
"Atreus' son and you other Argive lords,
Priam and his people have ordered me
to convey you, if you'll kindly listen,
the words of Paris, who has caused this war.
Those treasures he brought in his buoyant ships
to Troy—better if he had died before!—   390
will all be returned, together with more,
but he won't surrender Menelaus'
wedded wife, though the Trojans wish it.
I also present our people's appeal
for a truce so we may burn the bodies,
and later we can battle till heaven
gives victory to one side or the other."

   A hush of awe fell over those warriors
till finally brave Diomedes cried:

"No, we won't take Alexander's treasure   400
or Helen either! Any fool can see
we've got those Trojans just where we want them!"

  Those assembled Achaeans roared hurrah
for brave Diomedes' exhortation.
Now Agamemnon declared in reply:
"Idaeus, you hear our people's verdict,
and their decision pleases me as well.
But I've nothing against burning the dead:
corpses of warriors should not be begrudged
quick consolation from the licking flames.   410
Let Zeus be witness to our oaths of truce!"

  Then he raised his scepter before the gods,
and Idaeus went back to the city,
where those Trojan warriors sat assembled
awaiting the return of their herald.
So canny Idaeus came and proclaimed
his message—and they made themselves ready,
some to collect the dead, some to seek wood.
Opposite, the Achaeans hurried out,
some to collect the dead, some to seek wood.   420

  The sun was just barely touching the fields
as he rose from Oceanus' gentle flow
to climb the sky, when the two armies met.
And a hard job it was to know each man—
but they washed the clotted bloodstains away
and raised them onto carts, weeping hot tears.
Priam forbade sobbing, so they silently
piled their bodies on a pyre in sorrow
and returned to' the town when all were burned.
On the other side, those Achaeans too   430
piled their bodies on a pyre in sorrow
and returned to the ships when all were burned.

  In the dim half-light of the next day's dawn
a picked Achaean squad came together.
Over their pyre they heaped a funeral mound
as a common tomb and, right beside it,

built a great wall to protect their people,
with a set of tight-fitting entrance gates
where their chariots could thunder out to war,
and dug a formidable moat outside,   440
bristling with palisades at the bottom.

    Thus those Achaean warriors worked away,
while the gods assembled around lord Zeus
marveled at their mighty undertaking.
Poseidon Earthshaker spoke up the first:
"Ah, father Zeus, now no person on earth
will confide his thoughts or plans to the gods.
See how those haughty Achaeans have made
a wall by their ships and a moat outside
with never a sacrifice to the gods.   450
When its renown spreads as far as the dawn
they'll forget the wall Apollo and I
made for Laomedon with so much labor."

    And, very much vexed, Cronos' son replied:
"Aha, my earthshaking friend, you're worried!
Their wall might well alarm some other god
less mighty and powerful than you are,
but your renown spreads as far as the dawn.
Look here—once the flowing-haired Achaeans
have sailed away for their beloved homes   460
you smash that wall, sweep it all in the sea,
and cover the great beach again with sand
so not a trace of their labor remains."

    Thus those two immortals were conversing.
At sunset that Danaan wall was finished,
then they slaughtered oxen for their dinners
and many ships from Lemnos came ashore
carrying wine sent by king Euneus,
whom Hypsilë bore to mighty Jason.
For Atreus' two distinguished sons alone   470
Euneus had reserved a thousand jars.
The flowing-haired Achaeans purchased wine—
some in exchange for bronze, some for iron,

some for oxhides and some for live cattle,
some for slaves—and made a splendid banquet.
So all night long those Achaean warriors
feasted, as did the Trojans in their town—
and all night long wise Zeus planned more troubles,
thundering horribly. Pale fear seized them,
and they spilled their wine on the earth: none dared   480
drink till he made that libation to Zeus.
And they lay down, received the gift of sleep.

Book Eight: The Battle Broken Off

*Zeus forbids the Olympians to intervene in battle. The Greeks
are driven back to their wall.*

Now saffron-robed dawn covered all the earth
as thunderlord Zeus summoned a meeting
on steep Olympus' very highest peak
and delivered the following harangue:
"Listen here, all you gods and goddesses,
while I proclaim to you my royal will:
none of you gentleman or lady gods
dare go against me—do as I say
so my plan may be brought to fulfillment.
If I should see anyone sneaking off   10
to bring the Danaans help, or the Trojans,
I'll smash him with my awful thunderbolt
or toss him down into dank Tartarus
far, far away in the earth's deepest caves,
where the gates are iron and the threshold bronze,
as far under Hades as earth from heaven—
and then you'll know which god is mightiest.
Bah! come try me out, every one of you:
let a golden chain hang down from heaven
while all you gods and goddesses grab hold   20
and see if you can drag powerful Zeus
from heaven to earth, for all your tugging.
But if I should give only one good heave
I could haul you up, with earth and sea too,
and tie the chain to some Olympian peak
so everything would dangle in midair,
I'm that much stronger than gods and mortals."

And a hush of awe fell over them all,
they were so amazed at his forceful words.
But finally green-eyed Athena cried: 30
"Ah, father Zeus, our lord who rules on high,
it's perfectly clear you are very strong—
and yet we're sorry for those Achaeans
doomed by a dismal fate to die in Troy.
We shall obey and stay out of battle,
but can't we offer a bit of advice
so your anger will not destroy them all?"

And cloudgathering Zeus smiled and replied:
"There, there, dear girl, of course I was only
teasing—you do just as your heart desires."   40

And he harnessed up his bronze-hooved horses,
those swift fliers with flowing manes of gold,
put on his golden robes and took his whip
of well-worked gold, then mounted his chariot
and lashed the horses—and away they flew
there between earth and the starry heavens.
When he arrived at Ida, lair of beasts,
at Gargarus, his magnificent shrine,
the father of gods and men reined them in,
unharnessed them and covered them with mist,   50
and seated himself in all his glory,
gazing at Troy and the Achaean ships.

But meanwhile those Achaean spearmen dined
speedily in their camp, threw armor on,
while within the town the Trojans took arms,
fewer in number but furious to war
in defense of their wives and their children.
The gates were flung open, and out they poured
on foot and on chariot, with a great roar.

They came together at the battle place   60
with a crash of shields and spears and armored
warriors' fury, studded buckler battered
studded buckler, a dreadful din arose.

Together were screams and triumphant shrieks
of slain and of slayers, earth was drenched in blood.

   While it was morning and the sun still climbed,
spears took a terrible toll on both sides,
but after the sun stood astride the sky
mighty father Zeus poised his golden scales
and on them set two fates of wretched death,   70
one for the Trojans, one for the Argives,
then lifted them high—and the Argives' sank.
So their fates rested on bountiful earth,
while the Trojans' ascended toward broad heaven.
Next Zeus thundered mightily from Ida
and sent a lightning bolt at those Argives,
who stared amazed, as pale fear seized them all.

   And then Idomeneus didn't dare stay
nor Agamemnon nor the Aiantes,
only old Gerenian Nestor remained,   80
for his horse had been hit by an arrow
from Paris, husband of lovely Helen,
on top of the head, where its streaming mane
grows shortest at the front, a deadly place—
it leapt in pain as the point pierced its brain
and wildly dragged the chariot here and there.
Aged Nestor leapt down to slash it loose
with his sword, while Hector's horses thundered
straight toward him with a glorious charioteer:
Hector. He would have perished then and there,   90
but Tydeus' son Diomedes saw him
and bellowed horribly to Odysseus:
"Ho, you ingenious son of Laertes,
scuttling away as if you were afraid?
Don't let someone ram a spear in your back!
Help me save Nestor from that maniac!"

   Canny Odysseus paid no attention,
hurried away toward the Achaean ships.
So that son of Tydeus drove out alone
and stopped before the horses of Nestor   100

to address him in agitated words:
"Nestor, these youngsters are pressing you hard
and your legs are wobbly, your charioteer's
worthless, your nags slow and tired.
Just hop up here beside me, and you'll see
how these coursers of Tros go galloping
over the plain in pursuit or retreat.
They're the ones I captured from Aeneas.
Let our squires have your horses, while we two
drive through those Trojan armies so Hector   110
learns if my spear can be dangerous too."

  And aged Gerenian Nestor obeyed:
handed those horses to his attendants
Sthenelus and kindly Eurymedon,
mounted the chariot beside Diomedes,
took the shimmering reins tight in his hands,
and lashed that team toward the enemy hordes.
When Hector charged straight at them, Tydeus' son
hurled a spear but missed, hit his charioteer,
incomparable prince Eniopeus,   120
beside the nipple while he held the reins.
And he toppled to earth, so those horses
reared, as his life and strength abandoned him.
That loss filled Hector with a frantic grief,
but nevertheless he left him lying
to look for another driver—and soon
his team was not masterless, for he found
gallant Archeptolemus, who leapt up
behind those snorting beasts and took the reins.

  Now they would have been utterly ruined,   130
penned in their city like so many lambs,
but the father of gods and men saw them,
thundered horribly, sent a lightning bolt
crashing to earth by Diomedes' team
so dreadful sulfurous flames rose on the spot
and his horses cowered by their chariot.
Those shimmering reins fell from Nestor's hands
and, terribly dismayed, the old man cried:

"Oh, Tydeus' son, let's get out of here now!
Can't you see Zeus supports the enemy?   140
He granted victory to that warrior
for today at the very least, it's clear—
and no man can oppose the will of Zeus,
who has far more power than any mortal."

And dauntless Diomedes answered him:
"What you say is entirely correct, sir,
but I tell you it makes me indignant
Hector will boast before his Trojan hordes:
'Tydeus' son went scuttling off to the ships!'
May the grave gape for me that very day!"   150

But aged Gerenian Nestor replied:
"What a lot of foolishness, Tydeus' son!
No matter if Hector calls you coward,
he'll never convince his Trojan warriors
or those delicate women of Ilios
whose lusty husbands you smashed to the dust."

Then he turned his swift horses to retreat
through turmoil of war, as the Trojans roared
and showered deadly missiles after him.
That flashing-helmeted Hector shouted: 160
"Ho, Tydeus' son, your people honored you
with pride of place and meats and brimful cups,
but now they see you're weaker than a girl!
Bye-bye, baby doll, so sorry you can't
scale our city walls and win our women—
yes, before that happens, I'll take your life."

And Tydeus' son had half a mind to turn
his horses back and meet him face-to-face.
Three times Diomedes hesitated,
and three times wise Zeus thundered from Ida   170
to show the Trojans victory was theirs.
So Hector bellowed among his armies:
"You Trojans and Lycians and Dardanians,
be men, my friends, remember your courage!
Now I know Cronos' son has granted me

victory and routed the Achaeans.
Those fools believed their miserable wall
could keep our people back, but we'll breach it,
our horses will easily leap their moat.
And after we reach those fine ships at last   180
we won't forget to bring a few torches
and burn those ships and slaughter their warriors
who wander about them dazed with the smoke."

   And he roared to his own team of horses:
"Xanthus, Podargus, Aethon, and Lampus!
Now pay me back for the fodder you had
from Eëtion's daughter Andromache,
who gave you dinners of tenderest wheat
with watered wine whenever you wanted,
sooner than for me, her wedded husband.   190
Well, after them! faster! we'll capture that
shield of Nestor whose fame reaches heaven—
it's solid gold, its handle all of gold—
and when Diomedes is dead we'll win
his glorious armor, work of Hephaestus.
If we can slay those two, the Achaeans
might sail for their homes this very evening!"

   His boast so incensed haughty Hera she
shook on her throne, and great Olympus quaked—
and she called to powerful Poseidon: 200
"Dear me, my earthshaking friend, you never
pity our Achaeans when they perish,
though they bring fine offerings to your shrines
at Aegae and Helicë—help them, then!
If we gods would only stick together
we could defeat those Trojans and Zeus too—
he'd sit there moaning alone on Ida."

   Very much vexed, lord Poseidon replied:
"Ah, Hera, what a lot of silly talk!
Well, I wouldn't care to see Zeus at war   210
even against us all, he has such power."

Thus the gods were conversing—and meanwhile
that whole space between ships and Danaan wall
was jammed with horses and armored warriors
penned helpless together by Ares' peer
terrible Hector, whom Zeus supported.
Then he'd surely have burned their high-beaked ships,
but Hera made Agamemnon decide
to rouse his men for a very last stand.
That Danaan commander ran among them   220
waving his magnificent purple cloak
and stood by Odysseus' big-bellied ship
in the middle of the camp, where a cry
could reach giant Aias' tents on one side
and those of Achilles on the other,
since their ships were beached at the farthest ends.
He bellowed among his massed battalions:
"Shame and disgrace, pretty-faced Achaeans!
What's become of all those empty boasts
you babbled back in Lemnos as you gulped   230
cup after cup of our mellow red wine
and gobbled our tastiest cuts of beef,
then said you'd meet two hundred Trojans
single-handed—but we're no match for one,
Hector, who'll soon set our fine fleet aflame.
Ah, father Zeus, was ever a leader
made such a fool by you or more disgraced?
But I never neglected your altars
our ships passed by on my damned voyage here,
burned splendid sacrifice at every one,   240
I was so eager to sack their city.
Then grant me one wish only, glorious Zeus:
at least let our people escape alive,
don't let the enemy overwhelm us."

And the Father pitied him as he wept,
conceded his people would not perish,
swiftly sent an eagle, surest omen,
in its talons a tender baby fawn,
which it dropped beside the altar where they

sacrificed to Zeus, the source of omens.   250
Seeing the eagle had been sent by Zeus,
they attacked with even greater fury.

   Now no man among those many Danaans
was ahead of Tydeus' son in driving
beyond the deep moat to begin battle:
long before the rest, he slew a warrior,
Agelaus, who had wheeled his chariot
around to flee, but Diomedes' spear
drove between the shoulders, pierced to his chest—
and his armor boomed as he crashed to earth.   260

   Next came Agamemnon and Menelaus
and those two formidable Aiantes,
with Idomeneus and his companion
Meriones, peer of terrible Ares,
and Euaemon's son prince Eurypylus
and, as the ninth warrior, archer Teucer,
who stood beside Telamonian Aias
but when huge Aias moved his shield aside
took a careful aim with that mighty bow
and as his victim tumbled down lifeless   270
he'd dart back like a child to his mother,
while Aias hid him behind his bright shield.

   Which of those Trojans did Teucer dispatch?
Orsilochus first, then Ophelestes,
Dastor, Chromius, godlike Lycophontes,
brave Amopaon, and Melanippus,
stretched one after the other on the ground.
King Agamemnon rejoiced to see him
shattering Trojan battalions with his bow,
came to stand very near him, and declared: 280
"My dear Teucer, magnificent leader,
you'll be the glory of all our armies
and your father Telamon, who reared you
in his palace, though you were bastard born—
you do him honor, though he's far away.
And let me assure you of something else:

if thunderhurling Zeus and Athena
let us plunder their prosperous city
your reward shall be greatest after mine:
a cauldron, two horses, and a chariot,   290
with a lovely lady to share your bed."

    Then that cunning bowman Teucer answered:
"Atreus' son, you know how keen I am,
so why urge me on? While my strength remains
I'll keep on shooting the way I have
since our people last began the attack.
Already I shot eight long-barbed arrows
and each of them hit an enemy, but
the only one I missed was that mad dog."

    Next he strung one more arrow and shot   300
straight at Hector, furious to take his life,
but missed, hit another man on the chest:
peerless Gorgythion, Priam's gallant son,
born of that lovely Asymnian lady
Castianeira, fair as a goddess.
He bowed his head like a garden poppy
heavy with seed and the raindrops of spring—
so his head, heavy with its helmet, fell.

    And Teucer shot yet another arrow
straight at Hector, furious to take his life,   310
but missed him again—Apollo turned it
toward Archeptolemus, Hector's driver:
it bore through his chest as they rushed forward,
and he toppled to earth, so those horses
reared as his life and strength abandoned him.
That loss filled Hector with a frantic grief,
but nevertheless he left him lying
and ordered his brother Cebriones
to take the reins of those snorting horses.
Then glorious Hector leapt from his chariot,   320
bellowing horribly, seized a boulder,
and went for Teucer in a bitter rage.
That bowman had taken one more arrow

and fitted it to the string—but Hector
battered his shoulder where the collarbone
joins neck and chest, a most dangerous place:
just as he took aim, that jagged boulder
shattered the bowstring, his arm became numb,
and he slumped to his knees and dropped the bow.
But Aias guarded his fallen brother: 330
stood over him, covered him with a shield,
while he was raised by two trusty comrades—
Mecisteus and illustrious Alastor,
who brought him, deeply moaning, to the ships.

Once again mighty Zeus roused those Trojans
so they drove the enemy toward their moat,
Hector raging resistless before them.
As a swift hound bounds after some wild boar
or a tawny lion, snapping from behind
at his sides and rump, but won't come too near,   340
thus Hector pursued those enemy hordes,
slaughtering laggards—and they were routed.
After they crossed the moat and palisade
and many had fallen to the Trojans,
they came to a halt at last by the ships,
summoning one another, raised their hands
and implored the immortals to save them.
Hector drove back and forth outside their wall,
glaring like the Gorgon or fierce Ares.

When white-armed Hera saw, she pitied them,   350
and her words poured out to great Athena:
"Dear me, energetic daughter of Zeus,
no worry when our Achaeans perish?
Now all will be slaughtered most horribly
by a single warrior running amok,
that ferocious son of Priam, Hector."

The goddess green-eyed Athena replied:
"Ah, if only some Achaean spearman
would take his life right there in his homeland!
But our father's angry, and it's not nice—   360

that scoundrel, always messing up my plans!
Zeus forgets how often I saved his son
as he struggled with Eurystheus' labors:
whenever he wept and looked toward heaven
our father sent me running to help him—
but if I'd known Zeus would do such mischief
that time Heracles was ordered to go
and bring back Hades' horrible watchdog,
he'd never have escaped the streams of Styx.
Now Zeus despises me, plots with Thetis,   370
who has kissed his knees and caressed his chin,
begging him to back that brave Achilles,
but someday he'll call me 'Green Eyes' again.
So you harness up our glorious horses
while I go into the palace of Zeus
and arm myself for war. Then we shall see
if Priam's son Hector seems delighted
when we two appear on the battlefield.
No, many Trojans will be feeding dogs
with their fat and flesh by the Danaan ships!"   380

    And white-armed Hera did as she had said—
so those prancing horses were harnessed by
the queen of the gods, great Hera herself.
Meanwhile Athena, wise Zeus's daughter,
let her shimmering soft robe slither down
onto the floor of her father's palace,
donned the tunic of Zeus Thunderhurler,
and armed herself for miserable war.
She stepped on the fiery chariot, holding
her huge, stout, heavy spear that devastates   390
warriors who anger lord Zeus's daughter.
Now Hera flicked the horses with her whip,
and open groaned those gates kept by the Hours,
who watch over heaven and Olympus
and can split the thick clouds or keep them shut.
So they drove their team through the gleaming gates.

When Zeus saw them he was simply furious
and sent that golden-winged goddess Iris:
"Away with you, Iris, and tell those two
they'd better not tangle with me in war.   400
And if they should do it, this will happen:
I'll crush their horses under their chariot
and smash that chariot and dump them both out.
Tell them ten whole years will go rolling by
before their wounds from my thunderbolt heal,
so Green Eyes will learn what obedience means.
But I'm not so indignant with Hera—
she always works against me anyway."

   Stormfoot Iris rushed off with his message,
leapt from Ida's peaks to high Olympus.   410
And right beside Olympus' entrance gates
she met those goddesses and called to them:
"Just where are you two madly hurrying?
Zeus won't be glad if you help the Danaans!
And if you should do it, this will happen:
he'll crush your horses under your chariot
and smash that chariot and dump you both out.
He says ten whole years will go rolling by
before your wounds from his thunderbolt heal,
so you learn, Green Eyes, what obedience means.   420
He isn't so indignant with Hera—
she always works against him anyway—
but I think it's awful, you shameless bitch,
to dare raise your monstrous spear against Zeus."

   After saying this, Iris flew away,
and white-armed Hera cried to Athena:
"Come now, you daughter of shield-bearing Zeus,
let's not war with him because of mortals—
why, they can live or die, for all I care.
Zeus can very well make up his own mind   430
about that battle, as is most proper."

   She turned her horses back toward Olympus,
where the Hours unyoked those flowing-maned steeds,

tethered them to their ambrosial mangers,
leaned the chariot against an entrance wall.
And those two dropped down on their golden thrones
with the other gods, most disconsolate.

Now father Zeus drove his team from Ida
to join the immortals on Olympus.
There Poseidon unharnessed those horses,   440
covered the chariot, put it on its rack—
then Zeus took his seat on that golden throne
as tall Olympus quaked beneath his feet.
Only Hera and Athena sat apart
and wouldn't speak a word to him, but he
knew what was on their minds and addressed them:
"Why so downcast, Hera and Athena?
All worn out with destroying those Trojans,
you hate them with such a relentless rage?
Bah! nobody stands up against old Zeus—   450
all the Olympians can't change my purpose.
And how those fine legs of yours were trembling
before you even caught sight of combat!
But let me reassure you, dear ladies:
you would have no chariot to take you home
if I smashed you once with my thunderbolt!"

Great groans rose from Hera and Athena,
who sat side by side devising troubles
for the Trojans. Athena held her tongue
though father Zeus made her simply furious,   460
but Hera couldn't keep quiet and cried:
"You dreadful fellow, what a thing to say!
It's perfectly clear you are very strong—
and yet we're sorry for those Achaeans
doomed by a dismal fate to die in Troy.
We shall obey and stay out of battle,
but can't we offer a bit of advice
so your anger will not destroy them all?"

Whereupon cloudgathering Zeus replied:
"When dawn comes, my gentle-eyed queen Hera,   470

you'll see, if you wish, Cronos' mighty son
slaughtering even more Argive warriors.
And Hector's devastations will not end
till agile Achilles returns at last
while they battle over Patroclus' corpse
in direst straits by the sterns of their ships,
as heaven has decreed. And I don't care
how angry you are—run off to the ends
of earth and sea, where Iapetus and Cronos
live far away from the sun's lovely rays   480
or the tender breeze, in Tartarus' deeps,
go there if you wish, it won't worry me,
you're such an impossible bitch indeed!"

    And white-armed Hera refrained from reply.
Then the bright sunlight fell into the sea,
pulling night's shade over grain-giving earth—
sad for the Trojans, but the Achaeans
rejoiced at evening, answer to their prayers.

    And Hector called a Trojan assembly
at an open space beside that river   490
where the ground about was clear of corpses—
so all stepped down from their chariots to hear
Hector address them. In his hands he held
a sixteen-foot spear, and before him blazed
its razor-sharp edge with a golden ring.
Leaning on that weapon, Hector declared:
"Trojans and Dardanians and our allies,
today I hoped to destroy the Danaans
and enter our capital in triumph,
but darkness came first, and this alone saved   500
our enemies and their ships on the beach.
Now we must do the duties of evening:
prepare our suppers, let our horses loose
from their chariots, give them proper fodder,
then lead sheep and oxen from the city
immediately, bring bread and mellow wine
from our homes, and gather heaps of firewood.
And all night long till the coming of dawn

let's burn great bonfires to light up the sky
in case those flowing-haired Achaeans try   510
to flee for home over the sea's broad back.
They won't be escaping without a fight—
we'll give them a few Trojan souvenirs,
some sharp spears and arrows in their bellies
as they leap on their ships, so men will fear
forever to meet us in wretched war.
Our trusty heralds should go through the town
summoning boys and decrepit graybeards
to take up posts along the city walls,
while our women keep the bonfires blazing   520
in the halls of our homes and stay awake
so no enemies come while we are gone.
Enough for the moment, my dear Trojans,
but at daybreak I'll speak to you again
in a new assembly of our people.
May thunderlord Zeus and the other gods
help us drive away those ravenous dogs
the fates brought here on their seafaring ships!
Just keep a keen lookout the whole night through
and at dawn tomorrow we'll arm ourselves   530
to begin bitter battle by the ships.
Then we shall see if that Diomedes
can batter me back from the ships, or I
slay him and take some bloody booty home.
Tomorrow he'll learn if he can withstand
my dangerous spear—or we may see him
lying dead with many of his comrades
at sunset that day. Oh, I only wish
I were sure of being an immortal,
honored like Athena or Apollo,   540
as I know this day brings the Danaans ruin!"

    And those Trojan warriors roared approval.
So they unharnessed their sweating horses,
tethered them tight to the chariots with thongs,
then led sheep and oxen from the city
immediately, brought bread and mellow wine

from their homes, gathered great heaps of firewood
and burned offerings to the Olympians—
so the winds bore that odor to heaven.
But the blessed gods refused acceptance,   550
for they had come to hate holy Ilios
and Priam and his spear-slinging people.

   Thus, their hearts high with hope, those Trojans stayed
through the long night with many bonfires lit.
As stars are a-gleam about the bright moon
splendidly clear on some windless evening
and everywhere appear peaks and headlands
and valleys, till the firmament bursts forth
with all its stars and a shepherd is glad:
thus the bonfires of those Trojan warriors   560
glittered between the ships and Xanthus' streams.
A thousand fires burned on the plain, by each
fifty men seated in a gleam of flame,
while their horses munched white barley and rye
and stood by the chariots, awaiting Dawn.

Book Nine: The Refusal

Agamemnon offers gifts of reconciliation, but Achilles remains intransigent.

So the Trojans kept watch, while those Danaans
were gripped by panic, friend of chilly fear,
and all their lords felt desperate anguish.
As fish-filled billows heave beneath the gusts
of a northwest wind that bustles from Thrace
in a sudden rush, till the dark sea-surge
crests and hurls much seaweed along its shore:
thus those Achaean warriors were dismayed.

But Agamemnon, racked by a vast grief,
ordered his clarion-voiced heralds to call   10
the leaders of his armies one by one
but not to shout, and went with them himself.
When all had gathered, that son of Atreus
rose weeping, like a spring of murky streams
which pours its waters over some sheer cliff,
and groaning heavily, he addressed them:
"My heroic friends and fellow warriors,
Cronos' son Zeus made a great fool of me—
that cruel god! He bowed his head to promise
we should sack their city, return safe home,   20
but it seems he tricked me; now he decrees
I'll go back disgraced after many die.
Ah, this must be the will of mighty Zeus,
who has toppled towers in many towns
and will topple more, such is his power.
So every man here should do as I say:

let's set sail for our beloved homeland,
because I know we'll never take that town."

　A hush of awe fell over those warriors,
and they sat in silent desperation.　　　　　　　　　　30
Finally dauntless Diomedes cried:
"Atreus' son, I'll answer your foolishness
in this assembly, where I have the right.
You attacked my valor before us all,
called me a coward, a silly milksop,
and every one of us here heard your words.
Well, Zeus has treated you quite stingily,
gave you the scepter as sign of command
but declined to give something more: courage.
You strange fellow, do you really believe　　　　　　40
your people are such weaklings as you say?
If you're so very eager to return,
then do it! Home's that way, there are the ships
you brought along from Mycenae. But I
and the other Achaeans will stay on
till we sack that city—or all the rest
may set sail for their beloved homelands
while I and Sthenelus fight on alone
till we take that town, as fate has decreed."

　Those assembled Achaeans roared hurrah　　　　　50
for brave Diomedes' exhortation.
Then aged Nestor rose and addressed them:
"Tydeus' son, you're our finest in battle
and best among your age in strategy.
Nobody here will take your words lightly
or contradict them, but there's more to say.
You're young, young enough to be my own son,
my latest-born one—though you tell the truth,
such a splendid head is on your shoulders—
so listen to an older man's advice.　　　　　　　　　60
I'll tell the whole story, and no one here
should object, not even Agamemnon.
Clanless, lawless, homeless is a warrior
who strives against his own countrymen.

Now we must do the duties of evening:
prepare our suppers and post sentinels
along the moat that runs outside our wall—
so much for our younger people. Then you,
Agamemnon, as commander in chief,
serve a fine banquet for our commanders.   70
Your tents are full of wine our Argive ships
bring over the wide sea from Thrace each day,
so you have the means for entertainment.
After many have come together, hear
our good advice—and what a need we have
for a few wise words, with the enemy
burning many bonfires beside our ships!
Tonight brings our ruin or our salvation."

   And they gladly obeyed that lord's commands:
Sentinels hurried out in full armor   80
under the command of Thrasymedes,
valiant Ascalaphus and Ialmenus,
Meriones, Aphareaus, Deipyrus,
and Creon's son godlike Lycomedes.
Seven men were their captains, and with each
came a hundred young Achaean spearmen.
Thus they took their posts between moat and wall,
then kindled fires, and each man made his meal.

   And Atreus' son led all those commanders
into his tent, laid a feast before them.   90
So they reached their hands to the tender treats.
After they had eaten and drunk their fill,
that veteran whose plans were always best,
Nestor, began weaving the web of speech.
He addressed them with these well-measured words:
"Our distinguished leader Agamemnon,
I direct my words to you most of all,
for many men serve under your command
and thunderlord Zeus backs you in battle.
Therefore you must both give orders and hear   100
when our people make worthwhile proposals
and you have power to fulfill them.

So I'll tell you what seems the best to me.
We've had no plan superior to this one,
not for a long, long time, Agamemnon,
since you, my lord, took the girl Briseis
from Achilles' camp and made him angry,
much against our wishes. I surely tried
to dissuade you—but you were too haughty
and slighted someone honored by the gods,   110
stole his lady, took her away. But now
we must consider how to make amends
with words and gifts of reconciliation."

   Atreus' son Agamemnon answered him:
"True, dear fellow, I was very foolish,
mad—no doubt about it! A whole army
isn't worth one warrior adored by Zeus,
as he loves that man and damages us.
But since I gave in to my dreadful rage
I'll make amends with splendid recompense.   120
Yes, these are the presents he shall receive:
seven brand-new cauldrons, ten gold pieces,
twenty bright kettles, and twelve racehorses,
tough in running, each one a prizewinner.
A leader would not be lacking booty,
not without treasures of glamorous gold,
if he had what these racehorses have won.
I shall give seven women skilled in crafts,
my plunder after he captured Lesbos,
especially beautiful ones indeed,   130
among them the lady I took from him—
Briseus' daughter. And I'll swear a great oath
I never once have lain with her in love
as men and women do upon this earth.
All these shall be his immediately, then
if the gods let us sack Priam's city
he can heap his ship high with gold and bronze
before our Achaeans have split the spoils
and choose himself twenty Trojan women,
the loveliest after Argive Helen.   140

And if we ever return to Argos
he may take one of my daughters as wife
and be honored like my son Orestes.
I have three fine daughters—Laodicë,
Chrysothemis, and Iphianassa—
and he'll have whichever one he desires,
together with an opulent dowry,
more than a father has ever given.
Seven populous cities will be his:
Cardamylë, Enopë, and Hirë,   150
holy Pherae, deep-meadowed Anthaea,
fair Aepeia, and vineland Pedasus.
They lie by the sea on Pylos' borders,
with a people rich in herds of cattle
who will bring him offerings like a god
and obey his commands to the letter.
I'll do all this for him if he relents.
He must! Only Hades is unbending,
therefore men hate him more than any god.
He can submit to me—I'm his senior   160
and far more exalted in rank than he."

    And aged Gerenian Nestor answered:
"Our distinguished leader Agamemnon,
these are no mean presents you have offered.
Very well then, let's choose an embassy
to visit Peleus' son prince Achilles.
But I'll select the people if you wish:
venerable Phoenix will lead the way
with Aias, Odysseus, and our heralds
illustrious Odius and Eurybates.   170
Bring water for our hands so we may pray
for the mercy of Zeus Thunderhurler."

    And Nestor's words were approved by them all,
then heralds poured water over their hands,
young men brought bowls brimful of mellow wine,
poured libation, and everyone was served.
After they had prayed and taken their wine
they left king Agamemnon, Atreus' son,

and Nestor gazed piercingly at each man,
exhorting them—Odysseus most of all— 180
to appease Achilles as best they could.

  So they went their way by the booming sea
with many a prayer to Poseidon
that prince Achilles might be persuaded.
When they reached those Myrmidon ships and tents
they found him fingering a splendid lyre
richly inlaid, with a silver crossbar,
his spoils when he sacked Eëtion's city.
He strummed the lyre and chanted warriors' deeds
while Patroclus sat silent beside him, 190
raptly attent to that heroic song.
As Odysseus and the ambassadors
strode forward, Achilles leapt from his chair
in astonishment, still holding the lyre,
and Patroclus also rose at the sight.
Now Peleus' son Achilles greeted them:
"Welcome, dear friends—ah, now they must need me!
dearest of them all, despite my anger."

  Then that son of Peleus led them in,
seated them on couches and purple rugs, 200
and addressed Patroclus, who stood nearby:
"Menoetius' son, bring out a bigger bowl,
serve stronger wine, a cup for every man.
These are beloved comrades who have come."

  Patroclus did as his friend had ordered,
brought a great meat block into the firelight,
laid chunks of mutton and goat upon it
with a hefty hog's back dripping in fat.
Automedon held while Achilles carved—
he sliced the meat with care and spitted it 210
while godlike Patroclus fanned the flames high.
But after their crackling fire subsided
he set those spits on the scattered embers
over two andirons and salted them well.
After all was roasted, piled on platters,

Menoetius' son Patroclus offered bread
in baskets, as Achilles served the meat.
Next Achilles sat facing Odysseus
against the wall and ordered Patroclus
to burn holy offerings for the gods—   220
so they reached their hands to those tender treats.
And when they had eaten and drunk their fill
Aias winked to Phoenix. Odysseus saw,
filled a cup with wine, and raised it, saying:
"To your health, Achilles! We've had fine feasts
in the camp of noble Agamemnon
and in yours. Delicious food has been served,
though we cannot think of banquets, my lord,
but of the ruin we see before us,
and we're afraid. Who knows if we'll survive   230
unless you lead our people in combat.
Those arrogant Trojans and their allies
are camping very near our ships and wall
with many bonfires, and now they declare
nothing will keep them from burning our ships.
Mighty Zeus showed an omen on their right—
a flash of lightning—and Hector battles
ceaselessly, backed by Zeus, quite unafraid
of gods or men, such fury drives him on.
Now he prays for daybreak to come quickly,   240
says he'll hack the figureheads from these ships,
set all ablaze and slaughter our warriors
who wander about them dazed with the smoke.
I very much fear that the immortals
will fulfill Hector's boasts and we're fated
to perish here, far from grassy Argos.
So up with you, man! Only you can save
our Achaean armies from utter ruin.
You'll regret it if you refuse—but then
the damage will be done, so while you can,   250
consider how to rescue our people.
Dear fellow, remember your father's words
that day he sent you to Agamemnon:
'Son, Athena and Hera will grant you

strength if they so desire, yet you must keep
your temper—kindliness is better far.
Just stay out of quarrels and you'll have more
honor from all our Achaean people.'
You've forgotten the old man's words, but still
you can give up this grudge—Agamemnon   260
offers worthy gifts of conciliation.
Let me name all the magnificent things
Agamemnon has promised in his tent:
seven brand-new cauldrons, ten gold pieces,
twenty bright kettles, and twelve racehorses,
tough in running, each one a prizewinner.
A leader would not be lacking booty,
not without treasures of glamorous gold,
if he had what these racehorses have won.
And he'll give seven women skilled in crafts,   270
his plunder after you captured Lesbos,
especially beautiful ones indeed,
among them the lady he took from you—
Briseus' daughter. And he'll swear a great oath
he never once has lain with her in love
as men and women do upon this earth.
All these shall be yours immediately, then
if the gods let us sack Priam's city
you can heap your ship high with gold and bronze
before our Achaeans have split the spoils   280
and choose yourself twenty Trojan women,
the loveliest after Argive Helen.
And if we ever return to Argos
you may take one of his daughters as wife
and be honored like his son Orestes.
He has three fine daughters—Laodicë,
Chrysothemis, and Iphianassa—
and you'll have whichever one you desire,
together with an opulent dowry,
more than a father has ever given.   290
Seven prosperous cities will be yours—
Cardamylë, Enopë, and Hirë,
holy Pherae, deep-meadowed Anthaea,

fair Aepeia, and vineland Pedasus.
They lie by the sea on Pylos' borders,
with a people rich in herds of cattle
who will bring you offerings like a god
and obey your commands to the letter.
He'll do all this if you only relent.
But if you still despise Agamemnon   300
with his fine presents, pity the others
in their desperate need and you'll receive
honor and glory like a god himself.
Yes, here is your chance to slay that Hector—
he'll be so careless because he believes
no other Danaan is a match for him."

   And that quickfoot Achilles answered him:
"Laertes' son ingenious Odysseus,
it seems I must tell you very frankly
what I think and what I intend to do,   310
so you won't sit cooing at me all day—
yes, more than Hades' gates I hate a man
who tries to hide his plans with double-talk.
Very well, let me speak my mind out plain.
I won't be persuaded by Atreus' son
or anyone else, since I've had no thanks
for all I suffered in war to please him!
A man gets the same if he fights or not,
cowards and heroes win equal honor,
death takes hard workers as well as shirkers.   320
What good have I had from all these hardships,
constantly risking my life in combat?
I was like a bird who brings what she finds
to her chicks, with nothing left for herself,
while I kept watch through many sleepless nights
and spent bloody days on the battlefield
to win the wives of enemy warriors.
Twelve prosperous cities I sacked by sea
and eleven by land here in Ilios
and took piles of booty from every one   330
to lay at the feet of Agamemnon,

Atreus' son, who stayed behind by his ships
and apportioned a little but kept most.
Whatever he gave to our other lords
they still possess, but from me, me alone,
he took my wife. Well, let him sleep with her
and enjoy her. Why are we battling here,
we Achaeans? Why did we cross the sea
with Atreus' son? Wasn't it for Helen?
Then are the only ones who love their wives   340
those sons of Atreus? No, any real man
loves and cherishes his dear wife, as I
adored her too, though I won her in war.
Now he stole that lady, took her away—
he won't persuade me: I know him too well.
Odysseus, you and our other leaders
should put your own minds to saving the ships!
He already did so much without me—
made a great wall and a moat beside it,
bristling with palisades at the bottom—   350
but one thing he can't do: stop murderous
Hector. While I fought by the Achaeans
he didn't dare come far from his city wall,
stayed back by the oak tree and Scaean Gates.
I met him there once—he barely escaped.
Now, since I've no wish to battle Hector,
tomorrow I'll sacrifice to the gods,
launch my trim ships, and load them with cargo—
and then, if you care to, you shall see me
sailing over the Hellespont at dawn   360
with many excellent oarsmen aboard,
and if Poseidon grants us good weather,
on the third day we reach fertile Phthia.
I left many treasures home when I came,
and I'll take more back—gold and glowing bronze,
delectable women and gray iron—
but the best of all my battle booty
was stolen from me by Agamemnon,
Atreus' son. You tell him what I have said
in public, so his men will be angry   370

in case that double-crosser ever tries
to swindle one of them too—as for me,
the dog wouldn't dare look me in the eye.
He'll have no advice from me, much less help,
after he cheated me like that—I won't
let him fool me again. Once is enough.
He can go to hell: he's out of his mind.
And his presents aren't worth a straw to me.
Even if he gave ten times, twenty times
what he offers now, with a lot more too—   380
all that enters Orchomenos or Thebes
in Egypt, where the greatest treasures are
and from every one of their hundred gates
two hundred chariots thunder out to war—
if his gifts were as many as the sands
on all sea beaches, he'd never move me
till he pays the full price for his insult.
And I wouldn't marry that man's daughter
if she were lovely as Aphrodite
and ingenious as green-eyed Athena.   390
He can find someone else for his daughter,
someone of his own rank, nobler than me.
But if the gods keep me till I reach home
old Peleus will find me a wife himself.
Many ladies in Hellas and Phthia
are daughters of princes who rule cities,
and I can have my pick of any one.
While I was there I often planned to take
a dear wedded wife as my companion
and enjoy my father's splendid estate—   400
for to me life is worth far more than all
they say the busy city Troy once had
in peacetime, before we Achaeans came,
more than all the wealth in that marble shrine
of archer Apollo at steep Delphi.
In battle a man wins cattle and sheep,
and in trade he gets cauldrons and horses,
but once a man has breathed out his soul
neither trade nor battle will win it back.

My mother silverfoot Thetis tells me 410
two separate fates are leading me toward death:
if I stay here and continue combat
I won't go back but have undying fame,
while if I return to my dear homeland
I can live in decent obscurity
till I die in the fullness of my time.
And let me advise all the rest of you
to leave for your homes, because you'll never
sack that city—thunderlord Zeus himself
keeps its people under his protection. 420
You return to our Achaean leaders
and give them my message, as is proper,
so they can make some more sensible plan
for rescuing their armies and their fleet—
the one they have now simply will not do:
I'm far too angry to consider it.
But Phoenix shall stay and sleep here tonight,
then tomorrow morning he may go home
with me on my ships if he wishes to."

   A hush of awe fell over those warriors, 430
they were so amazed at his forceful words.
Finally veteran Phoenix declared,
weeping in his anxiety for the ships:
"Achilles, if you really plan to return
and don't intend to rescue our people
in your implacable indignation,
how can I, dear child, stay here without you,
alone? Aged Peleus sent me along
that day you went to join Agamemnon,
only a boy, knowing nothing of war 440
or assemblies where men show eloquence.
He made me the one who taught you to be
a speaker of words and a doer of deeds.
If you should go, dear child, I could never
remain without you, though a god promised
to take away my age and make me young
as the day I left my home in Hellas,

escaping the fury of my father,
who was incensed because of his mistress,
a girl he adored, ignoring his wife,   450
my mother, so she begged me on her knees
to seduce that lady, win her away.
I did it, but my father learned the truth,
cursed me, and swore by the dread Erinyes
that no child of mine would sit on his lap—
and his curse was carried out by the gods
underworld Zeus and grim Persephone.
And then I would have slain him with my sword,
but some god stopped me, made me consider
how the Danaans would hate me forever   460
and remember me as a parricide.
After that I found it unbearable
to stay in the palace of my father
though my many cousins and kinsmen came
begging me to remain at home with them,
slaughtered sheep and oxen by the dozens,
and hosts of corpulent white-tusked porkers
were roasted over the flickering flames
as we drank our fill of my father's wine.
Nine days long my kinsmen watched over me   470
in turns, kept their bonfires burning briskly,
one just under the courtyard portico,
another on the porch before my room.
But when the gloom of the tenth evening came
I broke the lock of those tight-fitting doors
and clambered over our great courtyard wall
easily, unseen by watchmen and maids.
So I escaped across all broad Hellas,
arrived at last in the land of Phthia,
where I found a welcome with king Peleus,   480
who loved me as a father loves a son,
his only child and the heir to his realm.
He made me rich, gave me many to rule:
Dolopians, who live on Phthia's borders.
I made you what you are, prince Achilles,
with my devotion. You'd let no one else

be with you at the feast, refused to eat
till I put you on my knees and prepared
pieces of meat for you and held your cup.
And how many times was my tunic wet   490
by the wine that you puked out helplessly!
I suffered much for you and labored much,
since I knew the gods would give me no son
of mine. I made you my child, Achilles,
expecting someday you would protect me.
So control your temper, Achilles, don't
be unrelenting! Even gods give in
though they're higher and mightier than you—
yes, even they can be moved by prayer
with incense, libations, and burned offerings   500
when men have transgressed and committed wrong.
Prayers are daughters of thunderlord Zeus,
limping and wrinkled, with eyes turned askance,
and they always follow behind Folly,
whose feet are so quick and nimble she
outruns them all, hurries over the earth
catching men, till Prayers come to release them.
Should someone honor these daughters of Zeus
they greatly bless him and hear his desires,
but in case he stubbornly refuses   510
they go their way and pray to Cronos' son
that Folly strike him till he pays the price.
And you too, prince Achilles, should respect
Zeus's daughters, as other people do.
If Atreus' son didn't offer presents,
if he were still relentlessly angry,
I'd never implore you to make your peace
or save our people in their greatest need.
You'll have glorious rewards now, more later,
and he sent men to beseech you, the best   520
in all our armies, the ones you yourself
love the most, so don't despise our appeal
though you were right to be angry before.
We've heard those stories of ancient warriors
in a towering rage—they too could be won

by proper presents and by persuasion.
Yes, I myself remember long ago—
and let me tell you about it, my friends—
Curetes battled against Aetolians
about their lovely city Calydon,   530
the Aetolians defending their city,
their enemies eager to ravage it.
Golden-throned Artemis had caused the war,
furious she received no harvest offering
from Oeneus, though the other gods did
and only Zeus's daughter was ignored—
a very foolish omission indeed.
So that daughter of Zeus was indignant
and sent a redoubtable white-tusked boar,
who went ramping through Oeneus' orchards   540
and tore up and toppled many tall trees,
their roots and blossoming branches and all.
Oeneus' son Meleager killed that boar,
assisted by hunters from many towns
and their hounds—few men could not have done it,
he'd put so many on the funeral pyre.
Then the goddess brought about contention
over his great head and his shaggy hide,
so those opposing hunters went to war.
As long as Meleager stayed in combat   550
the Curetes were worsted—didn't dare
leave their capital, although they were more.
But he lost his temper—like some others
in this world, however wise they may be—
and, raging at his mother Althaea,
remained home with his wife Cleopatra,
a daughter of slim-ankled Marpessa
and Idas, mightiest warrior on earth,
who wasn't even afraid to attack
great Apollo for the sake of his bride.   560
Marpessa's father and stately mother
gave her the name Halcyonë, because
when Phoebus Apollo snatched her away
her mother wailed like the halcyon bird.

Meleager lay sulking by his wife
after his mother cursed him to the gods
in grief because he murdered her brother.
Kneeling down, staining her tunic with tears,
she beat her fists on the bountiful earth,
begging Hades and dread Persephone   570
for her son's death—and the murky Furies
heard her frenzied cries out of Erebus.
Then about their gates came a thunderous
battering of walls, while the city elders
and chief priests entreated Meleager
to save them for an enormous reward:
on the richest part of the city's land
they promised him a prosperous estate—
fifty fine acres, half of them vineyard
and half open plowland cleared from the plain.   580
Next aged Oeneus implored him too:
standing on the threshold of his son's room,
he shook the folding doors in a frenzy,
while his sisters and mother beseeched him,
but he refused—and many friends as well,
his dearest and truest in all the world.
Yes, nothing they told him could move his heart
till his home was attacked, their city walls
set aflame by the raging Curetes.
Then Meleager's own beloved wife   590
tearfully begged him with tales about all
those sorrows of warriors whose fortress falls:
the men murdered, their city in ashes,
women and children enslaved to strangers.
Such horrors stirred even Meleager,
who leapt up, threw his gleaming armor on,
and saved his comrades in their hour of need—
but never received the gifts they offered,
despite what he did in rescuing them.
Now don't you make the same mistake, dear boy.   600
Remember how much harder it will be
to save our ships when they're aflame—take gifts
and help us. You'll have honor like a god.

If you come later, after refusing,
you'll be honored less, although you save us."

  And that quickfoot Achilles answered him:
"Phoenix, aged father, what do I care
for honors? I've enough of them from Zeus,
and all these shall be mine as long as breath's
in my body and I have strength to move.   610
And let me tell you another thing: don't
confuse me with this weeping and wailing
to please great Agamemnon. If you do,
I may well decide you're no friend of mine.
Better you should hate my enemies too.
Stay with me, share my honors and command.
Send these other men back and spend the night
on a soft bed here, and at break of day
we'll discuss whether we should return home."

  Then he signaled Patroclus silently   620
to prepare Phoenix' bed, so the others
might take the hint and depart. But Aias,
godlike son of Telamon, spoke up next:
"Very well, Odysseus, my dear fellow,
it seems we must go, since we won't receive
what we came here for. We'd better hurry,
bring our bad news to the Achaean lords
who are waiting for us. This Achilles
has become quite ferocious in his pride—
that unfeeling man! He has forgotten   630
his friends who love him more than anyone,
he's so unbending. Even murderers
of brothers or sons can be forgiven—
the culprit pays and escapes punishment
because his relatives stifle their pride
for a suitable recompense—while you
keep this stubborn temper over one girl
only, while we offer seven splendid ones
and a great deal more. So you should relent
and welcome men who come under your roof   640

for our entire army, who wish to be
nearest and dearest of your companions."

   And Peleus' son Achilles answered him:
"Magnificent Telamonian Aias,
I can only agree with what you say—
but I tell you it infuriates me
to be humiliated before our people
by Agamemnon, treated like a tramp.
So you two go and report my message:
I won't even consider bloody war   650
till that dangerous Hector, Priam's son,
forces his way to our Myrmidon camp
amid much slaughter, sets the fleet aflame.
But when he comes near my own high-beaked ship
I think his wildness will be tamed a bit!"

   So all took double-handled cups and poured
libations, then Odysseus led them back.
Patroclus ordered servants and slave girls
to prepare a resting place for Phoenix—
and as he commanded, they made a bed   660
with fleeces and rugs and soft gray linen.
Then that old lord lay and awaited dawn.
Glorious Achilles slept inside the tent
beside a lady he brought from Lesbos,
Diomedë, Phorbas' lovely daughter.
Patroclus lay opposite, at his side
graceful Iphis, a gift from Achilles
after he sacked Enyeus' city Scyrus.

   When those others reached Agamemnon's camp
the Achaean leaders leapt to their feet,   670
pledged them with golden cups, and questioned them.
Atreus' son Agamemnon spoke up first:
"Now come tell me, illustrious Odysseus,
will he save our ships from the enemy,
or did he refuse in relentless rage?"

That godlike patient Odysseus replied:
"Our distinguished leader Agamemnon,
he's entirely irreconcilable,
even angrier, scorns you and your gifts,
says you should make some more sensible plan   680
for rescuing our armies and our fleet,
declares that at dawn tomorrow morning
his people will put their ships in the sea.
And he would advise all the rest of us
to leave for our homes, because we'll never
sack that city—thunderlord Zeus himself
keeps its people under his protection.
Yes, he said it, and these were witnesses,
giant Aias and our two wise heralds.
But Achilles told Phoenix to sleep there,   690
then tomorrow morning he may go home
with them on their ships if he wishes to."

A hush of awe fell over those warriors,
amazed at the forcefulness of his words,
and they sat in silent desperation.
Finally dauntless Diomedes cried:
"Our distinguished leader Agamemnon,
better if we hadn't begged Achilles
and offered gifts—he's arrogant enough,
but this will make him even haughtier.   700
No matter, let him take his people home
or stay and enter battle whenever
he wants or some immortal god desires.
Now every man here should do as I say:
go take your rest when you've had enough
bread and wine, the sustenance of warriors,
but at the first sign of rose-fingered dawn
we'll form our battalions before the ships,
and you yourself, my lord, will lead the way."

Those assembled Achaeans roared hurrah   710
for brave Diomedes' exhortation.
Then they made libations, went to their tents,
and lay down and received the gift of sleep.

Book Ten: The Raid

The Greeks send Diomedes and Odysseus to reconnoiter the
enemy camp. The Trojans send Dolon with the same aim.

Now there by the ships those other leaders
slumbered all night, overcome by soft sleep,
but not Atreus' son lord Agamemnon,
so many troubles weighed upon his mind.
As when Hera's husband flashes lightning
that foretells some pelting rainstorm or hail
or a blizzard sprinkling the fields with snow
or the wide-open mouth of bitter war,
such enormous groans rolled from deep inside
Agamemnon's chest in his anxiety.   10
And each time he gazed toward the Trojan plain
he shuddered at how many fires were there,
with skirling flutes and muttering of men—
and each time he gazed toward the Danaan camp
he tore his hair out by the very roots
in appeal to Zeus and moaned mightily.
Finally he decided it was best
to approach aged Nestor first of all
in hopes together they might make some plan
for saving their people from utter ruin.   20
So he sat up in bed, donned his tunic,
bound elegant sandals about his feet,
put on a colossal tawny lionskin
that reached to the ground, and took his great spear.

    Menelaus felt troubled as well—he too
stayed sleepless as he worried what would come

of all who had crossed the seas for his sake
to Troy with terrible war on their minds.
Over his shoulders he flung a dappled
leopardskin, set a helmet on his head,   30
took a formidable spear in his hand,
and went to awaken Agamemnon,
king and commander of the Achaeans.
He found his brother putting on armor
by his own high-beaked ship—a welcome sight.
Atreus' son Menelaus cried out first:
"Why are you arming, dear brother? You plan
sending somebody to scout? I'm very
afraid no man will undertake that job,
going alone to spy on our enemies   40
through the ambrosial night—he'd be quite brave."

·   Atreus' son king Agamemnon answered:
"Both you and I need advice, Menelaus—
worthwhile advice that may save our people
now majestic Zeus has turned against us.
Hector's sacrifices must have won him.
Oh, I've never seen, never even heard
of so much damage being done in one day
as Zeus's beloved Hector did to us,
though he's not even the son of a god.   50
The Achaeans will remember that man
a long, long time, he brought them so much grief.
You hurry among our ships to summon
Aias and our Idomeneus, while I
wake aged Nestor and ask him for aid
in deploying our trusty sentinels.
They'll obey him best because his own son
and Idomeneus' comrade Meriones
are captains and commanders of the guard."

And that Menelaus replied to him: 60
"Very well then, but what do you suggest—
should I stay with them and wait till you come,
or return when I've given your command?"

Atreus' son king Agamemnon answered:
"Stay—if you don't we may miss each other,
such a maze of footpaths crosses our camp.
Waken our leaders wherever you go
and call each man with proper courtesy,
using his full name. Don't be overproud—
it seems we must do it ourselves, since Zeus
has doomed us to innumerable sorrows."

He sent his brother out with these orders,
then went to seek their veteran Nestor
and found him stretched out beside his black ship
on a soft bed, with all his rich armor:
a shield, two spears, and a brilliant helmet.
And next to him lay the breastplate he wore
when he armed himself for bitter battle,
leading his people, undaunted by age.
He lifted his head, rose on an elbow,
and called to Agamemnon, Atreus' son:
"Who are you, wandering through our camp alone
this gloomy night, while other mortals sleep?
Looking for a mule or for some comrade?
Speak up or don't come near! What do you want?"

Whereupon Agamemnon answered him:
"Illustrious Nestor, our pride and glory,
this is Atreus' son king Agamemnon,
a man harassed by Zeus as long as breath
stays in my body and I've strength to move.
I wander about because I can't sleep
with worries over our disastrous war.
Those Trojans make trouble after trouble,
so my heart hammers wildly, my legs shake,
my head is spinning, I feel I'm going mad.
But if you can help, since you're awake too,
come with me to inspect our sentinels
and see whether they have fallen asleep
and forgotten the watch with weariness.
The enemy camp's so near, who can say?—
they may be planning an attack by night."

70

80

90

100

And that aged Nestor said in reply:
"Our distinguished leader Agamemnon,
Zeus won't support Hector in everything,
as he seems to believe. Yes, you may see
he'll have more grief than us if Achilles
will only forget his miserable grudge.
Of course I'll come, but let's call the others—
Diomedes, ingenious Odysseus,
Oileus' son nimble Aias, and Meges.   110
Somebody else may be sent to summon
Telamonian Aias and Idomeneus,
since their ships are at the camp's farthest ends.
That Menelaus! I love and prize him,
but damn it, you won't blame me for saying
he shouldn't sleep on and leave you the work.
Better approach our Danaan commanders,
begging them to help us in our distress."

Atreus' son king Agamemnon answered:
"Sir, other times you might have scolded him   120
for negligence and arrant carelessness,
but it isn't because he's unwilling.
He simply waits for me to take the lead.
This time he woke first and hurried to me,
and I sent him to call the ones you named.
So let's be gone—we'll find them by the gates
with the sentinels, as I commanded."

That veteran Gerenian Nestor replied:
"Good enough then, they won't dare disobey
if Menelaus himself commands them."   130

And he wrapped his tunic around his chest,
bound elegant sandals about his feet,
then buckled on a heavy purple cloak,
two broad layers of thickly matted wool,
took a formidable spear in his hand,
and went along the lines of Danaan ships.
The first man he found was shrewd Odysseus,
and aged Gerenian Nestor woke him

with a shout. The sound ringing in his ears,
Odysseus stumbled from his tent and cried: 140
"Why are you two wandering here alone
through the ambrosial night? What has happened?"

  And veteran Gerenian Nestor replied:
"Ah, ingenious son of Laertes, don't
be angry—our people have such troubles.
Let's wake some other leaders and decide
whether or not we should set sail for home."

  When he heard this, Odysseus went inside,
took a cunningly crafted shield, and came.
They found Tydeus' son brave Diomedes   150
lying beside his tent, with his people
asleep all about him, heads propped on shields,
weapons upended in earth, the spearpoints
bright as mighty Zeus's lightning. That lord
lay drenched in slumber on piles of oxhides,
head pillowed on a brightly woven rug.
Veteran Nestor came striding forward,
prodded him with his foot, and he declared:
"Wake up, Diomedes—can't sleep all night!
Haven't you seen the Trojans camping there   160
so terribly near our high-beaked ships?"

  Prince Diomedes leapt up immediately
and addressed him in agitated words:
"You're a tough old man, sir, always busy!
Haven't we anyone younger than you
to do the job of waking our leaders
this evening? You're too much for us all, sir!"

  And veteran Gerenian Nestor replied:
"Indeed, my dear friend, we certainly have:
my sons, for example, and many more   170
among our people might be chosen too.
But now we're in our very greatest need—
I tell you, we stand on the razor's edge:
tonight means our ruin or salvation.

Now hurry off, if you respect my age,
call Telamonian Aias and Meges."

So over his shoulders Diomedes slung
a mighty lionskin, then took his spear
and woke those leaders and brought them along.

They joined their sentinels at the outpost   180
and found none of the commanders asleep,
but each sat wide awake in full armor.
Like dogs that keep restless watch about sheep
when they hear a lion creep through the forest
far in the mountains, and around him rise
cries of men and hounds, so all stay awake:
thus none of those lords had a wink of sleep
as they watched through that bitter night, gazed
toward the great plain, alert for an attack.
Veteran Nestor rejoiced at the sight   190
and addressed them in agitated words:
"Quite right, dear boys, let no one be napping—
that would provide the enemy much joy."

Then Nestor hurried on across the moat
with those gallant Achaean commanders.
Meriones and Antilochus came too,
since they had been invited with the rest.
When all had crossed over, they took their seats
in an open area clear of corpses,
where terrible Hector had been turned back   200
as darkness ended his devastations.
They conversed awhile with each other, then
aged Gerenian Nestor addressed them:
"Friends, would any man here have the courage
to go among those arrogant Trojans
and finish off some enemy straggler
or find out what their people are saying
about their purpose: have they decided
to remain here by the ships or instead
return to their city, now they have won?   210
Somebody could learn all this and come back

unscathed—and what a great name he would gain
as well as a magnificent reward:
yes, each of our Achaean commanders
would give him an incomparable black ewe
with a suckling lamb, an honor indeed,
and he'd always have a place at our feasts."

A hush of awe fell over those warriors,
but finally dauntless Diomedes cried:
"Well, Nestor, I'm not in the least afraid   220
to make my way through the enemy camp,
but if someone else accompanied me
I might feel easier about the job.
Two heads are better than one—if a man
goes all alone, he's kept so occupied
he has no time to make the proper plans."

And many were eager to follow him:
first those two redoubtable Aiantes,
then Meriones and the son of Nestor,
with Atreus' son valiant Menelaus   230
and stubborn Odysseus, keen for some feat,
eager to enter the enemy camp.
Then Agamemnon spoke out among them:
"Tydeus' son Diomedes, my good man,
take any of these as your companion,
so many veterans have volunteered.
But don't pass up the person you prefer
and select somebody less qualified
because he has higher rank than the rest."

He said this to spare blond Menelaus.   240
And dauntless Diomedes answered him:
"If I'm to choose my very favorite
how can I overlook our Odysseus,
who's always ready to undertake
any tough job, and Athena loves him.
We could go through blazing flame together,
such a clever head is on his shoulders."

That much-enduring Odysseus replied:
"Not too much praise or blame, Diomedes—
the Achaeans know my worth already.   250
Very well, let's go! Soon dawn will be here;
the stars are moving onward, night sweeps past:
no more than a third, I suppose, remains."

So both men put on their dreadful armor.
Thrasymedes presented Tydeus' son
a two-edged sword—he'd left his own behind—
and a shield, then he donned a fine helmet,
plain and of oxhide, the kind called skullcap,
often the attire of younger warriors.
And Meriones gave Odysseus a bow,   260
a quiver, a sword, a leather helmet
with many sturdy thongs stretched tight inside
to stiffen it—and bristling all about,
row after row of brilliant white boar tusks
and a soft felt lining in the middle.
Autolycus had stolen it in Eleon
by breaking into Amyntor's palace,
then presented it to Amphidamas,
that man gave it to his houseguest Molus,
who passed it on to his son Meriones,   270
and now it protected Odysseus' head.

When both had put on their dreadful armor
they left the other leaders, went their way,
and a heron was sent forth on the right
by Athena. Though they couldn't see it
through the gloomy darkness, they heard it cry.
Odysseus rejoiced at that sign and prayed:
"Now hear my petition, daughter of Zeus!
When I'm in trouble you stand at my side,
so favor me once again, Athena: 280
Let us return to the ships with glory
after we've done the Trojans some mischief."

Next that wild warrior Diomedes prayed:
"Tireless goddess, hear my entreaty too!

Guard me as you did my father Tydeus
in Thebes, where he went as a messenger.
He left his comrades by the Asopus
and came to the Cadmeians in friendship
but on the way back did horrible deeds
with your help, excellent daughter of Zeus.   290
Stand at my side, watch over me tonight,
and I'll sacrifice a heifer to you,
a sleek yearling that never bore the yoke,
magnificently gilded on the horns."

  Pallas Athena heeded their prayer.
And after imploring Zeus's daughter
they went their way like lions through the gloom,
through death and corpses, armor and dark blood.

  But neither would Hector let those Trojans
sleep—he also summoned an assembly   300
of the Trojan captains and commanders.
And when they had come together, he said:
"Which person here will promise me something?
He can be sure of a handsome reward:
a chariot and a pair of speedy steeds,
the best those Achaeans have at their ships,
for the one who dares win himself glory
by entering that enemy camp to learn
if they guard the ships as well as ever
or have they admitted defeat and plan   310
a speedy escape, so they're neglecting
to post a watch, out of sheer exhaustion."

  And a hush of awe fell over them all.
Now among the Trojans was one Dolon,
wealthy son of Eumedes the herald,
nimble in running but not much for looks,
the only brother among five sisters.
He cried among those Trojan commanders:
"Well, Hector, I'm not in the least afraid
to approach the ships and learn everything.   320
But first you must raise your scepter and swear

I'll have the horses and handsome chariot
that carry the peerless son of Peleus.
Oh, I certainly won't disappoint you!
I can creep through that camp until I come
to Agamemnon's ship, where their leaders
must be discussing whether they should flee."

  Then great Hector took the scepter and swore:
"Thunderlord Zeus himself be my witness:
no other Trojan will ride those horses—   330
they shall be your pride and joy forever."

  Thus he spurred him on with an empty oath.
And Dolon slung his bow over his back,
wrapped himself in the hide of a gray wolf,
took a weaselskin helmet and a spear,
and strode off for the ships—though he never
returned to render Hector his report.
After leaving those masses of warriors
he ran eagerly on—but as he came
ingenious Odysseus saw him and said: 340
"Hark, Diomedes, someone's over there!
What is his business, eh? To spy on us
or strip the armor from a warrior's corpse?
Well, we'll let him go wandering past us
a little, then rush behind and grab him.
If he's lucky enough to get away
we can cut him off, hem him toward our ships,
and he won't return to his camp alive."

  So they lay among corpses by the path
while that foolish Dolon came running past.   350
After he went as far as the furrow
of a mule, that beast better than an ox
in dragging the plow through deep fallow fields,
they dashed after him. He stopped when he heard,
in hope they were his Trojan companions
coming to say Hector had called him back.
But when they were a spear's throw off or less,
he knew they were enemies, took to his heels,

and those two hurried in headlong pursuit.
As two sharp-toothed hounds, experienced hunters,   360
relentlessly chase a hare or a doe
in some deep forest, and it runs screaming,
thus Tydeus' son and canny Odysseus
cut Dolon off, came relentlessly on.
He'd almost reached the Danaan sentinels
as he raced toward the ships, when Athena
strengthened Diomedes so no one else
would gain the glory of bringing him down.
Diomedes came after him and cried:
"Stand still or I'll run you through with my spear,   370
and this time I swear your death will be sure."

   Then Tydeus' son hurled but missed purposely:
that spear soared over Dolon's right shoulder
and stuck in the earth. He stopped, terror-struck,
staggering, teeth chattering in his mouth,
pale with fear. Those two ran on him panting
and seized his hands as he begged them with tears:
"Oh, spare my life, take a ransom! At home
I've bronze and gold and fine tools of iron!
My father would give you many treasures   380
if he heard I was alive at your ships!"

   But canny Odysseus said in reply:
"Now, now, fellow, don't worry about death!
But come now, tell me this, and truthfully:
Why are you going toward the ships alone
this gloomy night, while other mortals sleep?
To strip the armor from a warrior's corpse?
Did Hector send you out to spy on us?
Or have you come here of your own accord?"

   And all a-tremble, Dolon answered him: 390
"Yes, Hector gave me that mad idea,
promised me fiery Achilles' horses
and his incomparable chariot too
if I would hurry through the murky night
and enter that enemy camp to learn

if they guard the ships as well as ever
or have they admitted defeat and plan
a speedy escape, so they're neglecting
to post a watch, out of sheer exhaustion."

But canny Odysseus answered, smiling: 400
"You were ambitious, to want those horses
of fiery Achilles! They're hard enough
for any mortal on earth to manage
except for their master, a goddess' son.
But come now, tell me this, and truthfully:
Where did you last see your leader Hector?
Where is his armor? Where are his horses?
And their sentinels and the sleeping men?
And what about their plans? Do they intend
to remain here by the ships, or instead   410
return to their city, now they have won?"

Eumedes' son Dolon said in reply:
"Oh, I'll tell you everything, believe me!
Hector has summoned his commanders
to a council of war by Ilus' tomb,
away from the others. But sentinels?
No guards have been specially posted, sir,
only the ones who are tending bonfires—
these stay awake and encourage the rest
to keep a keen lookout. And our allies   420
are sleeping soundly without sentinels
since they have no homes to protect in Troy."

And that quick-witted Odysseus asked him:
"Very well, do they sleep near the Trojans
or apart? Speak up, man! I want to know."

Eumedes' son Dolon said in reply:
"Oh, I'll tell you everything, believe me!
Toward the sea are Carians and Paeonians,
Lelegians, Cauconians, and Pelasgians,
and toward Thymbrë are Lycians and Mysians,   430
those equestrian Phrygians and Maeonians.
But why do you ask me about all this?

If you wish to enter our Trojan camp,
the Thracians are sleeping there—they just came
with their king Rhesus, Eëoneus' son.
His horses are the loveliest I've seen,
whiter than snow, and they run like the winds;
his chariot's adorned with silver and gold,
and he brought his golden armor along,
quite a magnificent sight! Such armor   440
isn't for men but for the immortals!
All right then, take me away to your ships
or tie me hand and foot and leave me here
while you go ahead to learn for yourselves
whether I've told you correctly or not."

  Diomedes scowled at him and declared:
"See here, Dolon, you won't be returning
no matter how much good news you gave us.
If we released you, let you off scot-free,
sometime later you might be coming back   450
to spy on us or meet us in combat,
but if we finish you off here and now
you'll never make trouble for us again."

  And Dolon reached toward Diomedes' chin,
imploring him, but that son of Tydeus
swung a horrible sword, sheared through his neck—
and his head rolled in the dust as he spoke.
Next they tore off that weaselskin helmet,
with his wolfskin and bow and mighty spear.
Laertes' son Odysseus held them up   460
to Athena the plunderer and prayed:
"Rejoice in these, goddess! We thank you first
of all the immortals. Now guide us toward
those Thracian horses and sleeping warriors."

  He lifted all that booty in his arms,
set it on a tamarisk bush, and marked
the place with reeds and tamarisk branches
so it wouldn't be missed as they returned,
then wandered on, through armor and dark blood,

and quickly came to those Thracian spearmen   470
who slept exhausted, their glorious armor
lying tidily on the ground beside them
in three rows—and by each man, his horses.
Rhesus slept in the middle, his own team
tethered by their reins to the chariot rail.
Odysseus spied him through the night and cried:
"Hark, Diomedes, that warrior's the one
our prisoner Dolon told us about.
All right, show your valor, don't stand helpless—
cut those horses loose with your sword, or else   480
you kill the men and I'll take the horses!"

   Athena breathed might in Diomedes,
who stabbed left and right. Horrid groans arose
from dying warriors, earth grew red with blood:
as a lion finds an unshepherded flock
of sheep or goats, leaps fiercely among them,
thus Tydeus' son ranged among the Thracians
till twelve lay dead. And canny Odysseus
followed him, dragging away the bodies
of every warrior Diomedes stabbed,   490
so those handsome horses of the Thracians
could gallop away and not be afraid,
they were so unused to trampling corpses.
But when Tydeus' son came to king Rhesus
he stole his lovely life—the thirteenth man—
as he lay panting in a dreadful dream
that the son of Tydeus stood over him.
Meanwhile Odysseus cut their horses loose,
tied the reins together, and drove them off
with his bow, since he hadn't remembered   500
to take the whip from that splendid chariot,
then whistled to summon Diomedes.

   That warrior stayed pondering reckless deeds,
whether the chariot with the king's armor
could be driven off or dragged by its pole
or whether still more Thracians might be slain.

And as he stood rapt in meditation,
green-eyed Athena came near him and said:
"Tydeus' fiery son, better clear out now,
or soon you may be running for your life   510
when some immortal rouses the Trojans."

He recognized the goddess' voice and leapt
on one of those steeds. Odysseus smacked them
with his bow, and they galloped toward the ships.

But Apollo was keeping a close watch
and saw Athena with Diomedes,
then entered the Trojan camp in a rage
and woke a Thracian chief, Hippocoön,
Rhesus' noble cousin, who leapt from sleep,
saw the place empty where horses had been,   520
the men gasping wildly in pools of blood,
and called his comrade's name with a great groan.
Cries and clamor rose among the Trojans,
who ran to the place, gazed at the outrage
those two had done before they departed.

And when they came to where the spy lay slain
lordly Odysseus reined his horses in
as Diomedes dismounted and handed
that bloody booty to his companion,
then lashed the horses and away they flew,   530
very keen to reach the Achaean ships.
Old Nestor was first to hear them and cried:
"My heroic friends and fellow warriors,
can I believe my ears? Yes, it would seem
I hear the thundering of horses' hooves.
If only Odysseus and Diomedes
have taken a team from the enemy!
But I'm very afraid our brave fellows
have met some trouble among the Trojans!"

But even as he spoke, those two were there.   540
They leapt from their horses, and the leaders
wrung their hands and roared congratulations.
Aged Gerenian Nestor asked them first:

"Canny Odysseus, our pride and glory,
did you get those horses by entering
the Trojan camp? Or did some god give them?
Oh, they're awfully like glowing sunbeams.
I fight with the foremost—you won't find me
cowering back once battle has begun—
but I've never seen horses so glorious.   550
They must be a gift from some immortal—
we know you two are favorites of Zeus
and his great daughter green-eyed Athena."

    And that quick-witted Odysseus answered:
"Illustrious Nestor, our pride and glory,
the gods can give even better horses
whenever they wish, such is their power.
But if you'd like to know, these are fresh ones
from Thrace—Diomedes slew their master
with twelve of his best warriors beside him.   560
And near our ships we finished off a scout
that Hector and his haughty men had sent
to reconnoiter our own position."

    So he drove their horses over the moat
exulting, and all followed joyfully—
but when they came to Diomedes' tent
took sturdy thongs, bound those captured steeds
to the manger where his own nimble team
stood patiently munching their oats and rye.
Next Odysseus hung the bloody booty   570
on his ship's stern—Athena's offering—
and those two warriors plunged into the sea
to wash the sweat from shins and necks and thighs.
After the waves had washed that sweat away
from their fine bodies and they felt refreshed
they stepped into elegant polished baths.
When they had bathed and rubbed themselves with oil
they sat down to feast, from the great tureen
poured libations of wine to Athena.

Book Eleven: Agamemnon's Exploits

Agamemnon sweeps all before him on the battlefield. The Greek leaders Agamemnon, Diomedes, and Odysseus are wounded.

Now Dawn rose from her bed by Tithonus
with light for the blessed gods and mortals
while Zeus sent the Argives an envoy, Strife,
that difficult girl, with a sign of war.
She stood by Odysseus' big-bellied ship
in the middle of the camp, where a cry
reached the tents of huge Aias on one side
and those of Achilles on the other—
since their ships were beached at the farthest ends—
and gave a terrible, tumultuous yell,   10
so every Achaean felt his heart stirred
for the crash of implacable combat.
Then war became sweeter than returning
in the ships to their beloved homelands.

Now Agamemnon ordered his people
to put on armor, and he did the same:
strapped on his legs those elegant shinguards
so handsomely adorned with silver bands,
and over his chest the sturdy breastplate
Cinyras had sent to him from Cyprus,   20
since even there he heard the Achaeans
were about to sail for battle in Troy,
so he presented him with this armor.
Ten bands of blue enamel were on it,
with twenty of tin and twelve made of gold,
enamel serpents wriggling toward the neck,

three on each side, like rainbows Cronos' son
sets in the clouds as an omen for men.
And over his shoulders he slung a sword
studded with shimmering gold, its scabbard   30
crafted in silver on a golden chain,
then took his richly ornamented shield—
ten brazen rings in concentric circles,
and all about it twenty knobs of tin,
in the middle a dark enamel boss
engraved with the dreadful grim-eyed Gorgon
fiercely glaring between Terror and Rout,
and the shield had a silver strap adorned
with a snake made of dark-blue enamel,
three heads that twisted from a single neck.   40
Next he took a two-horned four-pronged helmet
whose horsehair crest bobbed horribly above,
and finally a pair of bronze-tipped spears,
keen ones that glittered to heaven, whereby
Hera and Athena thundered above
to honor that king of rich Mycenae.

    Next each spearman ordered his charioteer
to keep his horses tethered by the moat,
and armed to the teeth, they swarmed forth on foot
as cries undying rose before the dawn.   50
And they formed their ranks very near the moat,
charioteers to the rear, while mighty Zeus
roused horrible roars of battle and hurled
blood-drenched dewdrops from the sky as a sign
many strong heads would soon go to Hades.

    And on a hill opposite, the Trojans
gathered round Hector and Polydamas,
Anchises' son Aeneas, and those three
brothers illustrious as the immortals—
Polybus, Agenor, and Acamas—   60
and there before them Hector held his shield.
As searing Sirius appears among clouds
brilliant, till the dark clouds hide it again,
so Hector appeared now with the foremost,

now with the last, and his brazen armor
glittered like the lightning of father Zeus.

   Then the two hordes met like lines of reapers
who slash wide swaths in a wealthy man's field,
and sheaves of wheat or barley fall in heaps—
thus those warriors leapt at one another   70
murderously, and neither side would retreat.
Face-to-face like wolves they battled away,
while formidable Strife watched joyfully,
since she alone of the gods was present—
the others were leading their easy lives
in those handsome palaces each one had
among the peaks of craggy Olympus.
And all were grumbling over mighty Zeus
because he wished the Trojans victory.
But old father Zeus paid no attention,   80
sat apart in all his magnificence
gazing at Troy and the Achaean ships,
at flashing of bronze, at slayers and slain.

   While it was morning and the sun still climbed,
spears took a terrible toll on both sides,
but at the hour a woodman makes dinner
in some mountain glen—when his arms grow tired
felling tall trees and he can do no more,
for his stomach gnaws with thoughts of dinner—
those Achaeans, shrieking war cries, shattered   90
the enemy ranks. First Agamemnon
rushed before them all to kill Bienor
and then his driver illustrious Oileus,
who leapt defiantly from the chariot.
But as he attacked, Agamemnon lunged,
and his bronze helmet didn't stop that spear
which bore straight through to the bone, so his brains
spattered inside, his warmaking ended.
Atreus' son Agamemnon left them there,
chests gleaming bare when he took their tunics,   100
went on to slay Isus and Antiphus,
two brave sons of Priam in one chariot—

the first, bastard born, with reins in his hands,
Antiphus beside him. Once Achilles
had caught them herding sheep on Ida's slopes,
bound them with withes and held them for ransom.
But now Agamemnon hurled a great spear,
which hit Isus over the nipple, then
took prince Antiphus' life with a sword stroke
behind the ear. So he seized their armor,   110
knowing them well, having seen them before,
that time Achilles took both prisoner.
As a lion leaps on two baby fawns
in their mother's lair, steals their tender lives,
crunches them easily in his strong teeth—
and though the mother doe stands near, she can't
save them, such a dreadful trembling takes her,
and bounds away through the tangly forest
in frenzied retreat from that lunging beast:
thus none of the Trojans could save those two,   120
but all ran before lord Agamemnon.

    He caught Peisander and Hippolochus,
sons of Antimachus who once had urged
delightful Helen should not be returned,
since he hoped that Paris would give him gold,
and now Agamemnon took his two sons
as they struggled to control their horses,
for the gleaming reins had slipped from their hands,
those steeds ran wild—and there, like a lion,
stood Atreus' son. They begged from their chariot: 130
"Spare us, Agamemnon, take a ransom!
Our father Antimachus has great wealth
in gold and bronze and fine tools of iron.
You'd have an incomparable ransom
if he heard we were alive at your ships."

    Thus they wept and implored that commander
most gently, but heard an ungentle voice:
"If you're really sons of Antimachus,
who once advised the Trojan assembly
to murder Menelaus on the spot   140

when he came as envoy with Odysseus,
you'll pay for your father's outrage today!"

Then he drove Peisander from the chariot
with a spear thrust on the chest which spilled him
backward—and as his brother leapt to earth
Atreus' son killed him, lopped off head and arms,
sent him rolling through those throngs like a stone.
So he left them lying, hurried to where
most men were massed, and his comrades followed.
Now unmounted warriors slew unmounted,   150
and mounted warriors mounted, dust swirled up
from horses' thundering hooves, and the bronze
did horrible work, while Agamemnon
swept all before him, roaring to his men.
As a forest fire attacks dense woodland
when a furious wind whirls it, and thickets
are swept sheer away by the raging flames,
those hosts of Trojans were toppled to earth
by Agamemnon's spear, many horses
rattled empty chariots amid battle   160
without their brave drivers, who lay on earth
far more beloved by vultures than their wives.

Then Zeus took Hector away from the dust,
from slaughter, from blood, from restless tumult,
while Atreus' son followed, calling his men.
Past the tomb of old Dardanian Ilus
midway in the plain, past the wild fig tree,
they raced toward the town before that roaring
Agamemnon, huge hands besmeared with gore.
As they reached the oak tree and Scaean Gates   170
they stayed to wait for their other comrades
who still ran over the plain like cattle
when a lion comes at night to scatter
the herd, though one meets destruction at once—
he snaps her neck with his powerful teeth,
then gobbles up the blood and all the guts:
thus Atreus' son Agamemnon followed,
slaughtering laggards, and they were routed.

Many were tumbled facefirst or backward
from their chariots under his furious spear.   180
But when he neared their town and its steep wall
the father of gods and men came from heaven,
sat on Ida's peak with its purling pools,
a powerful thunderbolt in his hands,
and sent golden-winged Iris flying off:
"Now hurry down, Iris, and tell Hector
as long as he sees king Agamemnon
raging before them taking many lives
he must stay away and let the others
continue in their desperate struggle—   190
but after that man is wounded at last
and abandons combat, I'll give him might
till they reach the ships with awful slaughter
when the sun drops down and strong darkness comes."

   And windfoot Iris obeyed his command,
darted from Ida's hills to holy Troy.
There she found that redoubtable Hector
standing off the battlefield and watching.
Swift Iris scurried up to him and cried:
"Hector, you canny Trojan commander,   200
father Zeus has sent me to inform you
as long as you see king Agamemnon
raging before you taking many lives
you must stay away and let the others
continue in their desperate struggle—
but after that man is wounded at last
and driven from combat, Zeus will give you might
till you reach the ships with awful slaughter
when the sun drops down and strong darkness comes."

   After saying this, Iris departed—   210
so Hector leapt to earth in full armor
and hurried among them waving two spears,
urging them to finally make a stand.
So they rallied and faced the enemy,
who regrouped their ranks, and relentless war

began again as king Agamemnon
drove thundering into battle before all.

   Now tell me, you Muses on Olympus,
which one came first to face Agamemnon
among those Trojans and their famed allies?   220
Iphidamas, a tall, valiant warrior,
Antenor's son, reared in sheep-grazing Thrace,
where he grew up at the home of Cisseus,
his grandfather on the maternal side.
And when he became a strapping young man
Cisseus married him off to his daughter,
but just after marriage he heard of war
and went immediately with twelve beaked ships.
He had left these vessels in Percotë,
made the rest of his way to Troy on foot,   230
and now he came to meet Agamemnon.
After they came very near each other
that son of Atreus flung his spear but missed,
while Iphidamas stabbed him mightily
and the sturdy spear bore through the breastplate
but couldn't pierce his shimmering girdle:
its silver bent the point aside like lead.
Now Atreus' son Agamemnon leapt out
and, furious as a lion, wrenched that spear
from his hands, then cleft his neck with the sword.   240
So there he fell and slept an iron sleep,
poor man, fighting for home far from his wife,
who brought him no joy though she cost so much:
a hundred cattle, a thousand promised,
both sheep and goats, a high price for a bride.
Agamemnon took his glorious armor,
carried it off through those swarms of warriors.

   But his body was spied by prince Coön,
Antenor's eldest son, whose eyes clouded
with a vast grief for his fallen brother.   250
He ran near Agamemnon unnoticed,
stabbed him on the arm under the elbow,
and the gleaming spear sheared clear through his arm.

That son of Atreus shuddered at the sight
but wouldn't give up relentless combat
and, powerful spear in hand, pursued Coön,
who was just dragging his brother away
by a foot, calling his comrades for aid,
as great Agamemnon thrust that weapon
under his studded shield, sent him reeling,   260
then sheared his head off over his brother.
So those sons of Antenor met their fate
at Agamemnon's hands, sank to Hades.

He ranged among their armored battalions
with spear, with sword, with enormous boulders,
while the blood still trickled warm from the wound.
But when it had dried and the bleeding ceased
king Agamemnon was racked with anguish.
As women in labor feel piercing pain
sent by the Eilithyae, those midwife   270
daughters of Zeus who keep much suffering,
thus Atreus' stalwart son was tormented.
He leapt on his chariot in agony
and ordered his squire to drive toward the ships.
Then Agamemnon roared through his armies:
"My heroic friends and fellow warriors,
now all you others must defend our ships
since mighty Zeus seems to have decided
I can't continue in combat today!"

So that charioteer whipped the horses up,   280
and off they thundered toward the buoyant ships,
breasts foam-flecked, bellies dust-bespattered,
carrying an anguished king from battle.

But when Hector saw Agamemnon leave
he bellowed among his massed battalions:
"You Trojans and Lycians and Dardanians,
be men, my friends, remember your courage!
Their best warrior's gone, and I'll have glory
from Cronos' son Zeus, so drive your horses
forward, lords, and victory will be ours!"   290

His words gave a surge of strength to them all.
As when a hunter sics his white-toothed hounds
on some horrible boar or a lion,
thus Ares' peer redoubtable Hector
sent his Trojans after those Danaan hordes.
He himself swaggered among the foremost
and fell to battle like a furious storm
that roars down to stir the murky waters.

And who were the first, who last, to be slain
by Hector's spear while Zeus supported him?   300
Asaeus, then Autonous, Opites,
Dolops, Opheltius, and Agelaus,
Aesymnus, Orus, and bold Hipponous.
He slaughtered those Danaan commanders, then
fell on their warriors, as a west wind drives
glimmering clouds that skim up from the south,
swollen waves roll over the sea, and spray's
hurled far through the air by that furious gale—
so many Danaans fell before Hector.

Then they would have been utterly ruined,   310
flung themselves on their ships in a panic,
but Odysseus summoned Diomedes:
"Tydeus' son, stiffen up your courage!
Stand by me, man—a miserable shame
if awful Hector sets our ships aflame!"

And that Diomedes roared in reply:
"Of course I'll stay—but it won't help us much
now Zeus Thunderhurler has decided
to give those Trojans a glorious triumph!"

Next he stabbed Thymbraeus on the left breast   320
and brought him down, while canny Odysseus
dispatched Molion, that lord's godlike squire.
They let them lie, their warmaking over,
and went on to rout the Trojans, like boars
that suddenly turn on the hunting dogs—
thus those two stormed forward, as the Danaans
happily rested from Hector's onslaughts.

And they killed two warriors in a chariot,
sons of Percotian Merops, most skillful
fortune teller, who often begged his boys   330
to stay out of war—but they wouldn't hear,
for the fates of dark death had led them on.
Thus Tydeus' dauntless son Diomedes
took their lives and armor, while Odysseus
slew Hippodamas and Hypeirochus.

   Now Zeus, watching from Ida, held the cords
of war equal, so that carnage went on.
And Diomedes' spear sheared through the hip
of Agastrophus, who kept no horses
for a quick retreat—foolish thing to do!   340
They stayed to the rear as he was raging
on foot with the foremost, till he perished.
But when Hector observed those two, he charged
bellowing, as his battalions followed.
Prince Diomedes shuddered at the sight
and cried to Odysseus, who stood nearby:
"Here comes terrible trouble: Hector!
But we'll stand together and drive him off!"

   So he poised his ashwood spear and hurled it—
no miss! that weapon hit brave Hector's head   350
on top of his helmet, but bronze met bronze
and he was saved by those three great layers
of his crested helmet, Apollo's gift.
Now Hector reeled back among his people,
sank to his knees, and leaned upon the earth
with a heavy hand, as night took his eyes.
While that son of Tydeus ran to retrieve
his spear, which had fallen at some distance,
Hector caught his breath, leapt in his chariot
and drove back to battle, escaping fate.   360
Diomedes came after him and cried:
"Swine, you escaped again, but I almost
brought you down! Apollo saved you once more—
you must implore him when you enter war.
All right, I shall finish you off next time

if some immortal god assists me too.
And now I'll go after your companions."

Then he grabbed at Agastrophus' armor.
But Paris, husband of lovely Helen,
carefully aimed his bow at Diomedes   370
from behind the gravestone of Dardanian
Ilus, valiant captain in the old days:
just as that son of Tydeus was seizing
Agastrophus' breastplate and brazen shield
and ponderous helmet, Paris' arrow
flew through the air till it hit his right foot
at the instep, went hurtling through the sole,
and lodged in the earth. Gallant Paris leapt
from his hiding place and shouted, laughing:
"Dead aim today! I only wish it had   380
landed in your belly and brought you down!
That would have been good news for our Trojans,
who're trembling more like goats before a lion."

Prince Diomedes replied unperturbed:
"You big-mouthed girl-crazy fancy dandy,
come meet me face-to-face so you can see
if your bow and arrow are any use then!
Boasting because you only grazed my foot—
a woman or a boy could do as well!
A weakling's arrow cannot hurt a bit,   390
but if my spear even touches a man
it shows its sharpness, topples him to earth.
His wife's cheeks are streaked with tears, his children
fatherless, his blood reddens all the ground
as he rots, more birds than women round him."

Now canny Odysseus came rushing up
to shield Diomedes, who sat and drew
the arrow from his foot with dreadful pain,
then leapt on his chariot in agony
and ordered his squire to drive toward the ships.   400

Thus Odysseus was left alone: no man
remained beside him, they were so afraid.
Deeply troubled, he muttered to himself:
"What will become of me? Wrong to retreat,
worse still to stay here and be surrounded
alone, while the others have run away.
But why am I saying all this nonsense?
Cowards run off when the going gets rough,
while a serious warrior can only stay
to face the enemy, slay or be slain."   410

While stubborn Odysseus stood pondering,
the Trojan battalions came on and on
to trap him—but put trouble in their midst.
As hounds and powerful hunters harry
a wild boar, who charges from the thicket
gnashing white tusks in his curving jaws
with a dreadful clatter, and each man stands
steadfast before his relentless onslaught:
thus those Trojans swarmed around Odysseus.
First of all, he lunged at Deiopites,   420
stabbed him straight through the shoulder from above,
next killed Thoön and Eunomus, and then
as Chersidamas sprang from his chariot
struck him by the navel under his shield—
so he tumbled to earth, clutching the dust.
Odysseus left them, stabbed another man,
intrepid Charops, brother of Socus,
who saw him fall and came storming forward
and roared his defiance from very near:
"Very well, you quick-witted Odysseus,   430
make your boast over both Hippasus' sons
that you killed two brothers, took their armor,
or I'll have your life with my mighty spear."

Then prince Socus lunged at Odysseus' shield,
and that spearpoint sheared through its shimmering
surface, through his glorious breastplate itself,
and lodged in his side just under the skin—
Athena had deflected its impact.

Odysseus knew the wound wasn't fatal,
so he staggered away and bellowed out: 440
"Poor fellow, you won't be long for this world!
You made me leave the battlefield for now,
but today you'll meet your own death and fate
from my great spear, so I have more glory
and Hades the famous horseman your soul!"

And as Socus turned around to retreat,
Odysseus drove that dangerous weapon
between his shoulders and through to the chest.
He fell thundering as Odysseus roared:
"Socus, son of illustrious Hippasus,   450
death caught you too quick, you couldn't escape.
Ah, poor fellow, your papa and mama
won't be closing your eyes, but carrion birds
will beat big wings all about you, while I
have a sumptuous funeral if I die."

Next he tore Socus' enormous weapon
from his own side and from the studded shield,
and the blood burst forth with horrible pain.
When the Trojans saw Odysseus wounded
they crowded round, crying incessantly,   460
as he gave ground and called to his comrades.
Three times that son of Laertes shouted,
and three times Menelaus heard him cry,
so he summoned Aias, who stood nearby:
"Magnificent Telamonian Aias,
I heard our Odysseus calling for help
as if he were alone and in danger
and those Trojan spearmen had cut him off.
We'd better rescue him immediately!
If our friend battles on alone, he'll be   470
in trouble, and think how we would miss him."

Then off he strode, and that warrior followed.
They found canny Odysseus surrounded
by Trojans, like tawny mountain jackals
around some stag a hunter has wounded

with an arrow, but he bounds nimbly off
while the blood flows warm and his legs can move,
till finally that arrow takes its toll
and the ravenous jackals tear him up
in some shadowy glen—then a lion comes   480
to scatter them all and devours their prey:
thus stubborn Odysseus stood surrounded
by hosts of dangerous Trojans, as he
lunged wildly here and there to hold them off,
but Aias appeared, his shield like a wall,
and the Trojans retreated at the sight.
Menelaus led him by the hand
till his squire came with horses and chariot.

   Now Aias leapt on the Trojans to slay
Priam's son Doryclus and Pandocus,   490
Lysander, Pyrasus, and Pylartes.
As a river rushes down from the hills
swollen with melted snow and Zeus's rain,
sweeping many an oak or pine along
till it flings its flotsam into the sea:
thus giant Aias swept over the plain
in murderous contention. But Hector
knew nothing about it, he fought so far
to the left by the banks of Xanthus, where
most warriors' heads fell and cries undying   500
rose around Nestor and Idomeneus.
And among them Hector did dreadful deeds
with spear and horsemanship, ravaging ranks,
though the Achaeans declined to give ground
till Paris, husband of lovely Helen,
ended intrepid Machaon's prowess
with a three-barbed arrow that landed on
his right shoulder. His comrades feared for him,
the enemy kept pressing them so hard,
and that Cretan chief Idomeneus cried: 510
"Illustrious Nestor, our pride and glory,
put Machaon by you on your chariot
and take him back to our ships on the beach.

Many warriors aren't worth one physician
for excising arrows and spreading salves."

That aged Gerenian Nestor obeyed:
leapt up on the chariot, took beside him
Machaon, son of healer Asclepius,
then lashed the horses and away they flew,
very keen to reach those Achaean ships.　　　520

Cebriones stood by Hector in his chariot,
and seeing the Trojans retreat, he cried:
"Hector, you and I fight off to one side,
but meanwhile all our other battalions
are falling back in awful confusion.
Huge Aias is after them—it's easy
to spy him with his mighty shield. So we
better drive that way where the spearmen rage
with a most ferocious intensity
and die amid an endless battle cry."　　　530

Cebriones flicked those flowing-maned horses
with his shrill whip—and at the very sound
they galloped into the heart of combat,
trampling shields and corpses, as murky blood
churned from the earth by wheels and horses' hooves
spattered all the axle and chariot rail.
Thus Hector hurried onward, determined
to devastate ranks of Danaans, and roused
fierce turmoil as he ravaged them with spears.
He ranged among their armored battalions　　　540
with spear, with sword, with enormous boulders,
but avoided one warrior, huge Aias,
since that son of Cronos protected him.

Now father Zeus infused fear in Aias:
he stood dazed, slung his great shield on his back,
and, more like some wild beast, moved warily
away, step by step, often glancing back.
As a tawny lion in a cattle fold
is pursued by country people and hounds,
who watch all night to keep him from grabbing　　　550

their fattest cattle, and, greedy for meat,
he creeps by, but no luck!—a rain of spears
showers upon that hapless animal,
torches are hurled, and he slinks back furious,
then angrily lopes away at daybreak:
thus huge Aias retreated, extremely
afraid for the fate of the Danaan ships.
As farmer boys are fooled by a donkey—
a lazy one often beaten with sticks,
who leaps in the field and gobbles up grain   560
while they weakly batter his back but can't
get him out till he's had a bellyful:
thus Telamonian Aias moved away
from those haughty Trojans and their allies
who battered brilliant spears against his shield.
Again and again he would whirl around
in a rage, and those enemy spearmen
shrank back, till he turned once more to retreat.
So he kept them all from the Danaan ships,
battling alone between those two armies—   570
and some of the spears flung by mighty arms
hammered his shield as they hurtled onward,
but many fell short before reaching him
and stuck in the earth, hungry to cut flesh.

But when Euaemon's son Eurypylus
saw Telamonian Aias so hard-pressed
he ran to stand beside him, hurled a spear,
hit the son of Phausius, Apisaon,
over the liver and loosened his knees.
Eurypylus tried to seize that armor,   580
but prince Alexander was watching him,
then immediately drew a great bow taut
and shot a terrible arrow that hit
his right thigh: the shaft snapped, his leg grew numb.
So he staggered away, avoiding fate,
and bellowed among those massed battalions:
"My heroic friends and fellow warriors,
no time to retreat! Stand steadfast and save

our Aias in his need! I don't believe
he'll come out alive, but now we can try   590
to rescue our redoubtable Aias!"

And a host of warriors came hurrying
to aid Eurypylus, formed their phalanx
a-bristle with spears. Aias lumbered up
and turned around when he reached his comrades.

So they battled away like blazing flame,
while Neleus' sweating mares carried Nestor
and great Machaon from the battlefield.
But nimblefooted Achilles spied them
as he stood by the stern of his beaked ship   600
watching the struggle and dreary retreat,
and called to his companion Patroclus,
who heard from inside the tent and emerged
awful as Ares—thus his grief began.
And that son of Menoetius addressed him:
"Why did you call, Achilles? What is it?"
Illustrious Achilles said in reply:
"Ah, Patroclus, very dear to my heart,
now the Achaeans will be at my knees,
begging me to help them in their distress.   610
But you hurry out and ask old Nestor
the name of that man he brought back wounded.
From behind he looked like Machaon, but
I couldn't see his face, those horses came
thundering past us at such breakneck speed."

Patroclus did as his friend had ordered,
went running along the Achaean ships.
When Nestor brought Machaon to his tent
they stepped from their chariot onto the ground
while that squire Eurymedon unharnessed   620
their team. And they cooled their sweat-soaked tunics
standing in the breeze by the seashore, then
went into the tent and seated themselves.
Wine was mixed by fair-haired Hecamedë,
Achilles' prisoner in Tenedos

given to Nestor by those Achaeans
for his wise counseling of the people.
First she drew up a finely worked table
with blue enamel feet and placed on it
a bronze tray with an onion for relish   630
and honey and the sacred barley meal,
set by these a splendid gold-studded bowl
with four incomparable handles, each
adorned with golden doves that pecked at grain,
while two rods extended from rim to base.
Another man could hardly have raised it
brimful, but Nestor did so easily.
And in the bowl that godlike lady mixed
Pramnian wine, then grated cheese on top
with a sprinkling of fine white barley meal,   640
and called them to drink when all was ready.
After those two had satisfied their thirst
they began telling tales to each other,
when prince Patroclus appeared at the door.
Nestor observed him and leapt to his feet,
seized him by the hand and urged him to sit.
Patroclus declined that offer, saying:
"Sorry, sir, but I cannot be seated—
a distinguished, a most difficult lord
wants to know the name of that wounded man.   650
Ah yes, I recognize our Machaon,
so I must hurry to tell Achilles.
You're well aware, sir, how severe he is,
ready to blame a person for nothing."

    And aged Gerenian Nestor answered:
"Why has Achilles begun to worry
for our wounded men? He knows so little
what troubles we have, now all our leaders
are lying beside the ships disabled:
brave Diomedes wounded by a bow,   660
Odysseus and Agamemnon by spears,
and an arrow in Eurypylus' thigh,
while this one here just left the battlefield

with a deep arrow wound. But Achilles
has no pity at all for our people.
Is he waiting till the Achaean fleet
blazes away in the power of their flames
while they devastate us man after man?
My body's not quite what it was before,
but I only wish I were young and strong　　　670
as that day we warred with the Epeians
who were rustling our cattle: I brought down
valiant Itomeneus while I took sheep
in reprisal. So we fought for his flocks
when my spear hit him in their front ranks,
and those rustlers really took to their heels!
We won much booty that day, let me say:
fifty herds of cows, as many of sheep,
as many droves of pigs and herds of goats,
and a hundred fifty chestnut horses,　　　680
mares every one, with hosts of suckling foals—
we brought all those beasts into our city
the same evening, and great Neleus rejoiced
I'd had such luck though I was the youngest.
Next heralds went out at daybreak to call
everybody the Epeians had robbed,
and we gathered to divide the plunder
since many Pylians had lost property,
our country was so small and defenseless.
Heracles had made us suffer greatly,　　　690
slaughtered all our most formidable lords:
of the twelve sons born to glorious Neleus
I was the only warrior left alive,
so the arrogant armored Epeians
had exploited us very shamefully.
And now he claimed many head of cattle—
three hundred animals with their herdsmen—
since he himself had lost such valuables:
a chariot drawn by four champion horses
that had gone to race in competition　　　700
when king Aegeias confiscated them,
sent their driver away empty-handed.

So Neleus, still in a towering rage,
took plenty of booty and left the rest
for our people to divide equally.
We settled this affair and sacrificed
to the immortals—but on the third day
the Epeians came with hordes of warriors
in great haste, among them the Moliones
though they were boys and unused to battle.   710
That Pylian city Thryoessa lies
by the stream Alpheius on our border,
and first they planned to devastate its walls.
As they drove across the plain, Athena
came down from Mount Olympus to warn us
during the night—so we quickly took arms,
raging for the fray. But aged Neleus
wouldn't let me join them, hid my horses,
said I knew nothing of battle tactics.
I went anyway, led our charioteers   720
with Athena's aid, though I came on foot.
Where the Minyeius flows into the sea
beside Arenë, we awaited dawn,
we Pylian nobles, with swarms of warriors.
Then, armed to the teeth, we hurried forward
and at midday came to the Alpheius,
where we offered fine sacrifice to Zeus
with bulls for Alpheius and Poseidon
and a heifer for green-eyed Athena.
So each man dined with his own regiment   730
and we lay down to sleep in full armor
beside those streams. Meanwhile the Epeians
had begun their siege of Thryoessa
but quickly had a battle on their hands:
as soon as sun ascended over earth
we prayed to the immortals and attacked.
Pylians and Epeians met in combat,
and I was first to dispatch a warrior,
Mulius, a son-in-law of Augeias,
married to that ruler's eldest daughter   740
Agamedë, who knew all herbs on earth.

He stormed straight toward me, but my brazen spear
brought him down, then I leapt on his chariot,
drove with the foremost—and the Epeians
scattered when they saw great Mulius fallen,
finest and foremost of their mounted lords.
But I sprang on them like a dark whirlwind,
took fifty chariots, and two men with each
were toppled by my spear and bit the dust.
I'd have slain those two Moliones as well,   750
but their father earthshaking Poseidon
carried them off from battle wrapped in mist.
Then Zeus granted victory to our side:
we chased our enemies over the plain,
slaughtering them and taking their armor,
till our horses arrived at Buprasium
and Alesium by the rock of Olen,
where the goddess Athena turned us back.
I slew the last man, and our people drove
their thunderous chariots back into Pylos   760
and glorified Nestor beside wise Zeus.
Such was my bravery, but Achilles
is wasting his own courage—and I know
he'll regret it when our people perish.
Ah, friend, remember what Menoetius said
that day he sent you to Agamemnon.
I was there with ingenious Odysseus,
so we heard the instructions he gave you.
We'd come to Peleus' sumptuous palace,
gathering recruits throughout Achaea,   770
and there we found your father Menoetius
with you and Achilles, while old Peleus
burned fat bull thighs to Zeus Thunderhurler
in the great courtyard, held a golden cup
and poured libations with those offerings
as you and Achilles cut meat—then we
stood before the door. Achilles leapt up
amazed, led us in and begged us to sit
and gave us the refreshments due a guest.
After we had our fill of food and drink   780

you two agreed to accompany us,
so your two fathers gave you instructions.
Peleus admonished his son Achilles
to always be the bravest and the best,
while Menoetius gave you this advice:
'My boy, Achilles is your superior
and mightier by far, but you're older.
Offer a bit of wisdom now and then
and show him the way—he'll profit by it.'
You've forgotten the old man's words, but still   790
you can appeal to valiant Achilles.
Who knows? if heaven helps, you may move him,
and a friend's advice is always worthwhile.
But if he had some warning oracle
or his mother told him something from Zeus—
let him send you instead with your warriors,
and you may save our people even yet.
Wear Achilles' armor, so those Trojans
may take you for him and turn to retreat
and our Achaeans receive some respite   800
when they need it—they've had little enough.
Our fresh men could batter their weary ones
back to the city from their ships and tents."

  Patroclus was deeply stirred to hear this
and hurried off toward Achilles' quarters.
But when he reached the ships of Odysseus
beached about the Achaean meeting place
where their altars to the immortals were,
he met magnificent Eurypylus,
Euaemon's son, an arrow in his thigh,   810
limping from battle. Sweat streamed down his back
and head and shoulders as the murky blood
oozed from that gash, but his heart stayed steadfast.
Prince Patroclus pitied his suffering
and uttered a wail of lamentation:
"Ah, you miserable Danaan commanders,
so this is your fate, to glut Trojan dogs
with your white fat, far from friends and homeland!

But tell me, my dear Eurypylus, how
we can hold that terrible Hector back,   820
or will his spear make an end of us all?"

  That wounded Eurypylus answered him:
"No hope for our people now, Patroclus—
we'll soon be throwing ourselves on the ships.
All those warriors who once were our bravest
are lying disabled there in our camp,
while the Trojans grow steadily stronger.
But you can help me! Take me to my ship,
excise this arrow, wash the blood away
with lukewarm water, and apply those herbs   830
men say you learned from gallant Achilles,
who was taught them by the centaur Cheiron.
Of those two physicians in our armies,
Machaon lies beside the ships wounded
and could use a skillful healer himself,
while the other battles out on the plain."

  And Menoetius' son addressed him again:
"Ah, Eurypylus, how can such things be?
I have a message for prince Achilles
from aged Nestor, our people's bulwark,   840
but even so I can't abandon you."

  He flung an arm round his waist and led him
to his tent, where a squire spread oxhides out.
Patroclus put him down, cut that arrow
from his thigh and washed the dark blood away
with lukewarm water, then strewed bitter roots
over all, till the dreadful pains were still—
and his wound became dry, the bleeding ceased.

Book Twelve: The Struggle for the Wall

Hector storms the Greek ramparts, bursts the main gate
with a boulder. The Trojans pour through.

So there among the tents prince Patroclus
tended the wounded man, as those others
battled on in a swirling mass, though soon
the Danaans would have no help from their wall
or that deep moat they had dug before it,
with never a sacrifice to the gods
so their ships and all the battle booty
might be kept safe—built against the will
of the blessed gods, it didn't last long.
While Hector still lived and Achilles sulked,   10
Priam's great city remained undestroyed
and that formidable wall stayed intact.
Yet when the finest Trojans had been slain,
with many of their enemies slaughtered
and their capital sacked in the tenth year,
and the Danaans had gone home in their ships,
Poseidon and Apollo decided
to crush that wall with all the mighty streams
which flow from Ida's mountains to the sea—
Rhesus, Heptaporus, and Caresus,   20
Granicus, Aesepus, and Scamander
and Simois, by whose banks so much armor
fell in the dust, with warriors almost gods.
Apollo gathered the mouths of all these
and flung them at that bulwark nine days long,
while thunderlord Zeus rained incessantly.
Poseidon himself, holding his trident,

led the attack, shattered those foundations—
stones and logs the Danaans labored to lay—
then smoothed off the shores of the Hellespont   30
to cover the great beach again with sand
after that wall was gone, and turned the streams
back to their beds where they had flowed before.

  Poseidon and Apollo did all this
later—but now implacable combat
raged about their wall, beams of towers boomed
with hurtling spears, and lashed by Zeus's whip,
the Achaeans were hemmed about their ships
under the attack of gallant Hector,
who battled on like a raging windstorm.   40
As hounds and clamorous hunters surround
a lion or a boar, who turns furiously,
but, firm as a wall, they stand side by side
to meet his charge, while spears shower about him
and his magnificent bravery stays
unquenchable, though it proves his ruin—
and often he tries to shatter their ranks
and wherever he attacks they fall back:
thus Hector hurried among his Trojans,
urging them to cross the moat. But their swift   50
horses stood whinnying at the very
brink, terrified of that enormous moat,
so wide they could hardly leap over it
unscathed, with those dangerous beetling banks
falling sheer beneath, and at its bottom
row after row of spiky palisades,
a thickset sturdy dangerous defense,
not easy for horses drawing chariots
to cross, though men on foot were keen to try.
Then Panthous' son wise Polydamas cried: 60
"Hector and you other Trojan captains,
we're fools to try crossing their moat mounted!
We would soon come to grief with all those stakes
and the Achaean wall so very near—
impossible for any charioteer

to manage his horses in such a squeeze.
If all-highest Zeus should favor our side
and plan to destroy them in his fury
I'd be delighted if it happens soon
and they can die like dogs so far from home—   70
though if they turn after we reach the ships
and drive us down into that moat again
there won't be a single man left alive
to tell our families the terrible news.
But every man here should do as I say:
let the squires keep our horses by the moat
while we others follow Hector on foot
in one mass attack—and those Danaan hordes
won't batter us back if they're really doomed."

Polydamas' words pleased Hector, so he   80
leapt down from his chariot in full armor.
Nor did the other Trojans stay mounted:
all sprang to earth when they observed Hector.
Then each spearman ordered his charioteer
to keep his horses tethered by the moat;
they marshaled their ranks in five battalions
and moved to war behind their commanders.

The most and the best and those most eager
to breach that wall and battle by the ships
were led by Hector and Polydamas   90
with illustrious Cebriones, since Hector
had left his chariot with a lesser man.
The second group was led by Agenor
and the third by those two sons of Priam
Deiphobus and brave Helenus, with them
redoubtable Asius from Arisbë,
whose huge tawny horses brought him to Troy,
while the fourth group was led by Aeneas,
and his lieutenants were Antenor's sons
Acamas and gallant Archelochus.   100
But the allies were led by Sarpedon
with Glaucus and prince Asteropaeus,
warriors he had chosen as the finest

after himself, though he surpassed them all.
They jammed their shields together in a mass
and attacked in an awful fury, sure
their impetus would take them to the ships.
All those Trojans and their glorious allies
followed the advice of Polydamas
except for Hyrcatus' son brave Asius,   110
who declined to leave his horses and squire
and drove his chariot straight for the ships—
fool! he'd never escape the fates that day,
never return alive to windy Troy,
glorying in his horses and chariot,
for Deucalion's son Idomeneus soon
hurled a spear to seal his horrible doom.
He made for the left, where the enemy
entered their wall with thunderous chariots,
drove straight forward, found the tight-fitting gates   120
flung wide open, that massive bar drawn clear,
since the Achaeans weren't shutting them till
all their companions had escaped inside.
So Asius drove ahead, and his warriors
followed him roaring enormously, sure
their impetus would take them to the ships.
Idiots! Beside those gates stood two valiant
highhearted scions of the Lapithians:
the first Polypoetes, Peirithous' son,
and the second Leonteus, Ares' peer.   130
They took their stand before the entrance gates
like two towering oak trees in the hills
battered by wind and rain day after day
though their tremendous long roots remain firm—
thus they stood indomitably steadfast
where fiery Asius tried to storm that wall.
Those Trojans raised their oxhide shields and came
storming forward with horrible war cries
after Asius, Iamenus, Orestes,
Asius' son Adamas, and Oenomaus.   140
Though the two Lapithians had been inside
urging their fellows to defend those ships

when they saw the Trojans on the attack,
their companions screaming and retreating,
they rushed out to battle before their gates
like a pair of arrogant mountain boars
that meet the clamorous hunters and hounds
with sidewise lunges and crush the bushes
as clatter and crash of tusks can be heard,
till somebody stabs them to take their lives: 150
thus those brilliant spears came clattering on
tough breastplates, as they struggled steadily,
trusting in their strength and their friends above,
who showered boulders from that sturdy wall
defending themselves and the Danaan camp
and the ships: these tumbled down like snowflakes
when blustery wind gusts driving dark clouds
have scattered them over the face of earth—
so many stones came pouring from their hands
and the Trojans', with clangor of helmets   160
and studded shields as boulders battered them.
Then terrible Asius gave a great groan
and slapped his thighs and bellowed furiously:
"Ah, father Zeus, you're a lover of lies,
that's very sure. Why, I'd never have dreamed
they could resist the fury of our arms,
but here they seem more like hornets or bees
who build their hive by a rugged highway
and won't abandon that dangerous home
but defend their young against all comers—   170
so those two warriors refuse to give ground
till they have taken our lives or we theirs."

But his words failed to move the mind of Zeus,
who was set on giving Hector glory.

Others fought elsewhere—and even a god
would find it hard to tell the whole story,
how terrible flames rose around that wall
as the Danaans struggled desperately
to save their ships, and all the immortals
who helped them in battle were dumbfounded,   180

and the fierce Lapithians led their defense:
first indomitable Polypoetes
hurled his spear, hit Damasus' bronze helmet,
but that metal failed to detain its point,
which bore straight through the bone so his brains
spattered inside, his warmaking ended.
Now he slaughtered Pylon and Ormenus,
while Leonteus brought Hippomachus down
with a spearcast that pierced his gleaming belt,
then drew a sword from its scabbard and plunged   190
through the toil and moil of battle to slash
Antiphates, who toppled down backward,
next brought Menon, Iamenus, Orestes
one after another tumbling to earth.
As they were seizing that glorious armor,
Hector and Polydamas and their men—
the most and the best and those most eager
to breach that wall and set the ships aflame—
stood beside the moat in perplexity,
because just as they were about to cross,   200
an eagle flew high above on the left,
in his claws a huge, a blood-red serpent,
still alive and writhing and full of fight,
and it wriggled backward, bit the eagle
on the breast by the neck, so he dropped it
in pain, and it fell among those armies
as he flew shrieking away on the wind.
The Trojans shuddered at that squirming snake
which lay among them, an omen from Zeus,
and Panthous' son wise Polydamas cried: 210
"Hector, you've scolded me in assemblies
for good advice, you think it isn't right
a commoner should go against your words
in assembly or on the battlefield—
but let me tell you what seems best to me.
We won't be taking those Achaean ships,
since the outcome's sure, such a very clear
omen came as we stayed beside our moat:
an eagle flew high above to the left,

in his claws a huge, a blood-red serpent,   220
alive—but dropped it before he came home,
never brought it back as food for his chicks.
So even if we breach the gates and wall
and those enemy hordes retreat again,
we'll return that way in wild disorder,
leaving many warriors the Achaeans
have battered to earth by their high-beaked ships.
You'd hear the same from any soothsayer
wise and knowing of the gods' mighty signs."

   Hector answered scowling ferociously: 230
"Polydamas, this doesn't please me a bit—
I'd expected something better from you!
But if you really mean all this nonsense
you must be completely out of your mind,
advising us to forget Zeus's plan,
which he promised couldn't possibly fail,
and follow the flight of birds instead.
I say it makes no difference if they
soar to our right toward the rising sun
or left toward the night and murky darkness—   240
in any case we must obey great Zeus,
who rules over mortals and immortals.
The best omen's to defend your homeland.
And why should you be afraid of combat?
If all the others perish by the ships,
it's certain *you* won't be among them—
you'd scurry from battle too quick for that.
But see here, man, if you stay away now
or encourage somebody else to shirk,
my spear will take your life immediately!"   250

   Then off he drove—and his people followed
with an awful roar, while thunderlord Zeus
roused a blast of wind from Ida's mountains
and swept dusty clouds toward the ships, which dazed
the enemy, gave them a great triumph.
Trusting in Zeus's signs and their own strength,
they tried to breach that redoubtable wall,

tugged at the girders, toppled parapets,
and pried at beams the Achaean warriors
had sunk in the earth to support their towers—   260
thus they hoped to smash that massive bulwark—
but the enemy declined to give ground
and closed up their parapets with oxhides
as they showered arrows on the Trojans.

   So both Aiantes strode along that wall
calling the Achaeans to hold their ground,
scolded some gently, some ferociously
when they saw them shirk, and roared to their lords:
"Friends, some of us are weak, some powerful—
everyone can't be completely equal   270
in war, but all must do their part today,
you know that yourselves. Let no one retreat
because a few battle cries scare him off,
but stay tenaciously on the attack
till great Olympian Zeus concedes that we
may batter the Trojans back to their town."

   Thus those two encouraged the Achaeans.
And as snowflakes tumble to earth in swarms
some winter day when great Zeus brings mortals
a blizzard and showers down his arrows—   280
he lulls the winds, then pours steadily on
towering mountains and jutting headlands,
clovery meadows and farmers' rich fields,
and snow enswathes the gray sea's shores and bays
where waves knock it away, but all the rest
is wrapped in the storms of thunderlord Zeus:
thus those boulders flew back and forth in swarms,
some from the Trojans, some from Achaeans,
as war's clamor rose over all the wall.

   But even then those Trojans and Hector   290
could not have smashed the gates and their long bar,
but Zeus set his glorious son Sarpedon
on the Danaans, like a lion on cattle.
That Lycian leader took his massive shield

of hammered bronze which a skillful worker
had forged for him and stitched many oxhides
inside with a golden wire round the rim—
held this shield before him, brandished two spears,
and went his way like a mountain lion
long famished for the taste of tender meat,   300
who tries to sate his hunger by a raid
and even when he encounters shepherds
protecting their cattle with spears and hounds
won't be driven off till he leaps inside
a sheepfold and seizes one of the beasts
or is slain himself by some farmer's spear:
so furious was illustrious Sarpedon
to scale their wall and breach the battlements.
And he called Glaucus, his comrade in arms:
"Glaucus, why are we given privileges—   310
seats of honor and meats and brimful cups—
back in Lycia, where they treat us like gods?
Remember our estate by the river
with its wheat fields and flourishing orchards!
So we should be standing with the foremost
ready to enter relentless battle,
and those armored Lycian warriors will say:
'Nothing shameful about our commanders—
of course they enjoy our best cuts of meat
and our finest red wine, but they're men   320
of might, who fight with our Lycian vanguard.'
Ah, friend, if after we escaped this war
we were to be ageless and immortal,
I would never fight among the vanguard
or send you forth to win glory in war—
but now death's fates are waiting before us
in swarms, and no mortal can avoid them.
Let's go—either they or we will win fame."

  Glaucus did as his companion had said,
and they led their Lycians into battle.   330
Gallant Menestheus shuddered to see them,
since they were heading in his direction,

and peered along that massive Danaan wall
seeking somebody who could assist him—
and he spied those two fiery Aiantes,
with Teucer, who'd just arrived from his tent,
at their side. But his shout couldn't reach them,
such a racket echoed up to heaven,
battering of shields and crested helmets
and gates—all were shut, and the enemy   340
hammered madly, trying to shatter them.
So Menestheus shouted to his herald:
"Thoötes, summon our giant Aias
or both Aiantes, that would be better,
since we're in the most terrible danger:
here come those Lycian commanders, our most
formidable foes on the battlefield.
But if the Aiantes are hard-pressed too
at least send great Telamonian Aias
and Teucer, our magnificent bowman."   350

He did as his master had commanded—
went running along the Achaean wall,
summoned those two warriors called Aiantes:
"You heroic leaders of our people,
Menestheus implores you to hurry out
and help him, though only for a moment—
or if you both go, that would be better,
since he's in the most terrible danger:
there come those Lycian commanders, our most
formidable foes on the battlefield.   360
But if you Aiantes are hard-pressed too
at least send great Telamonian Aias
and Teucer, our magnificent bowman."

That giant Aias did as he had said,
leaving orders with Oileus' son Aias:
"Stay here beside Lycomedes, dear boy,
urge our people to keep up the struggle
while I go battle beside Menestheus.
And after I have helped them, I'll be back."

Then Telamonian Aias hurried off   370
together with his half-brother Teucer,
whose powerful bow was brought by Pandion.
And they came to the post of Menestheus
along the wall, came to men in trouble,
those dangerous Lycian lords and leaders
climbing their battlements like a dark storm—
and combat began again with a roar.

Giant Aias slew the first Lycian—
Sarpedon's dear companion Epicles—
battered him with a vast jagged boulder   380
from the top of their ammunition heap,
hard for a warrior to lift with both hands
as men are now, but he raised and hurled it
onto Epicles' four-pronged helmet, crushed
the head bones—and like a sea diver, he
plunged from the wall, and the soul left his bones.
Now as Glaucus climbed the ramparts, Teucer
shot an arrow that sheared through his forearm
where it remained bare, and he raged no more
but leapt to the ground very silently   390
so the Danaans wouldn't boast over him.
Though Sarpedon grieved at his departure,
he gave himself not a moment's respite,
stabbed Thestor's son gallant Alcmaon, then
withdrew his spear and that warrior followed
headfirst, his armor clanging about him.
Next Sarpedon seized their massive parapet
and tugged, so all collapsed, made a wide gap
on the wall above, where many could pass.

But Teucer and huge Aias attacked him   400
at the same moment: Teucer's keen arrow
hit the leather strap of his shield, though Zeus
saved his life that day by the Danaan ships,
while Aias thrust savagely with a spear,
which battered his shield and sent him reeling
from that parapet, unready to quit
in his rage to attain a great triumph.

Now lordly Sarpedon turned round and roared:
"Lycian warriors, what about your courage?
For all my power, I won't find it easy   410
to breach that wall unless all of you come!
So follow me now—the more the better!"

    And fearful of their leader's reproaches,
they pressed more closely about Sarpedon,
while the Danaans regrouped their ranks inside
that wall, a terrible task before them,
because neither could the Lycians shatter
their massive ramparts and attack the ships
nor could those Danaans drive the enemy
away from their wall when they'd come so near.   420
As two men with measuring rods argue
over boundary stones in a common field,
quarreling for their rights at close quarters,
thus, parted by parapets, those warriors
battered at one another's oxhide shields
and elegant bucklers of brilliant bronze.
Fierce weapons inflicted wounds on many
who turned around to leave their backs exposed,
and many of them through their very shields,
while everywhere towers and parapets   430
were spattered with blood of struggling warriors—
but those Achaeans refused to retreat.
Both sides held their ground, as when a spinner
balances weight against wool on a scale
to earn a wretched wage for her children:
thus that battle was evenly balanced
till Zeus gave gallant Hector a triumph,
made him first to breach the enemy wall.
He bellowed among his massed battalions:
"Up and over, my boys—we'll break through here   440
and make a fine fire of their glorious ships!"

    And as Hector had commanded, they all
rushed at the Achaean wall together,
climbed over its parapets holding spears,
while Hector lifted a boulder that lay

by the gate—broad at the base, and on top
razor-sharp, hard for two mighty warriors
to heave onto a wagon from the ground
as men are now, but he held it with ease,
Cronos' son had made it so light for him.   450
As a shepherd easily carries fleece
in one hand, and the weight seems like nothing,
lordly Hector carried that boulder toward
their tight-fitting gate with great double wings
buttressed by a pair of sturdy crossbars
inside, and a single bolt to hold all—
he stood before it, his legs spread apart,
and smashed that boulder square at the middle,
breaking both hinges, so the stone fell in
with its own dead weight, their gate groaned greatly,   460
and the bars gave way, both doors torn open
by that boulder's force. Hector sprang inside,
his face like sudden night, bronze glittering
horribly all about him, two huge spears
in his hands. Now no one could have stopped him
except for the gods—and his eyes gleamed fire.
He turned around in the crowd and shouted
for his men to force the wall then and there—
and some came clambering up, while others
poured through the gates, as those Danaans panicked   470
and ran for the ships with an endless roar.

Book Thirteen: The Battle at the Ships

*Poseidon aids the Greeks, now led by Idomeneus and the
two warriors named Aias—the Aiantes.*

After Zeus brought those Trojans to the ships
he left them there to suffer and struggle
unceasingly, then turned his brilliant eyes
away toward the lands of Thracian horsemen
and proud Hippemolgi, who drink mares' milk,
and martial Mysians and righteous Abians.
He turned his brilliant eyes to Troy no more,
for now he thought none of the blessed gods
would be coming to assist either side.

But that great Earthshaker kept a keen watch   10
as he sat marveling at the battle
on wooded Samothrace's highest peak,
from which all Ida might be plainly seen
with Priam's city and Achaean ships—
fresh risen from the sea, he took his seat
and pitied the Achaeans, raged at Zeus.

And down from that rugged mountain he came
with sweeping steps, so peaks and woodland shook
under lord Poseidon's immortal feet.
He took three mighty strides, and with the fourth   20
reached Aegae, where his famous palace lay
deep in the sea, a-shimmer with sheer gold.
And he harnessed up his bronze-hooved horses,
those swift fliers with flowing manes of gold,
put on his golden robes and took that whip
of well-worked gold, then mounted his chariot

and drove over the waves, while sea beasts frisked
on every side, for they knew their master.
The sea parted with joy, and on they flew
so fast the axle wasn't wet beneath   30
as those bounding coursers bore him toward Troy.

Deep in the waters lies a wide cavern
midway between Tenedos and Imbros:
there the Earthshaker reined his horses in,
unyoked them, gave them ambrosial fodder,
and fettered them with stout unbreakable
hobbles of gold to keep them from straying,
then entered those massed Achaean armies.

Meanwhile the Trojans, like fire or a storm,
furiously followed Priam's son Hector   40
with horrible roars, sure they'd take the ships
and slaughter every warrior beside them.
But that great Earthholder and Earthshaker
came from the deeps to aid the Achaeans:
with the shape and tireless voice of Calchas
he summoned those two warriors named Aias:
"Rescue our armies, you fine Aiantes—
remember your valor, forget retreat!
Now our people are in no more danger
from this rabid mob of Trojans trying   50
to climb our wall: we can handle them all—
except here, where I'm very much afraid
with that madman leading them on like flame,
Hector, who boasts his father was wise Zeus.
If only some immortal inspired you
to rally our people for resistance
we could drive him back, for all his fury,
though thunderlord Zeus himself supports him."

Then the Earthshaker struck them with his staff,
filled them with imperishable power,   60
marvelous lightness for their legs and arms.
As a powerful hawk rises in the air
and hovers above a towering cliff,

then scours the plain in pursuit of some bird,
thus glorious Poseidon darted away.
Oileus' son Aias recognized him first
and cried to great Telamonian Aias:
"That surely must have been some Olympian
who came to harangue us in mortal form,
not our canny soothsayer Calchas.   70
I could tell by the way he departed—
the blessed gods aren't hard to recognize—
so I feel indomitable fury
to start relentless battle once again:
my body rages for action, I say."

　　Giant Telamonian Aias replied:
"I feel the same way—my hands are itching
to hold a spear, my feet seem to eat
the ground up beneath me, I'm very keen
to meet that Hector in single combat."   80

　　Thus those armored warriors were conversing
as they felt the rage Poseidon had made,
while that Earthshaker roused the Achaeans
who stayed in the rear beside their swift ships.
They lay there absolutely exhausted,
hearts heavy with sorrow as they observed
those Trojan hordes swarming over their wall—
and tears streaked their cheeks at the very sight,
for they thought they were doomed. But Poseidon
hurried among them to rouse resistance,   90
called Teucer first, next illustrious Leitus,
Thoas, Peneleos and Deipyrus,
gallant Meriones and Antilochus,
addressing them in very forceful words:
"Shame and disgrace, Achaean babies!
I believed you'd defend the ships at least,
but you all seem so eager to retreat—
today brings our total ruin, I say.
Ah, what an incredible sight this is,
a dreadful, unexpected spectacle—   100
Trojans battling by our ships, though before

they were more like skittish deer in the woods
that feed jackals and leopards and wolves
as they wander timidly here and there:
thus none of those Trojan warriors would dare
face our fury for even a moment,
but now they battle far from their city
because our leader has wronged his people,
who're so indignant they refuse to try
defending their ships—they would rather die.   110
Well, even if it isn't wrong to blame
our distinguished monarch Agamemnon
for insulting the swift son of Peleus,
that's no reason to abandon battle—
good men don't stay irreconcilable.
It's truly awful to see you shirking,
our finest in combat! I wouldn't care
to mince words with any cowardly knave,
but it makes me furious to see you here.
Silly idiots, you'll bring more trouble   120
by skulking away—remember your shame,
your rage. Now's our most difficult hour!
Horrible Hector battles very near:
he has breached our gates and their great crossbar!"

   Thus the Earthshaker roused those Achaeans—
and round the Aiantes they regrouped ranks,
awful enough to daunt even Ares
or plundering Athena: their best warriors
stood steadfast before that Trojan onslaught,
hedged in with spears and overlapping shields;   130
so helmet pressed helmet, shield shield, man man,
and the horsehair crests on their helmets met
when they moved their heads, they were packed so tight,
and their outstretched spears formed a latticework
as strong men brandished them with thoughts on war.

   Now the Trojans charged together, Hector
raging ahead like a massive boulder
washed from a hillside by winter torrents
when waters undermine that ruthless rock—

it leaps high in the air, falls thundering 140
through the woods, and rushes on till it comes
to a level place, where it rolls no more:
thus Hector seemed ready to reach the sea,
cleaving his way through the enemy ranks
with horrible slaughter. But their phalanx
detained him: Danaan warriors stood steadfast
stabbing with swords and with double-edged spears
and battered that Hector staggering back.
He bellowed among his massed battalions:
"You Trojans and Lycians and Dardanians, 150
they won't hold me back forever, I'm sure,
no matter how close together they stand—
my spear will scatter them, since it seems
Hera's thunderlord husband backs our side."

His words gave a surge of strength to them all.
And a man pranced proudly out, Deiphobus,
one of Priam's sons, holding a trim shield
to protect his body as he advanced.
Molus' son Meriones took careful aim
and hurled a spear that hit his oxhide shield 160
but couldn't break through it, splintered in two
very near the socket—and Deiphobus
held it at arm's length, extremely afraid,
while illustrious Meriones went running
back among the Danaans in high anger,
having lost both his spear and a triumph,
and hurried along those ships on the beach
to collect another spear from his tent.

The rest fought on with a relentless roar.
Teucer was first to down an opponent: 170
intrepid Imbrius, deft with the spear,
who lived in Pedaeum before the war,
wed Priam's daughter Medesicastë,
but when the Achaeans came in their ships
he returned to Troy, received high honors,
was kept in Priam's palace like a son.
Teucer slashed behind the ear with a spear,

and as he withdrew it, Imbrius fell
like an ash tree on some mountain summit
toppled to earth with its tender branches,   180
and his armor clanged as he tumbled down.
Then Teucer ran up raging for plunder,
and Hector hurled a spear with deadly aim,
but he was keeping a close watch and dodged
just barely—so it hit Amphimachus
on the chest as he rushed into battle,
and his armor boomed as he crashed to earth.
As formidable Hector tried to seize
Amphimachus' finely fitted helmet,
Telamonian Aias lunged with a spear   190
and missed his flesh, so well was it guarded
by his shimmering bronze—the buckler's boss
parried that point—but he staggered away,
leaving the bodies to the enemy:
Stichius and Menestheus, Athenian chiefs,
brought Amphimachus back to his people,
and the two Aiantes took Imbrius' corpse.
As two fierce lions snatch a goat from hounds,
then bound away through the dense underbrush
holding it high above ground in their jaws,   200
so those Aiantes carried Imbrius' corpse
and stripped it bare. Raging for his dead friend,
Oileus' son swift Aias sheared off the head,
swung it around and flung it like a ball,
and it rolled in the dust to Hector's feet.

Poseidon was most indignant to see
his grandson Amphimachus had fallen,
and hurried along those ships on the beach
summoning troops to attack the Trojans.
That Earthshaker met Idomeneus   210
as he left a comrade who came to him
with a bad gash in the bend of the knee—
he had given his surgeons instructions
and was going toward the rear to prepare
for more combat. But lord Poseidon called

with the voice of Andraemon's son Thoas,
who ruled all Pleuron and steep Calydon,
where the people honored him like a god:
"Idomeneus, now what about our threats,
those bloodthirsty oaths against the Trojans?"　　220

That Cretan chief Idomeneus replied:
"Nobody, Thoas, as far as I know,
is to blame—we're all experienced warriors,
no man lost his nerve or stays skulking back
panicked by battle. Indeed it must be
the will of thunderlord Zeus, Cronos' son,
to have us die like dogs so far from home.
But, Thoas, you've always been our bastion
and keen at encouraging these others,
so rally our people for resistance!"　　230

Then earthshaking Poseidon answered him:
"Idomeneus, if any man shrinks back
may he never go home again alive,
may his body become a toy for dogs!
Just take up your armor, man, and let's go—
though we're only two, we may do something!
Even weak warriors work well together,
but we can stand up to the best there are!"

And back he went, a god in men's combat.
After Idomeneus came to his camp,　　240
he put on splendid armor, took a spear,
and hurried out like lightning Cronos' son
brandishes from a bright Olympian peak,
an ominous sign for mortals on earth—
so the bronze shone on his chest as he ran.
Then he met his trusty squire Meriones
on the way to find a spear for himself—
and that Cretan captain accosted him:
"Meriones, my good man, what has happened—
skipping off from the battlefield so quick?　　250
An arrowhead or a spearcast nipped you?

Or did you come to summon me? Well, I'm
not staying here but headed back to war!"

    Molus' son glorious Meriones declared:
"Idomeneus, you canny commander,
I came to look for a substitute spear,
since the one I had before was shattered
on the shield of that haughty Deiphobus."

    That Cretan chief Idomeneus replied:
"Is it spears you want? Take one, take twenty,   260
they stand beside the entrance of my tent—
Trojan weapons taken from slain warriors.
I'm not a bowman, who fights from afar,
so I have many spears and studded shields,
and helmets and great shimmering breastplates."

    Molus' son glorious Meriones declared:
"Sir, I also have plunder in plenty,
but my ships and my camp are nowhere near.
And I do my duty as well as you—
you'll find me standing among the foremost   270
when bitter battle breaks out again.
Some of the others may be unaware,
but you observe closely, I suppose."

    That Cretan chief Idomeneus replied:
"No need to tell me about your valor!
If our best people were being chosen
to go on ambush—that's the warrior's test
where we learn which commanders can do most:
a coward's face changes color, his nerves
are jerky, he fidgets round here and there,   280
rests first on one knee, then on another,
while his heart hammers loudly in his chest
and his teeth chatter as he thinks of death;
while a good man's cool and never too
anxious when he takes his place in ambush,
prays battle may begin that very day—
yes, even for ambush, you'd be first-rate.
If you should receive a wound in combat

it wouldn't be on your back, that's sure,
but on your chest or belly, from the front,   290
as you storm among our foremost warriors.
So let's not stand babbling like little boys,
or some of our people may resent it.
Go to my tent and choose yourself a spear!"

    Then prince Meriones, that peer of Ares,
hurried off to take another weapon
and furiously followed him into war.
As awful Ares moves into action
with Rout, his fearless and powerful son,
who puts the bravest man in a panic—   300
they march from Thrace to join the Ephyri,
or those formidable Phlegyans, and there
give triumph to whichever side they wish—
thus Idomeneus and his trusty squire
moved into war in their brilliant armor.
First Molus' son glorious Meriones asked:
"Sir, which of our units should we relieve?
There on our armies' right, or the center,
or over on the left, where it appears
our people need us most desperately?"   310

    That Cretan chief Idomeneus replied:
"We've other men to defend the center:
those two Aiantes, and Teucer, our best
at handling the bow and at close combat.
They'll surely manage that son of Priam
no matter how much he rages for war.
All his desperate fury won't help him
conquer their courage and powerful arms
if thunderlord Zeus doesn't come himself
to hurl a blazing torch on our swift ships!   320
Telamonian Aias yields to no man
who walks the earth and eats Demeter's grain
and is vulnerable to bronze or stone—
even Achilles couldn't defeat him
although Aias is slower on his feet.

So let's go to the left, and soon we'll see
if the ones who triumph are they or we."

   And Meriones, peer of fiery Ares,
led them where his master had commanded.

   But when the Trojans saw Idomeneus   330
and his squire in their shimmering armor,
they crowded round yelling incessantly,
and battle began beside the ships' sterns.
As shrill gusts of wind come whistling down
a day the dust lies thickest on the roads
and whirl it into a colossal cloud,
they met in dreadful combat, determined
to take the lives of many enemies.
That battlefield bristled with deadly spears
for tearing warriors' flesh, eyes were blinded   340
by blaze of bronze on their brilliant helmets
and burnished armor and glittering shields.
A man would have been hardhearted indeed
to watch that battle and feel no anguish.

   So Cronos' sons worked at cross-purposes,
making more troubles for warring mortals:
Zeus had planned a triumph for the Trojans
to help agile Achilles but didn't
wish their enemies completely destroyed,
only enough to honor Thetis' son,   350
while the Argives were led by Poseidon,
who came secretly from the sea, raging
that Zeus was giving the Trojans more aid.
Those gods were brothers, had the same parents,
but mighty Zeus was older and wiser,
so Poseidon didn't war openly
but slunk about in the shape of a man.
Now those two held a mighty tug-of-war,
stretched a rope over all, unbreakable,
unyielding, and it loosened many knees.   360

Then grizzled Idomeneus, Cretan lord,
sprang at the Trojans with horrible roars,
slew Orthryoneus first, a foreigner
who came to Troy when he heard of battle
and demanded Priam's loveliest daughter,
Cassandra, promising much in exchange:
to drive the Danaans from the land of Troy.
King Priam had bowed his head and granted
that girl, so Orthryoneus went to war.
As he strutted out, Idomeneus flung   370
a razor-sharp spear, and his breastplate failed
to stop the weapon, which pierced his belly,
and he fell crashing. That Cretan lord cried:
"Orthryoneus, you'd have been lucky
if you could have carried out your promise
to Priam, when he offered his daughter.
But see here, we can give you the same—
Agamemnon's most attractive daughter
shall be yours from Argos if you help us
sack that magnificent city of Troy.   380
Come to our ships, we'll reach agreement—
don't worry, dear boy, the terms will be fair."

Then Idomeneus dragged that body off
by the foot. And Asius, mad for revenge,
went storming out to aid his friend, so near
before his horses their breath beat on
his shoulders. But Idomeneus hurled first,
and the powerful spearcast pierced his throat—
so he fell like an oak or a poplar
or a tall pine tree cut down in the hills   390
to make the timber for a sailing ship:
thus he lay a-sprawl before his horses,
groaning and clutching at the bloody dust.
And Asius' charioteer was struck with terror,
stood dumbfounded, couldn't wheel his team round
to flee, whereupon Antilochus flung
a razor-sharp spear, and his breastplate failed
to stop that weapon, which pierced his belly,

so gasping out his life he toppled down,
and prince Antilochus drove his horses   400
back among those masses of Achaeans.

  Next Deiphobus ran near Idomeneus
to avenge great Asius, flung a bright spear—
but he was keeping a close watch and dodged
behind his well-balanced oval buckler
cunningly fashioned of oxhide and bronze,
with two wooden crossbars to stiffen it.
The weapon came hurtling past as he crouched,
and his shield boomed gratingly, barely grazed,
though it wasn't completely wasted: struck   410
intrepid Hippasus' son Hypsenor
over the liver and loosened his knees.
Then lord Deiphobus boasted horribly:
"So our Asius is avenged! I suppose
he'll be glad as he goes through Hades' gates,
since I sent a companion for the way!"

  Those Danaans felt a sickening sorrow,
and Antilochus was most dismayed
but didn't neglect that fallen friend
and covered him with a colossal shield   420
while he was raised by two trusty comrades—
Mecisteus and illustrious Alastor,
who brought him, deeply moaning, to the ships.

  But Idomeneus stormed forward, furious
to wrap more Trojans in dismal darkness
or perish himself defending the ships,
downed that beloved son of Aesyetes
named Alcathous, Anchises' son-in-law
by his first daughter, Hippodameia,
pride and joy of her delighted parents   430
since she was prettiest of her playmates,
best in handicrafts and the cleverest,
so a distinguished lord was her husband—
but now Poseidon delivered him to
Idomeneus: charmed his eyes, made him weak

so he couldn't retreat or dodge the blow.
Like a pillar or a towering tree,
he stood stock-still till Idomeneus thrust
a deadly spear at his chest, broke the bronze
that used to guard his body in the past,   440
and it resounded dully as it split.
Then he fell thundering, spear in his heart,
whose feeble beating made the butt end shake—
but there at last its fury was ended.
And Idomeneus bellowed terribly:
"Well then, Deiphobus, is this fair revenge—
three warriors for the one you bragged about?
Villain, come meet me in single combat
and learn what men are descended from Zeus!
Wise Zeus made Minos the Cretan monarch,   450
and his magnificent son Deucalion
became my father—I rule many men
in grassy Crete, and my ships have brought me
to plague your family and all your people!"

   Then Deiphobus stood in indecision
whether to look for someone who would help
or face lord Idomeneus all alone.
Finally he decided it was best
to seek Aeneas: he found him at the rear
standing idle, still angry at Priam,   460
his valor had received such small reward.
Deiphobus came running to him and cried:
"Aeneas, dauntless Dardanian leader,
rescue your sister's husband, if you care—
help us save the body of Alcathous!
Don't forget how he reared you in his home,
but now Idomeneus has brought him down."

   These words stirred Aeneas most mightily,
and, raging, he drove toward Idomeneus,
who didn't retreat like a pampered boy,   470
stood steadfast as a fiery mountain boar
faces a clamorous crowd of hunters
in a lonely place—his stiff back bristles,

his eyes are ablaze, and he grinds his teeth,
determined to batter off their attack:
thus Idomeneus declined to move back
and called his estimable companions
Ascalaphus, Aphareus, Deipyrus,
gallant Meriones, and Antilochus,
addressing them in agitated words: 480
"Here I need help, dear friends! I'm awfully
worried with Aeneas driving this way!
He has slain so many men already,
and he's in the very flush of youth.
But if we met at about the same age
we might battle it out on equal terms!"

   A host of warriors came hurrying to him
and stood side by side, shoulders bracing shields.
Opposite, Aeneas called his comrades
Deiphobus, Paris, and brave Agenor,   490
his fellow Trojan lords—and after them
the people followed, as a ram leads sheep
from field to stream, delighting the shepherd:
thus Anchises' son Aeneas rejoiced
when he saw those hordes who came to aid him.

   They met man-to-man about Alcathous,
brandishing spears. Bright bronze about bodies
rang horribly as they stabbed back and forth—
and most of all, two dangerous warriors,
fiery Aeneas and Idomeneus,   500
relentlessly raged to slay each other.
First Aeneas flung at Idomeneus,
but he was keeping a close watch and dodged,
so that weapon sank quivering in earth
though a powerful arm had propelled it.
Idomeneus hurled, hit Oenomaus,
shattered his breastplate, and his bowels burst out
as he fell to the earth, clutching at dust.
That Cretan lord tore the terrible spear
from his corpse but couldn't seize his armor,   510
such clouds of missiles showered all about

and his legs had lost a lot of their spring
for dodging spears or retrieving his own.
At close combat he was unbeatable,
but the bounce had gone out of his body.
As he slowly moved back, a spear was flung
by Deiphobus, furious for his dead friends,
but missed him barely, hit Ascalaphus,
Ares' son, hurtled straight through his shoulder,
and he fell to the earth, clutching at dust.   520
But booming-voiced Ares stayed unaware
his own son had fallen in bitter war:
sat on the highest peak of Olympus
under golden clouds, held by Zeus's will
with the other immortals kept from combat.

They met man-to-man about that body.
Deiphobus snatched its glittering helmet
as intrepid Molus' son Meriones
rushed at him with a spear and stabbed his arm
so the booty fell clanging to the ground,   530
then again lunged forward like a vulture,
withdrew that razor-sharp weapon, and ran
back among the Achaeans. Polites
supported his brother about the waist
and led him to the nimble-hooved horses
waiting at the rear of that battlefield
with their driver and their brilliant chariot.
These carried him, deeply moaning, away
as murky blood oozed from the open wound.

The rest fought on with a relentless roar.   540
Now Aeneas attacked Aphareus,
pierced his throat with a desperate spear thrust
so his head drooped sideward; he tumbled down
as dark death dismally enfolded him.
Next Antilochus watched till Thoön turned,
and furiously thrust his spear, cut the vein
that runs from the back up to the neck,
then he toppled over into the dust,
stretching both hands toward his dear companions.

Antilochus ran to seize his armor   550
with a wary eye on those Trojan hosts
who gathered round him, battering his shield—
but their deadly weapons left him unscathed
since powerful earthshaker Poseidon
protected Nestor's son Antilochus.
He battled on with the foremost, never
letting his spear rest even a moment,
but brandished and shook it incessantly,
feinting to hurl or attack hand-to-hand.

  As he fought among the throng, Adamas   560
spied him and stabbed at his shield from nearby,
but that colossal spearshaft was shattered
by dark-haired Poseidon, who grudged his life.
Part of the weapon stayed like a charred stake
in Antilochus' shield and part on earth—
and Adamas ran back, avoiding fate.
But glorious Meriones hurled and hit him
between crotch and navel, where most of all
Ares brings pain on miserable mortals:
as the spear drove in, Adamas leaned down   570
gasping like an ox that mountain shepherds
truss up and drag struggling helpless away—
thus he gasped for a moment, but not long,
till Meriones came to tear the weapon
from his flesh, and darkness covered his eyes.

  Now Helenus stabbed Deipyrus' temple
with a stout Thracian sword, smashed his helmet
to the ground, and one of the Danaan lords
gathered it up as it rolled among them—
and gloomy night floated over his eyes.   580

  Menelaus grieved greatly at that sight
and strode out bellowing, brandished his spear
at fiery Helenus, who drew a bow,
and both men let fly at the same moment,
one with the spear and one with an arrow.
Helenus' arrow hit Menelaus

on his bright breastplate, but it bounded off
as the harvested beans and chick peas leap
from a shovel over some threshing floor
when a farmer hurls them against the wind—   590
thus Menelaus' armor deflected
the bitter arrow and it skittered on.
His own spear landed on Helenus' hand,
which held the well-polished bow—its bronze
cut straight through his flesh and into the bow.
Helenus staggered back, avoiding fate,
that great ashwood spear dangling from his hand,
then his friend Agenor extracted it
and bandaged up the wound with twisted wool
his squire had carried as a catapult.   600

   And Peisander charged at Menelaus,
but an evil fate had led him to death
at your hands, illustrious Menelaus.
After they came very near each other
that son of Atreus flung a spear but missed,
while Peisander stabbed at his massive shield,
though the spear couldn't shear through that surface,
and its shaft snapped off beside the socket.
Peisander rejoiced, believing he'd won,
but Menelaus stormed forward swinging   610
a silver-studded sword, as the other
held the finely polished olivewood shaft
of his battle-ax—and those two men met.
Peisander smashed Menelaus' helmet
just under the plume, while Atreus' son slashed
at his forehead, cracked the bones, so bloody
eyeballs fell into the dust at his feet
as he sank. Menelaus put a foot
on his chest, tore off his armor, and roared:
"You all shall leave our ships in this same way,   620
arrogant Trojans, drunk with battle lust!
Dirty dogs, you have played me the lowest
trick there can be, you care so little
for the wrath of Zeus, protector of guests,

who'll devastate your city some fine day!
You kidnapped my wife and took her treasures
after she gave you hospitality,
and now you believe you can burn our ships
and murder these warriors who defend them,
yet we'll hold you back, for all your fury!   630
Oh, father Zeus, you're wiser than any
god or mortal—but this has come from you.
You are protecting insolent people,
reckless Trojan rowdies who never
have their fill of hideous battle's clamor.
A man may have enough of anything—
sleep or love or sweet song or the dance—
and all are much better than battle, but
these Trojans never get their fill of war!"

    Then lord Menelaus tore bloody armor   640
from that body, handed it to his friends,
and returned to stand among the foremost.
First he encountered Pylaemenes' son
Harpalion, who had followed his father
to war in Troy, but would never return:
he lunged at Menelaus with a spear
from very near, couldn't shatter his shield,
and hurried back among those Trojan hordes
peering about him in anxiety—
but as he departed, Meriones aimed   650
an arrow that hit his right buttock and
bit straight to the bladder beneath the bone.
So he sank in the arms of his comrades,
gasping his life away, lay like a worm
all a-sprawl, and his dark blood wet the earth.
Then the proud Paphlagonians cared for him:
set him in a chariot, brought him to Troy
with much grief. His father followed weeping:
a dear son dead, no blood price to be paid.

    Paris was furious to see him fallen,   660
for prince Harpalion had once been his host—
and, raging, shot a razor-sharp arrow.

One Euchenor was there, a seer's son,
rich in lands and brave, who came from Corinth
though he knew full well his terrible fate:
his aged father had often warned him
he'd either die of disease at his home
or be killed beside the ships in Ilios—
so he went, to avoid a deserter's fine
with the anguish of protracted illness.   670
Now that arrow bore under his ear, life
left his body and dread darkness took him.

   Thus they battled away like blazing flame.
But Zeus's beloved Hector did not know
his men were being slaughtered on the left
and the Danaans had nearly won the day
with the help of earthshaker Poseidon,
who urged them ahead and lent his own strength.
Hector continued battling at the place
he'd shattered the gate and enemy ranks,   680
where great Aias and Protesilaus
had their ships on the beach: that Danaan wall
was lowest and easiest to breach, and most
warriors fought on in a churning turmoil.

   Those Boeotians and long-robed Ionians,
Locrians, Phthians, and stately Epeians
couldn't keep him from the ships, batter back
that horrible Hector, more like a flame,
though picked Athenians came to assist them
commanded by Menestheus and Pheidas,   690
Stichius and Bias, with many others
under Meges, Amphion, and Dracius,
and Phthians under Medon and Podarcus—
the first a natural son of Oileus
and swift Aias' brother, who went to live
in distant Phylacë after he killed
his own stepmother's beloved cousin,
and the second one brave Iphlicus' son.
Armed to the teeth, these led their people
with the Boeotians, defending the ships,   700

and nimblefooted Aias, Oileus' son,
stood steadfast by Telamonian Aias.
As two dark oxen in a fallow field
who tug at the plow like one, and around
the base of their horns the sweat oozes out
and only the polished yoke divides them
while they struggle to finish their furrow:
so those two Aiantes stood side by side.
And behind giant Aias were many
trusty companions, who took his great shield   710
whenever weariness overcame him,
but no Locrians accompanied Oileus' son,
they were so afraid of facing combat,
for they'd brought no thick-plumed brazen helmets,
no bulging bucklers, no spears of ashwood—
armed only with bows and woolen slings,
they had come to Ilios and, wielding these,
bombarded the enemy from afar.
Thus some stood before them in full armor
contending with Hector and his comrades,   720
while others showered arrows from the rear,
and the Trojan spearmen remained dismayed.

   All would have miserably retreated
into their city from the ships and tents
if canny Polydamas had not roared:
"Hector, you won't listen to wise advice.
Because a god gives you skill in battle
you think you know more than anyone here.
But mortal men on earth have different gifts:
one is endowed with finesse in combat,   730
one in dancing, one in song and the lyre,
while to one mighty Zeus concedes a mind
that benefits many of his comrades
and saves many others from utter ruin.
So let me say what seems the best to me:
now red-hot battle blazes all around,
and our people have fled over that wall
and given up fighting or still struggle

outnumbered here in scattered skirmishes—
let's fall back and summon our commanders   740
to consider every possible plan,
whether we should attack those ships today
and trust a god for victory, or else
escape while we still can. As for myself,
I very much fear we shall be repaid
for yesterday, since one dangerous man
is waiting by the ships, but not for long."

That advice pleased gallant Hector, so he
leapt down from his chariot in full armor
and addressed him in agitated words: 750
"Summon our lords, Polydamas, while I
join our people in the fury of war.
I shall return when I've given orders."

So off he went, like a snowy mountain,
ran roaring among his followers,
who assembled around Polydamas
after Hector commanded their presence.
Now that son of Priam ran looking for
glorious Deiphobus and prince Helenus
with Asius and Asius' son Adamas,   760
but none of the men he sought stayed unscathed:
some were lying by the sterns of those ships,
toppled to the dust by their enemies,
while the rest lay wounded within the town.
But there on the left he soon encountered
Paris, that husband of lovely Helen,
urging his comrades to enter battle.
Hector came near him and cried bitterly:
"Damn you, Paris, pretty boy, girl-crazy,
where are Deiphobus and prince Helenus   770
with Asius and Asius' son Adamas
and Othryoneus? Oh, our steep city's
utterly ruined, nothing can save us!"

Godlike Alexander said in reply:
"Hector, you were right to scold me before

when you saw me retreating from combat,
but not this time—I'm not so cowardly
as I seem to be! Since you summoned us
all my people have been pressing forward
ceaselessly. But those you ask for are dead.　　　　　780
Only Deiphobus and prince Helenus
have returned to their homes, both with spear wounds,
though Cronos' majestic son saved their lives.
Just lead us into combat once again
whenever you desire—and then you'll see
we are brave enough while our strength remains,
though no man can struggle beyond his strength."

　　These words persuaded his brother Hector.
Now they hurried to where battle raged worst
around Cebriones and Polydamas,　　　　　790
Phalces, Orthaeus, and Polyphetes,
with Palmys, Ascanius, and brave Morys,
who brought all his spearmen from Ascania
the morning before and now entered war.
These people attacked like a fierce wind blast
that sweeps the earth beneath Zeus's thunder,
meets the sea with a roar, as many sheer
waves arch bright backs on the deep until they
break foaming, some before, then more and more—
so, rank after rank, their Trojan warriors　　　　　800
moved into battle with dazzling armor.
Ahead of those hordes went lordly Hector,
Ares' peer, with his formidable shield,
thick strips of oxhide overlaid with bronze,
helmet plume bobbing about his great head.
Behind that shield he hurried here and there
to hurl himself against the enemy,
who waited for him steadfast, unafraid.
Giant Aias strode out to challenge him:
"Look here, man, do you think you can scare us?　　　　　810
Well, our people are no greenhorns in war—
only Zeus has defeated us before!
You'd like to be looting these ships, but our

powerful arms are sure to protect them—
yes, sooner than that, your own rich city
will fall before the force of our armies.
It won't be long till you madly retreat,
begging father Zeus and the other gods
to make your horses swifter than falcons
as they gallop through the dust toward your town."   820

  Just as he said this, an eagle flew by
high to their right. The Argives cried hurrah
for that glorious omen, while Hector roared:
"Aias, you babbler, what nonsense this is!
I only wish I were sure of being
magnificent Zeus's and Hera's son,
honored like Apollo or Athena,
as I know today brings the Argives ruin.
And you'll perish too, if you dare to stay
and face my dangerous spear, which will tear   830
your lily-white skin—so the dogs and birds
devour your fat and flesh beside those ships."

  Then Hector led the way, and his army
followed with a most formidable din.
The Argives bellowed their replies and stood
steadfast before those swarming Trojan hordes
as both sides' cries rose to the brilliant sky.

Book Fourteen: Zeus Fooled

The wounded Greek leaders discuss their army's desperate situation. Hera dupes Zeus into lying with her.

As Nestor sat drinking, he heard their cries
and said to Asclepius' distinguished son:
"Ah, my dear Machaon, what shall we do?
That hubbub's coming nearer and nearer!
But you stay right here and sip our fine wine
till Hecamede can heat you a bath
and wash all the clotted blood from your wound,
while I go out to watch that battlefield."

So he seized the sturdy shield of his son
Thrasymedes, which rested in its rack   10
because the son had taken his father's,
then took a dangerous bronze-tipped spear,
strode from the tent, and witnessed disaster:
his people streaming in pell-mell retreat
before those Trojans, their great wall broken.
As waters darken with the deep ground swell
to fashion a path for the whistling winds,
and those rollers only begin to move
when father Zeus rouses a steady gale:
thus Nestor pondered and was of two minds,   20
whether to join his people in combat
or look for their leader Agamemnon—
but finally he decided it was best
to seek that son of Atreus. Meanwhile war
churned on, tough bronze ringing about bodies
as spears and swords took a terrible toll.

  First Nestor met those Achaean leaders
coming up from the beach badly wounded:
Diomedes, Odysseus, Agamemnon.
Their ships stayed farthest from the battlefield,   30
close by the sea, while others were drawn up
onto the plain, that wall built beside them,
since even an ample beach couldn't hold
their seafaring ships jammed close together
row after row so they filled the entire
shore enclosed within two promontories.
Thus, leaning on their spears, those commanders
went toward the battlefield all together,
extremely discouraged indeed—and met
old Nestor, a dejected group of men.   40
Atreus' son Agamemnon spoke out first:
"Illustrious Nestor, our pride and glory,
why are you wandering so far from war?
Oh, I'm very much afraid their Hector
will fulfill those boasts he was bellowing:
he would not return from combat until
they had burned our ships and murdered us all.
And see how it's happening as he said!
Damn it all, I know our Danaan people
have a grudge against me, like Achilles,   50
so they won't even fight to save their ships."

  And aged Gerenian Nestor replied:
"Yes, such is the case indeed, and even
Zeus the thunderhurler could not change it.
They breached the great wall we believed would be
an impregnable bulwark for our ships,
and see how they struggle all about us
ceaselessly. Impossible to say
which way the Achaeans are retreating,
such awful turmoil rages everywhere.   60
Now we'll take charge of planning strategy
but stay away from that action today,
wounded men are so useless in combat."

And Atreus' son Agamemnon answered:
"Nestor, since they're fighting beside our ships
and we weren't helped by our moat or that wall
we made with such labor so it would be
an impregnable bulwark for our ships—
ah, this must be the will of mighty Zeus,
to have us die like dogs so far from home.   70
I knew when Cronos' son was on our side,
and now it seems certain he concedes them
power like the very gods, and we're helpless.
But every man here should do as I say:
let's take our ships beached down by the water
in the first line, drag them into that sea,
then anchor them with stones until evening
gives our Achaean armies some respite,
and afterward we'll launch the entire fleet.
No shame to escape doom, even by night—   80
better escape with our lives than perish."

Odysseus scowled terribly and declared:
"What a lot of nonsense, Agamemnon!
Why, you should command some ragtag armies,
not warriors like ours, whom Zeus has given
bitter battle in an unending skein
till we die down to the very last man.
You'd like us to abandon that city
when we have suffered so much to win it?
Well, be quiet, or our people may hear!   90
No one alive should be telling us that
if any sense at all is in his head
and he has such numerous followers
as these battalions under your command.
Yes, the idea's simply ridiculous!
Right in the midst of battle you'd have us
launch our seafaring ships, so the Trojans
gain that great triumph they are longing for
while we die here. The moment our people
see the ships afloat, they'll surely lose heart   100

and watch the sea instead of fighting.
Then your advice will ruin us, my lord."

  Atreus' son Agamemnon answered him:
"Quite true, Odysseus, I don't deny it—
I cannot compel our Danaan people
to launch their ships. But if only someone
among all of our armies, young or old,
had a better plan to save us from ruin!"

  Whereupon dauntless Diomedes cried:
"That man is here—no need to look farther   110
if only you listen to my advice
and don't resent my being the youngest.
My father was also a nobleman—
turbulent Tydeus who's buried in Thebes.
Three illustrious sons were born to Portheus,
leaders in Pleuron and steep Calydon:
Agrius and Melas and brave Oeneus,
my grandfather, most distinguished of all,
whose own son Tydeus arrived in Argos
after a long and wandering exile   120
and there took Adrastus' daughter as wife,
lived in luxury with abundant lands:
wheat fields and orchards and sheep in plenty,
since he was our most accomplished spearman—
yet all of you know the tale already.
So I'm no ordinary commoner,
and you cannot ignore my good advice.
Now we should go onto the battlefield
but quickly retire and avoid action
so none of us receives a second wound.   130
At least we might encourage those shirkers
who nurse their grudges and lurk to the rear."

  Then they gladly did as he had proposed,
with king Agamemnon leading the way.

  But earthshaking Poseidon observed them
and came disguised as an aged warrior,
clutched great Agamemnon by the right hand

and addressed him in agitated words:
"Atreus' son, that terrible Achilles
must be glad to have our people perish,   140
such little sense is in the fellow's head!
I wish some immortal would bring him down!
But not all the gods are your enemies—
we still may see those Trojan commanders
raising the dust on the plain as they race
back to the city from our ships and tents!"

     And away he ran with a mighty roar
like nine thousand or ten thousand warriors
locked in relentless fury of combat—
such a vast bellow came from Poseidon's   150
chest. And every warrior felt new courage
for the crash of implacable combat.

     But golden-throned Hera kept a close watch
from an Olympian peak: she recognized
that brother of herself and her husband
bustling about battle—and she was glad.
Then on steep Ida's highest peak she saw
Zeus seated, and the sight disgusted her.
Whereupon Hera began to ponder
how thunderlord Zeus might be greatly fooled.   160
Finally she decided it was best
to visit Ida splendidly attired
in hopes old Zeus would wish to embrace her,
so she might pour a warm and gentle sleep
over his eyelids and his cunning mind.
She went to that stately dressing chamber
her son Hephaestus had fitted with doors
and a lock no other god could open
and, having entered, swung the bright doors shut.
First she bathed her body with ambrosia,   170
then anointed herself with olive oil
of delicate texture and heady scent
so sweet that if stirred in Zeus's palace
its fragrance would fill all heaven and earth.
She rubbed this into her voluptuous skin,

then combed her hair and braided the lovely
ambrosial locks that tumbled from her head
and took a marvelous robe Athena
had elaborately embroidered for her,
pinned it over her breast with golden clasps,   180
wrapped a hundred-tasseled sash about her,
and adorned herself with brilliant earrings
in three-stone berry clusters—a delight!
Next that enchanting goddess donned a veil
of new-spun cloth that shimmered like the sun
and bound handsome sandals about her feet.
After she was attired most splendidly
she left her chamber, called Aphrodite
apart from the rest, and murmured to her:
"Now will you do me a favor, dear girl?   190
Or will you refuse me out of anger
that I support the Danaans and you don't?"

Zeus's daughter Aphrodite answered:
"My honored lady, great Cronos' daughter,
of course I'll do whatever you desire
if it is in any way possible."

And queen Hera replied deceitfully:
"Concede me Love and Desire, with which you
subdue all men and the immortal gods,
for I plan to visit the ends of earth   200
where mother Tethys and old Oceanus
reared me so tenderly in their palace
after thunderlord Zeus had flung Cronos
far beneath the earth and the restless sea.
I only hope to patch up the quarrel
that has kept them sleeping apart so long,
they're in a rage that is so terrible.
If I were able to persuade those two
and make them a happy couple again
just imagine how grateful they would be."   210

And laughter-loving Aphrodite cried:
"It wouldn't be right for me to refuse,
since you sleep in the arms of mighty Zeus."

And out of her bosom she slipped a band
in which all charms were intricately worked:
Love was there, and Desire, and delightful
Flirtation, which fuddles even the wise.
She placed it in queen Hera's hands, saying:
"Now tuck this little band in your bosom:
all things are worked into it. Don't worry,   220
it will give you whatever you may wish."

Gentle-eyed queen Hera smiled in reply
and, smiling, tucked the band in her bosom.

So Aphrodite went to her palace
while Hera darted from Olympus—one
step on Pieria, one on Emathia,
then soared high over the topmost snowy
Thracian peaks, her feet never touching them,
and stepped on the sea waves after Athos
and came to Lemnos, the realm of Thoas.   230
There she met Sleep, Death's delicate brother,
clasped him by the hand and murmured to him:
"Sleep, you ruler of men and immortals,
listen to me now if you ever have,
and I'll surely be grateful all my days.
Lull those brilliant eyes of Zeus to slumber
as soon as I lie beside him in love
and you'll have an imperishable throne
of solid gold—my lame son Hephaestus
will make it for you, with a stool beneath   240
where you may rest your feet while sipping wine."

And delightful sweet Sleep said in reply:
"My honored lady, great Cronos' daughter,
I could easily lull some other god
to slumber—even that old river lord
Oceanus, ancestor of all the rest.
But you think I'd put father Zeus to sleep?

Ha, I wouldn't go anywhere near him.
I learned a lesson when I helped you once
that day his lionheart son Heracles   250
set sail after sacking the Trojan town.
Then I flung a spell over Zeus's mind,
drowned him in sweetness while you made trouble
by stirring up unfavorable winds
that carried his son to the isle of Cos
far from home. But Zeus woke in a fury
and tossed the gods about and looked for me
to fling me forever into the sea,
when I was saved by all-conquering Night—
I ran to her, and Zeus controlled his rage,   260
he was so afraid of swift Night's power.
And now you want me to do it again?"

But gentle-eyed queen Hera answered him:
"Now, now, Sleep, why worry about all this?
You really believe Zeus loves the Trojans
the way he cares for his son Heracles?
Look here, I'll give you one of the Graces
to be your own dear wife—Pasithea.
You've always longed for her, I do believe."

This was good news to Sleep, and he replied: 270
"Very well, swear by Styx's holy streams:
put one hand here on the surface of earth
and the other on the shimmering sea
and call our underworld gods to witness
I may really have her—Pasithea.
I've always been wild for her, as you know."

And immortal white-armed Hera did it:
swore as he ordered, naming all the gods
who live below Tartarus, called Titans.
After she swore that formidable oath   280
those two darted from Lemnos and Imbros,
hidden in mist, and hurried on their way.
But when they reached Ida, haven of beasts,
they left the sea, went soaring over earth

as the treetops quivered beneath their feet.
Sleep pulled up short before Zeus could see him
and perched on a lofty fir tree, tallest
on Ida, that rose to heaven itself.
There, hidden by branches, he took his place
in the shape of that whistling mountain bird   290
called Calchis by gods, Cymindis by men.

   But Hera swiftly approached Gargarus,
Ida's tall peak—and when Zeus observed her
he was quite overwhelmed by a desire
mighty as the time they first embraced,
keeping it a secret from their parents.
So that son of Cronos accosted her:
"Hera, why have you come from Olympus?
And without your horses and your chariot!"

   Then Hera addressed him deceitfully: 300
"Now I plan to visit the ends of earth
where mother Tethys and old Oceanus
reared me so tenderly in their palace.
I only hope to patch up the quarrel
that has kept them sleeping apart so long,
they're in such a simply terrible rage.
My horses are down below here waiting
to take me across the land and the sea,
but first I came from our Olympian home
so you wouldn't be angry if you heard   310
I'd gone to Oceanus without a *word*."

   Whereupon cloudgathering Zeus replied:
"Hera, there'll be time for all that later.
Now let me take you in my arms, my dear.
I have never felt such a mad passion
for any goddess or mortal woman,
not even when I embraced Ixion's wife,
who bore me a splendid son, Perithous,
or that delightful creature Danaë,
who gave birth to redoubtable Perseus,   320
or even the daughter of famed Phoenix,

who bore lord Minos and Rhadamanthys,
or Semelë or Alcmenë in Thebes,
who gave birth to stouthearted Heracles,
while Semelë bore daft Dionysus,
or even that ravishing Demeter
or glorious Leto—or even you—
as I do adore and desire you now."

Then Hera addressed him deceitfully:
"You dreadful fellow, what are you saying!   330
You really think we can lie together
here on Ida, where everyone can see?
And what if one of the eternal gods
should observe us and tell all the others?
I could never go to your home again
after that happened, I'd be so ashamed.
But if it's really your royal pleasure,
you have a chamber our beloved son
Hephaestus has made with tight-fitting doors.
We can very well go there to retire."   340

Whereupon cloudgathering Zeus replied:
"Hera, have no fear we shall be observed.
I'll cover us with such a golden cloud
the Sun himself can never penetrate,
though his eyes are more piercing than any."

Then that son of Cronos embraced his wife,
and beneath them the earth made fresh grass grow
with dewy clover, crocus, and thick soft
hyacinth, which kept them high above ground.
And they lay there wrapped in a golden cloud   350
from which the gleaming dewdrops trickled down.

Thus father Zeus slept high on Gargarus
with his wife, subdued by slumber and love,
while Sleep hurried off to the ships with news
for that great Earthholder and Earthshaker
and addressed him in agitated words:
"Poseidon, time to help the Achaeans!
Give them more glory now Zeus is asleep—

I drenched him in a delightful slumber,
and Hera tricked him into lying with her."   360

   Then Sleep went among the peoples of earth,
leaving Poseidon even more eager—
so he leapt out before them all, roaring:
"Achaeans, why hand Hector victory,
make him a glorious present of our ships?
Well, this is his boast, because Achilles
stays by the ships in a maniac rage!
But we won't miss him much if you others
only stand together in self-defense.
But every man here should do as I say: 370
take the biggest, sturdiest shields we have,
put your shimmering helmets on your heads,
hold the heaviest spears you can manage,
and follow me to battle—then we'll see
if that dangerous Hector dares face *me*.
And if any leader's shield is too small,
he should exchange it for a larger one."

   They gladly did as he had commanded,
and their ranks were formed by those wounded lords—
Diomedes, Odysseus, Agamemnon—   380
who commanded them to exchange armor
so better men might have better pieces.
After all had put on their brilliant bronze
they moved out behind mighty Poseidon,
in his hand a terrible fine-edged sword
like lightning, too much for any warrior
in battle, but all fall back before it.
Opposite, Hector marshaled the Trojans.
Thus that awful tug-of-war was pulled taut
by dark-haired Poseidon and great Hector,   390
one with the Trojans, one with the Danaans,
and the sea surged up to the ships and tents
as the two sides met with a dreadful roar.
More than the furor of sea pounding shore
when chilly north winds churn up the waters,
more than the thunder of a blazing fire

that devours a forest deep in the hills,
more than tall oaks resounding in the wind
that makes most dissonance in its fury,
was the sound of those Trojans and Danaans   400
roaring as they leapt on one another.

  First formidable Hector hurled a spear
at Telamonian Aias, and it hit
just where two leather bands came together—
that shield strap and the silver-studded sword's—
which saved his life. Hector was furious
he'd thrown his dangerous weapon in vain
and hurried back among his companions.
As he was moving away, Aias seized
a great boulder, one of many ship props   410
that rolled about their feet—he heaved it up,
struck Hector on the chest by his shield rim,
spun him around and around like a top.
As father Zeus blasts an oak tree that falls
ripped up by the roots, with a sulfurous stench,
and a man who stands watching shakes in fear
at Zeus's redoubtable thunderbolt—
thus the spear fell from mighty Hector's hand,
and he toppled down with shield and helmet
as his brilliant armor boomed about him.   420
Now all the Achaeans rushed out shouting
in a rage to drag him away, flung spears
in showers, but that brave son of Priam
stayed unscathed, so many stood at his side—
Polydamas, Aeneas, Agenor,
Glaucus, and the Lycian lord Sarpedon—
nor did the others fail: they made a wall
of their oval shields. His faithful comrades
lifted him up, brought him to the horses
waiting at the rear of that battlefield   430
with their driver and the glorious chariot
which carried him, deeply moaning, away.

When they came to the ford of that river
eddying Xanthus, immortal Zeus's child,
they lowered him to the ground, poured water
over his head. So he revived, looked up,
and belched black blood as he sat on his knees,
then tumbled back to the ground once again,
his eyes misted over, and lay there dazed.

And when the Achaeans saw Hector leave   440
they attacked with even greater fury.
First of all, nimble Aias, Oileus' son,
stormed forward swinging his spear, stabbed Satnius,
conceived by a water nymph to Enops,
who tended sheep by Satnioeis' streams:
Aias thrust that weapon into his side
so he fell backward, and all the others
surged together in desperate combat.
Panthous' son Polydamas rushed ahead
to rescue Satnius, hurled a spear that pierced   450
Prothoënor straight through the right shoulder,
and he fell to the earth, clutching at dust.

Now Polydamas boasted terribly:
"Seems this magnificent son of Panthous
hasn't thrown his spear entirely in vain—
it hit a Danaan, and now it will be
a staff for him as he creeps to Hades!"

Those Danaans felt a sickening sorrow,
and Telamonian Aias most of all,
the man had fallen so close beside him.   460
As Polydamas moved back, Aias hurled
a glittering spear, but he escaped fate
with a sudden dive, and that weapon met
Archelochus, since the gods planned his death:
went hurtling through the place where neck and head
joined at the top of his spine, cleft the nerves—
and as he fell, his head and mouth and nose
met earth far sooner than his legs and knees.
Now giant Telamonian Aias cried:

"All right, Polydamas, tell me the truth: 470
is that fellow's life worth Prothoënor's?
He looks to me like no common warrior
but a brother of gallant Antenor
or a son, he resembles him so much!"

   Those Trojans grieved extremely to hear this,
and Acamas bestrode his comrade's corpse,
stabbed Promachus as he tried to grab it,
and roared most horribly before them all:
"You Achaean bowmen, big boasting boys,
don't think we Trojans are the only ones   480
with troubles—you'll perish the same way too.
See your Promachus sleep! I brought him down,
and the blood price for my brother's murder
was promptly paid. That's why a warrior prays
some kinsman be left to avenge his death."

   Those Danaans felt a sickening sorrow
and fiery Peneleos most of all,
so he rushed upon prince Acamas—who
beat a quick retreat—then hurried after
Ilioneus, son of glorious Phorbas,   490
whom Hermes adored and gave great riches,
and his only child was Ilioneus.
Peneleos stabbed him under the brows,
that keen spear pierced to the nape of his neck,
drove an eyeball out, and he toppled back,
stretching out both hands. But Peneleos
slashed his head off with a sword, and it fell
still helmeted, that stubborn spearpoint stuck
in the eye. He raised it like a poppyhead,
showed it to all the Trojans, and boasted: 500
"Trojans, go tell Ilioneus' parents
to start lamentation in their palace,
because that wife of gallant Promachus
won't be glad her dear husband has come back
when we Achaeans set sail from your land!"

The Trojans trembled when they heard these words,
and each peeped round for a way to escape.

Now tell me, you Muses on Olympus,
which Achaean won bloody booty first
when Poseidon had turned the tide of war?   510
First giant Telamonian Aias came
to slay the Mysian commander Hyrtius,
while Antilochus cut down Mermerus,
Meriones killed Morys and Hippotion,
Teucer slew powerful Periphetes,
and Menelaus stabbed Hyperenor
in his side, so his bowels came oozing out
and the soul hurried from that open wound
as dismal darkness enfolded his eyes.
But Oileus' son Aias brought the most down,   520
since no man was so nimble in pursuit
when Zeus turned the enemy to retreat.

Book Fifteen: The Greeks Penned In

Zeus wakes in a rage, sends Apollo to heal Hector, who
again drives the Greeks back to their ships.

After they crossed the moat and palisade
and many had fallen to those Danaans,
they halted at last before their chariots,
dumbfounded, pale with terror. And Zeus woke
on Ida's peaks by golden-throned Hera,
leapt to his feet, and saw the battlefield:
Trojans retreating wildly, behind them
Poseidon leading that Danaan attack.
Then he saw gallant Hector as he lay
gasping in anguish and vomiting blood,   10
he had met so dangerous a warrior.
That father of gods and men pitied him
and roared to Hera, scowling horribly:
"Impossible female, you deceived me,
brought Hector down, defeated his people!
Well, you'll pay for this mischief soon enough,
when my whip beats some good sense into you!
Have you forgotten how I strung you up
with anvils on both your feet and handcuffed
in unbreakable gold? And there you hung   20
among the clouds, so the gods were furious,
but I caught the ones who came to free you,
tossed them from my threshold, and down they fell
powerless to earth. But still I had many
worries over my dear son Heracles
because you plotted with the wild North Wind
to carry him over the restless sea

till he stayed shipwrecked on the isle of Cos.
I rescued him from there and brought him back
to Argos after his many labors.   30
Remember this next time you try your tricks—
yes, you'll see what use your sweet talk will be
when you come up here to fool me again!"

   Now that gentle-eyed queen Hera shuddered
and addressed him in agitated words:
"I swear by Earth and broad Heaven above
and Styx's tumbling waters, the greatest
and most horrid oath for the immortals,
and by your sacred head and by our bed—
you know I'd never swear falsely by this—   40
it's not my fault earthshaking Poseidon
made trouble for Hector and the Trojans:
he came upon the idea by himself,
pitied the Achaeans as they perished.
But I should certainly advise him
to follow your orders, Thundercloud Lord."

   The father of gods and men smiled at this
and answered her in elevated words:
"Very well, my gentle-eyed queen Hera,
if you consent not to work against me   50
I believe Poseidon will change his mind
no matter how rebellious he may be.
So if you're really telling the truth
run among the immortals and summon
silverbow Apollo and our Iris,
so she may enter the Argive armies,
find Poseidon, and give him my orders
to abandon battle and go back home.
Meanwhile Apollo must rouse great Hector,
fill him with courage and quiet the pain   60
that torments him now, while his enemies
turn to retreat in tumultuous panic
till they fall back about the high-beaked ships
of Achilles and he sends his comrade
Patroclus—but Hector will bring him down

after he has slain so many Trojans,
even my own son noble Sarpedon.
This will put Achilles in such a rage
he can kill Hector as the Achaeans
turn to attack, and they'll take that city 70
with the stratagem planned by Athena.
But for now I shall stay implacable,
and no god may assist the Achaeans
till the wish of Peleus' son is fulfilled
just as I promised by bowing my head
that day the goddess Thetis hugged my knees,
begging me to back her brave Achilles."

And white-armed Hera obeyed that command,
leapt from Ida's peaks to high Olympus
swift as the mind of a well-traveled man 80
who ponders the lands he has seen and thinks
"wish I were here" or "wish I were there"—
thus queen Hera hurried eagerly on.
She arrived at Olympus, found the gods
in Zeus's palace. When they saw her come
all leapt to their feet and offered a pledge.
Hera ignored the rest and took a cup
from gracious Themis, who greeted her first,
addressing her in agitated words:
"Hera, why are you here? You look troubled. 90
Another spat with that son of Cronos?"

Haughty white-armed Hera said in reply:
"Ah, Themis, don't ask me—you know yourself
how extremely difficult he can be.
Have the gods begin their banquet while I
tell you and the other Olympians here
what awful things Zeus said. I can't believe
my news will bring merriment to mortals
or gods, if any still feast happily."

Whereupon queen Hera seated herself, 100
and all the Olympians were vexed. She laughed
with her lips alone, but those fine dark brows

were knitted, and suddenly she burst out:
"Ha, we're fools to be angry at old Zeus!
We still think we can walk up and stop him
by words or by force—but he sits apart
and doesn't care a bit, he knows so well
he's far superior to us in power.
So we simply must suffer what he sends.
Even now Ares has a shock coming: 110
that mortal man he loves most has fallen—
Ascalaphus, whom Ares calls his son."

   Then Ares slapped both his enormous thighs
with the flat of both his hands and intoned:
"Ah, don't blame me, you blessed Olympians,
if I should go to the ships for revenge,
though Zeus's thunderbolt may smash me down
to lie in blood and dust among the dead."

   Whereupon he ordered Terror and Rout
to yoke his horses and began to arm.   120
That would have brought even more relentless
quarrels between Zeus and the immortals,
but green-eyed Athena feared for the gods,
left her throne and hurried through the doorway,
tore off his helmet and his mighty shield,
ripped the bronze spear from his colossal hand
and berated manslaughtering Ares:
"Madman, idiot, don't ruin yourself!
You haven't a bit of sense in your head!
Remember what white-armed Hera told us?   130
And she just came from magnificent Zeus.
Would you fight it out to the bitter end
till he marches you back to Olympus
and makes more trouble for the rest of us?
He'll forget all about that battlefield
and rush over here to smash us around,
the innocent and the guilty as well,
so please, please don't be angry for your son.
Why, better and stronger mortals than he

have fallen in war, and others will fall.   140
We gods can't be running to save each one."

   She dragged fiery Ares back to his throne.
But Hera called Apollo from the hall
with Iris, the immortals' messenger,
and addressed them in agitated words:
"Great Zeus requests your presence on Ida,
and after he receives you in audience
you'd better do exactly as he says."

   Then white-armed queen Hera returned and sat
on her own throne, as those two hurried off.   150
They came to Ida with its purling pools
and Gargarus, where booming-voiced king Zeus
sat crowned with a fragrant cloud of incense,
and humbly stood before that thunderlord.
He wasn't a bit angry to see them,
they had come so quickly at his wife's call,
and addressed windfoot Iris first of all:
"Iris, you hurry down to Poseidon
and deliver this message word for word:
I desire him to abandon battle   160
and go join the gods or enter the sea.
If he declines to obey my order
tell him to consider more carefully
whether he has the courage to face *me*!
He knows very well I am mightier
and older too, but he's casual indeed
in opposing my invincible will."

   And windfoot Iris obeyed his command,
darted from Ida's hills to holy Troy.
As snow or hail comes tumbling from the clouds,   170
chill beneath the sweep of a fresh north wind,
Iris flew that speedily on her way.
She found earthshaking Poseidon and cried:
"Dark-haired Enfolder of Earth, I bring you
a message from Zeus the aegis bearer:
he desires you to abandon battle

and go join the gods or enter the sea.
If you decline to obey his order
he says to consider more carefully
whether you have the courage to face *him*!   180
You know very well he is mightier
and older too, but you're casual indeed
in opposing his invincible will."

   Very much vexed, glorious Poseidon said:
"Damn it, with all respect, he's gone too far
if he thinks he can hold me back, his peer.
We're brothers, sons of Cronos and Rhea—
Zeus and I and the lord of hell, Hades.
All was divided three ways between us
when we each drew lots—I won the gray sea,   190
while Hades was given gloomy darkness
and Zeus won heaven, among clouds and air,
but earth and Olympus are common ground.
So he can't push me around, he should stay
in the part of the world assigned to him,
he mustn't treat me like an inferior.
He can lecture his own sons and daughters
with these preposterous threatening words—
they are obliged to fulfill his commands."

   And that windfoot Iris cried in reply: 200
"Dark-haired Holder of Earth, are you quite sure
I should take Zeus this unpleasant message,
or won't you be wiser and change your mind?
You know the Furies help the eldest son."

   Then earthshaking Poseidon answered her:
"Ah, Iris, my dear, you've spoken the truth
as a good messenger should—I know it.
But I tell you it makes me indignant
to have him saying these disgraceful things
when I'm entirely his equal and peer.   210
Well, I'll swallow my anger for today,
but let me tell you this, and I mean it:
if he goes against Athena and me

and Hera and Hermes and Hephaestus
by sparing that city and refusing
to let our Achaeans devastate it,
he'll begin a feud that nothing can heal."

Then the Earthshaker left the Achaeans,
much to their dismay, and plunged in the sea.

But Zeus Cloudgatherer told Apollo: 220
"Phoebus, my good fellow, run to Hector
now mighty Poseidon has already
entered the sea, for fear of our anger—
otherwise there'd have been such an uproar
even the underworld gods would have heard.
And surely it's better for both of us
he had sense enough to stay clear of me,
or things would not have ended without sweat.
So you take my tasseled aegis in hand,
brandish it to frighten the Achaeans,   230
and protect illustrious Hector yourself:
give him more power till his opponents
retreat to their ships and the Hellespont,
and then I'll do whatever seems the best
so they may have a bit of rest from war."

Apollo obeyed his father's command,
darted down from Ida like a falcon,
destroyer of doves, swiftest winged thing,
and found that incomparable Hector
sitting up. He'd just regained consciousness   240
and gazed around, stopped sweating and panting,
when the will of glorious Zeus revived him.
Silverbow Apollo came near and cried:
"Hector, why are you lying far back here
in a daze? What's the matter with you?"

Flashing-helmeted Hector moaned feebly:
"Which great Olympian god are you who asks?
Don't you know war was raging by the ships
and as I ravaged the Danaans, Aias
struck me on the chest with a great boulder?   250

I thought I'd enter the gates of Hades
this very day, after breathing my last."

   But Apollo the archer answered him:
"Courage, dear fellow! Zeus sent this helper
to stand at your side and lend you a hand:
myself, golden-sword Phoebus Apollo,
who always protected you and your town.
Very well then, order your charioteers
to drive their thunderous horses toward the ships,
while I move before them to clear a path   260
and batter those Achaean spearmen back!"

   Now Apollo breathed fury into him.
As a mighty stallion stuffed with barley
breaks his rope and gallops over the plain
where he loves to bathe in a rippling stream—
exultantly throws his head up, the mane
floats over his shoulders, and he prances
to a place where the mares usually graze:
thus Hector rushed onto the battlefield,
roaring commands, when he heard that god's voice.   270
As a wild goat or a noble horned stag
is pursued by country people and hounds
till some sheer cliff or shadowy forest
saves him and they lose all hope of the kill,
then a bearded lion unexpectedly
stands in their way and they take to their heels:
so those Danaans attacked in a great mass,
stabbing with swords and with double-edged spears,
but when they saw Hector among the ranks
they were terror-stricken, and their hearts sank.   280

   One man spoke up—Thoas, Andraemon's son,
an Aetolian captain deft with the spear,
good at close combat and surpassed by few
in assemblies where men show eloquence.
And he addressed them with these measured words:
"I can't believe what I see with my eyes!
Hector has returned and escaped the fates,

just when our people hoped and expected
Telamonian Aias had brought him down.
Some god must have saved that son of Priam   290
who has slain so many fine men of ours
and will slaughter more, it seems, because he
must be assisted by thunderlord Zeus!
Then every man here should do as I say:
let the commoners go back to their ships
while all we Achaean commanders stand
side by side with our spears at the ready
and batter him back. Despite his frenzy,
he won't dare face our phalanx, I believe!"

And they gladly did as he had proposed: 300
captains who served Aias, Idomeneus,
Teucer, Meriones, and fiery Meges
called to their leaders, formed a battle line
facing Hector and his hordes—and behind,
the people streamed toward those Achaean ships.

Then Hector stormed forward with his warriors
in furious tempo, led by Apollo
wrapped in a cloud and holding the aegis,
that shimmering shield the smith Hephaestus
had given wise Zeus to frighten mankind—   310
and Apollo held it as they advanced.

Those Achaeans stood fast, and battle cries
rang out on both sides, arrows leapt from strings,
while many spears hurled by powerful hands
pierced the bodies of fiery young warriors,
though some fell short before reaching their goal
and stuck in the earth, hungry to cut flesh.
As long as Phoebus held his aegis still
spears took a terrible toll on both sides—
but when he looked straight at the Achaeans   320
and shook that aegis with a mighty roar
they became dazed, forgot all their courage.
Like a herd of cows or a great sheep flock
pursued through the darkness by two wild beasts

who surprise them while their shepherd is gone,
those Achaeans panicked as Apollo
shattered their ranks, gave Hector victory.

Then man killed man as the battle scattered.
Hector slew Stichius and Arcesilaus—
one a lord of the armored Boeotians,   330
the other Menestheus' trusty comrade—
while Aeneas downed Medon and Iasus,
the first a natural son of Oileus
and swift Aias' brother, who went to live
in distant Phylacë after he killed
his own stepmother's beloved cousin,
the second an Athenian commander,
son of Sphelus and Bucolus' grandson.
Next Polydamas dispatched Mecisteus,
Polites, Echius, Agenor, Clonius—   340
and as Deiochous ran away, Paris
pierced the base of his shoulder with a spear.

While they took the armor from those bodies
the Achaeans scrambled over their moat
and scattered here and there inside the wall,
as Hector bellowed among his armies:
"Leave the booty, men, and go for the ships!
If I should see anyone hanging back
I'll run him through on the spot—he won't
have proper cremation from our people,   350
but dogs will devour him before the town!"

Then he brought the lash down on his horses
and roared to his people along the ranks,
who bellowed their war cries and drove right on
with a dreadful din. Before them Phoebus
easily broke the moat's banks with his feet,
poured them in the middle to make a bridge
broad as the space a javelin travels
when a man tries his strength in funeral games.
The Trojans streamed over, Phoebus in front   360
holding the aegis—and he smashed that wall

quite easily, as a boy by the sea
builds castles of sand to amuse himself,
then crumbles them up with his hands and feet:
so, Apollo, you spoiled the Danaans' toil,
drove them back in a tumultuous panic.

At last they came to a halt by the ships,
summoning one another, raised their hands
and implored the immortals to save them.
Veteran Nestor prayed most fervently,   370
his hands upraised toward the starry heavens:
"Oh, Father Zeus, if any Achaean
ever made burned offerings in your name
and you promised him a safe return,
remember it, Olympian, help us now—
don't let the enemy overwhelm us!"

And wise Zeus thundered mightily above
to show he conceded Nestor's appeal.

When the Trojans heard that thunder of Zeus
they came in an even greater fury.   380
As dangerous waves on the wide-wayed sea
engulf some ship with a wind's awful might,
piling its billows higher and higher,
so the Trojans scaled that wall with a roar,
came driving in and stood on their chariots
to fight at close quarters by the ships' sterns,
while the Danaans clambered onto their decks
and struggled away with bronze-capped billhooks
the crew kept ready for naval combat.

And as long as those opposing armies   390
still battled at some distance from the ships,
Patroclus sat in Eurypylus' tent,
distracted him with talk while he applied
medicinal herbs to the open wound.
But when he saw Trojans scaling the wall,
its defenders screaming and retreating,
noble Patroclus groaned and slapped his thighs
with the flat of both his hands and intoned:

"It seems you need me here, Eurypylus,
but I can't stay, with war raging away.   400
Let your trusty servant take care of you
while I hurry back to urge Achilles.
Who knows? With heaven's help I may move him,
and a friend's advice is always worthwhile."

    Then he departed, while the Achaeans
stood steadfast and, though their numbers were more,
couldn't drive back those determined Trojans—
nor could the enemy shatter their ranks
and batter a path to the ships and sea.
As a plumb line makes a ship's timber straight   410
in the sure hands of some master craftsman
who has his skill from astute Athena,
thus that battle was evenly balanced.
And while their armies struggled here and there,
Hector stormed toward Telamonian Aias.
They met by a ship—and Hector couldn't
best his opponent and set it aflame,
nor could the Danaans repel his attack.
Now Aias hurled a spear, hit Caletor
on the chest as he brought fire toward that ship,   420
so he fell thundering and dropped his torch.
But when gallant Hector saw his cousin
lying in the dust beside that black ship,
he roared among his assembled armies:
"You Trojans and Lycians and Dardanians,
we need you desperately over here:
rescue our Caletor so the Danaans
can't steal his armor and despoil the corpse!"

    Next he flung his spear at giant Aias,
but it missed, hit Lycophron, Mastor's son,   430
who came to Aias' court from Cythera
after murdering a man in his homeland:
that dreadful weapon pierced under his ear
as he stood by Aias—so he tumbled
down from the stern, and strength abandoned him.
Aias shuddered and called to his brother:

"Teucer, look here! our dear friend has fallen,
Mastor's brave son, who came to our palace
and was given honors like our parents—
Hector killed him. Well, what about that bow   440
great Phoebus Apollo once gave to you?"

   So Teucer hurried up to his brother
holding that glorious bow and a quiver
and showered arrows upon the Trojans.
First to fall was Cleitus, Peisenor's son,
comrade of illustrious Polydamas,
as he held his thundering horses' reins.
He'd driven where combat raged the worst
to help gallant Hector—but soon he too
met the evil doom no man could deny: 450
that arrow shattered the nape of his neck,
and he fell to earth as his horses reared,
rattling an empty chariot. But quickly
Polydamas saw and ran to grab them,
let his comrade Astynous take the reins,
commanding him to keep those horses near,
and went back to battle with the foremost.

   Next Teucer took out another arrow
for Hector, who would have warred no more
if his bitter missile had hit its mark.   460
But Zeus protected that son of Priam
and stole great fame from intrepid Teucer,
broke the string of his redoubtable bow
as he drew it, so the bronze-tipped arrow
skittered off sideways—and he let it fall.
Teucer shuddered and called to his brother:
"Damn it all, our plans are being ruined
by some god, who smashed the bow from my hand
and shattered that brand-new string I put on
just this morning, good for many arrows."   470

   Telamonian Aias replied to him:
"Forget your archery, my dear fellow,
since it seems some god has gone against us—

take a spear, sling a shield on your shoulder,
and go back to battle with our vanguard!
We may be losing now, but we'll never
surrender the ships without a struggle!"

So Teucer left that great bow in his tent,
slung a massive shield over his shoulders,
set on his head a colossal helmet   480
whose horsehair crest bobbed horribly above,
took a formidable spear in his hand,
and hurried to stand beside huge Aias.

But when Hector saw Teucer's bow useless,
he roared among his assembled armies:
"You Trojans and Lycians and Dardanians,
be men, my friends, remember your courage,
for I have seen with my very own eyes
Zeus broke the bow of some Achaean lord.
It's easy to tell which side Zeus supports   490
when he grants one army the upper hand
and weakens the one he has abandoned
as he abandoned those Achaeans now!
We'll fight our way to the ships together,
and if any man's slain, let him lie there—
no shame to die defending your homeland!
At least you will save your wife and children
and your possessions, when the enemy
set sail for their own dear homeland at last!"

His words gave a surge of strength to them all,   500
and on the opposite side Aias cried:
"Shame, you Achaeans! We're sure to perish
if we don't stand steadfast in self-defense!
After Hector takes the ships, do you plan
returning to grassy Argos on foot?
Don't you hear how that son of Priam roars
for his people to set our ships aflame?
He isn't calling them to dance but war!
Now only one strategy can save us:
close combat hand-to-hand and man-to-man.   510

better live or die once and for all
than see our forces depleted slowly
by an army far inferior to ours."

His words gave a surge of strength to each man.
Then Hector slew Schedius, while huge Aias
dispatched Antenor's son Laodamas,
glorious commander of the foot soldiers,
then lord Polydamas struck down Otus,
comrade of Meges, Epeian leader,
who saw his friend fall, raced out for revenge,   520
but lord Polydamas leapt to one side
since Apollo wouldn't let him perish,
so that spear pierced Croesmus' chest—and he fell
thunderously, and Meges took his armor.
Then another warrior came running up,
dauntless Dolops, a cousin of Priam,
deadly to oppose on the battlefield,
and thrust a dangerous spear at Meges,
but he was saved by his weighty armor—
tight-fitting plates which Phyleus had brought   530
from Ephyrë near the river Selleis,
where king Euphetes gave it to him as
a bulwark in bitter battle, and now
it also kept his son from destruction.
But Meges jabbed his own keen-pointed spear
at the crown of Dolops' crested helmet,
severing that horsehair plume, so it spun
into the dust, all bright with scarlet dye.
Thus they continued their relentless duel,
while great Menelaus came unnoticed   540
to help his comrade Dolops, hurled a spear
that hurtled through Meges' chest from behind
and flew on—and he fell facefirst to earth.
They hurried to seize his brilliant armor,
while brave Hector bellowed to his kinsmen:
first Hicetaon's redoubtable son
Melanippus, who had pastured cattle
in Percotë far from any danger,

but when the Achaeans came in their ships
he returned to Troy, received high honors,   550
was kept in Priam's palace like a son—
and magnificent Hector called to him:
"Giving up, Melanippus? You don't care
those Danaans have slain your own dear cousin?
See them taking his resplendent armor?
Now no more battling with arrows alone—
we'll fight hand-to-hand till we kill each man
or they take Troy and massacre us all."

   Then off he strode, and that warrior followed.
Meanwhile huge Aias urged his armies on: 560
"Be men, my friends, remember your honor,
don't shame yourselves before your companions!
Men with self-respect have a chance to live,
but cowards come to a miserable end!"

   Though they were eager enough already,
this made them even more: they fenced the ships
with a hedge of bronze, as Zeus roused their foes.
Now Menelaus called Antilochus:
"Dear fellow, you're our youngest warrior here,
but none are quicker or more courageous   570
so I'd like to see you down some Trojan."

   Then he drove back onto the battlefield,
and Antilochus leapt out with a spear,
his eyes darting round. Those Trojans cowered
as it flew through the air—no miss! it hit
Hicetaon's brave son Melanippus
by the nipple as he rushed to combat,
so he thudded down, and night took his eyes.
Antilochus leapt on him like a hound
attacking some fawn a hunter has shot   580
as it left its lair, and it collapses—
thus, Melanippus, he came to plunder
your armor. But Hector saw him and stormed
straight for him. Antilochus didn't wait,
took to his heels immediately, ran off

like a beast of prey who's done some mischief,
killed a hound or a herdsman by his cows,
and escapes before a crowd has gathered.
As he hurried away, the Trojans roared
and showered deadly missiles after him—   590
so he turned round after reaching his men.

Then, more like ferocious lions, those Trojans
rushed toward the ships, obeying lordly Zeus,
who made them steadily stronger, confused
the Danaans, sent them running in panic,
since now he planned victory for Hector
till an enemy ship was set ablaze
and Thetis' presumptuous prayer might be
fulfilled. Meanwhile Zeus waited patiently
to see the glimmer of a burning ship—   600
then he intended to drive those Trojans
back toward the town and help their enemies.
Now he continued spurring Hector on,
though that man was already battle mad,
furious as spear-slinging Ares or flame
that rages through tangly woods in the hills.
So the foam came around his mouth, his eyes
blazed beneath those brows as he battled on,
and the helmet shook terribly about
Hector's head, he had such a defender,   610
Zeus, who gave him alone among them all
glory and fame, since his life would be brief
now Pallas Athena was bringing near
the day of his doom at Achilles' hands.
Again and again he attacked those ranks
where men were massed thickest, their armor best,
but couldn't break through, for all his fury:
they stood steadfast like a wall, like a cliff
that towers beside the gray sea to meet
a turbulent onslaught of shrill wind blasts   620
and swollen billows rolling over it—
so those Achaean spearmen held their ground.
Brilliant as fire, Hector leapt among them

as when ferocious waves engulf a ship
under wind-driven clouds and leave it all
covered with foam, while a terrible gale
bellows against the mainsail and the crew
shudder in fear, for they just escape death:
thus those Achaean warriors were dismayed.
He fell upon them like an awful lion   630
on cows that graze in their marshy meadow
accompanied by a novice herdsman,
who knows little of protecting cattle
and trots beside the foremost or the last,
but that lion plunges right in the middle
and gobbles up one as the others flee—
thus Zeus and Hector made those Achaeans
panic. First Hector slew Periphetes
Copreus' son, who had taken messages
between king Eurystheus and Heracles—   640
that miserable Copreus had a son
preeminent in war and the footrace
and cleverest of the Myceneans,
but he fell next before gallant Hector.
Turning to retreat, he tripped on the rim
of his great shield, that bulwark in battle,
and toppled backward, so the bright helmet
clattered horribly about his temples.
Hector saw him fall and came running out
and, right among his comrades, stabbed his chest   650
to take his life. For all their grief, his friends
couldn't help, Hector terrified them so.

Now they moved back till the outermost ship
surrounded them, but the Trojans came on
and those Danaans retreated still farther,
till they finally stood beside their tents
in one compact mass, ashamed and afraid
to scatter, and summoned their companions.
Veteran Nestor cried most fervently,
begging them in the name of their parents: 660

"Be men, my friends, remember your honor
in the eyes of your comrades! Don't forget
your home and parents and wives and children,
whether they be living or dead today—
yes, for the sake of those dear absent ones,
stand fast, I implore you, retreat no more!"

His words gave a surge of strength to each man,
and Athena raised the mist from their eyes
so the light came flooding in from both sides—
from the ships and from that hideous battle. 670
Thus Hector's hosts could be seen by them all,
by those who stayed behind without fighting
and those who battled about the black ships.

But Aias was no longer satisfied
to stand apart with the other Danaans,
strode back and forth on the decks of those ships
swinging a great pike used in sea fighting,
jointed with rings, thirty-three feet in all.
As a skilled equestrian harnesses up
a team of four superlative horses 680
to drive them thundering toward a city
along a straight highway, while passers-by
stare amazed as he leaps unerringly
from horse to horse and they gallop onward—
thus giant Aias moved from deck to deck
with mighty strides, voice rising to the sky
as he roared horribly for his warriors
to save their ships. Nor did haughty Hector
remain with his hordes of armored Trojans,
but as an eagle swoops on flocks of birds 690
that feed beside some river's grassy bank—
wild geese and herons and preening-necked swans—
so Hector darted for a dark-prowed ship
as cloudgathering lord Zeus hurled him on
with a powerful hand and roused his people.

Then combat broke out by the ships again—
and you might have thought two fresh armies stood

facing each other, so fiercely they fought.
And as they struggled, those Danaans despaired
of ever escaping sheer destruction,   700
while the Trojan warriors hoped fervently
to burn the ships and slay their defenders:
such were their thoughts as they met in battle.
Now Priam's son brave Hector seized the stern
of a seafaring ship that had brought Protesilaus
to Troy but didn't take him home again,
while around it Trojans and Danaans surged
together in tumult of close combat—
no battling with bows from a distance, but
they fought man-to-man with one intent,   710
wielding their whetted axes and hatchets
and enormous swords and double-edged spears,
while many a splendid black-hilted blade
was slashed from warriors' hands or shoulder straps
and all the dark earth was aflow with blood.
Meanwhile Hector held the stern of that ship
by its figurehead and called his people:
"Bring our torches, good men, bellow war cries!
I know great Zeus will grant us recompense
today: we'll take these Danaan ships that came   720
to bring us troubles because our elders
refused to let me fight off the landing
when I demanded it in assembly.
But if glorious Zeus made us fools before,
this time he's backing our Trojan people."

   So they stormed out with even more fury.
And Aias couldn't stand before those spears:
expecting death each moment, he moved back
on that seven-foot gangplank, left the deck.
There he stood on the watch and battered off   730
Trojans who tried to bring their torches up
as he roared horribly to his armies:
"Friends, Danaan warriors, servants of Ares,
be men, my friends, remember your courage!
You believe we've reinforcements behind

or a better wall that will save our skins?
No fortified cities of ours lie near,
no fresh spearmen to turn the tide of war—
but we stand alone on the Trojan plain,
sea smack at our backs, far from our dear homes,   740
salvation only in our own strong arms!"

Meanwhile he furiously wielded his spear.
And whenever a Trojan ran forward
carrying a torch at Hector's orders,
huge Aias met him with a savage thrust—
and there before the ships he brought down twelve.

Book Sixteen: Patroclus' Doom

Achilles' squire Patroclus enters battle, is slain by Hector.

Thus they battled on about that beaked ship,
while Patroclus approached prince Achilles
weeping like the spring of a murky stream
that pours its waters over some sheer cliff.
Gallant Achilles was struck with pity
and addressed him in agitated words:
"Why all these tears, Patroclus, like some girl
who begs her mama to be taken up,
tugs at her tunic and won't let her go
till she cuddles her blubbering baby—   10
that's the way you are today, Patroclus.
Have you news for our warriors or for me?
Something you heard from our home in Phthia?
They say old Menoetius is still alive,
Peleus still rules our Myrmidon people—
if they were dead, we'd have reason to weep.
Or are you mourning for our Achaeans
who perish because of their arrogance?
Speak up, tell me—don't keep it a secret."

So, great Patroclus, you groaned and answered: 20
"Ah, you incomparable Achilles, don't
be angry—our people have such troubles.
The warriors who were our finest before
are lying beside the ships disabled:
brave Diomedes wounded by a bow,
Odysseus and Agamemnon by spears,
and an arrow in Eurypylus' thigh.

Our physicians are trying to heal them—
but *you* are incurable, Achilles.
May I never hold such a grudge as this!   30
What name will you leave to posterity
if you let those Achaeans die like dogs?
Cruel commander, your parents weren't Thetis
and our great monarch Peleus—the gray sea
and sheer cliffs bore you, you're so pitiless.
But if an oracle has warned you off
or something your mother told you from Zeus,
send me instead with our other warriors,
and we may save our people even yet.
I'll go in your armor so those Trojans   40
may take me for you and turn to retreat,
and our Achaeans will have some respite
when they need it—they've had little enough!
Our fresh men could batter their weary ones
back to the city from the ships and tents."

Thus he implored him—the fool! It would be
his own foul death and fate that he begged for.
And, profoundly moved, Achilles answered:
"My dear Patroclus, what are you saying!
I know no oracle that worries me,   50
my mother has told me nothing from Zeus.
But I tell you it makes me indignant
when a man wants to rob someone his peer
and take back a gift, since he has more power—
an awful thing, after all I've suffered.
As battle booty, the Danaans gave me
a lady I captured, my rightful share,
but she was stolen by that son of Atreus
Agamemnon, treated me like a tramp.
Very well, we'll let bygones be bygones—   60
no use in feuding forever, though I
never expected to give up my grudge
till the tide of war had reached my own ships.
You take my incomparable armor
and lead our Myrmidons into battle,

now dark clouds of Trojans surround our camp
and our people stand with only the sea
at their backs, little space remaining,
while that whole city comes out to attack
fearlessly, since they don't see my helmet   70
glitter nearby. Yet their bodies would fill
the streams as they flee if Agamemnon
would treat me decently, as it should be.
Now no dangerous Diomedes stays
raging with his spear to save our people,
and Agamemnon's damned voice isn't heard
but only the bellows of murderous
Hector and his tumultuous Trojans
everywhere, and they're winning the war.
Go out on the battlefield, Patroclus,   80
and drive them off, don't let them burn the ships
and prevent our people from going home.
Now listen carefully while I tell you
how you can win me honor and glory
from all the Achaeans, so they'll return
that lovely girl, with glorious presents too.
After you have made them retreat, come back—
though Zeus himself should grant you victory
do *not* continue combat without me:
I'll have much less distinction if you do.   90
You mustn't let victory go to your head
and try to storm the walls of their city,
or a god may descend from Olympus
to stop you, Apollo loves them so well—
yes, after you've rescued the ships, return
and leave the others to battle it out.
O Zeus and Athena and Apollo,
if only death would take every Trojan
and all the Achaeans except us two,
so we alone might win that sacred town!"   100

    Thus they stood in earnest conversation
as Aias couldn't stand before those spears:
Zeus's will and the Trojan bombardment

drove him back. His helmet rang horribly
on his temples as again and again
cheekpieces were battered, his left shoulder
wearied carrying that shield, although they
couldn't cave it in with all their onslaughts.
So his breath became shorter, streams of sweat
poured over his body, and he had no   110
time to rest, as woe piled on woe for him.

   Now tell me, you Muses on Olympus,
how those Danaan ships were first set aflame.

   Hector came swinging an enormous sword,
which shattered Telamonian Aias' spear
near its point at the very end, and he
was left with a useless weapon whose head
flew far through the air and banged to the ground.
When giant Aias saw it, he shuddered
at the gods' great works, with majestic Zeus   120
ruining his plans and backing the Trojans—
and he lumbered off. So they put a torch
to that high-beaked ship and set it ablaze.

   As fire swirled over its stern, Achilles
slapped both his thighs and shouted in alarm
"Away with you now, my dear Patroclus!
I see flames racing up beside our ships.
Once our fleet is taken, we've no escape!
Take my armor, quick, and I'll call our men."

   Now Patroclus donned his brilliant armor: 130
strapped on his legs those elegant shinguards
so handsomely adorned with silver bands,
put over his chest the sturdy breastplate,
that star-strewn armor of prince Achilles,
slung on his back a silver-studded sword
and afterward his formidable shield,
then set on his head a well-wrought helmet
whose horsehair crest bobbed horribly above,
took two colossal spears which fit his palm
but not that huge, stout, ponderous weapon   140

of Peleus' son, which no other Danaan
could wield in combat except Achilles—
an ashwood spear Cheiron gave his father
from Pelion's peak to carry in combat.
Next Patroclus ordered Automedon,
whom he honored most after Achilles
and trusted most in the turmoil of war,
to harness up those thunderous horses
Xanthus and Balius, swift as the winds,
which the West Wind fathered to a harpy　　　　　　　150
grazing near Oceanus—and beside them
Patroclus tied the stallion Pedasus,
Achilles' spoil from Eëtion, and he,
though only mortal, paced immortal steeds.

　　Then Achilles ranged through his people's tents,
ordering them to arm. Like ravenous
wolves with unspeakable rage in their hearts
who kill a great horned stag among the hills
and rip it up, so their jaws are bloodied,
then race in packs to springs of dark waters　　　　　160
and their slender tongues lap the dark waters'
face, as they belch out blood and gore but still
remain undaunted with their bellies full:
thus those Myrmidon lords and commanders
came rushing round valiant Patroclus.
And among them, Peleus' son Achilles
marshaled their chariots and armored warriors.

　　Fifty were the ships that Zeus's beloved
Achilles had brought to Ilios, each
with fifty of his comrades at the oars,　　　　　　　170
while five trusted men were his lieutenants,
and he mightily commanded them all.
One regiment was led by Menestheus,
son of the river spirit Spercheius,
borne by Peleus' daughter Polydora
to that numinous water deity,
but in name to Borus, a mortal lord,
when he paid a great fortune to wed her.

And another was led by Eudorus,
natural son of Phylas' dear daughter   180
Polymelë, who made even Hermes
enamored as he saw her in the dance
for clamorous Artemis the archer,
so he crept to her room and lay with her
secretly, and she bore a glorious son,
Eudorus, superb in racing and war.
After Eilythyia, goddess of birth,
had brought him into the sun's brilliant light,
that stalwart son of Actor, Echecles,
took her in marriage for a high bride price—   190
while old Phylas reared Eudorus with care
and cherished him like his very own child.
But the third group was led by Peisander,
best Myrmidon in managing the spear
except for Achilles' brave companion,
and aged Phoenix commanded the fourth,
Laerces' son Alcimedon the fifth.
After Achilles had marshaled those ranks
behind their lords, he addressed them sternly:
"Myrmidons, remember how you boasted   200
over the Trojans while I was angry.
You so much loved to reproach me, saying:
'Cruel son of Peleus, raised on bitter gall,
keeping your people here beside the ships!
Well, we'll take our fleet and sail for home
if you stay in such a dreadful temper.'
You'd scold me just that way—and here it is:
the glorious work of war you so adored!
So if you have some valor, show it now!"

His words gave a surge of strength to them all,   210
and they stiffened up their ranks still tighter.
Like boulders set side by side for a wall
to protect some house from the whistling winds,
their shields and helmets were jammed together,
helmet pressing helmet, shield shield, man man,
and the horsehair crests on their helmets met

as they moved their heads, they were packed so tight,
and before them stood two lords, Patroclus
and Automedon, with one thought only:
leading Myrmidons to war. Achilles   220
went to his quarters and opened a chest
of well-worked wood, which silverfoot Thetis
had set on his ship and filled with tunics
and windbreaking cloaks and woolly carpets.
There he kept a cunningly fashioned cup
from which no man but himself could drink wine
and no god but Zeus received libations.
He took this cup and cleansed it with sulfur,
rinsed it in a stream of rippling water,
washed his hands carefully and dipped out wine.   230
Now he poured libations before his tent
and, gazing toward heaven, appealed to Zeus
"O Pelasgian Zeus, lord who lives afar
ruling Dodona among the Selloi,
your priests with unwashed feet who sleep on earth,
just as you heeded my prayer before
and ravaged their armies to honor me,
fulfill my supplication once again.
Though I'm staying here beside our ships,
I have sent my comrade into combat   240
with many warriors. Glorify him, Zeus,
grant him more valor so even Hector
learns if my squire's really formidable
or only dangerous whenever I
stand at his side in desperate battle.
But after he drives them off from the ships
let him return to our own camp unscathed,
with his armor and hosts of followers."

   Cronos' son Zeus heard that fervent prayer
and granted a part but denied the rest: 250
permitted him to drive war from the ships
but refused the return he requested.

After he finished libation and prayer
Achilles went in, put his cup away,
and emerged again, extremely eager
to watch the awful events of combat.

Now those armored warriors round Patroclus
hurried out to battle the Trojan hordes,
came pouring forth like a swarm of hornets
mischievous boys have disturbed with their sticks,   260
angering them for the sheer fun of it—
fools! they make trouble for very many:
just let some wayfarer come passing by,
and out they fly unquenchably furious
to defend their nests and their little ones—
thus those indomitable Myrmidons
poured from their ships in a constant furor.
Now Patroclus roared to his followers:
"Comrades of magnificent Achilles,
be men, my friends, remember your courage,   270
bring honor to this son of Peleus, best
in all our armies, with his valiant squires,
so illustrious Agamemnon may learn
he was mad to insult his best warrior."

His words gave a surge of strength to each man,
and they stormed forward in a mass, the ships
echoing horribly with their war cries.
And when the Trojans observed Patroclus
appear with his squire in brilliant armor,
they were shaken, their battalions wavered,   280
because now they thought Peleus' glorious son
had made up his quarrel with Agamemnon—
and each peeped round for a way to escape.

First Patroclus hurled a glittering spear
where enemy warriors were massed thickest
by the stern of Protesilaus' ship,
hit Pyraechmenes—Paeonian leader
from Amydon by the streams of Axius—
on his right shoulder, and he fell backward

groaning, as his people panicked round him,   290
Patroclus had given them such a scare
when he brought their gallant commander down.
Thus he drove them off, quenched the crackling flames.
The Trojans moved off from that burned-out hulk
with horrible roars, while the Danaans poured
among the ships in persistent furor.
As Zeus Thunderlord moves the murky clouds
away from a towering mountain range
and everywhere appear peaks and headlands
and valleys, till the firmament bursts forth: 300
thus after the Danaans had quenched those flames
they rested a bit, though war wasn't done,
the Trojans weren't yet wildly retreating
from Achilles' people by the beaked ships
but faced them still and gave ground grudgingly.

Then man slew man as the battle scattered.
Menoetius' powerful son Patroclus
flung a great spear, hit Areilycus' thigh
as he turned to flee; that point pierced his leg
and shattered the bone, and he fell facefirst.   310
Next Menelaus ran to stab Thoas
on the chest by his shield, and he collapsed.
And as Amiclus stormed out, Meges' spear
pierced his buttock where the very thickest
muscles are, tore it terribly open,
so dismal darkness enfolded his eyes.
Then Nestor's swift son Antilochus thrust
a weapon through Atymnius' side, and he
tumbled down facefirst. His brother Maris
came running to lunge at Antilochus   320
over the body, but Thrasymedes
met him as he came, stabbed unerringly
so that brazen spear ripped the arm away
from its muscles, shattered the shoulder bone,
and he thudded down and night took his eyes.
Thus, bested by two brothers, those two lords
sank to Erebus—Sarpedon's comrades,

sons of Amisodarus who had reared
the raging Chimaera, scourge of many.
Next Oileus' son nimblefoot Aias stormed   330
toward Cleobolus, who had tripped over,
drove a sword in his neck, stole all his strength—
the blade warmed with blood, and over his eyes
surged dark death and irresistible fate.
Now Lyco and mighty Peneleos
flung their spears at one another but missed,
then met with swords: Lyco slashed his helmet,
but that weapon broke apart at the hilt,
while Peneleos swung ferociously,
severed his neck with a stroke, so only   340
skin held it, his head hung, and he collapsed.
Next Meriones overtook Acamas
mounting his chariot, stabbed his right shoulder,
and he fell as his eyes misted over;
while Idomeneus hurled unerringly,
hit intrepid Erymas in the mouth,
and that spear pierced the brain, split his white bones—
so his teeth were loosened, while both eyes filled
with blood that spurted from mouth and nostrils
as he lay agape in death's murky cloud.   350

Now every Danaan leader slew a man:
as ravenous wolves attack lambs or kids,
pick them from flocks that a foolish shepherd
lets scatter on the hills—and when they see,
they quickly seize the helpless little ones—
thus those Danaans fell on the enemy,
who only thought of disgraceful retreat.

Huge Aias was furious to hurl his spear
at Hector, but that son of Priam stayed
away and, shoulders covered with the shield,   360
observed those whirring arrows, thudding spears.
Though he knew the tide of battle had turned
he stood steadfast, tried to save his comrades.

As clouds scurry over a murky sky
from Olympus when Zeus prepares a storm,
a panicky clamor came from those ships
when the Trojans were routed. Great Hector's
horses carried him off, left his other
warriors jammed together before the moat,
but many of those magnificent steeds   370
broke the yoke pole and galloped away free,
while Patroclus followed with awful shouts,
raging incessantly. Roar of retreat
filled all the plain when they scattered, dust
rose under the clouds as coursers thundered
back to the city from those ships and tents.
Where most were retreating, Patroclus drove
with hideous bellows, and many fell
under his axles as their chariots spilled.
Over the moat leapt his swift-hooved horses—   380
immortal steeds the gods gave Peleus—
and onward he drove looking for Hector,
but that warrior's chariot carried him off.
As a tempest batters the whole black earth
some day of autumn when Zeus pelts his rain
pell-mell in a rage against those people
who give false judgments in the marketplace,
drive justice out and scorn the gods' vengeance,
then swollen rivers flow in their full flood
and torrents tear great gorges from the hills   390
while they hurtle down with a mighty roar
toward the dark sea, ruining fine farmlands:
those Trojan horses came with such a roar.

When Patroclus had cut off the hindmost
he hemmed them back toward the ships, wouldn't let
those frenzied men enter the town, but there
between ships and river and lofty wall
slaughtered them all, took revenge for many:
first caught Pronous with a deadly spearcast
where the chest was left bare beside his shield,   400
so he crashed down—and Thestor, Enops' son,

was killed the next, as he crouched cowering
on his chariot, dazed with terror, dropped
the reins. Patroclus thundered up to thrust
a spear in his right jaw, which pierced the teeth
and dragged him down like an angler who sits
on some craggy headland to haul a fish
with line and shiny hook from the waters—
thus that gleaming spear dragged him down agape
and flung him on his face as life left him. 410
When Eurylaus stormed out, Patroclus
struck him with a boulder that split the skull
inside his heavy helmet so he fell
facefirst as death enveloped him—and next
Epheus, Amphoterus, Epaltes,
Damastor's son Tlepolemus, Echius,
Erymas, Evippus, Polymelus
tumbled to earth under Patroclus' spear.

But when Sarpedon saw his companions
fleeing before that son of Menoetius 420
he bellowed among his massed battalions:
"Shame on you, Lycians! Why such a hurry?
Well, I'll meet him myself, and we shall learn
the identity of this maniac
who has slain so many fine men of ours."

He leapt from his chariot in full armor—
and, when he saw him Patroclus did too.
Then as two bent-beaked crooked-taloned vultures
battle with strident cries on some high peak,
they rushed at each other, roaring wildly. 430
But Cronos' son Zeus was struck with pity
and said to Hera, his sister and wife:
"Now it seems my beloved Sarpedon
is doomed to die at prince Patroclus' hands.
And it's difficult to decide indeed
whether I should snatch him away alive
and have him brought to the land of Lycia
or let him be slain by Menoetius' son."

That gentle-eyed queen Hera answered him:
"You dreadful fellow, what are you saying!   440
A mere mortal, doomed long ago by fate,
and you plan to save him from death again?
Well, we other gods will never approve!
And let me assure you of one thing more:
if you should send Sarpedon home alive
some other immortals may also wish
to rescue their own dear sons in battle.
Many men fighting by Priam's city
are sons of gods, who could all be envious.
But since you so much adore Sarpedon,   450
let him die on the battlefield today
at the hands of powerful Patroclus—
and after his life and soul have left him
tell Death and sweet Sleep to take him away
till they reach the rich land of Lycia, where
his brothers and kinsmen will bury him
properly with a mound and a pillar."

So the father of gods and men obeyed,
scattered bloody raindrops over the earth
to honor his dear son, whom Patroclus   460
would soon be slaying far from his homeland.

After they came very near each other
Patroclus hurled at Sarpedon but hit
his magnificent squire Thrasymelus
in the lower groin, so his limbs grew limp.
Sarpedon hurled too but missed Patroclus,
hit the right flank of his horse Pedasus,
who, gasping his life away, neighed and fell
moaning in the dust as his soul flew off.
Those others reared, their yoke creaked and the reins   470
tangled, since the third horse lay in the dust—
but Automedon warded off danger,
drew the mighty sword that hung by his side,
cut the dead steed loose from its harness, then
the others straightened, strained their reins taut
as those two men met again in combat.

Once more lord Sarpedon hurled a spear, which
hurtled over his opponent's shoulder
and left him unscathed. But prince Patroclus
flung yet another spear with deadly aim,   480
struck Sarpedon's chest by his beating heart,
and he fell like an oak or a poplar
or a tall pine tree cut down in the hills
to make the timber for a sailing ship—
so he lay a-sprawl before his horses,
groaning and clutching at the bloody dust.
As a lion enters the herd to kill
an arrogant tawny bull with the cows
and he dies bellowing in that beast's jaws,
thus the Lycians' illustrious commander   490
writhed in death and called to his companion:
"Glaucus, dear fellow, now more than ever
you'll need all your finesse with the spear—
make horrible war your only desire.
First order our Lycian lords and leaders
to defend the body of Sarpedon
and you too protect me with your weapon.
Shame and disgrace for you all your days
if they steal this armor and strip my corpse
while I lie here by the Achaean ships!   500
Stand steadfast, I say, summon all our men!"

Even as he spoke, death covered his eyes.
Next Patroclus put a foot on his chest,
tore the weapon out, and his bowels followed—
so spear and life left him at the same time.
Those Myrmidons seized his snorting horses
as they galloped off without their chariot.

Then Glaucus felt a sickening sorrow,
agonized he couldn't help his comrade,
pressed his bloody arm tightly, tormented   510
by the wound lord Teucer had inflicted
as he tried to storm the Achaean wall,
and prayed to that archer god Apollo:

"Listen, prince, in the rich land of Lycia
or in Troy, since you hear prayers everywhere
when men are troubled as I am today.
This wound is hurting me terribly, pains
shoot up and down my arm, the oozing blood
cannot be staunched and my shoulder's numb—
impossible to even hold a spear!   520
And they've slain our great leader Sarpedon,
a son of Zeus, who didn't help his child.
Now heal my wound, far-worker Apollo,
ease these dreadful pains, concede me courage
so I may summon all my battalions
and join the struggle for Patroclus' corpse."

    Phoebus Apollo granted his prayer,
made pain cease immediately, dried the blood
in his gaping wound, gave him bravery.
And Glaucus rejoiced when he recognized   530
that glorious god so quickly heard his prayer.
First he called his Lycian lords and leaders
to defend the body of Sarpedon,
then mightily strode through those Trojan hordes,
found Polydamas and brave Agenor,
looked for fiery Hector and Aeneas
and addressed them in agitated words:
"Hector, you forget your faithful allies
who are sacrificing their lives for you
so far from their homes, though you won't save them.   540
There lies our Lycian leader Sarpedon,
a man who ruled our people with justice,
brought down by Ares and Patroclus' spear.
But stand beside him, friends, do your duty,
or they'll despoil him, mutilate his corpse,
those Myrmidon spearmen are so furious
for the warriors we slaughtered by their ships."

    Heart-wrenching grief took the Trojans, since he
had been their bulwark on the battlefield,
although a foreigner, and brought along   550
hordes of formidable Lycian warriors.

And raging to save Sarpedon, they came
after great Hector, while the Achaeans
were led by shaggy-hearted Patroclus,
who summoned those two warriors named Aias
"Now hold your ground, my dear Aiantes,
as you've always done or even better!
There lies the Lycian who scaled our wall first:
Sarpedon. Now we'll disgrace his body
by stripping it bare, and slaughter any   560
companions of his who dare defend it."

   But they were keen for combat already.
When both sides had assembled in full force,
Trojans, Lycians, Myrmidons, Achaeans
met man-to-man about Sarpedon's corpse,
roaring as their armor crashed together,
while Zeus drew dismal darkness over all
to make that dreadful struggle even worse.
First the Trojans drove their opponents back
by slaying a Myrmidon commander,   570
intrepid Epeigeus, Agacles' son,
who had ruled the rich city Budeium
before—but after he slew a kinsman,
he begged Peleus and Thetis for refuge,
and they sent him with their son Achilles
to terrible combat in grassy Troy.
As he seized Sarpedon's armor, Hector
struck him with a stone, split the skull open
inside his heavy helmet so he fell
facefirst, and mighty death enveloped him.   580
Patroclus felt frantic grief for his friend,
swept through the enemy ranks like a hawk
that scatters jays and starlings before it—
thus, Patroclus, you stormed at those Trojans
in a fury over your fallen friend
and struck prince Sthenelaus on the neck
with a boulder that crushed both sinews there.
So Hector and his foremost ranks gave ground—
and far as the flight of a javelin

some spearman throws to show his strength in games   590
or in war, when enemies press him hard,
those Achaeans battered the Trojans back.
But Glaucus, Lycian lord and commander,
turned around to dispatch great Bathycles,
Chalcon's dear son who had lived in Hellas,
where he was the wealthiest Myrmidon—
as he hurried in hot pursuit, Glaucus
spun quickly round, pierced his chest with a spear,
and he fell thundering. The Achaeans
grieved to see it, while those Trojans rejoiced   600
and swarmed about him, though their opponents
came resolutely pressing on and on.
Next Meriones killed an armored Trojan,
Onetor's son Laogonus, priest to Zeus,
glorified by the people like a god:
thrust a spear under jaw and ear, so life
left his body and dread darkness took him.
And now Aeneas hurled at Meriones,
who advanced under cover of his shield,
but he was keeping a close watch and dodged   610
by ducking down, so the long spear landed
upright behind him, butt end a-tremble,
but there at last its fury was ended—
that weapon sank quivering in the earth
though a powerful arm had propelled it.
Lord Aeneas roared exasperated:
"You dance well, Meriones, or else my spear
would have ended your dancing forever!"

    And Molus' son Meriones bellowed back:
"For all your courage in war, Aeneas,   620
you won't defeat every Danaan leader
who meets you in war—you too are mortal!
If you get a taste of my spear, I'm sure
your strength and valor won't help you at all—
I'll gain a triumph and Hades your soul."

But gallant Patroclus admonished him:
"No time for chatter today, Meriones!
Listen here, dear fellow—these taunts and boasts
won't make them abandon Sarpedon's corpse.
Tall talk's for assemblies, but now we need   630
unending battle more than heaps of words!"

Then off he strode, and that warrior followed.
As woodcutters' axes in a valley
clatter so the echo resounds afar,
thus earth reverberated with that crash
of bronze and leather and shimmering shields
when they stabbed with swords and double-edged spears.
And no man present would have recognized
Sarpedon's corpse, with spears and blood and dust
completely covering him from head to foot.   640
They swarmed all about his body like flies
which buzz and murmur through a farmer's pens
in springtime, when milk overflows the pails—
thus they swarmed about that body. But Zeus
didn't turn his bright eyes from those warriors
and, as he observed them, meditated
much about the dying of Patroclus,
whether great Hector should slay him as well
in the combat over Sarpedon's corpse
and tear the bronze armor from his shoulders   650
or whether he should slaughter even more.
Finally Zeus decided it was best
to let Achilles' redoubtable squire
drive Hector and his Trojan battalions
back toward the town while taking many lives—
that son of Cronos made Hector afraid:
he leapt on a chariot, called his people
to retreat, knowing Zeus had tipped his scales.
The Lycians too didn't stand—they panicked,
every man of them, when they saw their lord   660
struck down and lying among the corpses
with many others fallen above him.
So those Danaans took Sarpedon's armor,

with its shimmering bronze—and Patroclus
ordered his comrades to carry it off.
Now Zeus Cloudgatherer told Apollo:
"Hurry, dear Phoebus, cleanse the clotted blood
from Sarpedon's wound, then take him away
and bathe him in the river far from war,
anoint him well, and clothe him handsomely.   670
And after that our nimble messengers,
the twin brothers Sleep and Death, will quickly
carry him to the rich land of Lycia,
where brothers and kinsmen will bury him
properly with a mound and a pillar."

     Apollo obeyed his father's command
and strode from Ida to the battlefield,
where he wafted Sarpedon gently off
and bathed him in the river far from war,
anointed him well, clothed him handsomely,   680
then gave him to two nimble messengers,
the twin brothers Sleep and Death, who quickly
set him down in the rich land of Lycia.

     And roaring to his horses, Patroclus
relentlessly pursued the enemy—
fool! if only he'd obeyed Achilles,
dark death would not have taken him that day.
But no man has a will like mighty Zeus,
who routs the bravest, steals their victory
easily, though he sent them out himself—   690
and now he roused Patroclus to battle.

     Which warrior did you bring down first, which last,
Patroclus, when the gods called you toward death?
Adrastus first, Autonous, Echeclus,
Megas' son Perimus, Melanippus,
with Elasus, Moulius, and Pylartes,
one after the other, while the rest fled.

     And Troy would have fallen that very day
thanks to Patroclus, who raged everywhere,
but Apollo stood on the city wall: 700

trouble for him, the Trojans' salvation.
Three times Patroclus stormed a parapet,
three times powerful Apollo smashed him
back with a jab of those immortal hands.
But when he flung himself up the fourth time
Phoebus Apollo bellowed horribly:
"Get down, Patroclus! It isn't fated
for that town to be taken by your spear
or the spear of Achilles, your better."

So Patroclus moved some distance away   710
avoiding the anger of Apollo.

Hector reined his team at the Scaean Gates,
stood thinking whether to rejoin battle
or summon his people within the wall.
And as he pondered, Apollo came near
in the form of a sturdy hard spearman—
Asius, lord Hector's maternal uncle,
brother to Hecabe and Dymas' son,
who came from Phrygia by the Sangarius.
With this man's appearance, Apollo cried: 720
"Hector, why did you leave war? Don't do it!
If only I were mightier than you
you'd soon be sorry for this cowardice!
Now drive your chariot straight for Patroclus,
and Apollo may help you bring him down!"

Then back he went, a god in men's combat.
And Hector ordered Cebriones to lash
his horses forward, while Apollo plunged
into the crowd to confuse those Danaans
and give their opponents a great triumph.   730
Priam's son Hector ignored the others
and drove his horses straight for Patroclus.
But that warrior leapt down from his chariot,
in his left hand a spear and in the right
a gleaming jagged boulder, which he held,
fingers round it, and hurled with all his might,
hit Hector's companion and charioteer

Cebriones, natural son of Priam,
between the eyes as he held the reins.
That boulder drove both brows together, broke   740
the bone, so his eyes tumbled to the dust
at his feet—and like a sea diver, he
plunged to the earth, as the soul left his bones.
Then, formidable Patroclus, you roared:
"Oh, how easily this fellow can leap!
Why, if he were a sailor on the sea
he could hunt oysters, fill many bellies
by diving overboard even in storms
the way he just leapt from his chariot now.
It seems the Trojans have divers too!"   750

   Whereupon he rushed at Cebriones' corpse
like a tawny lion wounded on the chest
whose fury finally brings his ruin:
thus, Patroclus, you pounced on Cebriones.
But Hector too leapt down from his chariot,
and they met by that corpse like two lions
struggling for a dead stag in the mountains,
famished, determined to battle it out:
in such a rage those two came together—
Menoetius' son Patroclus and Hector—   760
furious to slash each other with the spear.
First Hector seized the head of Cebriones,
Patroclus a foot, and all those others
surged together in desperate combat.
As East Wind and South Wind struggle away
in a mountain glade, shaking the forest—
oak trees, ash trees, and delicate dogwood
that batter their long branches together
with an awful clatter of smashing wood:
so those warriors leapt at one another   770
murderously, and neither side would retreat.
Around Cebriones' corpse fell many spears
and feathered arrows whizzing from bowstrings,
while many boulders boomed against those shields—

and there in a great swirl of dust he lay
mightily mighty, forgetful of war.

   As long as the sun stood astride the sky
spears took a terrible toll on both sides,
but just when farmers unyoke their oxen
those Achaeans turned the tide of battle,   780
dragged the body from among those roaring
Trojans, tore the armor from its shoulders,
while Patroclus attacked in a frenzy.
Three times he rushed out furious as Ares,
with awful shouts, three times brought nine men down.
As he came storming forward the fourth time,
then, Patroclus, came the end of your life:
Phoebus Apollo met you in combat,
a terrible god but invisible,
he was hidden in such a murky mist.   790
First Apollo smashed Patroclus' broad back
with the flat of a hand, so his head spun
and the helmet fell to earth from his head
and rolled clanging under the horses' hooves,
its incomparable plumes all besmeared
with blood and dust. Never once until then
had dust stained that magnificent helmet
while it protected the head and fine brow
of prince Achilles—but now Zeus gave it
to Hector, though his own destruction neared.   800
That mighty spear was completely shattered
in Patroclus' hands, his tasseled shield
tumbled to the ground with its oxhide strap.
And next Apollo cut his breastplate loose.
So he stood there terror-struck, paralyzed,
in a daze—and from close behind, a spear
was rammed in his back by a Dardanian:
Panthous' son Euphorbus, best of his age
in battle and running and horsemanship,
who had already slain twenty Danaans   810
the first time he came to learn about war,
and now he hurled at you, brave Patroclus,

but couldn't bring you down. And he withdrew
that spear, hurried among his men, afraid
to face his opponent, even unarmed.
Patroclus, overcome by the god's blow
and that weapon, reeled back toward his comrades.

  But when Hector saw gallant Patroclus
staggering from the battlefield wounded
he rushed through the ranks, stood right beside him,   820
and thrust a brilliant spear into his groin,
and—bitter grief for the Danaans!—he fell.
As a lion overwhelms a tireless boar
in wild contention on some mountaintop
about a springlet where both wish to drink,
till the panting boar can struggle no more:
thus that slayer of many, Patroclus,
lost his own life to Priam's son Hector,
who bellowed exultantly over him:
"Patroclus, you wanted to sack our town   830
and make the graceful Trojan women slaves,
carry them home on your seafaring ships—
fool! before these women, Hector's horses
gallop into war. Yes, I protect all
our battle-hardened Trojans with my spear,
while you'll be eaten by the vultures here!
Ha, your Achilles didn't help you now!
I suppose he said when he sent you out:
'Patroclus, you terrible fellow, don't
come back to the ships until your weapon   840
has bloodied murderous Hector's tunic.'
And you still believed it would be easy!"

  Then, gallant Patroclus, you cried feebly:
"This time, Hector, the boast is yours! You won
because of powerful Zeus and Apollo,
who battered the armor from my body,
but if twenty men like you had met me
my spear would have taken care of them all.
My conquerors were fate and Leto's son
and Euphorbus—you were only the third.   850

And let me assure you of one thing more:
you too won't be living long—already
death and powerful fate are at your side
so Achilles will kill you very soon."

Even as he spoke, death enfolded him—
and the soul flew from his corpse to Hades
bewailing its fate, leaving strength and youth.
And Hector bellowed to the lifeless man:
"Patroclus, why babble about my death?
Who knows if Thetis' son prince Achilles   860
may not lose his life to my own spear first!"

So Hector tore the bronze spear from that wound
and shoved him back to the earth with his foot,
then raced wildly after Automedon,
formidable Achilles' glorious squire,
who was carried off by his great horses,
immortal steeds the gods gave Peleus.

Book Seventeen: Menelaus' Feats

Seesaw struggle for Patroclus' body. Achilles' horses mourn Patroclus.

But brave Menelaus, Ares' beloved,
didn't fail to see Patroclus fallen.
He strode out in all his brilliant armor
and stood above him like a mother cow
lowing over a calf, her firstborn one—
so Menelaus bestrode that body,
shield and dangerous spear held before him,
ready to slay any man who came near.

   Nor did great Euphorbus fail to notice
Patroclus lying dead—he hurried up   10
and bellowed fiercely to Menelaus:
"Ho, you turbulent tough son of Atreus,
leave the body and my bloody booty!
No other warrior was ahead of me
stabbing gallant Patroclus in battle,
so let me have the fruits of my triumph
or soon I'll be taking your own life too."

   Then, very much vexed, Menelaus replied:
"Oh, father Zeus, how ugly is boasting!
There's no such fury in leopards or lions   20
or horrid wild boars, whose rage is greatest
when they race through the woods on a rampage,
as in these dangerous sons of Panthous!
But even Panthous' son Hyperenor
had a short life after mocking at me,
declaring I was the weakest Danaan—
he didn't go home on his own two feet

to delight his dear wife and his parents.
And you shall die too, if you only dare
meet me in war! Better scamper away,   30
don't do anything so dangerous, or
you may learn too late how foolish you were!"

 Panthous' son Euphorbus roared in reply:
"Now, brave Menelaus, you'll pay the price
for killing Hyperenor, boasting how
you widowed a wife in her bridal bed
and brought his parents unspeakable grief.
But their mourning would have an end if I
take your head and your terrible armor
and place them in Panthous' and Phrontis' hands.   40
Well, let's battle it out—and soon we'll see
if you or I have a glorious triumph!"

 And he hurled a spear at Menelaus,
whose sturdy shield deflected it. And then
that incomparable son of Atreus
stormed forward with a prayer to father Zeus
and, as Euphorbus shrank back, stabbed him hard
at the base of his throat, an open place—
and through his tender neck that spearpoint pierced,
so his armor boomed as he crashed to earth.   50
And blood soaked his hair, fair as the Graces',
those braids held tight by gold and silver bands.
As some farmer rears an olive sapling
in a lonely place where springs bubble up,
and swayed by the breath of all the breezes,
its milky blossoms begin to burgeon,
but suddenly a raging storm appears,
rips it up by the roots, and lays it out:
thus Panthous' son spear-slinging Euphorbus
was slain and despoiled by Menelaus.   60
As a fierce lion bred in the mountains
grabs the finest cow of a grazing herd—
he snaps her neck with his powerful teeth,
then gobbles up the blood and all the guts
in a mad frenzy—while hounds and herdsmen

raise a racket round him but do not dare
come near, for pale fear leaves them paralyzed:
so none of those Trojans were brave enough
to face that illustrious Menelaus.
Then he would have won Euphorbus' armor,   70
but silverbow Apollo begrudged it
and took the shape of Ciconian Mentes
to approach Priam's redoubtable son
and address him in agitated words:
"You can't catch Achilles' horses, Hector!
No mortal on earth would find it easy
to handle that team of turbulent steeds
except for their master, a goddess' son.
But now their dangerous Menelaus
stands over Patroclus—he slaughtered our   80
magnificent companion Euphorbus."

   And back he went, a god in men's combat,
as Hector's heart darkened with dismal grief—
and he gazed along those ranks of warriors,
saw one man seizing booty, another
sprawled on the ground, blood gushing from a wound,
and strode out in all his brilliant armor
bellowing wildly, like Hephaestus' flame
unquenchable. Menelaus heard it
and, deeply troubled, muttered to himself: 90
"Oh my, if I abandon this armor
and Patroclus, who lies here for my sake,
our people will be rightfully angry,
while if I face the Trojans all alone
for fear of disgrace, they'll surely trap me—
and here they come now, Hector and his hordes!
But what a lot of nonsense I'm saying!
When a warrior tries to take on someone
backed by a god he's asking for trouble,
so no matter if our people see me   100
flee from Hector: he has help from heaven.
Ah, if only I could find huge Aias
I'd go back to battle beside him though

the gods themselves opposed us—we alone
might save that body for prince Achilles."

   As Menelaus stood there pondering,
Hector led his Trojans steadily on—
so he moved away from Patroclus' corpse
with many a backward glance, like a lion
driven from a fold by farmers and hounds   110
with their spears and shouts, so a chilly rage
fills him as he reluctantly retreats:
thus blond Menelaus left Patroclus.
But when he reached his men, he turned around
and looked for great Telamonian Aias.
Soon he spied that leader on the left flank,
urging his comrades to enter combat,
Apollo had made them so afraid.
Menelaus stood beside him and cried:
"Aias, dear friend, let's rescue Patroclus!   120
We can bring his body for Achilles
though Hector has the armor and it's bare."

   Telamonian Aias was deeply stirred
and strode to battle with Menelaus.
After Hector seized Patroclus' armor
he dragged him off to decapitate him
and toss the body to the Trojan dogs—
but Aias came near with his towering shield.
So Hector retreated into the throng,
mounted his chariot, and ordered his men   130
to take the elegant armor away.
Now Aias hid Patroclus with that shield,
stood over him like a lion above cubs
who leads his young through the forest and meets
a horde of hunters, stiffens haughtily,
and lowers dark brows to cover his eyes:
thus Aias bestrode Patroclus' body
as fiery Menelaus stood nearby,
sorrow filling his heart more and more.

Whereupon that Lycian leader Glaucus   140
scolded Hector with a ferocious scowl:
"You're handsome, Hector, but not much in war!
So you won all your fame by skulking back!
But better consider how your people
can save the city alone: we Lycians
won't be battling the Danaans anymore
around your town, such little thanks we've had
for all the fighting we did to please you!
How will you ever protect plain warriors
when you left your companion Sarpedon   150
and let the enemy take his armor!
He helped you and your city while he lived,
but you couldn't keep the dogs from his corpse.
Now if the Lycians obey my commands
we'll go on home and leave you to your doom.
Your people could use some of that courage
which strengthens spearmen who enter combat
to defend their homes against enemies—
then Patroclus' corpse would soon be in Troy!
If this warrior were off the battlefield   160
and lay in Priam's prosperous city,
the Danaans would surely be giving back
Sarpedon's armor and his body too,
since Patroclus served their most distinguished
commander with his many followers.
But you ran at the mere sight of Aias,
didn't dare stay face him eye-to-eye,
he's so far superior to you in war!"

And gallant Hector answered him, scowling
"Ah, Glaucus, what a lot of gibberish!   170
Friend, I considered you the cleverest
in all wealthy Lycia, but now it seems
you haven't a bit of sense in your head,
saying I am afraid to face Aias.
Thunderous battle chariots can't scare *me*.
Yet no man has a will like mighty Zeus,
who routs the bravest, steals their victory

easily, though he sent them out himself.
Just stay beside me now, and soon you'll see
if I cower back all day, as you say,   180
or stop many of those mad Achaeans
from battling about Patroclus' body."

    Then Hector bellowed among his armies:
"You Trojans and Lycians and Dardanians,
be men, my friends, remember your courage
while I put on Achilles' battle gear,
my booty when I brought Patroclus down."

    So flashing-helmeted Hector hurried
from the turmoil of war and quickly came
to where his companions, not far away,   190
were taking that booty toward the city.
There apart from war they traded armor:
Hector left his for safekeeping and he
received Achilles' immortal armor,
which the gods had once presented Peleus,
who gave it to his son in his old age—
though the son didn't grow old wearing it.

    But when father Zeus saw him from afar
donning Achilles' glorious battle gear,
he shook his head and murmured to himself: 200
"Poor fellow, you aren't thinking of your death,
but it's near. You won immortal armor
of a lord you fear, as many men do,
by slaying his valiant, kindly comrade
and tore the brilliant bronze from his body
wantonly. Well, you shall triumph today—
but in exchange for this you won't return
to give Andromache that fine armor."

    Thus Cronos' son spoke and bowed his dark brows,
made the armor fit Hector perfectly,   210
while Ares entered him to fill his limbs
with fury. He strode among the allies
with awful bellows, showed himself to all
in the armor of Peleus' peerless son.

So Hector strode back and forth, haranguing
Mesthles, Glaucus, Medon, Thersilochus,
Asteropaeus, Chromius, Hippothous,
Phorcys, and the soothsayer Ennomus,
addressing them in elevated words:
"Now hear me, countless clans of our allies!   220
It wasn't because I lacked followers
I called you from the cities all around
but so you might save our wives and children
from these savage battle-mad Achaeans.
Therefore I've impoverished my people
to reward you with generous presents.
Now turn your faces toward the enemy
and live or die—that's the game of battle.
If any spearman brings Patroclus' corpse
back to our Trojans and drives Aias off,   230
he may keep half the ransom for himself
and have vast honors like my very own."

  So they raised their spears and stormed straight forward
toward the Achaeans, extremely eager
to drag the body from giant Aias—
fools! he took many men's lives beside it.
Telamonian Aias called his comrade:
"Ah, Menelaus, I know we'll never
escape alive if we battle alone!
But I worry less for Patroclus' corpse,   240
which soon shall be glutting the Trojan dogs,
than I do about my own life and yours
with this dark cloud of battle coming near:
Hector, and our ruin's plain to see.
So call our commanders to help us here!"

  Atreus' son Menelaus obeyed him
and bellowed among those massed battalions:
"My heroic friends and fellow warriors,
who drink at the cost of Atreus' sons
Agamemnon and Menelaus, and rule   250
by authority from thunderlord Zeus,
I can't possibly see all our leaders

with awful battle raging everywhere,
but come unsummoned—imagine the shame,
Patroclus a toy for the dogs of Troy!"

Oileus' son nimble Aias heard his voice,
hurried toward him through the battle turmoil,
followed by Idomeneus and his friend
Meriones, peer of bloodthirsty Ares,
and as for the rest, who could name each man   260
that came behind them to join the struggle?

Then Hector stormed forward with his warriors.
As waves break into currents at the mouth
of a surging river while, all around,
headlands resound as the salt sea slams them,
those Trojans came roaring. But the Danaans
stood by Patroclus' corpse with one intent,
made a hedge of their shields to protect him,
and around their helmets Cronos' son poured
thick mist, having loved Patroclus before   270
while he was alive and Achilles' squire,
so now Zeus would not have him torn by dogs
and roused his comrades to defend his corpse.

First the Achaean spearmen were battered
back from his body, though not a warrior
fell before the onslaught of those Trojans
who dragged Patroclus' corpse away, and they
retreated a bit till they were rallied
by Aias, their bravest and handsomest
except for Peleus' redoubtable son: 280
he strode through the Trojans strong as a boar
who whirls around and easily routs
hounds and lusty hunters in a valley—
thus illustrious Telamonian Aias
easily scattered those Trojan hordes
who stood before Patroclus determined
to take his body and gain great glory.

As Pelasgian Lethus' son Hippothous
was dragging that body off by the feet,
a sword belt tied around both the ankles,   290
for Hector's and the Trojans' sake—though soon
he too met the doom no man could deny—
Telamonian Aias lunged fiercely out
and stabbed at the cheekpiece of his helmet
so his horsehair-crested armor shattered
when that formidable spear found its mark,
and his brains burst out along its socket
all bloody. His strength left him as he let
the foot of great Patroclus tumble down
and fell on the corpse facefirst, very far   300
from fertile Larissa, where his parents
had little joy in rearing him, so brief
his life became, cut short by Aias' spear.

And Priam's son Hector hurled at Aias,
but he was keeping a close watch and dodged
just barely—so that weapon hit Schedius,
far the noblest Phocian, who ruled many
from his palace in famed Panopeus,
relentlessly bore through his collarbone,
came out beside the base of his shoulder,   310
and his armor clanged as he crashed to earth.

Next Telamonian Aias stabbed Phorcys
as he stood over Hippothous' body,
shattered the breastplate, and his bowels burst out—
and he fell to the earth, clutching at dust.
So Hector and his foremost men gave way
while the Danaans roared, dragged those bodies off,
seized their fine armor, and moved on forward.

And then they would have sent those Trojan hordes
streaming helplessly into their city   320
and won more glory than Zeus had decreed,
but archer Apollo roused Aeneas,
taking the shape of aged Periphas,
a herald who had once served his father

Anchises in their Dardanian palace.
With this man's appearance, Apollo cried:
"Aeneas, how can you guard steep Ilios
if the gods oppose you? Yet I knew some
who trusted in their power and valor
though mighty Zeus himself was against them.   330
And now that son of Cronos backs our side,
yet even so your people have panicked."

   And Aeneas peered at the speaker's face,
recognized archer Apollo and cried:
"Hector and you other Trojan captains,
what a disgrace if the Danaans send us
streaming helplessly into our city!
But some immortal god who just stood here
declares Olympian Zeus is on our side,
so forward, lords! They won't have it easy   340
carrying Patroclus' corpse to their ships!"

   Then he rushed out far before the others,
and they rallied to face the enemy.
First Aeneas flung his weapon and hit
Leocritus, friend of Lycomedes,
who grieved exceedingly to see him fall,
ran very near and hurled a brilliant spear,
which struck Hippasus' son Apisaon
over his liver and loosened the knees
of that most accomplished Paeonian chief   350
after illustrious Asteropaeus,
who grieved exceedingly to see him fall
and hurried forward furious for revenge—
but no use! their shields made a solid wall
as they stood by Patroclus with their spears.
Aias strode among them giving orders:
none of them should abandon that body
and no man battle far before the rest
but all stand fast to fight at close quarters—
thus he commanded them, as murky blood   360
drenched the earth, and warrior after warrior
fell from among those relentless Trojans

and the Danaans, since they too weren't unscathed
though far fewer of their people perished,
they planned so well to protect each other.

  So they fought on like fire, and you'd never
have thought the world had a sun or a moon,
such impenetrable mist had settled
over those men who fought round Patroclus.
Meanwhile the other Trojans and Achaeans   370
continued battling intermittently
beneath the bright glare of sunlight—nowhere
a cloud over mountains and all the plain—
and avoided the enemy's weapons,
keeping out of range. Those in the middle
were plagued by mist and battle as that bronze
took a heavy toll of their best. Yet two,
famed Thrasymedes and Antilochus,
didn't know Patroclus was dead, believed
he stayed alive and fought with the foremost,   380
for they were posted far out on the flank,
as Gerenian Nestor had commanded
when he called them to combat from their ships.

  Now all day long relentless contention
raged most horribly, sweat and weariness
came pouring over knees and shins and feet
and arms and eyes as they battled away
about the body of Achilles' squire.
As a man commands his servants to stretch
a magnificent bull's hide soaked in fat—   390
then, standing in a circle, they take it
and tug, till moisture leaves and fat enters
while that hide is stretched to the maximum:
thus both sides tugged the body back and forth
in a narrow space, those Trojans trying
to drag it toward their town, the Achaeans
toward the buoyant ships, about them battle
so fierce even Ares or Athena
would not have found it too sweet for their needs.

Thus Zeus made labor for men and horses   400
over Patroclus' corpse that day. But still
Achilles knew nothing of his friend's death,
that battle was raging so far away
under the city walls. He hardly dreamed
Patroclus was dead, believed he'd return
alive and unscathed, never thought his squire
would sack the town without him, or with him—
his mother had often assured him that
when she brought him news about Zeus's plans
but never told him of this great grief: 410
his very dearest friend dead in battle.

The rest of them pressed round Patroclus' corpse,
came together in horrible carnage.
One or another Achaean would say:
"Friends, no glory gained in cowering back
beside our beaked ships—better, far better,
for dark earth to devour us all here
if we let the enemy drag that corpse
into their town for a glorious triumph!"

And one or another Trojan would say: 420
"Friends, though we're fated to die together,
stand steadfast in your places, don't give way!"

These words made them even more determined.
So they struggled on, and an iron roar
rose to brass heaven through the restless air—
but Achilles' swift horses at the rear
were weeping, when they learned their charioteer
had been battered to the dust by Hector.
Diores' valiant son Automedon
lashed them again and again with his whip   430
and spoke to them gently and roared curses,
but they wouldn't go toward the ships and sea,
nor would they gallop toward the battlefield,
stayed motionless as a stone monument
that marks the grave of a man or woman—
thus they stood stock-still beside their chariot,

heads riveted downward. And lukewarm tears
poured from beneath their eyelids as they mourned
their dear charioteer, drenched the glossy manes
that drooped beneath their breastbands on both sides.   440
Cronos' son Zeus pitied them in their grief
and shook his head and murmured to himself:
"Poor things, why did we give you to Peleus,
a mortal, when you two are immortal?
So you might have sorrows with humankind?
Yes, nothing's more miserable than man
of all that breathes and creeps on the earth's face.
But your fine chariot cannot be ridden
by illustrious Hector—I won't let him.
Isn't it enough he has the armor?   450
I shall pour more strength in your hearts and hooves
so you may take Automedon away
while the Trojans have a mighty triumph
and reach the beaked ships amid much carnage
as the sun drops down and strong darkness comes."

   Then he breathed fury into those horses,
who shook the dust from their manes and quickly
brought the chariot onto the battlefield.
Grieving for his friend, Automedon rode
like an eagle who swoops on flocks of geese,   460
and easily galloped out to attack
and easily fled those roaring Trojans.
But none of their warriors fell before him,
since he rode alone and couldn't manage
a spear and a chariot at the same time.
At last he was spied by a companion,
Laërces' lordly son Alcimedon,
who drove very near him and demanded:
"Automedon, which god has fuddled your wits?
You must have gone plain out of your mind,   470
riding alone among the enemy
though your dear friend's dead and haughty Hector
swaggers around in Achilles' armor."

Diores' son Automedon replied:
"Alcimedon, what man can be your peer
driving those fiery immortal coursers
except for our beloved Patroclus
while he lived? But now death has taken him.
So you hold the whip and shimmering reins
while I dismount to meet them in combat."   480

Then Alcimedon leapt on the chariot,
quickly seized the whip and shimmering reins,
and Automedon sprang down. But Hector
called to Aeneas when he saw those two:
"Ho, Aeneas, you canny counselor,
here come those horses of prince Achilles
thundering to war with puny charioteers.
If you're ready to help me, I am sure
we can capture their team—those two won't dare
stay around here when they see *us* coming!"   490

And Anchises' son Aeneas obeyed.
Now they rode straight forward behind those shields
of dry tough oxhide overlaid by bronze,
with them Chromius and gallant Aretus,
raging in relentless expectation
to slay more warriors and take their horses—
idiots! they could never escape unscathed
from Automedon, who prayed to great Zeus
so his murky heart was filled with fury
and quickly cried to his dear companion: 500
"See here, Alcimedon, keep our horses
breathing on my neck, because it seems
that dreadful Hector won't be satisfied
till he rides behind Achilles' fine team
and slaughters us both and routs our people
or somebody makes an end of him first."

He called the Aiantes and Menelaus:
"Lords and commanders of the Achaeans,
leave your bravest warriors here to defend
Patroclus' body from the enemy   510

and come save two men who are still alive!
We're being attacked by their most dangerous—
Hector and formidable Aeneas!
It's all in the lap of the gods—so I
shall fling my spear and let wise Zeus decide."

Automedon hurled that ashwood weapon,
which hit Aretus' finely crafted shield,
bored through its shimmering metal and then
straight through his girdle and into his groin.
As a farmer takes a broadax in hand   520
to stab a sturdy ox behind the horns,
cutting the muscles, and it plunges down,
so gallant Aretus leapt and collapsed
with that spear quivering in his midriff.
Now Hector hurled at prince Automedon,
but he was keeping a close watch and dodged
by ducking down, so that long spear landed
upright behind him, butt end a-tremble,
and there at last its fury was ended.
Next they would have battled it out with swords,   530
but the two Aiantes came to part them
in answer to their companion's call,
so Hector and Aeneas and Chromius
retreated before those two Achaeans,
left magnificent Aretus lying
dead. And Automedon, swift Ares' peer,
tore off that armor and bellowed his boast:
"Now we'll grieve somewhat less for Patroclus,
though the man I killed isn't half as good!"

He seized that bloody booty and set it   540
on the chariot, then mounted, hands and feet
bloodied like a lion that devours a bull.

And once more there around Patroclus' corpse
came awful combat roused by Athena,
whom Zeus had sent to help the Achaeans
since now he planned a new course for that war.
As Cronos' son hangs a gleaming rainbow

from heaven as a portent of battle
or a chilly tempest that makes mortals
stop work on earth and terrifies their flocks,   550
so Athena, wrapped in a gleaming cloud,
urged the Achaean armies to advance.
First she approached Atreus' son Menelaus
with the shape and voice of aged Phoenix
and murmured insistently in his ear:
"Hang your head, Menelaus! A disgrace
to see Achilles' faithful companion
torn by the dogs beneath that Trojan wall!
Stand steadfast, I say, summon all your men!"

    And Atreus' son Menelaus answered: 560
"Granddad Phoenix, if only Athena
would protect me again, I'd be ready
to defend our Patroclus to the end,
his death has touched me so very deeply.
But Hector rages like horrible flame
and won't give up now he knows Zeus backs him."

    Then green-eyed Athena was delighted
he named her first of all the immortals
and flooded more strength into his body,
poured in him the fury of a horsefly   570
that persists in biting although each time
it's brushed away, since it loves to taste blood—
thus she filled his murky heart with courage,
and he ran to Patroclus, hurled his spear.
Now Eëtion's son Podes stood nearby—
a brave, rich man much honored by Hector
for his good fellowship at the table—
and that dreadful weapon hit his girdle
as he turned to escape, drove straight through it,
and he fell thundering. So Atreus' son   580
dragged his body back to the Achaeans.

    Next Phoebus Apollo approached Hector
disguised as Phaenops, who had come to him
from Abydus and they swore amity.

With this man's appearance, Apollo cried:
"Hector, which Danaan will ever fear you
again? You scurried off from Menelaus,
who was helpless before, but now he's won
Patroclus' body and slain your comrade
glorious Podes, our bulwark in battle."   590

   A black cloud of sorrow covered Hector,
and he strode forward in brilliant armor
while Zeus took his magnificent aegis,
enfolded Mount Ida in murky mist,
and brandished that storm cloud, and thunder rolled
to show the Trojans that they would prevail.

   First to retreat was brave Peneleos:
he stood steadfast facing the enemy
when Polydamas came near, hurled a spear
which grazed his shoulder, cutting to the bone.   600
And Hector stabbed Alectryon's son Leitus
on the bare wrist, put him out of action—
and off he ran, peering anxiously round,
since he couldn't do battle with a spear.
While Hector was driving in hot pursuit,
Idomeneus' spear hit his breastplate and
snapped off at the socket, as the Trojans
roared. Then Hector hurled at Idomeneus
as he stood on a chariot, but missed him,
hit Meriones' illustrious charioteer   610
and trusty boon companion, Coeranus,
for Idomeneus brought no chariot there,
and the Trojans would have had a great triumph
but Coeranus drove his speedy team near
to rescue him from certain destruction
and lost his own life to Hector's weapon—
it bored into his neck under the ear,
tore his teeth out by the roots, pierced his tongue.
So he fell from the chariot, dropped the reins.
Now Meriones bent to gather them up   620
and called his companion Idomeneus:

"Hop up here, man, and we'll drive to the ships!
It's plain to see our people are losing!"

And prince Idomeneus lashed the horses
back toward the ships in an awful panic.

Aias and Menelaus knew very well
Zeus had given the Trojans victory,
and Telamonian Aias cried out first:
"Menelaus, any idiot can see
Zeus himself is supporting the Trojans!   630
Their spears hit home no matter who throws them—
that son of Cronos must keep them on course—
while ours never even come near their goal.
Now we'd better make some sensible plan
for rescuing the body and returning
alive to delight our comrades in arms
who watch us anxiously because they fear
Hector's murderous fury won't be stopped
till he sets our Achaean ships ablaze.
If only we could find some messenger   640
to give our Achilles the news—he still
has not been told his dear companion's dead—
but I can't see a man to do the job
with this damned fog over all our armies.
Ah, father Zeus, set us free from the fog,
grant us clear sky, let us see with our eyes!
Have us die if you wish—but in the light!"

And the Father pitied him as he wept,
immediately scattered mist and darkness
till sun shone over the whole battlefield.   650
Telamonian Aias called his comrade:
"Menelaus, hurry and try to see
if our Antilochus is still alive
and order him to inform Achilles
his friend, his very dearest one, is dead."

And Atreus' son Menelaus obeyed,
went away as a lion leaves a stable,
weary of tormenting hounds and farmers

who stay on the watch all night to save
their fattest cattle—and, greedy for meat,   660
he creeps by, but no luck! a rain of spears
showers upon that hapless animal,
torches are hurled, and he slinks back furious,
then angrily lopes away at daybreak:
so Menelaus left Patroclus' corpse
most unwillingly, afraid his people
would cease defending it in their defeat,
called Meriones and the two Aiantes:
"Heroic Achaean lords and leaders,
remember poor Patroclus' kindliness!   670
While he lived he was courteous to all,
but death and murky fate have taken him."

And Atreus' son Menelaus went off,
peering about like that eagle they say
sees keenest of any winged creature:
from high in the air he observes a hare
cowering under a leafy bush, then
swoops down to seize it, steals its tender life—
thus, Menelaus, your glittering eyes
ranged everywhere among those regiments   680
to see if Antilochus stayed alive.
And soon he detected him on the left,
urging his comrades to enter combat.
Blond Menelaus came near him and cried:
"Antilochus, my good fellow, I bring
terrible news! If only it weren't so!
Surely you've seen with your very own eyes
how that powerful god backs the Trojans,
and our most glorious warrior has fallen—
Patroclus, whom we miss enormously.   690
You run to the ships and tell Achilles
to come and save his companion's body
now great Hector has taken the armor."

Antilochus was stunned to hear these words,
stood motionless and speechless, as his eyes
flooded with tears and his voice became choked.

But he obeyed Menelaus' orders
and hurried away, leaving his armor
with Laodocus, who held his horses near.

Thus he went weeping from the battlefield   700
with sorrowful news for swift Achilles.
Then, lord Menelaus, you had no mind
to help the hard-pressed men Antilochus
left, though they sorely needed a leader.
He sent his squire Thrasymedes instead
and ran himself to defend Patroclus,
calling those two spearmen named Aiantes:
"I've sent that fellow as messenger
to swift Achilles, though I don't believe
he'll relent, for all his rage at Hector,   710
since he has no armor to wear in war.
Now we'd better make some sensible plan
for rescuing the body and returning
unscathed from those ferocious Trojan hordes."

Giant Telamonian Aias replied:
"Very true, my dear friend Menelaus,
so you and Meriones lift that body
and take it away, while we Aiantes
remain behind to hold off the Trojans
with one heart and one name, as we always   720
stand side by side on the battlefield."

Then they lifted that body from the ground
with a mighty heave—and behind them all
those Trojans roared to see it raised on high
and stormed straight for them, like hounds that bound
before the hunters at a wounded boar
and race ahead, raging to tear him up,
but when the boar wheels round in a fury
they scatter back terrified here and there:
so the Trojan hordes crowded after them   730
stabbing with swords and with double-edged spears—
but every time the two Aiantes turned

to make a stand, they paled, and no man dared
leap forward to contest Patroclus' corpse.

　Thus they hurried to carry that body
toward the buoyant ships—and about them war
raged fierce as fire that rises suddenly
to devour a town, and houses crumble
in a vast glare, where the wind sweeps it on:
so the Trojan spearmen and charioteers   740
followed those two in a constant furor.
Like some powerful mules who heave hugely
along a rugged mountain path to drag
a great tree trunk for a ship's mast, and they
struggle and strain as they come sweating on:
thus they brought Patroclus' corpse. Behind them,
those two Aiantes stood like a wooded
ridge that rises immense and impassive
to keep the tumbling torrents of winter
in check, send them flooding over a plain—   750
and all the river's might cannot smash it.
Thus those Aiantes held the Trojans back,
but still they followed, especially two:
Aeneas, Anchises' son, and Hector.
As a cloud of starlings or jackdaws fly
with frenzied cries when they happen to spy
a falcon bringing death to little birds,
the Argives left Hector and Aeneas
with frenzied cries, and lost all heart for war.
Many fine weapons fell about that moat   760
as they fled, and no end of combat came.

Book Eighteen: Achilles' Shield

Achilles appears on the battlefield, dismaying the Trojans.
Hephaestus makes him a new shield.

As they battled away like blazing flame
Antilochus brought Achilles the news.
He found that commander before his ships,
pondering over the events of war.
Deeply troubled, prince Achilles muttered:
"Ah, damn it all, why are our Achaeans
streaming madly back toward the ships again?
I only hope the gods won't bring those griefs
my mother once predicted when she said
that while I lived, the finest Myrmidon   10
would be leaving the bright light of the sun.
It must be our Patroclus has been slain—
the fool! I told him to put out the flames
but not to do battle with great Hector."

And as that son of Peleus stood brooding,
illustrious Antilochus approached him,
weeping hot tears, and delivered his news:
"Achilles, my dear friend, I have dreadful
news for you! I only wish it weren't so.
Our Patroclus is dead. They're fighting for   20
his body, and Hector has the armor."

Black clouds of grief enveloped Achilles—
and he took grimy dust in both his hands,
poured it over his head, streaked his fine face,
staining that fragrant tunic with ashes.
Mightily mighty, he lay in the dust

and tore and smeared his hair in a frenzy,
as the women he and Patroclus won
howled with lamentation and rushed around
incomparable Achilles, then all   30
beat their bosoms and fainted to the ground.
Antilochus stood weeping and wailing
and held prince Achilles' hands while he wept
so he wouldn't cut his throat with the knife.
Horribly he groaned—and his mother heard,
sitting in the sea's deeps by her father,
and shrieked. So the water nymphs rushed around,
daughters of Nereus who dwell in the deeps:
Flaucë, Thaleia, and Cymodocë,
Nesaea, Speio, soft-eyed Halië,   40
Cymothoë, Actaea, Limnoreia,
Melitë, Iaera, Amphithoë,
Doto, Proto, Pherousa, Dynamenë,
Dexamenë, Doris, Callianeira,
with Panopë, lovely Galatea,
Nemertes, Apseudes, Callianassa—
and Clymenë, Ianeira, Ianassa,
Maera, Orithyia, fair Amathea,
and other Nereids who dwell in the deeps.
The gleaming cave was full of them, and they   50
beat their breasts as Thetis led the mourning:
"Listen to me, sisters, so all may hear
what terrible troubles I have to bear.
Oh miserable me, unhappy mother
of a peerless heroic warrior, born
to command. He shot up like a sapling,
I reared him like a tree on a hillside
and sent him away with the high-beaked ships
to battle at Ilios—but I'll never
welcome him back to the halls of Peleus.   60
As long as he lives and sees the sun's light
he has grief, and I can't help him a bit.
But now I shall visit my child to hear
what cares have come on him so far from home."

So she left their cave, as the rest followed
weeping, and the murky sea waves parted
about them. When they came to grassy Troy,
they stepped out on the shore together
where the ships were clustered round Achilles.
His mother sat beside him as he groaned,   70
clasped her son's head with a piercing shriek and
addressed him in agitated words:
"My child, why these tears? Have you some trouble?
Speak up, tell me. All has been accomplished
by Zeus, just as you implored him to do:
the Danaans have been trapped at their ships' sterns
in desperate straits and need you greatly."

Achilles groaned heavily and replied:
"Yes, Mother, Zeus has fulfilled my prayer—
but what good is it with my dear friend dead,   80
Patroclus, noblest of my companions.
And his murderer, arrogant Hector,
has stolen all the elegant armor
the gods presented Peleus that same day
they married you to a mortal monarch.
If only you had stayed with the sea nymphs
and Peleus had taken a mortal bride!
All this was to bring you unending grief
for a son you'll never welcome home
alive. In any case, I wouldn't care   90
to go on living among men unless
my spear topples Hector into the dust
and he pays for our Patroclus' murder."

But silverfoot Thetis answered, weeping:
"Ah, my child, then you won't live long either,
because soon after Hector, you die too."

Mightily moved, swift Achilles replied:
"I want to die soon, since I failed to help
my comrade when they killed him—he fell far
from home, and I could not keep him from death.   100
Well now, since I too won't be going home

and couldn't save Patroclus or any
other comrades of mine Hector slaughtered
as I stayed idle here beside my ships
while no other Achaean is my peer
in awful war, though some are in debate—
oh, if gods and men could only end strife
and anger, which maddens even the wise
and, so much sweeter than trickling honey,
grows in the chest of a warrior like smoke,   110
as Agamemnon made me angry now.
Very well, we'll let bygones be bygones
and control our temper because we must.
But I shall find my dear friend's murderer,
Hector, and meet my own doom whenever
Zeus and the other immortals send it.
Even Heracles couldn't escape death
though thunderlord Zeus adored him dearly—
fate and Hera's anger defeated him—
and if the same fate awaits me, I too   120
shall lie dead. But now I'll have more glory,
and many Trojan or Dardanian dames
will be wiping tears from delicate cheeks
with both their hands, wailing incessantly,
and then they'll know I returned to battle.
Just don't try to hold me back—you cannot."

   The goddess silverfoot Thetis answered:
"Yes, my beloved child, it isn't wrong
to prevent your poor friends from perishing—
but your brilliant armor has been taken   130
by the Trojans. That arrogant Hector
swaggers around wearing it, though he won't
boast for long, since his own end approaches.
Now you stay away from the battlefield
until you see me coming here again—
and tomorrow at daybreak I'll return
with a splendid new set from Hephaestus."

Then she turned away from her son and spoke
to her sister Nereids, who waited there:
"Now leap in the broad bosom of the deep   140
and tell our father, Old Lord of the Sea,
all. Meanwhile I shall go to Olympus
and implore Hephaestus to give my son
a splendid set of glittering armor."

So they plunged beneath the waves of the sea
as silverfoot Thetis darted away
to seek that splendid armor for her son.

While she went to Olympus, those Danaans
clamorously retreated before Hector
till they came to the ships and Hellespont,   150
and for all their struggles, they couldn't save
the corpse of Achilles' squire Patroclus,
being so embattled by those warriors
with Hector, like flame in his bravery.
Three times Hector snatched at Patroclus' foot
eager to seize him, shrieking to his men—
and three times those ferocious Aiantes
battered him off. Haughtily he followed,
sometimes charging out to attack, sometimes
standing and roaring, but never moved back.   160
As a famished lion stays by a carcass
though the shepherds try to chase him away,
those two tough Aiantes couldn't drive
intrepid Hector from Patroclus' corpse.
And now he'd have seized it, won great glory,
but windfoot Iris sped to Achilles
from queen Hera, who sent her secretly
with orders for him to enter combat.
She stood beside him, murmured in his ear:
"Formidable son of Peleus, hurry,   170
rescue that body—they're fighting for it
beside the beaked ships amid much slaughter,
our side trying to defend Patroclus,
the Trojans contesting his helpless corpse,
and arrogant Hector leads their attack.

Now he wants to chop off Patroclus' head,
set it on a stake of his city wall!
Well, away with you—imagine the shame,
Patroclus a toy for the dogs of Troy!
Your disgrace if they should mutilate him!"   180

   Whereupon nimble Achilles inquired:
"Iris, which god commanded you to come?"

   Then windfoot Iris murmured in reply:
"Zeus's wife Hera sent me secretly
without informing that son of Cronos
or the other Olympian immortals."

   And Peleus' son swift Achilles answered:
"How can I enter battle? They've taken
that armor, and my mother said to stay
until I see her coming here again   190
with a splendid new set from Hephaestus.
I could wear no other man's battle gear
except for the shield of giant Aias,
but he's battling far out before them all
to defend the body of my dead friend."

   Then that goddess windfoot Iris declared:
"Yes, we know you lost your glorious armor,
but show yourself at the moat as you are.
Those Trojans might be afraid and retreat
so our Achaeans would have some respite   200
when they need it—they've had little enough."

   After saying this, Iris departed,
and Achilles leapt up, while Athena
threw her aegis over his huge shoulders,
set a golden cloud round his mighty head,
made shimmering flame blaze from his body.
As smoke rises skyward from a city
on a distant isle besieged by its foes,
and all day long they meet in dreadful war
before their city walls, but at sunset   210
their beacon fires flicker forth, and the glare

shines high and wide, a signal for neighbors
to hurry with their ships and rescue them:
thus that glitter rose from Achilles' head.
And he strode to the moat but stayed away
from the battlefield, as his mother said,
just stood and bellowed while Athena shrieked
from afar. Turmoil among the Trojans!
Like a trumpet call that rings out clearly
when murderous enemies surround a town,   220
so clearly resounded his clarion roar.
And as they heard Achilles' iron voice
they were dismayed, those flowing-maned horses
turned the chariots back in anxiety,
their drivers afraid of the steady flame
rising horribly over his helmet
when green-eyed Athena had made it blaze.
Three times Achilles roared over that moat,
three times the Trojans stirred in confusion,
and twelve of their finest warriors perished   230
by their own spears and chariots. Those Danaans
joyfully dragged prince Patroclus away
and set him on a stretcher, where his friends
mourned about him—and Achilles followed,
weeping hot tears as he saw his comrade,
mangled and torn by murderous weapons.
He had sent him off with his own horses
but never would welcome him back again.

   Then Hera commanded the tireless sun
to enter Oceanus before his time—   240
so darkness fell, and the Danaans rested
from the evil carnage of brutal war.

   And on the other side, the Trojans too
left the battlefield, unyoked their horses,
then met in assembly before they dined.
Everyone stood through that meeting: none dared
take seats, they were so greatly dismayed
now Achilles had come back to battle.
First to speak up was shrewd Polydamas,

a man who knew how to weigh all matters,   250
companion of Hector, born the same night,
but one was skilled in speech and one in war.
He addressed them with these well-measured words:
"Consider the matter, friends! As for me,
I believe we should enter our city
before one more night by the ships has passed.
While that man feuded with Agamemnon,
the Danaans weren't so difficult to face,
and I was ready to camp out here
hoping we'd take their ships that very day.   260
But now I most exceedingly fear
their Achilles, a man so furious he
won't stay on the plain where our battalions
meet in the frenzy of awful Ares—
he'll fight for our city and wives instead.
Better take refuge inside our walls,
since night has stopped Achilles for a while,
but if that warrior comes out tomorrow
and finds us here, we'll know him all too well.
Then we'll be glad to reach our city,   270
whoever can escape, and dogs will feed
on many of ours—I pray it's not so.
But if my advice meets your approval
we can camp at our place of assembly,
while those sturdy ramparts with their great gates
protect our prosperous metropolis,
and at dawn tomorrow we'll arm ourselves
to fight from the walls. Too bad for him then
if he tries to take our turreted town!
He'll head for the ships when his horses tire   280
driving back and forth beneath our walls;
he won't have the heart to battle his way
inside—our dogs will devour him sooner."

Hector answered, scowling ferociously:
"Polydamas, this doesn't please me a bit.
You want us to be cooped inside our walls!
Haven't we had enough of being shut in?

Our city was once famous everywhere
for its fabulous wealth of gold and bronze—
but all this is gone, our glorious treasures   290
traded to Phrygia and to Maeonia
since mighty Zeus became angry at us.
And just when Cronos' son supports our side,
lets me pen the Achaeans by their ships,
don't give us such stupid advice, you fool—
I'll never approve it, you may be sure!
But every man here should do as I say:
take supper among your own battalions
and stay wide awake and keep a keen watch—
and if you're worried for your possessions   300
divide them among our community
but don't present them to the Achaeans!
And at dawn tomorrow we'll arm ourselves
to begin bitter battle by the ships.
No matter if Achilles should appear—
too bad for him if he wants it, but I
shall never retreat before him. We'll meet
face-to-face, and one of us will triumph:
awful Ares often kills the killers."

Then those Trojan warriors roared approval—   310
idiots! Athena had stolen their wits:
they applauded Hector's ill-conceived plan
and none Polydamas', though his was right.
Thus they dined in their camp—but the Danaans
mourned all night long for lordly Patroclus.
And Achilles led the lamentation,
placing murderous hands on his comrade's chest
amid great groans, like some bearded lion
whose cubs are taken by a deer hunter—
and when he returns to find them absent   320
he follows the spoor through hills and valleys,
raging with fury to overtake him:
so noble Achilles moaned, and muttered:
"Oh, what stupidities I said that day
I reassured Menoetius in our halls,

promised his son would be returning home
with heaps of booty after I sacked Troy.
But Zeus will not fulfill all mortals' plans—
we'll redden the same earth with our blood
here in Ilios. I won't return either   330
to be welcomed back by aged Peleus
and my mother, but earth will hold me here.
Now, Patroclus, since I'll follow you soon
you will not be buried till I bring back
the head and armor of fiery Hector,
who has slain you, and cut twelve Trojans' throats
before your pyre to avenge your murder.
Meanwhile you can lie here as you are
but day and night be lamented with tears
by these Trojan and Dardanian ladies   340
we two have won on the field of battle
when we plundered their prosperous cities."

  Now gallant Achilles ordered his men
to place a pot on the fire and quickly
wash the clotted blood from Patroclus' corpse.
So they set a tripod on the embers,
poured water in, put faggots beneath it.
And flames surged up, the water became warm.
When it had boiled in that bright bronze vessel
they washed Patroclus, anointed his skin,   350
filled his wounds with an unguent nine years old,
then laid him out and wrapped him in linen
from head to foot, with a white robe on top.
So all night long Peleus' son Achilles
and the Myrmidons groaned for Patroclus—
but Zeus told Hera, his sister and wife:
"Well now, my love, you've had your way again,
brought Achilles back to battle. Indeed
these Achaeans must be your own children!"

  Then gentle-eyed queen Hera answered him: 360
"You dreadful creature, what are you saying!
Why, even a mortal, far inferior
to me in wisdom, will help someone else.

And I'm the highest Olympian goddess,
being both oldest and your wedded wife,
while you are lord of all the immortals,
so why can't I bring the Trojans trouble?"

   Thus those two immortals were conversing
as Thetis came to Hephaestus' star-strewn
eternal palace, Olympus' glory,   370
a building of bronze he had made himself.
She found him sweating before his bellows
while he hastily made twenty tripods
to stand about the walls of his palace
and fastened golden wheels beneath each one
so they could scurry of their own accord
to the gods' gatherings—a wondrous sight!
All were complete except for the handles,
which he was just attaching with rivets.
As he labored away most cunningly   380
the sea nymph silverfoot Thetis arrived.
She was greeted by shining-veiled Charis,
that glorious goddess Hephaestus had wed,
who clasped her hand and addressed her kindly:
"Dear Thetis, why have you come to our home?
What an unexpected pleasure indeed!
Do step inside and stay with us awhile!"

   And delightful Charis led Thetis in,
seated her on a silver-studded chair,
elaborately worked, a footstool beneath,   390
and called the famous craftsman Hephaestus:
"Ho, Hephaestus, Thetis wants to see you."
That bent-legged god of the smithy replied:
"What an extremely great honor indeed!
Thetis once saved me when I took that fall
because my silly mother was ashamed
of my lameness. Yes, I'd have suffered much
if I hadn't been welcomed by Thetis
and Eurynomë, Oceanus' daughter.
Nine years with them I made much finery—   400
brooches and bands, earrings and necklaces—

deep in their cave, with Oceanus' waters
endlessly roaring and foaming around,
and none of the gods or mortal men knew
but gracious Eurynomë and Thetis.
Now she has come. Well, I'm certainly bound
to do what I can for my rescuer.
Bring her some pleasant refreshments while I
tidy up my bellows and all my tools."

So huge Hephaestus rose from the anvil   410
limping, though his slender legs moved nimbly.
He laid the bellows away and gathered
his working tools in a silver cupboard,
next took a sponge to wipe his face and hands,
his powerful neck and his shaggy chest,
put on a tunic, seized his sturdy staff,
and came out limping, supported by two
servants of gold, like two living girls.
Sense is in their heads, and they have speech
and strength, for the gods have taught them to work.   420
They bustled along beneath him as he
hobbled to Thetis and drew up a chair,
then clasped her hand and addressed her kindly:
"Dear Thetis, why have you come to our home?
What an unexpected pleasure indeed!
Of course I'll do whatever you desire
if it is in any way possible."

Silverfoot Thetis answered him, weeping:
"Hephaestus, must any Olympian goddess
bear so many dreadful tribulations   430
as the ones Cronos' son has given me?
I received from him a mortal husband,
powerful Peleus, went to that man's bed
much against my will. Now he lies at home
overcome by age, and I suffer more:
Peleus and I had a glorious son, born
to command. He shot up like a sapling;
I reared him like a tree on a hillside
and sent him away with the high-beaked ships

to battle in Ilios—but I'll never   440
welcome him back to the halls of Peleus.
As long as he lives and sees the sun's light
he has grief, and I can't help him a bit.
As booty in war, he received a girl,
but great Agamemnon snatched her away—
so my son sat eating his heart out
while his people were penned beside their ships.
Next the Achaean ambassadors came
to promise many excellent presents,
and though he refused to help them himself   450
he put Patroclus in his own armor,
sent him into combat with many men.
All day they fought beside the gates, and then
would have taken that town, but Apollo
killed prince Patroclus as he was raging
among the foremost, gave Hector glory.
I come to implore you for a favor:
let my poor doomed son have a new-forged shield,
a helmet and shinguards with ankle clasps
and a breastplate. He lost his when his friend   460
was slain, and now he lies in a frenzy."

   That bent-legged god of the smithy replied:
"There, there, now, no need to worry, my dear.
I only wish I could hide him from death,
that day that he meets his terrible fate,
as surely as he'll have wondrous armor
to amaze the world forever after."

   So Hephaestus hobbled to his bellows,
bent them fireward, and ordered them to work.
And those twenty bellows puffed at the pots   470
with just the proper blasts that were needed
to assist his labor and accomplish
all Hephaestus required to do the job.
On his fire he put tin and stubborn bronze
with precious gold and silver, after that
set a great anvil on its block and took
hammer in one hand, tongs in the other.

First he made an enormous sturdy shield,
surrounded by a gleaming triple-tiered
rim with a silver strap to hold it fast.   480
And on that five-ringed shield Hephaestus made
many adornments with intricate skill.

There he fashioned earth and heaven and sea,
with the tireless sun, a moon at the full,
and all those constellations of the sky:
Pleiades, Hyades, strong Orion,
and the Great Bear, known also as the Wain,
who circles in her place by Orion
and alone has no bath in Oceanus.

And there he made two prosperous cities—   490
in one marriages and festive banquets,
brides being led through the streets by brilliant
torches as the wedding march was chanted,
young men whirling in the dance, among them
a skirl of flutes and lyres, while the women
stood in the doors to marvel at that sight.
And a crowd had gathered where a quarrel
had arisen about the proper fine
for a murder: one man offered to pay,
another declined to accept the sum,   500
and both had requested arbitration.
The crowd stood cheering for their favorites
as heralds held them back, and the elders
sat on smooth stones in the sacred circle,
and each one held the herald's staff in turn
when he sprang up to announce his verdict.
And in the middle lay two gold pieces
for the one whose judgment was accepted.

But two armies in bright armor besieged
the other town—and they stood quarreling   510
whether to attack or to offer terms
of half the wealth that capital possessed.
Yet the city people planned an ambush:
they left their wives and their little children

to guard the wall, with men too old for war,
and marched out led by Ares and Athena,
gods of gold attired in golden clothing,
huge and magnificent, as gods should be,
while the people at their feet were smaller.
When they reached a place good for ambushing,   520
a river where men drove their flocks to drink,
they sat down in all their lambent armor
and sent two nimblefooted sentinels
to watch for the sheep and shambling oxen,
which came along soon, with their two shepherds
piping at flutes in perfect innocence.
So the ambushers rushed out and swiftly
rounded up the cattle and fleecy sheep,
then slaughtered that pair of hapless shepherds.
As the besiegers sat in council, they   530
heard that hubbub, rushed to harness horses,
and drove their thundering chariots to the spot.
There they formed ranks along the riverbanks,
and again and again the bronze hit home,
among them Strife and Turmoil and dread Fate,
who grabbed wounded and unwounded alike
and dragged off another, dead, by the foot,
so her robes were red with the blood of men.
They battled away like living mortals
and hauled off corpses the others had slain.   540

And there he set a soft, rich fallow land
on the third plowing, with many farmers
driving their oxen across back and forth.
Whenever they reached the end of that field
a man brought mellow red wine in a cup
and handed it to them, then they returned,
eager to reach the end of their furrow.
The field grew black behind them, as if real,
though it was gold: and this was the wonder.

And there he set an estate, with reapers   550
holding sharp sickles as they mowed a field.
The grain lay in rows all along the swath

where workers were tying it up with straw.
Three binders stood by, while just behind them
boys bustled about, gathering up grain
for their bundles—and a king, staff in hand,
stood silent by the swath, a happy man.
In the distance heralds prepared a feast,
a colossal roasted ox, as women
cooked barley soup for the workers' dinner.   560

   And there he set a ripening vineyard
of elegant gold, though the grapes were black
and the vines were propped upon silver poles,
round them a ditch of dark-blue enamel
and a tin fence. In led a single path
where villagers came to gather their grapes,
young men and women very merrily
carrying sweet fruit in wicker baskets.
Among them a boy plucked a plangent lyre,
sang the dirge for the departing summer   570
while the others cried hurrah as they came
leaping and beating the time with their feet.

   And there he carved a herd of high-horned cows
in gold and tin, who lowed as they hurried
from the stables toward their pasture meadow
by the bobbing reeds of a swift river.
And golden herdsmen came right at their side,
four of them, and nine swift hounds frisked after.
But among the first cattle, two lions
had grabbed a mighty bull and dragged him off,   580
bellowing wildly, chased by dogs and men:
they had torn the bull's belly open, then
were gulping blood and guts, while the herdsmen
tried to sic their quick hounds on—but no use!
They shied away from biting the lions
and stood by barking but stayed out of reach.

   And there the bent-legged god made a pasture
in a lovely glen, a glade of white sheep
with stables and pens and huts thatched over.

And there the bent-legged god made a dance floor   590
like the one built long before in Knossos
by Daedalus for fair-haired Ariadne:
lusty young men and graceful young women
danced in a ring, hands on each other's wrists.
The women wore fine linen and the men
elegant tunics gleaming soft with oil—
and the women wore lovely wreaths, the men
daggers of gold that hung from silver slings.
Now they scurried around on skillful feet
with consummate ease, as when a potter   600
sits by his wheel and sets it a-spinning,
now they hurried toward each other in rows.
A large crowd stood and watched the spectacle
with an intense joy, while two acrobats
whirled among the dancers, giving the beat.

And there he put Oceanus' vast power
around the rim of his enormous shield.

And after finishing that massive shield
he made him a breastplate brighter than flame
and made a heavy tight-fitting helmet,   610
intricately carved, with a golden crest,
and made him shinguards of flexible tin.

When the bent-legged god had completed all,
he laid it before Achilles' mother,
who leapt hawklike from snowy Olympus
with the gleaming armor from Hephaestus.

Book Nineteen: The Rage Renounced

Agamemnon and Achilles are reconciled. The horse Xanthus
predicts Achilles' death.

Saffron-robed Dawn rose from Oceanus' streams
with light for the blessed gods and mortals
as Thetis came with Hephaestus' presents.
She found her dear son hugging Patroclus
with piercing shrieks, while all his companions
mourned around him. Then that goddess came near
and clasped him by the hand as she murmured:
"My child, we must leave him, despite our grief.
He's dead because the immortals willed it.
But look! I have armor from Hephaestus,   10
handsomer than a man has ever worn."

   Now the goddess Thetis set that armor
before Achilles, and its splendor clanged.
The Myrmidons shrank back in awe—none dared
look at it—but Peleus' illustrious Achilles
grew even wilder at the sight: his eyes
blazed beneath their lids like a pair of flames
as he gladly held those glorious gifts.
When he had taken his fill of gazing,
he addressed her in agitated words: 20
"Ah, Mother, only a god could have made
such a magnificent set of armor.
So I shall put it on—although I fear
meanwhile our Patroclus will be assailed
by the terrible swarms of carrion flies
that breed their worms to corrupt men's corpses,
so his mortal remains will rot away."

The goddess silverfoot Thetis answered:
"Dear child, you need not worry about this—
I'll do my best to keep away those flies   30
that prey on corpses of fallen warriors,
and even though he lies an entire year
his flesh will stay whole, or better than now.
But you call the people to assembly,
give up your grudge against Agamemnon
and quickly arm yourself for bitter war!"

Now she filled him with enormous courage,
poured ambrosia in Patroclus' nostrils
to keep his flesh whole and uncorrupted.
So Achilles strode along the seashore,   40
rousing those Danaans with horrible roars.
Even the people waiting at the beach—
pilots who guided the ships with rudders
and stewards who apportioned provisions—
came to assembly, because Achilles
had appeared after his long rest from war.
Two of their lords limped forth with the others—
Tydeus' son Diomedes and Odysseus—
leaning on spears, their wounds were so painful,
and took their seats before the assembly.   50
Last of all came mighty Agamemnon,
suffering terribly from that spear wound
Antenor's son Coön had given him.
After the Achaeans had assembled,
Achilles rose among them and declared:
"Atreus' son, was it really the best thing
you and I gave in to our resentment
and had this stupid quarrel for a girl?
If only Artemis' bow had slain her
that day I captured her in Lyrnessus,   60
then fewer Danaans would have bit the dust
due to my ruinous maniac rage—
good news for the Trojans, but our people
will not forget it for a long, long time.
Very well, we'll let bygones be bygones

and control our temper because we must.
Yes, I shall give up my grudge—a man can't
stay in such a rage forever. But you
call our Achaean people to battle
so I may meet the enemy and learn   70
if they stand fast *then*. No, I believe most
will be glad for a moment's rest if they
escape my spear in the fury of war!"

   All those assembled Achaeans were glad
to hear Achilles had renounced his wrath.
Next Agamemnon spoke up from his place,
not coming forward into the middle:
"Friends, Danaan warriors, servants of Ares,
listen to a speaker with courtesy—
such interruptions are most distracting.   80
With all this noise, how can anyone hear
or speak? Even the best would be tongue-tied.
I address Peleus' son, but you others
should pay close attention to what I say.
Of course our people had often told me
and scolded me too, though I'm not to blame
but Zeus and fate and murky Erinys,
who put this idiocy in my heart
the day I stole the spoils of Achilles.
What could I do? A god made it happen.   90
Any man may be cheated by Folly,
that daughter of Zeus with delicate feet
who treads the air tiptoe over men's heads
and catches them one after the other.
Once she even caught Zeus, who is mightier
than all gods and mortals, they say—but he
was fooled by a female, haughty Hera,
that day his distinguished son Heracles
was due to be born from queen Alcmenë.
Cronos' son had boasted on Olympus: 100
'Listen to me, you gods and goddesses,
I have an important message for all:
today our midwife nymph Eilithyia

brings forth a mortal who will rule many,
a man in my own august lineage.'
And Hera addressed him deceitfully:
'Come, I don't believe you really mean it!
Well then, Olympian, take a solemn oath
that warrior will command many peoples
who falls between a woman's feet today   110
and can boast he is descended from you.'
Zeus had no suspicion whatsoever
and swore a great oath in his foolishness.
So Hera hurried down from Olympus
to Achaean Argos, where she well knew
the wife of Sthenelus, Perseus' son,
carried a seven-month child in her womb.
Hera caused it to come before its time,
then held back Alcmenë's own delivery
and spoke to that mighty son of Cronos: 120
'Old Dazzlebolt, let me tell you something:
a magnificent monarch has been born—
Eurystheus, grandson of gallant Perseus,
an Achaean leader in your own line.'
These words gave Zeus a most ferocious jolt,
and burning with fury, he grabbed Folly
by her bright braids, swore an enormous oath
Olympus and starry heaven would never
again see Folly, who cheats everyone.
So he whirled her around and flung her down   130
from starry heaven—and she fell to men.
Later he'd groan over her when his son
Heracles slaved at Eurystheus' labors.
I suffered the same while that great Hector
was slaying our people by their ships' sterns:
sly and insidious Folly obsessed me.
But since I was so completely deceived
I'll make amends with splendid recompense—
and you lead us in battle, Achilles.
You shall receive all Odysseus promised   140
when he came with our people's embassy—
or, if you wish, be patient for a while

and my squires will bring these gifts from my ship,
so you see what splendid things shall be yours."

   And that quickfoot Achilles answered him:
"Our distinguished leader Agamemnon,
offer all the splendid presents you wish
or keep them, I don't care. Now we need war
immediately—no time to stand babbling
and wasting time, when we have work to do: 150
you'll see our Achilles out front once more,
devastating enemies with his spear.
Just keep this in mind while you do battle."

   And canny Odysseus said in reply:
"No doubt of your valor, prince Achilles,
but don't lead our Achaean armies out
until we eat, since it won't be a brief
struggle, once those opposing phalanxes
are locked in Ares' horrible fury.
So you urge our people to take food—   160
bread and wine, the sustenance of warriors.
A man can't keep up combat all day long
without a bite to eat in his stomach—
hunger and thirst begin to torment him,
so no matter how eager he may be,
his legs grow wobbly, he trips and stumbles.
But a man with enough to eat and drink
stays always keen to meet the enemy,
his spirit steadfast; he feels not the least
weariness till the battle is done.   170
Dismiss our troops, then, command them to dine
while mighty Agamemnon brings those gifts
so all our people may witness and see
what wonderful presents you shall receive.
Then he'll stand up in assembly and swear
he never once has lain with her in love
as men and women do upon this earth—
but you must be gracious and kindly too.
A banquet shall be held in your honor,
a rich one with everything you deserve—   180

and you, Atreus' son, keep a clearer head
in the future. No harm for a monarch
to make amends, if he got angry first."

And Atreus' son Agamemnon answered:
"Odysseus, I'm delighted to hear this—
and you've told it all very beautifully.
Yes, I shall take the oath with all my heart,
and a man can't swear false before the gods.
So Achilles should hold back a moment
and the rest of you stay here till the gifts   190
are brought from my ship and we make amends.
These are my orders for you, dear fellow:
pick the best young men in all our army
to bring those glorious presents Achilles
was promised before, with the women too.
Trusty Talthybius should prepare a boar
for sacrifice to Zeus and to the sun."

But quickfoot Achilles interrupted:
"Our distinguished leader Agamemnon,
save all that for some other occasion,   200
when a pause in bitter battle appears
and I'm less angry than I am today.
Our faithful comrades are lying mangled
by Hector's spear while Zeus supported him,
and you two want us to eat! As for me,
I'd rather start combat immediately
with no food whatever, and at sunset
we'll feast after we have avenged this shame—
until then I shall let no food and drink
touch my lips, while my beloved comrade   210
lies there in my camp all lacerated,
feet turned toward the door, as our people mourn
about his corpse. So I don't care for that—
but for death and blood and warriors' moans."

And canny Odysseus said in reply:
"My incomparable friend Achilles,
you're far superior managing the spear,

but I've a better head on my shoulders
because I am older and I know more.
Then listen carefully to what I say: 220
warriors soon become weary of combat
when the keen blade scatters more straw than grain
and the harvest's scanty as the balance
tips, since Zeus has decided the winner.
It's not with our bellies we mourn the dead—
day after day so many warriors fall,
how would there ever be an end to grief?
Better, far better, to bury the slain
and harden our hearts and weep just that day.
The people dreadful combat leaves alive   230
must be thinking of food and drink so they
may incessantly meet the enemy
in their sturdy armor. Let no one wait
for another summons to enter war,
because this is it: there'll be trouble
for men who hang back! All together, then,
begin bitter battle once again!"

  So off he went, with noble Nestor's sons
and Meges and Thoas and Meriones,
brave Lycomedes, and Melanippus.   240
They hurried to Agamemnon's quarters
and carried out their task as commanded:
took seven cauldrons their lord had promised,
twenty bright kettles, and twelve racehorses,
brought the seven women clever in crafts,
with that enchanting Briseis as the eighth.
Next Odysseus weighed out ten gold pieces
and led the young men back with their presents.
These were set in the meeting place, and then
king Agamemnon rose, as Talthybius   250
stood beside him holding a bristly boar—
and that son of Atreus drew the dagger
which always hung by his giant scabbard,
slashed bristles from the boar, raised them toward Zeus
and prayed, while the Achaeans sat silent

in reverent attention to his words.
Gazing toward heaven, Agamemnon intoned:
"All-highest mighty Zeus be my witness
with Earth and Sun and the dark Erinyes
who take dreadful vengeance on oath breakers: 260
I laid no hand on that lady Briseis
in love or in any other manner,
never touched her once while she stayed with me.
Should this be false, may the gods carry out
the punishments all perjurers deserve."

So he slit the throat of that bristly boar—
and Talthybius whirled it round and flung it
in the gray sea's abyss, food for fishes.
Then illustrious Achilles addressed them:
"Oh, father Zeus, what fools you make of men!   270
I should never have been in such a rage
at Atreus' son, he wouldn't have taken
that girl so cruelly, if Zeus had not planned
to devastate our Achaean people.
Now take your meals, so battle can begin."

He dismissed the meeting—and the people
scattered, every warrior to his own ship,
as the Myrmidons gathered up those gifts,
carried them to gallant Achilles' camp,
and left them in charge of the women there,   280
then his squires drove the horses to his herd.

But Briseis, golden Aphrodite's peer,
saw Patroclus' body mangled by spears
and flung herself upon him shrieking, tore
her lovely face, her breasts and tender neck,
and that lady more like a goddess cried:
"Patroclus! dearest friend in my distress!
When I went from this tent you were alive,
and now I find you dead, my honored lord,
on my return—grief after grief for me!   290
My parents gave me a lusty husband,
but I saw him cut down before our town,

and those three beloved brothers of mine
fell battling in their homeland just as he.
But when Achilles slaughtered my husband
by Mynes' city, you wouldn't let me
weep, you promised me that son of Peleus
would take me back to Phthia in his ships,
where his men would celebrate our marriage—
so I mourn for your kindness, now you're dead."   300

   Sobbing she said this, as the women groaned
for Patroclus and for their own griefs too.
The Danaan lords came around Achilles,
urging him to eat, but he moaned and said:
"I beg you, dear comrades, if you'll listen,
don't ask me to take food or drink today—
I am far too miserable for that.
Let me stay as I am until sunset."

   Whereupon he sent those leaders away
except for Odysseus, Atreus' two sons,   310
Nestor, Idomeneus, and old Phoenix,
who stayed to console him—but he would take
no comfort till he entered bloody war.
He sighed heavily with remembrance and said:
"Ah, my poor beloved friend, it was you
who served me all those delicious dinners
as our Danaan warriors were rushing out
to meet the Trojans in wretched battle—
and you lie here lacerated, while I
decline the food and drink they offer me,   320
I miss you so much. Nothing worse could come,
not even the death of my own father—
who sits at home weeping for my absence
as I battle far away in Ilios
because of that cursed female Helen—
or the death of my dear son in Scyrus,
though who can say if that boy's still alive.
Until now it had always been my hope
I alone would die far from my homeland,
while you returned to the land of Phthia   330

so you might bring my son back from Scyrus
in your seafaring ship and show him all—
my treasures and servants and stately halls—
because by now old Peleus must be dead
or else barely alive and suffering
from the ravages of age, while he waits
for the awful news that I have fallen."

He said this weeping, and the leaders groaned
as each remembered what he'd left at home.
Cronos' son saw them mourn and pitied them,   340
so his words poured out to great Athena:
"My child, you've forsaken your own warrior—
don't you care for Achilles anymore?
Just see how he sits before his beaked ships
mourning his dear comrade—while the others
have their dinners, he refuses food.
Now you pour nectar and sweet ambrosia
into his breast so he won't be hungry."

This was all green-eyed Athena needed—
and, like some shrill-voiced broad-winged falcon, she   350
leapt from heaven. And while the Achaeans
flung on their armor, she found Achilles,
infused him with nectar and ambrosia
so no gnawing hunger pains would plague him,
then hurried back to her father's palace,
and the Danaans came running from their ships.
As snowflakes tumble from Zeus in swarms,
chill beneath the sweep of a fresh north wind,
their brilliant helmets and tough studded shields,
breastplates of metal and ashwood weapons,   360
were carried from those Danaan ships in swarms.
And the glare rose up to heaven, earth laughed
with flashing bronze, echoed with treading feet,
while Achilles armed himself among them.
He ground his teeth together, and his eyes
blazed like a pair of flames, most terrible
grief in his heart. Raging at the Trojans,
he dressed himself in Hephaestus' armor:

strapped on his legs the elegant shinguards
so handsomely adorned with silver bands,   370
and over his chest that sturdy breastplate,
slung on his back a silver-studded sword
and after this the massive sturdy shield,
whose shimmering shone afar like the moon.
As sailors gaze over the sea and spy
a fire that gleams high up in the mountains
on some lonely farm, but blustery winds
bear them over the water, far from friends,
thus the gleam from that magnificent shield
rose to heaven. Next he took the helmet   380
and set it on his head, bright as a star—
and all about it bobbed the golden plume
Hephaestus had fastened over the crest.
That son of Peleus tried his armor on
to see if it fitted him snug but free—
and it buoyed him up like a pair of wings.
Now from his father's sheath Achilles drew
a huge, stout, ponderous weapon which none
of the other Danaan warriors could wield,
an ashwood spear Cheiron gave his father   390
from Pelion's peak to carry in combat.
Then Alcimus and Automedon yoked
those horses, put their handsome breast straps on,
fit bits between their teeth, tugged the reins taut
to the chariot. And Automedon seized
the glittering whip, sprang on that chariot,
as swift Achilles mounted beside him,
all brilliant in his armor like the sun,
and bellowed horribly to his horses:
"My famous coursers Xanthus and Balius,   400
consider how to bring this charioteer
back to our people when battle is done—
don't leave him dead as you did Patroclus."

    And from under that yoke the horse Xanthus
spoke—bowed his head quite suddenly; the mane
streamed from beneath his breastband to the ground

as divine white-armed Hera gave him speech:
"This time we'll save you, Achilles, although
your own end is near, and we aren't to blame
but a mighty god and resistless fate.   410
It wasn't our slowness or laziness
that gave the Trojans Patroclus' armor
when powerful silverbow Apollo
killed him in combat, gave Hector glory.
We two can run as fast as the West Wind,
swiftest of them all, while you are fated
to be slain by a god and a mortal."

   Thereupon the Erinyes stopped his voice.
And, profoundly moved, Achilles answered:
"Xanthus, why predict my death? You needn't.   420
I know myself I am doomed to die here
far from my father and mother—but still
I won't stop till those Trojans tire of war!"

   Then he drove his horses on with a roar.

Book Twenty: War Among the Gods

The gods battle for their favorites. Poseidon saves Aeneas
from Achilles.

There at the ships the Achaeans took arms
around you, insatiable Achilles—
and, facing them, the Trojans did the same.
Meanwhile mighty Zeus commanded Themis
to summon the gods, so she scurried out,
ordering them to meet at Zeus's palace.
No river stayed away save Oceanus
nor any nymph who haunts those lovely groves
and river springlets and grassy meadows.
When they came to the halls of Cronos' son   10
they sat on that glittering portico
Hephaestus had made with masterful craft.

    Thus all assembled. Nor did Poseidon
ignore her command—he rose from the sea
and took a seat among them and asked Zeus:
"Why did you call us together, my lord?
Have you some strategy for that struggle
now battle's about to begin again?"

    And cloudgathering king Zeus answered him:
"Now, now, Earthshaker, you know very well—   20
I care for them although they're perishing.
I'll stay here on my peak of Olympus
and watch the spectacle, while you others
go among those Trojans and Achaeans
to help whichever side most pleases you.
If we let Achilles enter battle
no man alive will ever hold him back.

Even before, they trembled to see him,
and in this fury for his friend, I fear
he'll go beyond his fate and take the town."   30

Then Cronos' son made unending combat.
So the gods went to war for their favorites:
With the ships, queen Hera and Athena,
powerful Poseidon and the helper
Hermes, cleverest contriver of all,
while lame Hephaestus swaggered among them
limping, though his spindly legs moved nimbly.
But with the Trojans were fiery Ares,
shaggy-haired Phoebus, archer Artemis,
Leto, Xanthus, and fair Aphrodite.   40

While the gods stood apart from mortal men
the Achaeans won, because Achilles
had appeared after his long rest from war,
and every Trojan trembled in terror
before that dangerous son of Peleus
in his shimmering armor, Ares' peer.
But when the Olympians entered their throng
up leapt mighty Strife, and Athena shrieked,
now standing at the moat outside the wall,
now howling by the resounding seashore.   50
Opposite, like a dark storm, Ares roared
piercingly from the Trojan citadel
or hurrying over Callicolonë.

Thus the blessed gods urged the two sides on,
and heartbreaking battle burst forth again.
Then the father of gods and men thundered
horribly—and, from below, Poseidon
shook the vast earth and its steep mountain peaks,
swayed the feet of many-fountained Ida
with its crests and Troy and the Danaan ships.   60
And Hades Lord of the Shades was afraid,
leapt from his throne and bellowed in terror
powerful Poseidon would tear the ground
so men and immortals might see his home,

a dank, wretched place even the gods loathe—
such was the roar as those gods met in war.
And facing great earthshaker Poseidon
stood Apollo with his winged missiles,
as green-eyed Athena faced fierce Ares
and Hera met Phoebus' huntress sister　　　　　　　70
Artemis, goddess of golden arrows,
while Leto opposed lucky Hermes and
glorious Hephaestus that deep-flowing stream
the gods call Xanthus and men Scamander.

So gods warred against gods, while Achilles
stayed raging to meet fiery Hector,
Priam's son, that man he most of all
sought with a sheer insatiable hate—
but archer Apollo sent Aeneas
to face Achilles, filled him with fury.　　　　　　　80
Taking the shape of Priam's son Lycaon,
far-shooter Phoebus Apollo shouted:
"Well now, Aeneas, what about those boasts
you made to our leaders over your wine,
that you'd battle Achilles man-to-man!"

And magnificent Aeneas answered him:
"Lycaon, I'd never be so foolish
to match my might with that son of Peleus—
it wouldn't be the first time I met him.
Once already he chased me down Ida,　　　　　　　90
that time he came rustling cattle and sacked
Lyrnessus and Pedasus—but wise Zeus
rescued me then, gave my legs the strength
to escape Achilles and Athena,
who granted him many a great triumph
as he ravaged Trojans and Lelegians.
Gallant Achilles is invincible
when some immortal stands there beside him—
whatever happens, his spear keeps on course
till it hits a victim. But if some god　　　　　　　100
would only help me too, he'd find it hard
to win the day, though he were made of bronze."

And Zeus's son Apollo answered him:
"Come now, fellow, pray to the immortals!
You're a son of the goddess Aphrodite,
while his mother's only a lesser one,
and thunderlord Zeus was your grandfather.
So drive your horses straight for Achilles,
don't be afraid of his big boasting words."

Then Apollo filled him with might, and he   110
strode to battle in his brilliant armor—
but Hera spied that son of Anchises
moving toward Achilles through their armies
and called the gods to assembly and said:
"Very well, Poseidon and Athena,
let's quickly consider what should be done.
There goes Aeneas in all his armor—
Apollo sent him against Peleus' son—
and we must turn him back immediately,
or one of us could stand with Achilles,   120
pour fury in him and encourage him,
so he knows he's loved by the finest gods
and the other immortals are windbags
who fancied they could protect those Trojans.
We three have come here on the battlefield
to keep Achilles from being injured
today, though later he must take what fate
has spun for him the day that he was born.
Yet if we don't tell him beforehand, he
may shrink when he meets us in war—a god   130
in mortal form is hard for men to bear."

And earthshaking Poseidon answered her:
"Now, now, Hera, you mustn't lose your head.
We're so superior it isn't right
for gods to battle against each other.
Now we'd better look for a place apart
where we can watch, and leave war to men.
But if Ares or Phoebus should appear
or try to keep Achilles from combat,
we can make some trouble for them as well!   140

Yes, they'll leave the battlefield soon enough
and scurry on home to Olympus when
they've had a taste of our glorious power!"

Then that dark-haired sea lord led them away
to the crumbling wall of great Heracles,
which the Trojans and Athena had made
to protect him from that dread sea monster
whenever it chased him up on the plain—
there Poseidon sat with the other gods,
shoulders wrapped in impenetrable clouds,   150
while their foes sat on Callicolonë
around you, archer Phoebus, and Ares.

So the gods faced one another, planning
strategy, and neither side would begin
wretched battle, though Zeus had ordered it.

Now the plain was filled with men and horses
aflame with bronze; earth groaned beneath them as
they came together. Two men, best by far,
rushed between those armies, mad for battle:
Aeneas and Peleus' son Achilles.   160
First Aeneas strode forth menacingly
with a tough shield, as his heavy helmet
bobbed above, and brandished a bright spear.
And Achilles met him like some lion
when an entire people has assembled
to take his life: he pays no attention
and goes his way, but a young man stabs him,
so he crouches down with wide-open mouth,
foam round his teeth, and growls deep inside,
lashing at ribs and flanks with his tail   170
as he steels himself for resistance, then
lunges at them, glaring, till he kills
someone, or dies himself in the attempt—
Peleus' son Achilles was that furious
to face Aeneas in single combat.

   After they came very near each other
redoubtable Achilles bellowed out:
"Aeneas, why are you so far out here
all alone? Want to meet me in combat
because you aspire to the Trojan throne   180
instead of Priam? But even though you
defeat me, he won't surrender his realm—
he has sons, he isn't out of his mind.
Or did the Trojans promise an estate,
an excellent tract of fields and farmland,
if you kill me? It will not be easy.
I chased you once with my spear already:
remember that day with your cattle herds
when you scurried down from Ida's foothills
quickly enough—didn't even look back!   190
You escaped to Lyrnessus, which I sacked
with help from Athena and father Zeus,
took many attractive ladies captive,
though Zeus and the other gods rescued you.
Yet this time he won't save you as you think!
Scamper off today, I advise you, stay
away from me on the battlefield or
you may learn too late how foolish you were!"

   And fiery Aeneas roared in reply:
"See here, Peleus' son, you won't frighten me   200
as if I were some silly child—I too
can bellow insults and contemptuous words.
I know your ancestry as you know mine,
from the stories men told in the old days,
though neither has seen the other's parents.
They say your father was peerless Peleus,
the sea nymph Thetis your mother, while I
can boast my parents were lord Anchises
and the goddess golden Aphrodite.
One of these mothers will be mourning for   210
her son today, since we won't return
after just a little childish chatter.
But if you wish, I'll tell you my lineage,

though many men know it well already.
Mighty Zeus was father of Dardanus,
who founded Dardania when holy Troy
was not yet constructed here on the plain
and the people still lived on Ida's slopes.
Dardanus had a son, Erichthonius,
wealthiest monarch among all mortals   220
with three thousand horses in his meadows,
mares that exulted in sleek frisking foals.
The North Wind fell wildly in love with them
and covered them as a dark-maned stallion,
so twelve fine foals were born of their union.
They bounded over the bountiful earth,
skimming its wheat fields, not breaking an ear,
and they bounded over the sea's broad back,
skimming above its very highest waves.
Erichthonius' son Tros ruled the Trojans,   230
and three magnificent sons were his heirs:
Ilus and Assaracus and godlike
Ganymedes, handsomest man on earth,
so the gods let him pour the wine for Zeus
and he lived among them on Olympus.
One of Ilus' sons was Laomedon,
who fathered Tithonous and king Priam,
Lampus, Clytius, and great Hicetaon.
And Assaracus' grandson Anchises
was my own father, while Priam was Hector's.   240
This is my lineage and I'm proud of it.
But thunderlord Zeus can give men valor
as his most sovereign will determines.
So let's not stand babbling like little boys
while awful battle rages everywhere.
Blabbing invective's an easy matter:
people pile insults up to the sky,
their tongues are agile and delight to wag—
no end to the idiocies they invent.
Whatever you say, you get back the same.   250
Why should we stand here angrily wrangling
like a couple of silly women who

lose their temper in some petty quarrel
and go running out on the street to shriek
more lies than truth in their stupid fury.
No, I won't retreat from arrogant words
till we two battle it out man-to-man—
so see if you like the taste of my spear!"

Then Aeneas hurled at Achilles' shield,
which resounded wildly with the impact,   260
and that son of Peleus held it away,
fearing the dangerous spear would tear
straight through its metal with no more ado—
very foolish of him! he didn't know
the gods' glorious gifts are not easily
destroyed by the force of mortal warriors.
For all its great power, Aeneas' weapon
couldn't pierce that gold the god had given:
ripped two of the heavy layers, but three
remained from the five Hephaestus had made—   270
two were bronze, with two tin layers inside
and one of gold, which held the awful spear.

Nimble Achilles hurled his weapon next,
hit Aeneas' shield just beside the rim,
where its bronze was weakest and the oxhide
thinnest: that spear of Pelian ashwood
tore through it with a formidable boom.
Aeneas crouched down, held his shield away
afraid, as the spear hurtled by and stuck
furious in earth after splitting two rings   280
of his sturdy shield—then he staggered up,
head swimming with fear, extremely shaken
by that narrow escape. And Achilles
drew a redoubtable sword, stormed forward
roaring horribly, while Aeneas seized
a huge boulder, too much for two warriors
as men are now, but he held it with ease.
Then he would have brought it thundering down
on the shield or helmet of Achilles,
whose sword would have quickly finished him off,   290

but earthshaker Poseidon observed them
and cried to those assembled immortals:
"Dear me, I'm so sorry for Aeneas,
who soon will die and descend to Hades
because he obeyed Apollo's commands—
idiot! that god won't rescue him now.
But why should an innocent man suffer
for troubles of others, when he gives such
delightful offerings to us Olympians?
Well, we must rescue him immediately,   300
or Zeus may be angry if Achilles
should take his life—he's fated to escape,
so there will be no end to that family
of Dardanus, whom Cronos' son loved best
among all his sons from mortal women.
Zeus has come to hate the house of Priam,
and lord Aeneas will rule the Trojans
with his sons and grandsons ever after."

Gentle-eyed queen Hera said in reply:
"Very well, Earthshaker, do as you please—   310
rescue Aeneas or let him be slain
by Achilles, for all his bravery.
But we two, Pallas Athena and I,
have sworn strong oaths among the immortals
never to defend those Trojans from doom,
not even when all their city's ablaze
with flames the Achaean warriors have made."

When powerful Poseidon heard her words
he hurried among the hurtling weapons
till he reached those two opposing warriors   320
and poured murky mist over the eyes
of Peleus' son Achilles, tore his spear
from the elaborately crafted shield
and set it down again before his feet,
then swung lord Aeneas high above earth—
and over their ranks of men and horses
that warrior soared from the god's mighty hand

and fell far away from the battlefield,
where all the Cauconians were taking arms.

    Now the Earthshaker came hurrying up   330
and addressed him in agitated words:
"Aeneas, which god made you so insane
as to match your power with Peleus' son,
your superior and dearer to the gods?
Better retreat when you see him coming,
or you'll go to Hades despite your fate!
But after Achilles has met his doom,
stay battling fearlessly in our vanguard,
for no other Achaean can kill you."

    Whereupon glorious Poseidon left him   340
and swiftly took the mist from Achilles'
eyes. That son of Peleus stood dumbfounded
and, deeply troubled, muttered to himself:
"Ha, what an incredible sight this is!
My spear lies here on the ground, and the man
I aimed it at vanished without a trace.
Aeneas too must be dear to the gods—
and I believed he was only boasting.
Good riddance to him! He won't dare face me
again after such a narrow escape.   350
So I'll call all our fiery warriors
and learn how tough those other Trojans are!"

    Now he bounded through the ranks, bellowing:
"Now forward, my fine Achaeans, so we
meet them indomitably, man-to-man!
For all my power, I'll find it hard
to take on those enemy hordes alone.
Not even great Ares or Athena
could manage combat ferocious as this,
though as long as my breath and strength remain   360
you won't see me holding back a moment
but shattering their ranks—and I believe
no Trojan will be glad to see my spear."

Thus swift Achilles urged his armies on,
and Hector roared among *his* battalions:
"Don't let Achilles scare you, comrades!
In speech a man can contend with the gods
but not in war—they're far too powerful.
Although Achilles may fulfill a part
of what he said, he cannot do it all.   370
I'll face him although his hands are like fire,
his hands like fire and his fury like steel!"

So those Trojans moved forward, spears upraised,
and the two sides met with a deafening din.
Next Apollo called that son of Priam:
"Hector, don't meet prince Achilles alone—
await his attack among your people
but stay away from his spear and his sword."

Hector shrank back to his Trojan cohorts
afraid, when he heard that voice of the god.   380
But Achilles leapt on the enemy
with horrible war cries, killed Iphition,
son of city-plundering Otrynteus,
borne by a water nymph near the snowy
slopes of Tmolus in his wealthy homeland:
as he stormed forward, that son of Peleus
hit his head with a spearcast, split the skull
so he fell thundering—and Achilles cried:
"Farewell, Iphition, you dreadful fellow!
You'll perish here very far from your home   390
by Hermus and Hyllus, fish-teeming streams,
and Lake Gygaea, your family estate."

As Achilles spoke, night covered his eyes.
So the wheels of Achaean chariots tore
him apart—and over him Peleus' son
slew Demoleon, bulwark in battle,
drove a deadly spearpoint through his temple:
that bronze helmet couldn't hold its impact,
and it bore straight through the bone, so his brains
spattered inside, his warmaking ended.   400

As Hippodamas leapt from a chariot
to retreat, Achilles' spear hit his back,
and he gasped out his life, cried like a bull
that bellows, being dragged about a shrine
by the young priests—and Poseidon is glad:
thus he bellowed as the life left his bones.
Next Achilles pursued Polydorus,
a son of Priam, who forbade that boy
to enter war, for he was his youngest
and dearest child, best runner in Ilios—   410
so he merely made a show of his speed
on foot with the foremost, till he perished:
Achilles' brazen spear went hurtling through
the place on his back where gold belt buckles
met at the overlap of his breastplate:
pierced his chest, lodged by the navel, and he
fell groaning to his knees, a murky cloud
over him, pressed his bowels back as he sank.

  When Hector saw his brother Polydorus
stretched out on the ground with a dreadful wound,   420
his eyes became misted; he couldn't bear
to stay away more but rushed to battle
brandishing a spear like flame. Achilles
leapt forward when he saw him and roared:
"There goes the man who wronged me most of all,
killed my beloved companion—and now
we won't hang back from each other again!"

  And he called to Hector, scowling fiercely:
"Come on, and I'll make a quick end of you."

  And Priam's son Hector cried, unperturbed: 430
"See here, Achilles, you won't frighten me
as if I were some silly child—I too
can bellow insults and contemptuous words.
You may be far mightier than I am, but
the immortals decide who wins in war—
I may slay you too, despite your power,
for my glorious spear is dangerous too!"

And he hurled that weapon, but Athena
blew it away from gallant Achilles
with a gentle puff—it flew back and fell   440
at Hector's feet. Next that son of Peleus
sprang at him in an insatiable rage,
roaring most horribly—but Apollo
seized Hector with ease, hid him in a mist.
Three times Achilles raced to the attack,
three times stabbed in vain at the drifting mist,
and as he stormed forward the fourth time,
a man possessed, gave a dreadful cry:
"Swine, you escaped again, but I almost
brought you down! Apollo saved you once more—   450
you must implore him when you enter war.
Very well, I'll finish you off next time
if some immortal god assists me too.
And now I can catch your companions here."

   So he stabbed Dryops' neck, and that warrior
fell before his feet. Achilles left him,
struck dauntless Demuchus, Philetor's son,
on the knee with a spearcast, then came near
swinging an awful sword and took his life.
Next he met Laogonus and Dardanus,   460
sent them tumbling to earth from their chariot,
one with a spearcast and one with the sword.
Alastor's son Tros came as supplicant,
implored him to be taken prisoner,
pity a person his very same age—
fool! Achilles had no thoughts of mercy:
here was no kindly, no courteous man
but a maniac! As that warrior knelt
in hapless appeal, Achilles stabbed him
through the liver with a sword; his tunic   470
was flooded with blood, his eyes became dim
as he fell. And Achilles thrust a spear
above Mulius' ear so its bronze point bore
straight to the other ear, then brought his sword
down on the head of gallant Echeclus:

the blade warmed with blood, and over his eyes
surged dark death and irresistible fate.
Then that son of Peleus stabbed Deucalion
beside his elbow: the great spear pierced
his arm—and he stood helpless, paralyzed,   480
death before him. Achilles swung a sword,
lopped off head and helmet, so the marrow
oozed from his spine and his corpse lay on earth.
Now Achilles rushed after Peiras' son
Rhigmus, who came to Troy from grassy Thrace—
hurled a keen spear at his midriff and he
toppled down. And while his squire Areithous
turned the chariot to flee, Achilles' spear
pierced his back, he fell, and his horses reared.

And as fearful fire rages in valleys   490
when mountainsides dry and deep woods blaze,
while blustery winds drive those flames ahead,
so he followed them raging everywhere
with his spear—and dark blood covered the earth.
As a farmer harnesses broad-browed bulls
to tread the barley on a threshing floor
and those snorting bulls quickly crush the grain,
thus Achilles' thunderous coursers came
trampling over shields and corpses, so blood
churned from the earth by wheels and horses' hooves   500
spattered all the axle and chariot rail,
and Peleus' terrible son hurried on
mad for glory, his huge hands smeared with gore.

Book Twenty-one: The Battle at the River

The river Xanthus (Scamander) tries to hold Achilles back.
The gods meet in battle.

When they came to the ford of that river
eddying Xanthus, immortal Zeus's child,
Achilles parted them, drove some over the plain
toward the town, where the Achaeans had fled
from fiery Hector just the day before.
Some streamed ahead in retreat, as Hera
made thick mist to hinder them—and the rest,
trapped by the silvery river's eddies,
tumbled in while its sheer streams bellowed,
its banks resounded. Roaring fearfully,   10
they swam here and there, whirled in the current.
As locusts take refuge in a river
from a forest fire, but those tireless flames
scorch them as they cower on the surface:
thus Xanthus' sonorous waters were jammed
with horses and warriors fleeing Achilles.

   That Myrmidon lord left his bronze spear propped
on tamarisk branches beside the bank,
plunged in with his sword to do evil work,
and stabbed left and right so horrible groans   20
rose from dying men, the streams grew red with blood.
As fish fill the nooks of a sheltered cove
when a dolphin pursues them, and they flee
in panic as he snatches all he can—
thus the Trojans cowered in those waters
beneath the steep banks. And when Achilles

wearied with slaughter, he took twelve young men
to pay the price for Patroclus' murder,
led them out from the water, dazed like fawns,
then bound their hands behind them with the belts   30
they wore about their elegant tunics,
ordered his people to take them away
and rushed back again, raging to slay more.

    Now Achilles met a son of Priam
ascending that bank—Lycaon, whom he
had captured before by Priam's orchards
chopping fig-tree shoots for a chariot rail
in the dead of night, when that poor man met
unexpected trouble: prince Achilles.
That time Achilles put him on a ship   40
and sold him in Lemnos to Euneus,
but he was ransomed dearly by a friend,
Eëtion, who sent him to Arisbë,
where he escaped, came to his father's home.
Eleven days long he celebrated
after his arrival—but on the twelfth
fell again in the hands of Achilles,
who soon would send him to Hades' dwelling.
When that son of Peleus spied him there
unarmed—without helmet or shield or spear,   50
since all had been abandoned as he swam
half faint with weariness in the river—
he muttered, deeply troubled, to himself:
"Ha, what an incredible sight this is!
I wonder if every Trojan I have slain
will come up again from the murky gloom
the way this fellow has escaped his doom.
I sold him in Lemnos, but it appears
even the deep sea couldn't keep him back.
Well, he'll have a taste of my mighty spear   60
so we can see with our very own eyes
if he also returns from there or stays
in the earth, which holds even the strongest."

As he pondered, Lycaon came near, dazed,
eager to implore him, most desperate
to escape his death and miserable fate.
Peleus' son Achilles raised his weapon,
but Lycaon crouched, scurried under it
to kneel before him—so that spear flew past
and stuck in the bank, eager to cut flesh.   70
Then he held Achilles' knees with one hand,
that formidable spear with the other,
and addressed him in agitated words:
"Pity me, magnificent Achilles—
I throw myself on your mercy, my lord.
Remember how we broke bread together
after you captured me in the orchard
and sold me in Lemnos, far from my land,
for the price of a hundred fine oxen.
Now my ransom was three times that, and I   80
came home twelve days ago after much
suffering, and again you've taken me—
awful fate! I must be hated by Zeus,
I was borne for so brief an existence
by my mother lovely Leothoë,
daughter of our Lelegian lord Altes,
who rules Pedasus on the Satnioeis
and married her to powerful Priam—
but you'll be murdering both their sons.
You slaughtered my brother Polydorus   90
as he fought among our foremost warriors
and now my own end's near—I don't believe
I shall ever escape from you again.
But listen, my lord, let me tell you this:
I'm only a half-brother of Hector
who murdered your brave and kindly comrade."

Thus Priam's glorious son begged Achilles
but heard a most ungentle voice reply:
"Fool, don't babble to me about mercy!
Before my dear Patroclus met his fate   100
I was far more ready to spare the lives

of Trojan warriors, took many captive.
But now I won't pardon a single one
the gods may deliver into my hands—
not a one, least of all Priam's sons.
Yes, my friend, you perish too—why whimper?
Death took Patroclus, a far better man.
And you see how handsome and tall I am?
My parents were a king and a goddess,
but I am doomed to die as well as you: 110
some morning or evening or afternoon
my life shall be taken in battle too
by a spear or an arrow from the string."

    This made Lycaon's heart and knees give way,
and he crouched down helplessly, stretching out
both his hands. But Achilles drew a sword
and stabbed him by the collarbone: it sank
in to the hilt, so he tumbled facefirst
all a-sprawl, his dark blood moistening the earth.
Then Achilles seized his foot and flung him   120
into the river and bellowed this boast:
"Now lie among the fishes, let them lick
the blood from your wound! Your own dear mother
won't mourn you on a bier, but Xanthus here
will whirl you down to the sea's broad bosom.
Fishes will dart through the murky ripples
to nibble at Lycaon's gleaming fat.
And you'll all die too, till we reach that town
while I follow you slaughtering stragglers!
Just don't expect this silvery river   130
to help, though you sacrificed many bulls
and hosts of prancing horses in his streams—
you shall all die horribly as you pay
for Patroclus and those many Danaans
you murdered by the ships in my absence."

    This increased the fury of that river,
who pondered how to restrain Achilles'
depredations and rescue the Trojans.
Now Peleus' fierce son, brandishing his spear,

leapt frenzied at great Asteropaeus,   140
a son of Pelagon, whom the Axius
fathered by princess Periboea
when that deep river lay with her in love.
Asteropaeus stood fast before him,
holding two spears, and was given courage
by Xanthus, furious for those Achilles
had mercilessly slaughtered in his streams.
After they came very near each other
illustrious quickfoot Achilles bellowed:
"Which mortal man are you who dares face me?   150
I've made many fathers weep for their sons!"

     And gallant Asteropaeus answered:
"Achilles, why ask about my lineage?
I came to Troy from far-off Paeonia
with hosts of Paeonian warriors, and this
is my eleventh day here in Ilios.
My grandfather was the river Axius,
whose waters are lovelier than any,
my father our famed spearman Pelagon—
so now let's do battle, prince Achilles!"   160

     Thus he boasted—and that son of Peleus
raised his great spear. But Asteropaeus,
being ambidextrous, flung two spears at once:
one hit the surface of his shield and yet
couldn't pierce that gold the god had given,
the other barely grazed his right forearm,
drew murky blood as it hurtled on past
and stuck in the earth, hungry to cut flesh.
Next Achilles hurled his own deadly spear,
in a rage to take his opponent's life,   170
but missed him, hit the high riverbank,
and that ashwood weapon ran halfway in.
Then Achilles drew his razor-sharp sword
and sprang upon him as he tried to tear
that spear from the bank with all his power.
Three times he shook it most frantically,
three times it stayed fast—and on the fourth try

would have bent it till the spearshaft shattered,
but Peleus' son took his life with the sword:
stabbed him on the belly by the navel   180
so his bowels burst out, and night veiled his eyes
as he writhed. Achilles leapt on his chest
to seize that armor and bellowed his boast:
"Well, farewell then! Zeus's progeny are
superior to those of a river god.
You say your grandfather was a river,
but I trace my line from thunderlord Zeus:
my father Peleus rules the Myrmidons,
and his own father was a son of Zeus,
who's mightier far than any stream,   190
and his progeny are more powerful too.
Let's see if this enormous river here
can help you now. But nothing withstands Zeus,
even the regal streams of Achelous
or that deep-flowing mighty Oceanus,
source of all rivers and of every sea
and the mountain springs and the deepest wells—
yet even he fears Zeus's lightning bolt
and his thunder when it rolls from heaven."

So he tore his bronze-tipped spear from the bank,   200
left Asteropaeus lying lifeless
on the sand, wetted by the dark waters,
as silvery eels and fishes came near
to nibble at the fat about his kidneys.
Next Achilles pursued the Paeonians
who scattered along that swirling river
when they saw their stalwart commander slain
by the awful might of Achilles' sword.
He killed Thersilochus, Astypylus,
Mnesus, Aenius, and Ophelestes,   210
and then would have slaughtered many more,
but the river became furious and roared
with human voice from the deeps of his streams:
"See here, Achilles, you've done more killing
than anyone else, since gods support you,

but even if Zeus lets you slay them all,
just do your dirty work away from me.
My delightful streams are crammed with corpses,
my waters dammed, can't proceed in their path,
being so choked with those men you murdered.   220
Now stop it, I say! You amaze me, sir!"

    And quickfoot Achilles cried in reply:
"Yes, I'll do as you command, Scamander,
though I won't stop slaying Trojans till they
are penned in their city and great Hector
meets me man-to-man in single combat."

    Again he rushed madly to the attack,
and that deep-streamed river called Apollo:
"Ho, Silverbow Lord, so you won't obey
the commands of Zeus, who often told you   230
to stand by our Trojans and assist them
till evening falls and darkens fertile earth."

    Now glorious Achilles plunged from the bank
into that river, who met him surging,
made the murky streams churn, and swept away
corpses of warriors Achilles had slain,
then, bellowing like a bull, he hurled them
onto the land—but saved the survivors,
hid them in wildly turbulent eddies.
And the surf surged all about Achilles   240
to smash his shield back, so he couldn't keep
his feet but clutched a colossal leafy
elm tree, which ripped out by the very roots
and tore the bank away and tumbled down
so its heavy branches dammed the river's
flow. He leapt from those tumultuous eddies,
hurried headlong away toward the great plain,
afraid. But the river rose after him
dark-crested, ready to end Achilles'
devastations and rescue the Trojans.   250
Peleus' son bounded far as a spearcast
with all the impetus of an eagle,

mightiest and swiftest winged thing:
thus he rushed away, his brilliant armor
clattering horribly, while that river
poured after him with an enormous roar.
As when some farmer digs a gravel ditch
to lead a stream among plants and gardens
and pries out boulders that block its passage—
but on comes that murmurous water, sweeping   260
pebbles before it, and where the ground slopes
flows so fast it overtakes its maker:
so again and again those swollen streams
overtook Achilles, for all his speed.
And every time that son of Peleus tried
to make a stand and learn if all the gods
who hold broad heaven were pursuing him,
the flooded river's formidable waves
hammered at his shoulders. And up he'd leap,
furious, but the river slowly tired him,   270
eating the ground out from under his feet.
So Achilles gazed toward heaven and groaned:
"Oh, father Zeus, will no god pity me
and save me from the river just this once?
But I blame none of the heavenly gods
as much as my mother, who lied to me
when she said I should die beneath that wall
by archer Apollo's awful arrows.
Ah, if only Hector had brought me down,
then one brave man would have slain another—   280
but now I'm doomed to a miserable death
penned in these streams like some pig-herding boy
swept from his feet by the torrents of spring."

  Thereupon Poseidon and Athena
approached him in the form of two warriors,
clasped Achilles' hand to reassure him.
Powerful Poseidon addressed him first:
"No need for you to worry, Peleus' son,
you have such fine helpers among the gods—
Athena and me, and Zeus supports us.   290

You are not doomed to die in a river—
he can't keep up his attack that long—
but hear some advice from us, dear fellow:
don't desist from detestable battle
till you come to their city and drive them
inside—but after you take Hector's life
return to the ships with your victory!"

   Then they went back among the immortals.
Very much encouraged, Achilles rushed
toward the plain, as waters poured everywhere,   300
carrying armor of many warriors
and their corpses. He leapt high in the air,
pressed against the current, wouldn't be held
with Pallas Athena urging him on.
And neither would Xanthus abate, but raged
even more furiously, raised crested waves
higher, and roared to the river Simois:
"Now join me against this warrior, brother,
or soon he'll be sacking Priam's city,
and none of the Trojans can withstand him.   310
Help me immediately! Pour more water,
set your streams to running tumultuously,
raise greater waves and a mighty turmoil
of trees and stones, so we stop this madman
who would even battle against the gods.
He won't be helped by his strength or his looks
or that stupendous armor, which will lie
covered by clammy slop and slime, as he
sinks in the sand with a heap of shingle
over all—his men won't gather his bones,   320
I'll bury him so deep in mud and ooze.
Yes, his tomb will be here: he needs no mound
when the Achaeans make his funeral!"

   Then he rushed at Achilles in a rage,
boiling with blood and foam and men's bodies.
And that dark flood of the heaven-fed river
rose towering, nearly knocked him over,
while Hera shrieked with fear prince Achilles

would be swept away by the raging streams
and quickly cried to her son Hephaestus: 330
"Now hurry, my crookfoot child—we believed
you'd be a match for eddying Xanthus!
Help that man immediately! Make a fire,
and there beside the sea I'll rouse a blast
of blustery winds from the south and west
to devour warriors' bodies and armor
as it carries your flames. Consume the trees
by Xanthus' banks and scorch him too—and don't
let him turn you back with a few wild words:
keep up the relentless attack till I   340
command you to cease that conflagration."

So Hephaestus made unwearying flames:
first they swept the plain, consumed those corpses
which lay there in heaps, slain by Achilles,
and the bright streams on the parched plain vanished.
As autumn winds sweep a rain-soaked orchard
to swiftly dry it, joy for the farmer,
that Trojan plain became parched, the bodies
charred. Next he turned his flames on the river,
consumed elms and willows and tamarisks,   350
burned clover and rushes and galingale
that lushly grew by its lovely eddies,
as the eels and fishes, in agony,
plunged here and there through the turbulent streams
tormented by canny Hephaestus' blasts.
Even that river was singed, and shouted:
"Hephaestus, no god can contend with you,
and you're far too much for me, fire-spitter!
Now stop it, I say! Achilles can drive
those Trojans from their town! Why should I care?"   360

He cried this while his silver eddies seethed.
As a cauldron set to boil over fire,
melting the lard of a market-fat pig,
begins to seethe when wood's put beneath it,
so those lovely streams bubbled with the flames—
and the river ceased to flow, tormented

by Hephaestus' heat. Then Scamander prayed
to haughty Hera in agitation:
"Hera, why does your son attack my streams
so outrageously? Well, I'm not to blame   370
as much as the other Trojan helpers!
I shall give in, if you so desire,
but have him do it too! I'll swear an oath
never to defend those Trojans from doom,
not even when all their city's ablaze
with flames the Achaean warriors have made."

When white-armed Hera heard the river's words
she quickly cried to her son Hephaestus:
"Stop, Hephaestus, my child! It isn't right
to attack a god for a mortal's sake."   380

Now Hephaestus quenched his unwearying fire,
and the lovely waters flowed as before.

Thus that river's fury ended, and they
quit their quarrel when Hera restrained them.
But the other gods began contending
bitterly in two different factions
and met with a hubbub as broad earth rang,
heaven clanged like a trumpet. Great Zeus heard
from his throne on Olympus and chuckled
with delight to see the gods do battle.   390
So they marched right to it: fiery Ares
hurled himself at plundering Athena,
waved his spear at her and cried spitefully:
"Why make the gods quarrel, you shameless bitch,
arrogant, impudent troublemaker?
Remember how you urged Diomedes
to attack me in war, led his weapon
till it lacerated my lovely skin?
Ha, you'll pay for it now, I do believe!"

Then he stabbed at her tasseled storm-cloud shield,   400
that dreadful thing even lightning can't pierce—
but Ares battered his spear against it.
Next green-eyed Athena reeled back and grabbed

a jagged black stone that lay on the plain,
once the boundary marker for a farmer,
smashed it on Ares' neck, and he collapsed.
Seven acres long he lay, hair besmeared
with dust, and his armor clanged about him.
Pallas Athena tittered and boasted:
"You big fool, you didn't know my power   410
if you believed you were a match for me!
What I did should please your mama Hera,
who's angry you abandoned the Danaans
and sided with their haughty enemies."

So she turned her delightful eyes away—
and Aphrodite led him by the hand,
tottering, groaning again and again.
But when divine white-armed Hera spied them
her words flew out to green-eyed Athena:
"Dear me, energetic daughter of Zeus,   420
see that wretched female taking Ares
from battle. Well, after her! Don't let her!"

Now Athena joyfully raced ahead,
overtook her, and slapped her on the breast—
and poor Aphrodite fell in a heap.
Thus those two lay on the bountiful earth
as Athena's boastful words fluttered out:
"I only wish all the Trojans' helpers
were brave and sturdy like Aphrodite,
who came to overthrow our Achaeans   430
and helped ferocious Ares against me.
Then that war would have ended long ago
after we sacked the city of Ilios."

And gentle-eyed Hera smiled to hear this.
But the great Earthshaker called Apollo:
"Well now, Phoebus, what are we waiting for?
The others have started, we'll be disgraced
if we go home without doing combat!
You start, since you're younger—it isn't right
I should, I'm so much older and wiser.   440

Ah, what an idiot! You have forgotten
all we suffered in the land of Ilios
after we two came at Zeus's command
to serve Laomedon a solid year
and that man promised us pay at the end.
I girded Troy with a wonderful wall
impregnable to attack forever,
while you herded their wandering cattle
in the wooded valleys of Mount Ida.
And when the time came to collect our pay   450
that rascally Laomedon refused—
sent us away and threatened us, he did!
Declared he'd have us tied up hand and foot,
sell us as slaves on some distant island,
hack off our ears with his hefty broadax!
We both went home in a fury that day
after he swindled us out of our pay.
But now you're backing his people and won't
help us destroy those arrogant Trojans
utterly, with all their wives and children."   460

    And Apollo the archer answered him:
"Ah, Poseidon, you could call me insane
if I fought you for the sake of mortals—
poor things! really more like leaves, one moment
full of fury, gobbling up earth's produce,
the next moment quite dead. Silly idea!
Let the others fight! I won't hear of it!"

    So prince Apollo turned away, ashamed
to battle against his own dear uncle.
But his sister Artemis, queen of beasts,   470
cackled after him as he departed:
"What's this, Apollo, leaving Poseidon
a total victory without combat?
Silly fool, what good are your arrows now?
But don't let me hear you boasting again
in my father's palace, telling the gods
you could take on Poseidon any day."

Far-worker Apollo didn't answer,
but the demure wife of Zeus was furious
and roared to that golden-arrowed goddess: 480
"Shameless bitch, how dare you go against me!
You're not my equal, I tell you, even
armed with the bow! Zeus made you a lioness
among women—lets you kill anyone—
but better be in the hills shooting deer
than try to battle your superiors here!
If you want to learn about war, you'll see
how much stronger I am when you meet me!"

Then Hera grabbed both her arms at the wrists
with one hand, took her bow with the other,   490
and, grinning ferociously, boxed her ears
as she squirmed. Arrows fell from her quiver,
and that goddess fled wailing, like a dove
who, chased by a hawk, flutters to a cave
and by a sheer stroke of fortune escapes:
thus Artemis left her bow, ran weeping,
while Hermes the messenger called Leto:
"I won't war against you, Leto—it's hard
to contend with thunderlord Zeus's wives!
Go ahead, boast to all the immortals   500
you won by your own enormous power!"

So Leto gathered the bow and arrows
scattered here and there in the swirl of dust
and followed her daughter when she had all.
But Artemis came to Zeus's palace
and sat there weeping on her father's knees,
ambrosial robes a-tremble. Father Zeus
pressed her to him, asked with a tender laugh:
"Now, now, my love, which god has treated you
so unkindly, as if you'd been naughty?"   510

That goddess of the clamorous hunt replied:
"Why, your own wife white-armed Hera did it—
she started the immortals quarreling."

Thus those two immortals were conversing
while Apollo Far Shooter entered Troy,
worried the sturdy wall of that city
would fall to the Danaans before its time.
But the other gods came to Olympus,
some angry, some glorying in victory,
and sat by their father, while Achilles   520
ravaged more ranks of warriors and horses.
As smoke rises from a burning city
to heaven when the gods' wrath fans those flames
and brings much trouble on suffering men,
so Achilles brought the Trojans trouble.

Aged Priam sat on his city wall
and spied that monstrous Achilles driving
his people in pell-mell retreat, no fight
left in them—and descended the tower
with a great groan and called his gatekeepers: 530
"Throw the doors open until our people
are all in the town! Here comes Achilles,
driving them on! Now we're surely doomed!
But after our Trojans are safe inside,
ram the great bolt of our double gates shut,
or that maniac may leap inside the wall!"

So they flung the bars back, opened those gates,
and rescued their armies, while Apollo
rushed out to keep the Trojans from ruin.
Straight for the city and its lofty wall,   540
thirst-parched, smeared with dust churned up from the plain,
they raced, as Achilles followed, madness
in his heart, raging to win more glory.

And Troy would have fallen that very day,
but Phoebus Apollo roused Agenor,
Antenor's proud son, peerless with the spear,
infused him with courage and stood nearby,

leaning on an oak tree, covered with mist,
ready to keep death's heavy hands from him.
Yet when he saw Achilles coming near   550
he stopped and stood pondering gloomily
and, deeply troubled, muttered to himself:
"Oh my, if I retreat from Achilles
where my comrades are fleeing, he'll catch me
on the spot, and I die a coward's death.
But suppose I leave them to be butchered
by that son of Peleus and make a dash
toward the Ilean plain: I might arrive
at Ida's slopes and hide in the bushes,
then wash away my sweat in the river   560
and return to the city by night.
Ah, what a lot of nonsense I'm saying!
If he sees me turning off toward the plain
he'll catch me easily with his speed—
and then I can never escape my doom,
he is so much stronger than any man.
Well, suppose I stay and wait for him here—
his flesh too may be pierced by a weapon,
he's also mortal, with only one life,
though Cronos' son lord Zeus gives him glory."   570

    Thus he awaited Achilles' attack,
ready to battle it out to the last.
As a leopard leaps from a deep thicket
to meet the hunters, and his haughty heart
stays fearless when he hears the hounds baying—
and, though a hunter attacks and stabs him
so a wound drips blood, he can't be kept back
till he springs on them or is killed himself:
so Antenor's son noble Agenor
remained in his place and wouldn't retreat   580
but kept behind the shelter of his shield,
brandishing an enormous spear, and roared:
"Glorious Achilles, you really believed
you'd sack our prosperous city today—
idiot! much will be suffered for it still!

Within its walls stand many brave warriors
before their parents and wives and children,
protecting them well. But you'll perish here
no matter how mad you are for battle!"

And he hurled his spear most mightily, hit   590
agile Achilles just beneath the knee
so his intricately forged tin shinguard
clattered horribly as bronze battered bronze,
though it couldn't pierce that gift of the god.   ·
And prince Achilles stormed toward Agenor—
but Apollo stole his victory, snatched
that son of Antenor, hid him in mist,
sent him peacefully off the battlefield.
Then the Far Worker lured swift Achilles
from combat, took a shape like Agenor,   600
and that son of Peleus raced after him.
Away they ran across the fertile plain,
Achilles hemming him toward the river,
not far behind—this was Apollo's trick,
so every moment he hoped to catch him—
while the Trojans gladly swarmed through the gates
till their city was jammed with fleeing men.
They no longer dared stay outside the walls
waiting for the rest, to see who was safe
and who lay dead, but all poured frantically   610
into the town if their feet could take them.

Book Twenty-two: Hector Falls

*Achilles slays Hector, dishonors his corpse. Hector's family
laments his death.*

So there in the city, panicked like fawns,
those Trojans cooled their sweat and quenched their thirst,
resting on ramparts, while the Achaeans
braced shoulders on shields and moved forward.
But Hector, trapped by an evil fate, stayed
outside his city at the Scaean Gates.
Meanwhile Apollo roared to Achilles:
"Ho, Peleus' son, why pursue me, a god,
you miserable mortal? You never knew
I'm an Olympian, you were so furious.   10
Have you forgotten those Trojan warriors
who fled to their town while you ran off here?
Well, you won't kill me—I'm no man who dies!"

   Very much vexed, swift Achilles answered:
"Ah, ruinous Apollo, you fooled me,
making me chase you here—if you hadn't,
many more would have died before their walls!
You stole my victory and rescued them
easily, since you needn't fear revenge.
But I'd repay you if I had the power."   20

   Then he ran proudly back toward the city
like a prizewinning horse with a chariot
who races full speed across a great plain:
thus glorious Achilles hurried ahead.

   And aged Priam was first to see him
as he ran all glittering like the star

that comes in winter and appears so clear
among those constellations of the night,
and men have given it the name Dog Star—
it shines the brightest but forebodes trouble 30
and brings burning heat upon poor mortals:
so the bronze shone on his chest as he ran.
Now the old monarch groaned and beat his head,
stretched his hands toward heaven and shrieked wildly,
begging his son, who stood before the gates
eager to meet Achilles in combat.
Priam cried piteously with arms upraised:
"Oh, Hector, my beloved child, don't wait
out there alone: you'll surely be murdered
by that formidable son of Peleus. 40
Merciless man! I wish the gods loved him
as I do—then dogs and vultures would soon
be eating him, and my heart would be eased.
He stole so many splendid sons of mine,
killed them or sold them into slavery,
and just now I found two more were missing—
Lycaon and gallant Polydorus,
my children by lovely Laothoë.
If those boys have been taken prisoner
we'll ransom them with all the gold and bronze 50
her father Altes has given to her—
and should they be dead, in Hades' kingdom,
their mother and I will have misery,
but our people won't lament them so long
if Achilles doesn't slaughter you too.
Come back to the city, my boy, and save
the men and the women of Ilios, don't
let that fierce son of Peleus take your life!
And pity poor me while I'm still alive,
a wretched old man dragging out his years, 60
doomed to be slain after many horrors:
my dear sons murdered, my daughters enslaved,
my palace plundered, innocent children
dashed to the ground in that dreadful carnage,
my son's wives captured by the Achaeans.

And at last, by my own front gate, fierce dogs
will tear me to pieces when some bronze spear
has taken the life from my body—
those same dogs I reared at my own table,
who will lap up my blood in a frenzy   70
and loll at my gate. Oh, it isn't wrong
for a young man to be mangled in war—
all seems proper, whatever may happen—
but when an old man's gray hair and gray beard
and private parts are disgraced by dogs,
nothing more piteous comes to poor mortals."

   And as he spoke, the old lord tore gray hairs
from his head—but didn't persuade Hector—
while his mother stood weeping and wailing,
then loosened her robe to expose her breast   80
and shrieked to him, weeping distractedly:
"Hector, child, pity and respect this breast
if ever it satisfied your hunger—
remember this, and defend the city
from inside the wall! Don't stand there alone!
Merciless man! if he kills you, you won't
be mourned on a bier by your mother, boy,
or by your lovely wife—but far from us
the dogs will devour you beside those ships!"

   Thus they tearfully implored their dear son   90
again and again but couldn't move him,
and he stood awaiting great Achilles.
As a mountain serpent waits for a man,
full of fury after eating foul herbs,
and writhes in its hole, glaring horribly—
so Hector stood with unquenchable rage,
his shield propped against a ledge of the wall,
and, deeply troubled, muttered to himself:
"Oh my, if I should retreat to our town
Polydamas will put the blame on me.   100
He told me to take our army inside
that terrible night Achilles returned,
but I didn't listen. I wish I had!

Now that my foolishness has ruined them,
I'm ashamed to face our Trojan people,
since some common soldier may be saying:
'Hector's awful pride has destroyed us all.'
No, better, far better, to go back home
after defeating that son of Peleus
or else die gloriously before our town.   110
But what if I lay down my mighty shield
and my helmet, lean this spear on the wall,
then go straight out to meet prince Achilles,
promise him Helen with all those treasures
Alexander's seafaring ships brought back
to Ilios, the cause of our contention—
and the Achaeans might receive a share
of whatever our people still possess.
Our elders would swear a most solemn oath
to conceal nothing, while we measure out   120
half the wealth our prosperous city has.
Ah, what a lot of nonsense I'm saying!
If I did this, I'd receive no pity
or mercy or respect—he could kill me
like a woman, when I meet him unarmed.
We wouldn't be scampering through the woods
to flirt together like a boy and girl,
like a girl and boy who flirt together!
No, better battle it out right away,
and Olympian Zeus will choose the victor!"   130

   While Hector pondered, Achilles advanced
fierce as the helmet-shaking god of war,
brandished a spear over his right shoulder
terribly, bronze a-glitter like the glare
of brilliant flame or of the rising sun.
Hector trembled at the sight, didn't dare
stay there, dashed wildly away from the gates
with that son of Peleus in hot pursuit.
As a mountain hawk, swiftest winged thing,
swoops easily after some timid dove   140
who darts away, and he plunges after

with piercing shrieks, keen to overtake her:
thus Achilles rushed on, while Hector ran
with all his might beneath the Trojan wall.
Past the lookout and the windswept fig tree
they raced on that wagon trail from the wall
and came to the lovely spring where two streams
rise to feed Xanthus' eddying currents:
one of them flows with warm water, and smoke
surrounds it as though it were blazing flame;   150
the other, even in summer, flows cold
as hail or snow or as a block of ice—
and next to these are two ample basins
of handsome stone, where the Trojan women
went to wash their very finest clothing
in peacetime, before the Achaeans came.
They raced on past, one after the other,
a mighty man chased by a far mightier,
swiftly, since they weren't running for a sheep
or an oxhide shield, first prize in a race,   160
but for the life of illustrious Hector.
As two fine horses round the turning posts
at a fast gallop, some great prize at stake,
a tripod or a lady, in funeral games:
so they circled Priam's city three times
on speedy feet, the immortals watching.
Then that father of gods and men declared:
"Oh my, I see a man I dearly love
being chased about their wall—poor Hector!
He made fine sacrifices in my name   170
on Ida's slopes or in his citadel,
but now incomparable Achilles
pursues him round that city of Priam.
So it seems we Olympians must decide:
should we hurry to save him once again
or shall Achilles lay that brave man low?"

   The goddess green-eyed Athena replied:
"Why, Father, old Dazzlebolt, I'm surprised!
A mere mortal, doomed long ago by fate,

and you plan to save him from death again?   180
Well, we other gods will never approve!"

    And Zeus the cloudgatherer answered her:
"There, there, dear girl, of course I was only
teasing. You do just as your heart desires;
I won't stand in your way for a moment."

    This was all green-eyed Athena needed,
and she darted down from Olympus' peaks.

    But swift Achilles still pursued Hector.
As in the hills a hound flushes a fawn
from its lair, chases it through wooded glens,   190
and it slithers away in a thicket,
but the hound implacably tracks it down:
thus Hector could not hide from Peleus' son.
Each time he dashed for the Dardanian gate
to gain the shadow of that sturdy wall
where his friends could help with shots from above,
Achilles would cut him off, turn him back
toward the plain, staying on the city side.
As a man in a dream flees another
who cannot catch him, nor can he escape,   200
Hector kept only a few steps ahead.
And how would he have avoided his doom
had not Apollo come for the last time
to give him more vigor and speed his knees?
Next Achilles gestured to show his men
they weren't to hurl their weapons at Hector,
so no one else would be his conqueror.
And when they approached those springs the fourth time,
mighty father Zeus poised his golden scales
and on them set two fates of wretched death,   210
one for Achilles, one for Hector, then
raised them at the middle—and Hector's sank
down to Hades, while Apollo left him.
Thus green-eyed Athena neared Achilles
and, standing by him, murmured in his ear:
"Now, Peleus' peerless son, I hope we two

will bring our Argives enormous glory
by slaying that insatiable Hector.
No, he won't escape us today, I say,
though archer Apollo should give his all   220
and go groveling before father Zeus.
So you stay here and catch your breath while I
persuade him to come meet you in combat."

He gladly obeyed Athena's command,
stood leaning on his keen bronze-pointed spear.
Then she left him and hurried to Hector
in the shape of illustrious Deiphobus
and, standing by him, murmured in his ear:
"My dear friend, it seems you're having trouble
with that swift Achilles hot on your heels!   230
But we'll stand together and drive him off!"

Flashing-helmeted Hector answered her:
"Ah, Deiphobus, I always loved you best
of all the brothers in my family,
but now I'm fonder of you than ever.
When you saw me, only you weren't afraid
to leave the town, though the rest stayed inside."

The goddess green-eyed Athena replied:
"True, my dear friend! How often our parents
knelt with our companions and implored me   240
to stay, they feared that man so extremely,
but I was full of fury to help you.
Very well, up and at him—we won't spare
our spears, and soon we'll see if Achilles
slaughters us and takes some bloody booty
back to his ships, or you kill him sooner."

Thus Athena cunningly led him on.
After they came very near each other,
that flashing-helmeted Hector bellowed:
"Peleus' son, I'll retreat from you no more!   250
Three times you chased me around the city
since I lost my nerve, but now I'm ready
to stand fast before you, kill or be killed.

Let's swear by the immortal gods, those best
witnesses and keepers of people's oaths:
I won't mistreat your body if wise Zeus
grants me endurance and I take your life—
I'll keep your glorious armor, Achilles,
but give your body back. You do the same."

And nimble Achilles shouted, scowling: 260
"Hector, madman, don't babble about oaths!
Lions and people make no agreements,
wolves and lambs will exchange no promises,
but live in incessant enmity.
Thus we'll have no friendship, no solemn oaths
till one of us has fallen in the dust
and gluts murderous Ares with his blood.
Now remember what you know of battle:
you need all your skill in handling the spear—
and no escape! Soon Pallas Athena   270
will help me take your life, and you shall pay
for all my dear companions you murdered."

So he poised his ashwood spear and hurled it,
but Hector was watching closely and dodged
by ducking down, so it hurtled past him,
rammed in the earth. Athena seized that spear
and returned it to Achilles, unseen.
Then Hector called to Peleus' peerless son:
"A total miss, Achilles! You never
knew of my doom from Zeus, you just dreamed it!   280
Miserable swindler, slippery talker,
big boasting words cannot scare me away.
You won't drive a weapon in my back
but in my chest, as I charge straight for you,
if it must be so. All right, here's my spear—
take it along with you in your body!
Our Trojans will be delighted when you
are dead, you've given them so much trouble."

So he poised his ashwood spear and hurled it,
and it hit Achilles' shimmering shield   290

but bounded back. And Hector was furious
he'd thrown his dangerous weapon in vain
and stood dumbfounded, since he had no more,
then shouted to white-shielded Deiphobus
requesting a spear—but he wasn't there.
Thus Hector knew all, and said to himself:
"Ah, the gods are summoning me toward death.
I believed Deiphobus was standing by,
but he isn't, and Athena tricked me!
Now horrible death has come very near   300
and no escape. It must have been the plan
of Zeus and the Far Shooter, who always
helped me before—but here fate has trapped me.
Well, I won't go down without a struggle:
I'll do something glorious before I die."

    And then Hector drew the razor-sharp sword
that hung so huge and heavy by his side
and leapt out like some high-flying eagle
who plunges through murky clouds to the plain
to seize a lamb or a cowering hare: 310
thus he stormed forward, brandishing his sword.
And full of ferocious rage, Achilles
attacked, before him that elaborate
incised shield, tossed his shimmering four-horned
helmet surmounted by a golden plume
Hephaestus had fastened over the crest.
As a star rises among stars at night—
Hesperus, loveliest in the heavens—
so shone the pointed spear that Achilles
brandished in his right hand for Hector's doom   320
as he scanned him seeking a place to stab.
His body was covered by that armor,
his booty when he brought Patroclus down,
but an opening showed where neck and chest
met at the gullet, the deadliest spot—
and as Hector came on, Achilles stabbed,
and through his tender neck that spearpoint sheared.
Yet the bronze didn't sever his windpipe,

so he still could murmur a few last words.
He sank in the dust—and Achilles roared: 330
"Hector, when you stole Patroclus' armor
you thought you'd be safe, forgot about me—
idiot! there among our seafaring ships
he left an even stronger avenger,
who has brought you down. Now you shall be torn
by dogs, while he has a decent burial."

   Flashing-helmeted Hector cried feebly:
"I beg you by your life, by your parents,
don't let the Achaean dogs devour me!
Accept all those treasures, the gold and bronze   340
my father and mother will present you,
and return my body so our people
may burn it with proper ceremony."

   But nimble Achilles shouted, scowling:
"You swine, don't babble about my parents!
I'm so angry that I could carve you up
and eat you raw, for the harm you have done.
No man alive can keep the dogs from you,
not even for ten times, for twenty times
the usual ransom, with more promised too—   350
not even if your weight were paid in gold
by Dardanian Priam would your mother
be mourning her dear son upon a bier,
but dogs and vultures will devour you here."

   And that illustrious Hector gasped, dying:
"Ah yes, I know you all too well: you won't
be persuaded—your heart is of iron!
Beware, or I may bring the gods' anger
that day Apollo and Paris slay you
by the Scaean Gates, for all your bravery."   360

   Even as he spoke, death enfolded him,
and the soul flew from his corpse to Hades
bewailing its fate, leaving strength and youth.
Then Achilles cried to the lifeless man:

"Well, die! I'll meet my doom whenever Zeus
and the other immortals may send it."

Next he tore his bronze spear from the body,
set it aside, and ripped the armor off,
all bloodied. The Achaeans ran around
to gaze amazed at Hector's form and face,   370
and each one made a new wound when he came.
A man would catch his neighbor's eye and say:
"Hey, Hector seems a lot softer today
than the time he put the torch to our ships!"

These were their words as they stabbed at his corpse.
After Achilles had taken that armor
he stood among the Achaeans and called:
"My heroic friends and fellow warriors,
the gods have allowed us to kill this man
who did more damage than all the others.   380
For the moment we'll continue combat,
till we learn if the Trojan spearmen plan
to abandon their town, now Hector's dead,
or keep on fighting even without him.
But what a lot of nonsense I'm saying!
A warrior lies by the ships unburied:
our Patroclus, whom I shall not forget
as long as I live and breathe on the earth.
Though people forget their dead in Hades
I'll remember my dear companion there.   390
All right, boys, how about a victory song?
Haul the body back to our buoyant ships—
we've won great glory by slaying Hector,
a man the Trojans honored like a god."

Next he planned foul treatment for Hector's corpse:
slashed close behind the tendons of both feet
from heel to ankle, ran two straps through them,
tied them to his chariot, but let the head
drag, then mounted himself with that armor,
whipped the horses up, and away they flew.   400
Hector was dragged in a dust cloud, his dark

hair streaming wildly, his head—once so fair—
smeared with dust, now Zeus had abandoned him
to humiliation in his own homeland.

So dust covered his head, while his mother
tore her hair out, ripped her shimmering veil
away, and screamed when she saw her dear son.
Priam too wailed piteously, while the people
shrieked and moaned everywhere in the city.
It was more as if all their towering town   410
of Ilios were being burned to the ground.
They could hardly keep that grief-stricken king
from rushing through the gates in his frenzy.
Then he rolled in manure and implored them,
calling one after another by name:
"Oh, friends, if you love me, let me go out
alone to the ships of the Achaeans
and entreat that reckless, ruthless warrior
to have shame before his men and pity
my old age. He has a father like me,   420
Peleus, who raised him to be a scourge
on Troy and trouble for me most of all,
he killed so many splendid sons of mine.
But I grieved for none of them as this one,
who'll bring me down to Hades with sorrow—
Hector. If only he'd died in my arms!
Then his poor wretched mother and myself
might have had our fill of mourning for him."

Sobbing, he said this, as the people groaned.
And Hecabe led the lamentation: 430
"My dear child, oh misery! How can I
live on without you? Every day and night
you were my pride and a blessing for all
the people of Ilios, who received you
like a god, such was your fame and glory
while you lived, though now fate has taken you."

Sobbing, she said this. But Hector's wife still
hadn't heard the news: no messenger came

to say her husband stayed outside the gates.
Deep in her palace, his wife was weaving   440
a double-fold purple cloak with flowerlets.
And she summoned her servant girls to put
a great pot on the fire, so there would be
a hot bath for Hector when he returned—
fool! she little knew he lay far from baths,
slain by Athena at Achilles' hands.
But when she heard that shrieking and wailing
from the wall, she reeled and dropped the shuttle,
and her words fluttered out to her servants:
"Two of you come with me to see the war!   450
I heard the voice of my husband's mother
shrieking—and my heart's in my mouth, my knees
feel weak. This means trouble for Priam's sons!
I pray it isn't so. But I'm very
afraid Achilles has cut Hector off
alone, driven him out onto the plain
and made an end to that dreadful courage
which possessed him. He wouldn't stay behind
but always fought far before the others."

    She rushed from the hall like a madwoman,   460
heart hammering, beside her handmaidens.
And when she came to their throng on the wall
she stood staring toward the plain and saw him
being dragged before the town: those horses
pitilessly bore him toward the ships.
So a murky haze enveloped her eyes,
and she fell over backward in a faint,
her splendid headdress tumbled to the ground:
that diadem, that net, that woven band
and the veil golden Aphrodite gave   470
when glorious Hector took her as his wife
from her home for such an enormous price.
And her husband's sisters came running round
to lift her, stunned with grief, among them.
After she had recovered consciousness

she wailed among the women of Ilios:
"Oh, Hector! we both were born to the same
fate, you here in Priam's stately palace,
I in Thebes beneath wooded Mount Placus
at the home of Eëtion, who reared me   480
for a dreadful doom—better he had not.
Now you go to Hades deep in the earth,
leaving your wife to her bitter sorrow,
widowed in your palace, our child so young—
poor miserable boy—and you can be
no comfort for him, Hector, now you're dead.
Even if he escapes this dreadful war
he is sure to have troubles afterward,
since other people will covet his lands.
An orphaned child has no more companions   490
but hangs his head always, cheeks streaked with tears,
and runs to his father's friends when in need,
tugging in vain at their cloaks and tunics
till a man who pities him holds a cup
to wet his lips a bit but not his throat.
Then some boy whose parents are both alive
shoves him away from the table and says:
'Beat it! Your father doesn't eat with us!'
Back to his mother comes the weeping boy—
Astyanax, who sat on his father's knees   500
and would eat only marrow and sheep fat,
and when he became drowsy with playing
slept on a bed in the arms of his nurse,
with nothing but happy thoughts in his head.
But his father's death means trouble for our
Lordling, as the Trojan people called him,
because you alone were our salvation.
And there by the ships, far from your parents,
after dogs have gnawed you, worms will devour
your naked body, though you've clothes at home,   510
those lovely finespun ones your women wove.
Now I'll burn them all, so useless they are—

you cannot be wearing them where you lie—
and thus we shall remember your splendor."

Sobbing, she said this, as the women groaned.

Book Twenty-three: The Funeral Games

Patroclus' ghost appears to Achilles. Funeral games for Patroclus.

So they mourned in the town, while those Argives
came to their ships and the broad Hellespont
and scattered, every warrior to his ship,
but Achilles would not dismiss his men
and called to his battle-loving comrades:
"Equestrian Myrmidons, my dear comrades,
keep your thundering horses in harness
till we drive our chariots past Patroclus
to grant him the proper lamentation.
When we have taken our fill of mourning,   10
we may unyoke them and make our suppers."

  And all wailed together with Achilles.
Three times they drove round Patroclus' body,
grieving, as Thetis increased their sorrow.
The sands were wet, those warriors' armor wet
with tears, they mourned so illustrious a lord.
And Achilles led the lamentation,
placing murderous hands on his comrade's chest:
"Rejoice, Patroclus, even in Hades!
Now you'll have all I promised you before: 20
to drag Hector here, let the dogs eat him,
and cut the throats of twelve Trojan nobles
before your pyre to avenge your murder."

  Next he planned foul treatment for Hector's corpse:
left it lying facedown in the dust beside
Patroclus' bier. And the people removed
their gleaming armor, unyoked those horses,

and sat by Achilles' ship in endless
rows—and he ordered a funeral feast.
Many sleek bulls bellowed about the knife   30
as they died, many sheep and bleating goats
and hosts of corpulent white-tusked porkers
were roasted over the flickering flames
while, cup after cup, libations were poured.

   And Peleus' illustrious son Achilles
was brought to Agamemnon by the lords
with difficulty, so frenzied was he.
When they came to their commander in chief
those nimblefoot Achaean heralds placed
a great pot of water over the fire   40
so Achilles could wash the blood away.
But he vehemently refused and swore:
"No, by Zeus, all-highest, most powerful,
water will never touch my head again
till Patroclus rests in his funeral mound
and I cut my hair to lament this loss,
since I'll have no greater grief in my life.
Very well, set out our miserable meal.
But at daybreak, Agamemnon, my lord,
we'll bring firewood and prepare what's proper   50
for a dead man to take into the gloom,
so the tireless flames may burn his body
and our people can return to their tasks."

   They gladly obeyed Achilles' commands:
a sumptuous dinner was set before them,
and they feasted of that abundant meal.
After they had eaten and drunk their fill,
each warrior entered his tent to slumber.
But Peleus' son lay by the thunderous sea,
heaving great groans among his Myrmidons   60
on an open beach where the surf surged in.
When sleep had seized him, easing his heartache
in its sweet flood—he was so exhausted
pursuing Hector before windy Troy—
the spirit of poor Patroclus appeared,

with the very same shape and splendid eyes
and voice, and wearing just the same clothing.
It stood above Achilles' head and said:
"You sleep and forget me, prince Achilles,
as never in life, though you do in death.   70
Bury me soon so I pass Hades' gates—
the shades of the dead will not allow me
to join them over the Stygian river,
and I wander vainly above Hades.
Give me your hand, I beg you, because once
you burn my body I'll never return.
Never again will we sit together
spinning our plans, now I have been taken
by that awful fate I got at my birth.
And you too, godlike Achilles, are doomed   80
to die beneath their city's massive walls.
Now this is my last request for you: don't
let them bury us apart, Achilles,
but together, as we lived in your home
when my father brought me from Opoeis
because of that unfortunate murder
when I killed the son of Amphidamas
accidentally in a childish quarrel—
but Peleus sheltered me in his palace,
reared me with kindliness, made me your squire.   90
So let one urn hold the bones of us both,
that golden urn your mother once gave you."

    And that quickfoot Achilles answered him:
"Ah, my dearest friend, why have you appeared
to ask me this? Of course I shall do it,
exactly the way you have requested.
But now come nearer so we may embrace
and grieve together only a moment."

    Then Peleus' son stretched his hands out and grasped
thin air: like smoke the spirit sank in earth   100
with an eerie squeal. Achilles leapt up
amazed, slapped his hands together, and cried:

"Ha, then there's something even in Hades,
a spirit and a phantom shape at least,
because all night long poor Patroclus' soul
hovered above me weeping and wailing,
his very image as he was in life!"

So every man began to groan again—
and rose-fingered Dawn appeared as they wept
over the corpse. Meanwhile Agamemnon   110
went through the camp, assembling men and mules
to gather wood—and sent as commander
Idomeneus' trusty squire Meriones.
Then off they went, with their hefty axes
and tough-woven ropes and stubborn pack mules,
and upward, downward, sideward, back and forth
they trudged till they reached the slopes of Ida,
where they immediately began to hack
at those towering oaks, which thundered down.
Now the Achaean warriors cut the wood   120
and tied it to mules, who dug their hooves in
and struggled through the bushes to the plain.
Idomeneus' trusty squire Meriones
commanded them to carry logs, and they
left these on the shore, where Achilles planned
a great tomb for Patroclus and himself.
And after each man had brought his firewood
they sat down and waited. Now Achilles
ordered those formidable Myrmidons
to harness their horses and arm themselves—   130
and all of them rose, donned their brilliant bronze,
and mounted, spearmen beside charioteers,
their chariots in front, then swarms came on foot,
and in the middle they brought Patroclus.
Next they cut their hair to cover the corpse—
and behind them Achilles held the head,
grieving for the friend he sent to Hades.

After they reached the designated place
they laid Patroclus down, made heaps of wood.
Then Achilles remembered something else: 140

walked away from their pyre and sheared the hair
he'd grown for that river god Spercheius
and gazed over the wine-dark sea and cried:
"Spercheius, my father made a useless vow
I would celebrate my safe return home
by cutting my hair and sacrificing
fifty uncastrated rams in your streams,
by your holy grove and fragrant altar.
He swore this, but you ignored his appeal.
And now, since I too won't be going home,   150
Patroclus may take this hair to Hades."

    Then he laid it in his dear comrade's hand,
and all of them burst into tears again.
The sun would have set upon their mourning,
but Achilles addressed Agamemnon:
"Atreus' son, you have most authority
over our people, so give them commands
to cease the mourning and make their dinners.
Patroclus' dearest friends will care for him,
and our Achaean lords may stay here."   160

    After king Agamemnon heard these words
he sent the people away to their ships—
but the mourners remained, heaped wood in piles
till they made a pyre a hundred feet square,
and sadly laid the dead body on top.
Then many an excellent sheep and ox
were flayed and dressed before the funeral pyre.
Achilles gathered fat from every one
to cover the corpse, heaped skinned beasts nearby,
laid jars of honey and oil on the bier,   170
then put four glorious horses on that pyre,
groaning and moaning loudly all the while.
Nine dogs there were that fed from his table,
and he slaughtered two of these for the pyre,
next cut the throats of twelve noble Trojans
with his sword—an evil business indeed—
set the flames to flicker implacably
and groaned and called his beloved comrade:

"Rejoice, Patroclus, even in Hades!
Now you have all I promised you before.   180
Yes, here we've put those twelve noble Trojans
to burn with you on the pyre—and Hector
won't be devoured by flames but by the dogs."

   This was his boast, but no dogs gnawed Hector:
golden Aphrodite kept them away
night and day, anointed him with rose oil
to protect his body from corruption.
Now Phoebus Apollo summoned dark clouds
and covered that place where the dead man lay,
so no scorching rays of the sun would come   190
and shrivel up the flesh about his bones.

   But Patroclus' funeral pyre failed to burn.
So prince Achilles devised a new plan:
he turned away and prayed to the North Wind
and the West Wind, promising sacrifice,
then poured libations from a golden cup,
begged them to kindle the wood and set flames
crackling over the corpse. Quickly Iris
heard his prayers, carried them to the winds
gathered in the blustery West Wind's home   200
at a banquet table—so she came and stood
on the stone threshold. When they saw her there
each one leapt up to offer her his seat,
but she declined to join them and declared:
"Can't sit! I'm going over Oceanus
where they sacrifice to the blessed gods
in Ethiopia, and I want my share.
Achilles begs the North Wind and West Wind
to come, promises them splendid offerings
if they will kindle the funeral pyre   210
for Patroclus, whom all the Danaans mourn."

   Whereupon she scurried off, and they rose,
driving the clouds before them with a roar,
rushed over the waters and raised the waves
with whistling blasts, then came to deep-soiled Troy,

fell on the fire, which flared ever higher.
All night long they hurled themselves on that pyre,
shrieking shrilly, and all night Achilles
dipped wine in a fine double-handled cup
from a golden bowl, poured his libations,   220
and called to the soul of poor Patroclus.
As a father wails while burning the bones
of his newly wed son, a dreadful loss,
thus Achilles wailed burning his friend's bones
and dragged himself about with ceaseless groans.

When the morning star came to proclaim day
and Dawn spread saffron robes over the sea,
Patroclus' pyre began to flicker down,
and the winds went rushing back to their homes
over the billows of the Thracian sea.   230
Now Peleus' son strode away from the pyre,
lay down wearily, and sweet sleep took him—
while Agamemnon summoned his leaders.
The noise of their coming woke Achilles,
so he sat up straight and addressed them:
"Atreus' son and you other Danaan lords,
quench the funeral pyre by pouring wine
everywhere those powerful flames have come.
Then gather the bones of our dear comrade
carefully—they aren't hard to recognize: 240
we put him in the center of that pyre,
with warriors and horses on the edges.
And we'll lay his bones in a golden urn
till I take my own journey to Hades.
No need to prepare a great mound for him
but a proper one only—then later
it can be made high and wide by the men
who are left by our ships when I'm dead."

They did as gallant Achilles ordered:
poured wine to quench the pyre of Patroclus,   250
where flames had come and the ashes were deep,
then, weeping, gathered their gentle friend's bones
in a golden urn with two layers of fat,

veiled it with linen, set it in a tent.
Next they laid stone foundations for a mound
about the funeral pyre, piled earth inside,
and turned to go. But that son of Peleus
stopped the people, commanded them to sit,
and ordered up prizes: pots and kettles
with horses and mules and sturdy oxen,   260
stately women and gray chunks of iron.

   First he set out prizes for the drivers:
a servant girl clever at handicrafts
and a pot that held twenty-two measures
for the winner; next an unbroken mare
six years old, a mule foal in her belly.
And as third prize he set out a kettle
that held four measures, never touched by fire,
for the fourth two pieces of solid gold,
and as fifth a magnificent goblet.   270
Now Achilles stood and shouted to all:
"Atreus' son and you other Achaeans,
here are fine prizes for our charioteers.
If you raced in another man's honor
the first prize would be mine, no doubt of that,
since my horses run faster than any—
they're immortal ones Poseidon granted
my father Peleus, who gave them to me.
But I'll stay back with these powerful beasts.
And what a glorious charioteer they had—   280
a kindly man who often oiled their manes
after washing them in limpid water.
So they stand here in lamentation, manes
trailing onto the ground, brokenhearted.
Well, anyone who believes in his team
better get them ready to race today!"

   And the charioteers stirred in excitement.
Immediately that son of Admetus
rough-riding Eumelus leapt to his feet,
and dauntless Diomedes stood up next   290
to yoke the team he took from Aeneas,

though Apollo had rescued their master.
Next Atreus' son blond Menelaus rose
to harness a span of thundering steeds:
his Podargus and Agamemnon's mare
Aithë, given him by Echepolus
to be excused from warring in Ilios
and stay at home enjoying those riches
Zeus had granted him in broad-lawned Sicyon—
and now Menelaus made her ready.   300
And the fourth to rise was Antilochus,
redoubtable son of aged Nestor,
whose chariot was drawn by those nimble-hooved
Pylian coursers. His father hurried up
and offered his son a stream of advice:
"Antilochus, you're young but Poseidon
and thunderlord Zeus have taught you to drive,
so you've no need of instruction from me,
you have such finesse in handling a span.
Too bad these horses of yours are slowest.   310
Though other men have faster ones, they can't
control their team as cleverly as you.
Therefore, dear boy, use all your cunning skill,
or you may miss out on these prizes too.
Skill serves a woodcutter better than force;
skill lets a pilot bring his ship to port
when turbulent sea winds toss it about;
skill makes one charioteer defeat another.
Some drivers may give the horses their heads
and carelessly let them swerve back and forth   320
so they go wandering over the course—
while a good man, though his team is weaker,
swings deftly back and forth and remembers
how to extend his horses at the start,
keeps a keen eye on the driver ahead.
Now listen, I'll describe the turning post.
It's a dried-out stump about six feet high,
an oak or a pine the rains cannot rot,
with a pair of stones set on either side
where the two tracks meet at a wide smooth space—   330

a memorial for some long-dead warrior,
or it may have been a landmark before—
and prince Achilles has made it your goal.
Drive near that post as you possibly can,
lean in your chariot only a little
to the left, encourage the right-hand horse
with shouts or the spur, and give him free rein.
Let your left-hand horse come so near that post
it seems to graze the hub of your wheel,
but be careful you don't collide with it,   340
or you'll come to grief with this glorious team
and make the other drivers delighted.
All right, son, keep a weather eye open.
And if you're ahead at the turning post
no man on this earth can overtake you,
though he were driving mighty Arion,
that flying-hooved steed of heavenly stock,
or Laomedon's team, bred in this land."

  And veteran Nestor sat down again
after he had duly spoken his piece.   350

  Fifth to harness horses was Meriones.
So they mounted, put lots in a helmet,
Achilles shook them, and Antilochus'
leapt out first. Eumelus drew second place
and blond Menelaus received the third
and Meriones came next, while last of all
fell to Diomedes, though he was best.
Achilles showed them that turning post
far out on the plain, where an umpire stayed—
godlike Phoenix, his father's follower—   360
to observe the race and report its course.

  Then all raised their reins at the same moment,
called to encourage their horses, and lashed
them eagerly—so those impatient teams
sped off from the ships, and under their chests
dust rose and stood like clouds or a whirlwind;
while their manes came streaming out behind them.

Now those chariots thundered on the rich earth,
now they bounded in air—and the drivers
held the reins tight, hearts hammering wildly   370
in hope of victory, and each man roared
as his horses raced on, raising the dust.
But after their teams had turned down the track
back toward the gray sea, the worth of each steed
appeared, they strained to the limit, and soon
Eumelus' swift mares galloped out ahead,
and behind them Diomedes' stallions,
those mettlesome horses of Tros, so close
they seemed ready to trample his chariot
and their breath warmed his back and shoulders   380
as the sturdy stallions thundered ahead.
And now they'd have passed or drawn alongside,
but Apollo was vexed with Tydeus' son
and battered the brilliant whip from his hand,
so angry tears came streaming from his eyes
to see those mares go faster than before
while his own team ran slack without a whip.
And when Athena saw how Apollo
had deceived him, she came rushing behind
to return his whip, gave his horses strength,   390
and pursued Eumelus in a fury
and shattered his yoke: those nimble-hooved steeds
swerved and their chariot pole clattered to earth,
so he tumbled beside the whirling wheels,
skin all ripped on his elbows and nose,
forehead formidably bruised, while his eyes
flooded with tears and his voice became choked.
Next Tydeus' son swerved his thunderous team
and surged far in the lead, since Athena
had infused his horses with more fury,   400
while Menelaus followed in second place.
Antilochus called to his father's steeds:
"Get a move on, you two—faster! faster!
but never believe you can overtake
Diomedes' team, green-eyed Athena
has given them such incredible speed.

Just catch those horses of Menelaus
immediately, or you'll both be disgraced
by Aithë, a mare—what's wrong with you here?
Well, let me assure you, my fine fellows,   410
our Nestor won't care for you anymore,
he'll cut your throats with his razor-sharp sword
if your laziness makes us come in late!
So step lively, boys, give it all you have,
and meanwhile I'll keep a keen eye open
for a narrow place where we can slip past!"

Then, fearful of their master's reproaches,
they strained to the utmost—and very soon
Antilochus spied a break in the track,
a gully where the pent-up winter rains   420
eroded the road, made a deep hollow.
There Menelaus drove so none could pass,
but Antilochus turned his swift horses
outside the track and followed to one side.
That son of Atreus was frightened and cried:
"You're mad, Antilochus! Hold your team back!
The way's too narrow for passing me, man!
If we collide, it will ruin us both!"

But Antilochus drove frantically on,
whipped his horses as if he hadn't heard.   430
As far as a discus some young warrior
hurls from the shoulder to prove his power
they ran side by side, but Menelaus
let his mares drop back, stopped spurring them on,
afraid those coursers would come together,
overturn the chariots, and spill them both
into the dust in their fury to win.
Blond Menelaus bellowed angrily:
"Ho, Antilochus, you reckless rascal,
damn it, we thought you had more sense than that!   440
But you won't win the prize so easily!"

Then he roared to his own team of horses:
"Keep it up, I say, don't slacken the pace!

Those others will be wearying sooner,
since neither is young as he was before!"

And fearful of their master's reproaches,
they galloped faster, soon came close behind.

The Achaeans sat watching those horses
race ahead, raising the dust on the plain.
First to see was Cretan Idomeneus,   450
who sat on high ground apart from the rest.
He heard a voice shouting in the distance
and knew it, saw the steed that sped out front—
an all-bay one except for his forehead,
dappled with a white spot round as the moon—
so he stood and shouted to the people:
"My heroic friends and fellow warriors,
am I the only one who sees these horses?
Another team is ahead, I believe,
another driver—must have been trouble   460
for those mares who were running first before!
They rounded the turning post far in front,
but now the mares are nowhere to be found
though I've looked all over the Trojan plain.
It appears their driver has dropped the reins
and couldn't hold them as they made the turn.
He must have fallen and smashed his chariot,
while his horses ran wild outside the course.
Have a look for yourselves—I'm old, you know,
and can't see clearly, but it seems to be   470
an Aetolian, a distinguished noble,
Tydeus' turbulent son Diomedes."

And Oileus' son Aias cried scornfully:
"Nonsense, Idomeneus—those horses are
still far away as they race on the plain.
You're hardly the youngest Achaean here,
and your sight's blurry, all right, but you
love to talk big. Sit down and be quiet,
since men much better than you are present.

The mares are in front as they were before,   480
and lord Eumelus stands holding the reins."

That Cretan leader answered angrily:
"Damn it all, Aias, you're good at wrangling
but at little else, you thickheaded ass!
Well, let's bet a kettle or a cauldron,
and Atreus' son Agamemnon will say
which team is ahead. You'll learn when you pay!"

Then Oileus' son Aias leapt to his feet,
ready to answer with more angry words,
and their quarrel would have gone still further,   490
but Achilles himself stood up and cried:
"Now stop this stupid argument, you two.
You wouldn't like to hear another man
making such an unconscionable fuss!
Sit back in your places, keep your eyes peeled,
and those fine horses will be arriving
soon enough. Then you'll both see for yourselves
which one of our chariots is out ahead."

As he spoke, that son of Tydeus came near,
whipping his team up frantically—and they   500
leapt high in the air while they galloped on,
flakes of dust bespattering the driver,
and his chariot garnished with gold and tin
followed the horses so only little
trace of those wheel tires remained behind
in the powdery dust, so quick they flew.
And he drove into their assembly, sweat
streaming over his horses' necks and chests.
Diomedes leapt down from the chariot,
leaned his gleaming whip on the yoke. And then   510
his squire hurried up to claim those prizes,
the pot and the lady, presented them
to Diomedes' men, and unyoked the team.

Next Antilochus drove his horses in.
He'd beaten Menelaus by a trick,
but even so that great commander came

close as a chariot wheel follows a horse
who pulls his lord full-speed over the plain
and his tail hairs whisk on the tires as they
come thundering ahead, with only a small   520
space between him and the chariot: so near
Menelaus drove to Antilochus' rear,
though a discus throw had been between them,
but he soon caught up—Agamemnon's mare,
flowing-maned Aithë, was in such fine form—
and if the course had been any longer
Menelaus would surely have passed him.
Idomeneus' trusty squire Meriones
came a spear's throw after Menelaus,
because his horses ran slowest of all   530
and he was the least accomplished driver.
But Admetus' son prince Eumelus came last,
dragging his broken chariot through the dust.
Gallant Achilles was struck with pity
and shouted among those assembled throngs:
"See how our best driver finishes last.
But it's only right he should have something—
second prize. Diomedes can have first."

    Then those Achaean warriors roared hurrah.
And Eumelus would have received the mare,   540
but magnificent Antilochus rose
and appealed to Peleus' son for justice:
"Confound it, Achilles, you can't do that!
You'd like to deprive me of my prize
because he had trouble with his chariot
and he's a good man. Well, if he had prayed,
the immortal gods would have helped him out.
But since you love him and pity him so,
you have heaps of gold and bronze in your camp
and sheep enough, with horses and women—   550
give him any of these as recompense
and our Achaean people will approve.
In all events, I won't concede the mare—
whoever wants her can battle with me!"

Peleus' son Achilles smiled to hear this,
pleased with his companion Antilochus,
and answered him in elevated words:
"If you'd like me to choose another prize
for our Eumelus, I certainly shall:
Asteropaeus' elegant breastplate,   560
cast in solid bronze with rings of bright tin—
quite a magnificent treasure indeed!"

Then he ordered his squire Automedon
to bring the breastplate from its storage place—
and Eumelus received it with delight.

Atreus' son Menelaus rose too, still
furious with Antilochus. A herald
gave him the speaker's staff, bawled for silence
as that godlike commander addressed them:
"Antilochus, you show-off and trickster,   570
a shame to have cheated my glorious team
by pushing your slower horses ahead!
All right, you Achaean lords and leaders,
decide impartially between us two,
or later some of our warriors may say:
'Menelaus lied about Antilochus
and took the mare, though he came in later,
since his rank and power were superior.'
I'll tell you what we must do, and no one
should disagree with me, since this is fair: 580
Antilochus, my dear boy, step up here
and stand as our people's custom decrees:
hold the bright whip you were driving with now,
touch your horses, and swear by Poseidon
you didn't block my chariot with a trick."

But canny Antilochus answered him:
"Bear with me, sir! You're very much older
and your rank is higher, Menelaus.
You know young people can go to extremes—
they have quick tempers, a dash of rashness—   590
so forgive me, please. Of course you may take

that mare I won—and whatever of mine
you fancy I shall give immediately
rather than lose your favor forever
and stand as a sinner before the gods."

   Now that son of Nestor led the mare up
and presented her to Menelaus,
whose heart was glad, as when wheat ears receive
fresh morning dew and all the fields bristle—
thus you exulted, great Menelaus,   600
and addressed him in these exalted words:
"Yes, Antilochus, of course I'll forget
my fury. You weren't so reckless before,
and now your youth got the better of you.
Next time don't try cheating on your betters.
No other man could have persuaded me,
but you've suffered much on the battlefield
for my sake, with your father and brother.
I shall be gracious to you, and the mare
is yours to keep, so that all may be sure   610
I'm never too proud or overbearing."

   Then he took the cauldron—and Noemon,
Antilochus' comrade, led the mare off,
while Meriones claimed those pieces of gold
as fourth prize—but no one received the fifth,
that double-handled bowl, so Achilles
gave it to that aged Nestor, saying:
"Here, good old man, you must have something too
in memory of glorious Patroclus,
who will be seen no more. This prize is yours   620
since you won't be boxing or wrestling today
or tossing the javelin or sprinting,
old age weighs so heavily on you."

   So Nestor joyfully received the bowl
and addressed him in elevated words:
"Yes, dear boy, you've told the truth precisely:
my legs are wobbly, friend, and my fine arms
don't have the power that they had before.

Ah, if only I were as young and strong
as that day they buried Amarynceus   630
and held their funeral games at Buprasium.
I had no match among all those warriors—
Epeians and Pylians and Aetolians—
defeated Clytomedes as boxer
and pinned Ancaeus in the wrestling match,
left Iphlicus far behind in the sprint
and outthrew Polydorus with the spear,
although Actor's sons won the chariot race,
two against one, furious for victory
with the most important prize still at stake.   640
Those men were twins, one drove steadily on,
one drove steadily, while the other whipped.
That's how I used to be, and the youngsters
do such work now, since age has taken me—
but once I was better than anyone.
All right, you hold games for your friend as well.
I'm glad to receive this gift, delighted
you haven't forgotten my services
and the honor due me from our people.
May the immortals grant you blessings too."   650

   That son of Peleus went off through the crowd
when aged Nestor had finished his thanks.
Next he offered them prizes for boxing:
brought a sturdy mule, ordered it tethered—
a stout six-year-old, most stubborn to break—
with a goblet as prize for the loser.
So Achilles stood and shouted to all:
"Atreus' son and you other Achaeans,
now I need two men, the best in our camp,
to raise their fists and box. If Apollo   660
gives victory to one, in our judgment,
this incomparable mule will be his,
with a goblet as prize for the loser."

   Then up leapt a towering valiant man,
Epeius, champion among the boxers,
who laid his hand on the mule and declared:

"Step right up, whoever wants the goblet!
But nobody else will receive this mule
since I'm unbeatable with my two fists.
Isn't it enough I'm useless in war?   670
No one can be skillful in everything.
Yes, let me assure you, the man I meet
will have his hide ripped, his bones pulverized.
His kinsmen better be waiting around
to take him off when I finish with him."

    And a hush of awe fell over them all.
Only one warrior rose, Euryalus,
godlike grandson of gallant Talaus,
who came to Thebes after Oedipus died
and beat them all in the funeral games.   680
Dauntless Diomedes bustled about,
encouraging him for that encounter,
and girded him with a loincloth, then
bound strips of leather about his knuckles.
So those two boxers strode into the ring,
raised their fists and squared away, then began
to batter one another back and forth.
Most horribly they ground their teeth, sweat poured
from their bodies—but Epeius stepped in,
spotted an opening, slugged Euryalus   690
on the cheek, and his legs buckled under.
As a fish leaps from the north wind's ripples
onto some beach, till the dark wave hides it,
so he rose with the blow. And Epeius
picked him up as his comrades came around,
led him staggering from the assembly,
spitting out thick blood, head hung to one side.
Now they set him down, half stunned, among them
and went themselves to receive the goblet.

    Next Peleus' son set out other prizes,   700
offered them to the people for wrestling:
for the winner, an elegant cauldron
those Achaeans valued at twelve oxen,
while the loser would have a servant girl

expert in handicrafts, worth four oxen.
So Achilles stood and shouted to all:
"I need two men to try for these prizes."
Telamonian Aias leapt to his feet,
and up rose Odysseus, canny trickster.
So both of them strode into the middle   710
and came to grips with their enormous hands
like rafters a clever carpenter builds
to protect some house from the whistling winds.
Stout backs creaked beneath determined tugging
of formidable hands, sweat poured in streams,
while on their shoulders many bloody weals
swelled from the skin, as those two steadily
struggled to win the elegant cauldron.
Odysseus could not throw his opponent,
nor could Aias, the other held so firm,   720
and just as the people had become tired
of watching their match, giant Aias cried:
"Laertes' son shrewd Odysseus, lift me
or I'll lift you, and let wise Zeus decide."

And he raised Odysseus, who played a trick:
kicked his knee from behind, made him stagger
and topple, while that son of Laertes
fell on his chest, as they all watched amazed.
Then ingenious Odysseus had his turn
and raised him but couldn't throw him over,   730
so he tripped him up—and both men tumbled
side by side, their bodies dust-besmeared.
Now they'd have risen to wrestle again,
but Achilles himself stood up and said:
"Stop the fight, you two, don't wear yourselves out!
Take equal prizes and call it a draw
so the others have a chance to compete."

And they happily did as he had said:
wiped the dust away, put their tunics on.

Next Achilles set out prizes for the sprint—   740
a silver mixing bowl of fine design

that held six measures, loveliest on earth,
cunningly made by Sidonian craftsmen,
brought by Phoenicians on the misty sea
and presented to powerful Thoas,
then given by illustrious Euneos
to Patroclus as Lycaon's ransom,
and now that son of Peleus offered it
for the Danaan fastest in footracing.
As second prize he brought a sturdy ox   750
and as last, half a nugget of pure gold.
So Achilles stood and shouted to all:
"I need three men to try for these prizes."
And Oileus' son Aias leapt to his feet,
followed by Odysseus and that nimble
Antilochus, best runner of the young.
Next Achilles showed them the turning post,
and they were off to a fast start—but soon
Oileus' son drew ahead, Odysseus
close behind as some graceful lady's   760
breast from a shuttle when she deftly draws
woof through warp, brings the weaving rod near
her breast, so close that son of Laertes
stepped in his tracks before the dust settled,
and Odysseus' breath beat on Aias' neck
as he raced ahead, the people cheering
excitedly for him to give his all.
And as they neared the finish, Odysseus
prayed silently to green-eyed Athena:
"Now, goddess, give my feet a little lift!"   770
Pallas Athena heeded his appeal,
threw marvelous lightness over his legs.
Then just before they reached the finish line,
Aias slipped and fell—Athena tripped him—
where the ground was covered with manure
from bulls Achilles killed for Patroclus,
and excrement filled his mouth and his nose.
So ingenious Odysseus took the bowl
for first prize, and nimble Aias the ox.
He stood there holding his ox by the horn,   780

spitting out filth, and sputtered furiously:
"Ah, damn it all, the goddess made me fall!
She helps Odysseus like his own mother!"

The Danaans laughed merrily at these words.
Then Antilochus carried off last prize
smiling, and cried among the Achaeans:
"You see, my friends, it happened once again—
older men are still the gods' favorites.
Aias is only a bit my senior,
but this one was born long, long ago.   790
He's a spry old codger, all right—no man
except for Achilles can run so fast."

Thus he deftly added commendation
for that son of Peleus, who answered him:
"Praise deserves its reward, Antilochus—
your prize shall be raised a half nugget more."

He handed it over, a welcome gift.
Next Achilles showed a ponderous spear
with a helmet and a colossal shield,
Patroclus' plunder from prince Sarpedon.   800
So Achilles stood and shouted to all:
"Now I need two men, the best in our camp,
to put on armor, take bronze-tipped spears,
and give an exhibition of fencing.
Whoever touches the other's flesh first
and draws dark blood through his sturdy armor
will have this silver-studded sword from me,
my fine booty from Asteropaeus,
and they may have this battle gear to share,
and both shall be my guests at a banquet."   810

Telamonian Aias leapt to his feet,
and up rose Tydeus' son Diomedes.
When both had put on their brilliant armor
they strode to a space among those warriors,
glaring terribly, as all watched amazed.
After they came very near each other
three times they charged, stabbed three times with their spears:

Aias thrust through his opponent's shield
but missed the flesh, for that breastplate held fast,
while prince Diomedes jabbed steadily   820
over Aias' shield, aiming at his neck,
till the Danaans became afraid for him
and called them to stop, take equal prizes.
But Achilles gave Tydeus' son the sword,
with its scabbard and finely crafted strap.

Next Peleus' son showed a lump of iron
which Eëtion had hurled in former days,
but he was slain by nimble Achilles,
who took it, with his other possessions.
So Achilles stood and shouted to all: 830
"Now I need three men to try for this prize.
No matter how large his estate may be,
it should serve the winner for five whole years—
he wouldn't dispatch a shepherd to town
for lack of iron if this were around."

Then up leapt intrepid Polypoetes,
Telamonian Aias and Epeius
and that vastly powerful Leonteus.
They stood side by side while Epeius flung
that iron mass—and the Achaeans laughed.   840
Redoubtable Leonteus hurled the next,
and Aias, as third, gave a hefty heave
that sailed past the marks of both those others.
But when Polypoetes took the iron,
it flew far as a shepherd flings his staff
to send it spinning over all his herds—
and went past the rest, as the people cheered.
So the friends of strong Polypoetes rose
and brought that lump of iron to the ships.

Next he offered prizes for the archers—   850
ten axes with two heads and ten with one—
had the mast of a dark-prowed ship set up
far off in the sands, tied a dove to it
by a slender cord, and ordered archers

to shoot away: "Whoever hits the dove
will have all these double-headed axes,
but if a man hits the cord, not the bird,
he shall receive the single-headed ones."

   Up leapt that keen bowman Teucer and then
Idomeneus' trusty squire Meriones.   860
They shook lots in a shimmering helmet,
and Teucer's fell out. Thus he had first shot
but forgot to promise great Apollo
a glorious sacrifice of firstborn lambs
and missed the bird—Apollo begrudged it—
hit the cord that fastened her by the foot,
and that sharp arrow broke it clean apart,
so she darted to the sky with her cord
dangling earthward, as the Achaeans roared.
Meriones immediately took the bow   870
and an arrow he held while Teucer aimed,
then promised great Apollo he should have
a glorious sacrifice of firstborn lambs.
High up beneath the clouds he spied that dove
circling and shot—nipped her under the wing,
and the arrow sheared through and fell again
at Meriones' feet as that luckless bird
fluttered to the mast of the ship and perched
head hanging, thick feathers drooping, but soon
life left her body, and she tumbled down   880
as the Achaean warriors watched amazed.
Meriones won the axes with two heads,
and Teucer took the single-headed ones.

   Next Peleus' son brought a colossal spear
and a precious cauldron carved with flowers,
set them out for the javelin throwers.
And up leapt king Agamemnon and then
Idomeneus' trusty squire Meriones.
Now agile Achilles addressed those two:
"Atreus' son, we know you're far superior,   890
our mightiest and best in spear finesse—
so take this cauldron away to your ships,

and Meriones will have the splendid spear
if you desire. It's my wish, at the least."

　Atreus' son Agamemnon assented,
ordered Talthybius to claim that treasure,
as Achilles gave Meriones the spear.

Book Twenty-four: Hector Ransomed

Priam ransoms Hector's body, brings it back to Troy. Hector is buried.

So those games were ended, and the Danaans
scattered among their ships. Then each man thought
of supper and slumber—but Achilles
wept with remembrance of his friend, and sleep
avoided him as he tossed endlessly,
yearning for great Patroclus' bravery,
for all they'd done and suffered together
in wars of men and on the bitter waves.
Fresh tears streaked his cheeks at the memory
as he lay sprawled on his side, and sometimes   10
on his back or on his face, or he stood
or wandered wildly along the shore. Dawn
found him as she shone over the sea beach,
then he harnessed up his bronze-hooved horses,
tied Hector's body behind the chariot,
dragged it three times around Patroclus' tomb,
returned to rest in his tent, and left it
lying facedown in dust. But Apollo
pitied lord Hector and protected him,
covered his corpse with the golden aegis   20
so Achilles could not disfigure it.

Thus he insulted brave Hector's remains—
but the immortal gods felt compassion
and implored Hermes to steal the body.
This thought pleased all of them except Hera
and Poseidon and green-eyed Athena,
who still raged relentlessly at Ilios

and Priam, because of Paris' folly
in spurning these other two goddesses
and choosing the one who granted his lust.   30
On the twelfth day after Hector had died
Apollo spoke among the immortals:
"You gods have hard hearts indeed! Did Hector
never make sacrifice at your altars?
But now it seems you won't save his body
so his wife and his mother and children
and his people and his father Priam
may bury him with due ceremony.
Instead you help murderous Achilles,
a man with no sense of right, no kindness,   40
and a heart ferocious as some lion
who goes out in all his arrogant might
to attack a flock and grab his dinner.
This fellow has no pity, has no shame,
which makes mortal men do the proper thing.
People have suffered worse losses than his—
a brother, perhaps, or even a son—
and dried their tears after mourning awhile,
for the fates have given men enduring souls.
But this one ties Hector to his chariot   50
and drags him around his companion's tomb—
a disgusting sight it is, I must say.
He should beware, or we may be furious:
in his madness he insults senseless earth."

    Then white-armed Hera cried angrily:
"So this is what you intend, Silverbow,
to treat Achilles and Hector the same,
although Hector had a mortal mother
while Achilles was child of a goddess
whom I myself reared and gave to a man,   60
Peleus, a favorite of us Olympians.
All the gods came to her wedding—you too
appeared with your lyre, you tricky fellow."

And cloudgathering Zeus replied to her:
"There, there, now, Hera, control yourself—
those two won't receive the same, though Hector
was dearly beloved by the immortals
and me: he worshiped us so faithfully,
never left my altar without its feasts
and offerings and libations, as is right.   70
I want no talk of stealing that body—
Achilles would surely learn, since it seems
his mother runs to help him day and night.
Yet if some god would summon Thetis here
I'd tell her how she might make Achilles
accept Priam's gifts and release the body."

Stormfoot Iris rushed off with his message
and halfway between Imbros and Samos
leapt into the murky waters, which roared
above her. Down she plunged like a plummet   80
fastened to a tiny piece of oxhorn,
which sinks bringing death for savage fishes.
She found Thetis in her cave, those other
sea nymphs gathered round in crowds, while she
bewailed the fate of her peerless son, soon
to die in Ilios, so far from his home.
Swift Iris scurried up to her and cried:
"Come with me, my dear—wise Zeus summons you."
And divine silverfoot Thetis replied:
"Why does that great god call me? I don't care   90
to go among immortals, I have so
many, many griefs—but I shall do it."

Then that delightful goddess took a veil
of murky purple, the darkest she had,
and hurried after windfoot Iris
as the sea waters parted before them.
They stepped out on the shore and leapt to heaven,
where they found that glorious son of Cronos
with all the blessed gods attending him.
She sat by Zeus as Athena gave place,   100
and Hera handed her a golden cup

to welcome her. Thetis took it and drank,
then the father of gods and men declared:
"Ah, poor Thetis, you came to Olympus
despite your sorrows—I know about them.
Well, let me tell you why I summoned you.
Nine days long the immortals have quarreled
about Hector's body and Achilles—
the others would like Hermes to steal it,
yet I've defended prince Achilles' rights   110
so I may keep your reverence and love.
Now you hurry down to inform your son
the gods are angry and I'm especially
indignant he won't give up his fury
and let Hector have a decent burial—
if he refuses, there will be trouble
from me. And I'll send Iris to Priam,
ordering him to go ransom his son
with gifts that will make Achilles relent."

Silverfoot Thetis did as commanded,   120
darted down from the peaks of Olympus
to prince Achilles' camp, where she found him
groaning again and again as his men
bustled about preparing their breakfast,
for which a shaggy ram had been slaughtered.
So his gracious mother sat at his side
and stroked him with her fingers, murmuring:
"Child of mine, how long will you continue
this endless grief, forgetting to take food
and sleep? But better embrace a lady   130
since you haven't long to live: already
death and powerful fate are at your side.
Now listen, I bring a message from Zeus:
The gods are angry, and he's especially
indignant you won't give up your fury
and let Hector have a decent burial.
Accept a ransom, give up that body."

And Peleus' son swift Achilles answered:
"Yes, the corpse shall be released for ransom
if Olympian Zeus has commanded it."   140

So there among the ships mother and son
were conversing in great agitation
as Cronos' son sent quick Iris away:
"Iris, you hurry down from Olympus
and take this message to Priam in Troy:
I wish him to go ransom his dear son
with gifts that will make Achilles relent.
He had better travel unattended,
though a herald, some older man, may drive
a light mule cart to carry back the corpse   150
of the warrior great Achilles has slain.
Tell him he need have no fear for his life,
I'll give him such a faithful guide—Hermes—
who will bring him straight to Achilles.
After he comes in the enemy camp
he may be quite certain of his safety:
Achilles is no madman or rascal
and hears supplication with courtesy."

Stormfoot Iris rushed off with his message,
came to Priam's palace, found frantic grief: 160
those sons of Priam sat in the courtyard,
wetting their clothes with tears, while the king
lay muffled in his robe—and all about
the old man's head and neck was that manure
he'd gathered in his hands as he groveled.
His daughters and sons' wives sobbed everywhere,
remembering those many valiant warriors
toppled to the dust by their enemies.
Zeus's messenger stood by him and spoke
softly—but Priam shuddered at the sound: 170
"Great Dardanian Priam, don't be afraid—
it's no distressing news I have brought you.
Listen! I am a messenger from Zeus,
who worries for you though he's far away.
The Olympian says to ransom Hector

with gifts that will make Achilles relent.
You had better travel unattended,
though a herald, some older man, may drive
a light mule cart to carry back the corpse
of the warrior great Achilles has slain.   180
He says you should have no fear for your life,
he'll give you such a faithful guide—Hermes—
who will bring you straight to Achilles.
And when you come in the enemy camp
you may be quite certain of your safety:
Achilles is no madman or rascal
and hears supplication with courtesy."

    After saying this, Iris rushed away—
and Priam ordered his sons to prepare
a light mule cart with a wicker body.   190
Then he went down to his vaulted storeroom,
fragrant of cedar and heaped with treasures,
called his wife Hecabe to him, and said:
"My lady, a messenger came from Zeus
who orders me to go ransom our son
with gifts that will make Achilles relent.
But tell me, how does the idea strike you?
As for myself, I'm extremely eager
to enter that camp of the Achaeans."

    But his beloved wife shrieked and answered: 200
"Oh my, what's become of all that wisdom
you were celebrated for everywhere?
How could you go among their ships alone
and face the one who has murdered many
fine sons of yours? Your heart is of iron!
If he sees you, gets you into his hands,
that savage rascal, don't expect pity
or respect! We can mourn for Hector here
without his body, since this is what fate
has spun for him the day I gave him birth: 210
to glut the dogs far from his parents
in the camp of that violent man, whose heart
I could tear out and eat, so I might be

avenged for my son, who died most bravely
in defense of our city and people,
with never a thought of shameful retreat."

   But aged king Priam replied to her:
"Nonetheless I shall do it—and you won't
hold me back like some bird of ill omen.
If any man on earth had told me this,   220
even a priest or a skilled diviner,
we could call it a lie and ignore it,
but I heard the goddess' voice and saw her.
I'll obey her instructions, and if I
am doomed to die by the Achaean ships,
so be it. Achilles can take my life
after I hold my son and weep my fill."

   Next the old king opened his stately chests
and took twelve robes of exceeding beauty,
twelve single-fold cloaks, and as many rugs,   230
as many mantles, and as many robes,
then carefully weighed out twelve gold pieces,
took two brilliant kettles and four cauldrons,
with a glorious cup the Thracians gave him
when he came to them on an embassage—
even this wasn't spared in his fervor
to ransom his son. He drove the people
from his portico, scolded them roundly:
"Go away, damn you! Have you no troubles
to mourn for at home, without plaguing me?   240
Isn't it enough Zeus has made me lose
my noblest son? Soon you'll know what it means
when those Achaean warriors slaughter you
so easily, now he's dead. As for me,
may I go down to the house of Hades
before seeing my city sacked and destroyed!"

   Then he chased them with his staff—and they ran
before that frantic old man. He harangued
his sons Helenus, Paris, Agathon,
Pammon, Antiphonus, and Polites,   250

Deiphobus and Hippothous and Dius,
in a wild tirade of imprecation:
"Step lively, useless brats! I wish you all
had died by the ships instead of Hector!
Miserable me, I had sons the best
in our land of Ilios, but none are left,
not Mestor nor that intrepid Troilus
nor our redoubtable Hector, who seemed
more the son of a god than a mortal.
Ares has slain them, and I'm left this shame: 260
liars, fast talkers, dance-floor commanders,
pillagers of their people's goats and sheep!
Now get the wagon ready for me, quick,
and load it with these things so I can go."

   And fearful of their father's reproaches,
they hurried to fetch a handsome wagon,
then fastened a wicker basket on it,
and from its peg they took a boxwood yoke
with knobs and guide hooks for holding the reins
and brought out a rope some fourteen feet long.   270
They carefully set that yoke to the pole,
where it bent up, put the yoke ring on it,
tied this to the knob with a triple turn
of its rope, and bound both ends to the cart.
Next they brought the magnificent ransom,
Hector's price, piled it on that polished cart,
and yoked up a team of sturdy-hooved mules,
the Mysians' generous gift to Priam.
For Priam himself they harnessed horses
the old king kept for his very own use.   280

   While cart and chariot were being prepared
for the herald and for aged Priam,
queen Hecabe came near, deeply troubled,
holding mellow wine in a golden cup
to offer libations before he left.
She stood before his horses and declared:
"Now pour this wine to father Zeus and pray
for a safe return, you are so eager

to go among the ships, despite my wish.
And implore that powerful Thunderlord   290
who looks down from Ida on all Ilios
to send a suitable bird of omen
on your right—whichever is his favorite—
so you may see with your very own eyes
it's safe for you to go among the ships.
But if booming-voiced Zeus should refuse it,
do not, I beseech you, enter their camp,
no matter how determined you may be."

     And godlike Priam answered his wife:
"Very well, my dear, I'll do as you say—   300
prayer to Zeus is never out of place."

     Now Priam ordered a servant woman
to bring water for his hands, and she came
carrying a basin and a pitcher.
After he washed his hands, he took the cup
and made libations there in the courtyard.
Gazing toward broad heaven, Priam prayed:
"Most glorious great Zeus who rules from Ida,
may I be welcome in Achilles' camp!
Graciously send me a bird of omen   310
on my right—whichever is your favorite—
so I may see with my very own eyes
it's safe for me to go among the ships."

     Cronos' son Zeus heard that fervent prayer,
swiftly sent an eagle, surest omen,
that hunter in dusk men call the Dark Bird.
Broad as the strong-bolted entrance door
of a wealthy merchant's vaulted storeroom
was its wingspread—and it appeared to them
on their right, flew straight across the city.   320
And all the Trojans rejoiced at that sight.

     Now Priam hurried to mount his chariot
and drove from the echoing portico.
The mules tripped ahead with their swift wagon
driven by the herald Idaeus, then

came the horses, that old king whipping them
quickly through the town—and kinsmen followed
lamenting as if he went to his death.
After they descended onto the plain
his sons and his daughters' husbands turned back   330
into Ilios—but Zeus observed those two
coming from the town, pitied the old man,
and summoned Hermes, his beloved son:
"Hermes, I know it's your dearest pleasure
to accompany people who need you.
Away with you then, guide Priam tonight
so none of the enemy warriors see him
until he comes to that son of Peleus."

   Messenger Hermes did as commanded.
Around his feet he fastened those golden   340
sandals that carry him over the sea
and lands of earth as swiftly as the wind—
next he took his wand that enchants men's eyes
when he wants, or wakes them again from sleep.
Thus, wand in hand, Hermes darted off
and soon came to the Hellespont and Troy,
where he took the shape of a princely boy
with down on his cheek, the most charming age.

   When those two had driven past Ilus' mound
they stopped to let their mules and horses drink   350
in the rippling river, since night was near.
Just at this moment the herald observed
Hermes the Helper, and cried to Priam:
"Look there, my lord! Whatever shall we do?
I see a warrior—he may cut us down.
Oh, let's escape in our chariot or throw
ourselves at his feet and beg for mercy!"

   Dumbfounded, terrified, Priam waited,
and the hair on his aged body rose
as he stood dazed. But the Helper approached,   360
took the old king's hand, and asked him kindly:
"Sir, why are you leading horses and mules

through the ambrosial night, while others sleep?
Have you no fear of those fierce Achaeans,
your bitter enemies so very near?
And what if they spy you through the darkness,
carrying these magnificent treasures?
You're not so young and your friend here is old
to be defending yourselves from attack.
But I will not harm you—I'll even be   370
your guide, you seem so much like my father."

   Now that aged godlike Priam replied:
"What you say is all very true, dear boy.
Some god must be holding his hand over me
to bring me to a traveler like you
at the right time, a fine-looking man
and wise—noble in birth, I do believe."

   Then Hermes the messenger answered him:
"An entirely proper assumption, sir.
But tell me, and please be frank about it: 380
are you carrying these many treasures
to some foreign country for safekeeping,
or have you all abandoned Ilios
now such a noble warrior has been slain,
your son, who fought always with the foremost?"

   Now that aged godlike Priam replied:
"Let me know who you are, my fine fellow—
you tell so well of my poor son's doom."

   Then Hermes the messenger answered him:
"You ask about Hector to test me, sir.   390
I often saw him on the field of war,
driving the Danaans back to their ships
amid the most dreadful devastation.
We stood there amazed, because Achilles
was angry and wouldn't let us battle.
I'm one of those captains who came with him,
a Myrmidon, son of lord Polyctor,
a wealthy man and your very same age.
Of his seven sons, I am the youngest,

chosen by lot to join the armies here.   400
I came out on the plain because at dawn
our men begin battle about the town—
they're weary of waiting, and our leaders
cannot control their eagerness for war."

   Now that aged godlike Priam replied:
"If you're really one of Achilles' men
tell me the truth, and omit nothing, please:
is my son at the ships, or has his corpse
already been thrown to the Argive dogs?"

   Then Hermes the messenger answered him: 410
"No, the dogs have not yet devoured him, sir—
he lies beside the ship of Achilles
in our Myrmidon camp. It's the twelfth day,
but his flesh is undecayed and the worms
that eat slain warriors have not been seen.
Prince Achilles pitilessly drags him
around the tomb of his friend each day at dawn
but can't disfigure him. You'd be amazed
to see him fresh as dew and clean of blood,
without a stain—yes, the wounds are closed   420
over all those places where he was stabbed.
The blessed gods have cared for your son
even in death, they love him so dearly."

   The old king was delighted and declared:
"It's good to give the immortals their due.
That beloved son of mine would never
forget the Olympians in his palace,
so they remember him, although he's dead.
Now let me give you this fine goblet,
and you guide me with the gods' assistance   430
till I reach the camp of prince Achilles."

   Then Hermes the messenger answered him:
"You test me, sir, since I am much younger.
I can't take gifts behind Achilles' back,
he's so terrible, so awe-inspiring,
and he would be furious if he learned—

but I'd lead you all the way to Argos
gladly, on foot if you wished or by ship,
and with my guidance your safety is sure."

   Now the Helper leapt on Priam's chariot,   440
took whip and reins in his immortal hands,
and breathed vast power in horses and mules.
When they reached the Achaean moat and wall
they found those sentinels at their dinners,
but Hermes the Helper flung sleep over
all, threw the bolts back and opened the gates,
brought Priam inside with his fine presents.
And when they came to Achilles' quarters—
made by the Myrmidons for their leader
from enormous pine beams and a roof   450
of shaggy thatch gathered in the meadows
and, all around it, a courtyard fenced in
by sturdy stakes, their gate with a single
pinewood bar that took three warriors to shut
and three to open, so huge was that bolt,
although Achilles could do it alone—
Hermes opened the door for the old lord,
brought those magnificent presents inside,
descended from the chariot, and declared:
"Sir, an immortal god stands before you,   460
Hermes. Father Zeus sent me as your guide.
And now I must return, so Achilles
won't see me here, since it is not proper
for a mortal to entertain a god.
But you go inside and kneel before him,
implore him by his father and mother
and by his own child, so you may move him."

   Then Hermes flew off for high Olympus,
and Priam leapt from his chariot to the ground,
leaving his trusty herald Idaeus   470
with horses and mules. The old man entered
Achilles' quarters, found him seated there
apart from the rest, with two men only—
Alcimus and gallant Automedon—

in attendance. He'd just finished dinner,
and the light table remained at his side.
Priam entered unseen and approached him,
clutched Achilles' knees and kissed those dreadful
hands that had slain so many of his sons.
As a man who killed someone in a rage   480
escapes to the home of some wealthy lord
far away, where they gaze at him amazed,
thus godlike Priam amazed Achilles,
while the others exchanged surprised glances.
And aged Priam implored him, saying:
"Remember your own father, Achilles,
suffering a bitter old age like me
now the neighboring peoples press him hard
because he has no one to defend him.
As long as he hears you are still alive   490
he rejoices, hoping day after day
his beloved son will return from Troy.
Ah, miserable me! my sons were the best
in our land of Ilios, but none are left.
There were fifty when the Achaeans came,
nineteen of them born from the same mother,
the others from my palace concubines,
but furious Ares has laid them all low—
and my last one, who guarded us alone,
has fallen in defense of our city: 500
Hector. I come to the Achaean ships
with an enormous ransom for his corpse.
Respect the gods, Achilles—pity me
for your father's sake! I am more piteous,
since I've suffered more than any mortal:
to kiss the hands of him who killed my son."

   This made Achilles long for his father.
He took the old man's hand, pushed him gently
away—and both were lost in memory:
one wept for Hector at Achilles' feet,   510
while Achilles grieved for his father and
Patroclus, so their sobs rang through the house.

But after Achilles had wept his fill
and the desire for mourning had left him,
he sprang from his chair and helped Priam up,
for he pitied his gray hair and gray beard,
then addressed him in agitated words:
"Poor man, you've suffered much tribulation.
How could you go among the ships alone
and face the one who has murdered many   520
fine sons of yours? Your heart is of iron!
Now do take a seat on this chair and we
may forget our sorrows for a moment,
since grim lamentation is so useless.
The gods have spun this fate for wretched men:
to live in pain, while they themselves have none.
Two jars are on the floor of Zeus's home,
one with gifts of evil, one with blessings.
And a man Zeus has given both kinds mixed
sometimes encounters evil, sometimes good—   530
but a man with the bad is an outcast
and stalks wildly over the face of earth,
honored neither by gods nor by mortals.
Thus it was the gods gave Peleus gifts
from the time he was born, so he surpassed
all men in wealth and ruled the Myrmidons
and, though a mortal, married a goddess.
But some god brought sorrow too: he had no
children to rule his kingdom after him
except for one son, who is doomed. I won't   540
serve him in his age, now I'm far away—
a plague on you and your Trojan people.
We hear you, old man, were once happy too.
All that lies between Macar's realm Lesbos
and highland Phrygia and the Hellespont
was splendidly ruled by you and your sons,
but since the immortals brought these troubles,
battle and slaughter surround your city.
Take it patiently, don't grieve forever!
No use lamenting the death of your son—   550
it won't resurrect him, you may be sure."

   Now that aged godlike Priam replied:
"Sir, I cannot be seated while Hector
lies here unburied. Release him quickly
so I may see him. Take the great ransom
we bring. May you enjoy it and return
safely to your home, now you have spared me
and let me live on here beneath the sun."

And agile Achilles answered, scowling:
"Listen to me: it was my idea   560
to return your Hector, since Zeus has sent
a messenger, my own mother Thetis.
Another thing, Priam: I know full well
some god has led you to the Danaan ships.
No mortal, even the boldest, would dare
enter our camp—couldn't slip by the watch
or open the bar of our massive gate.
Now don't upset me, with all my sorrows,
or I just might not want to spare you, sir,
though suppliants have Zeus's protection."   570

   So the old lord was frightened and obeyed.
And Peleus' son leapt up like a lion,
followed by his two formidable squires
Automedon and Alcimus, dearest
of his comrades after Patroclus' death.
They unharnessed the horses and the mules,
then led Priam's herald inside and there
seated him on a chair. And from the cart
they brought that splendid ransom for Hector
but left two woven cloaks and a tunic   580
to shroud the body for its journey home.
And Achilles called women to wash it
somewhere king Priam could not observe them
lest the aged monarch lose his temper
at sight of his son, rouse Achilles' wrath,
and he'd kill him and sin against Zeus.
After they washed and anointed the corpse
they wrapped it in a cloak and a tunic,
then Achilles raised it onto a bier

which his people placed on the polished cart.   590
He groaned and called his beloved comrade:
"Patroclus! Don't be angry if you hear,
even in Hades, I have given back
Hector—his father ransomed him dearly,
and you shall have a share before your tomb."

   Then agile Achilles entered again,
sat in the same elegantly carved chair
against the wall, and addressed king Priam:
"Your son has been returned, sir, as you asked:
he lies upon a bier, and at daybreak   600
you may take him away. Now dine with me.
Even Niobe remembered to eat
though twelve of her children died in her halls—
six daughters and six magnificent sons:
silverbow Apollo had slain the sons
and Artemis the daughters, indignant
that Niobe had insulted Leto
by boasting to her she had more children,
so those two immortals destroyed them all.
Nine days they lay in a welter of blood,   610
since Cronos' son had made the people stone—
but on the tenth day the gods buried them,
and she ate when she wearied of weeping.
Now somewhere among the lonely mountains
in Sipylus, home of those fabled nymphs
who dance in rings round Achelous' waters,
she broods for her sorrows, become a stone.
We too, my dear man, had best remember
food—and you can mourn your beloved son
with many tears when you return to Troy."   620

   Achilles leapt up, had a sheep slaughtered,
and his companions flayed and prepared it,
carved the meat with care and slipped it on spits
and laid it on the crackling flames to roast.
Now his squire Automedon passed out bread
in baskets, as Achilles served the meat.
So they reached their hands to those tender treats.

After they had eaten and drunk their fill
mighty Priam marveled at Achilles,
tall and handsome like one of the gods,   630
while Achilles marveled at great Priam,
watching his fine face and hearing his words.
But when they had gazed at one another
to their hearts' content, Priam spoke up first:
"Show us to our beds immediately, sir,
so we may have a wink of sleep at last.
Since the time you killed my beloved son
I haven't closed my eyes for a moment
as I groaned and brooded over my griefs,
groveling in the manure of my courtyard.   640
Now I have eaten and a little wine
has passed my throat—but before I had none."

    And prince Achilles ordered his servants
to set bedsteads beneath the portico,
then spread elegant purple rugs on top
with woolly cloaks to cover the sleepers—
so the girls went outside bearing torches
and hurriedly made those two beds ready.
Next he spoke to Priam in mocking tones:
"Better sleep outside tonight, old fellow!   650
One of our lords may come, they love so much
to sit here planning their plans as usual!
If one should see you with me and inform
king Agamemnon, there might be trouble
returning that body without delay.
Now tell me—and truthfully, if you please—
how long you need for Hector's funeral,
so meanwhile we may celebrate a truce."

    Now that aged godlike Priam replied:
"If you allow us to bury Hector,   660
then grant me one more request, Achilles:
we are trapped in our town, and it takes time
to find wood for a pyre, and we're afraid.
So allow us to mourn him nine days long,
then on the tenth we'll bury him and feast

and on the eleventh heap his tomb high
and on the twelfth do battle, if we must."

    Whereupon gallant Achilles answered:
"Old Priam, it shall be as you desire—
for just that time we'll refrain from battle." 670

    And with this he gripped the old man's right wrist
as a sign he should have nothing to fear.
The herald and Priam lay down to sleep
there outside, many worries on their minds,
while prince Achilles took his rest within
beside that delightful lady Briseis.

    Now the other gods and mortal warriors
slumbered all night, overcome by soft sleep,
but Hermes the Helper stayed wide awake
as he pondered how to guide old Priam 680
from those ships unseen by the gatekeepers.
He stood above the monarch's head and said:
"Careless of you, sir, to be snoozing here
simply because Achilles has spared you.
You ransomed your son, paid plenty for him,
but your own ransom will be three times more
for your sons still left, if Agamemnon
or the other Danaans chance to see you."

    The old man was frightened, woke the herald.
So Hermes harnessed their horses and mules 690
and quickly drove through the camp, unobserved.

    When they came to the ford of that river
eddying Xanthus, immortal Zeus's child,
Hermes darted off for tall Olympus,
while Dawn spread her saffron robes over earth—
and wailing and moaning, those two men drove
toward their town, as mules brought the corpse. No one,
man or woman, knew that they were coming
till Cassandra, golden Aphrodite's peer,
went up to Pergamus, spied her father 700
standing on the chariot by his herald—

and saw what lay outstretched on the wagon.
She screamed, and shrieked for the city to hear:
"Oh my Trojans, come look at our Hector
if ever you welcomed him from battle
alive, while he was our city's delight."

   Soon all the town was emptied of people
seized with intolerable grief, and they
met Priam with the corpse beside the gates.
First Hector's beloved wife and mother   710
tore their hair, hurled themselves on the wagon
to hold his head, while all wailed about him.
That whole day long until the sun went down
they would have mourned Hector before their gates,
but the old king shouted from his chariot:
"Now make way for the mules—and afterward
take your fill of mourning in my palace!"

   They stood apart so the wagon could pass,
and Hector was brought to the palace, then
laid upon a bed, and there beside it   720
singers sat leading dirges and chanted
songs of sorrow as all the women groaned.
Andromache led their lamentation,
holding the head of man-slaying Hector:
"My husband, you died young and left me
widowed in our home, our child a baby
born of two miserable parents—he won't
be grown before our city is ruined,
because you alone were its great guardian,
who kept its wives and children safe from harm.   730
Now they'll be taken away on the ships
with me among them, as you follow, child,
to a place where you do disgraceful work
for a cruel master, or some Achaean
will seize your arm and hurl you from the wall,
furious that Hector had slain his brother
or father or son, there are so many
who have bitten the dust at Hector's hands,
since your father wasn't gentle in war!

So our people are mourning everywhere, 740
and your parents have unspeakable grief,
Hector, and I most misery of all.
When you died you didn't stretch out your arms
from a fine bed or tell me something wise
I might remember day and night with tears."

Sobbing she said this, as the women groaned.
Then Hecabe led their lamentation:
"Hector, very dearest of my children,
you were loved by the gods while you still lived,
so now they protect you even in death. 750
Achilles took my other sons alive,
sold them in slavery over the sea
in Samos or Imbros or hazy Lemnos.
And after he stole your life with the spear
he dragged you around the grave of his friend
Patroclus—that didn't resurrect him!
Now here in our house you lie dewy fresh,
more like someone silverbow Apollo
has stung with his gentle arrows and slain."

Sobbing she said this, as they all wailed on. 760
Then Helen took up the lamentation:
"Hector, dearest of my husband's brothers—
yes, my husband is Paris, who brought me
to Ilios, though I wish I'd died sooner—
already the twentieth year has passed
since I abandoned my beloved home,
but you never had a rude word for me.
And when you heard me cursed by someone else,
your brothers or sisters or brothers' wives
or mother—though your father was kind as mine— 770
you tried to persuade them and restrain them
in your great gentleness, with gentle words.
So I weep for you and my wretched self,
since no one remains in the city now
kind or good to me, but all despise me."

Sobbing she said this, as the people groaned.
Then aged Priam called his followers:
"All right, my Trojans, bring wood to the town!
No need to fear ambush, since Achilles
promised when I departed from the ships   780
he'd leave us alone until the twelfth day."

Now they yoked their sturdy oxen and mules
and quickly assembled before the town.
Nine days long they gathered heaps of firewood—
but when the tenth dawn shimmered over earth
they brought Hector from the city, weeping,
laid him on the pyre, and set it aflame.

And just as dawn's rosy fingers appeared
the people met at his funeral pyre.
Once all those Trojans had come together   790
they poured out brilliant wine to quench the fire
where embers still smoldered—and after that
friends and brothers collected his white bones
mournfully, thick tears rolling down their cheeks.
So they placed the bones in a golden urn
and covered it with their soft purple robes,
then set that urn in a grave, and on top
piled an enormous heap of close-set stones
to make a burial mound, while sentinels
kept watch against an Achaean attack.   800
After the mound was complete, they returned
and met to celebrate a sumptuous feast
in the palace of Priam, loved by Zeus.

And thus they buried illustrious Hector.

GLOSSARY OF
THE PRINCIPAL NAMES
AND PLACES

There has never been a universally accepted system for the transliteration of Greek proper names into English. In general, the most common system, that of the Latin writers, has been followed here.

Abydus - a city on the Hellespont

Acamas - (1) son of Antenor, leader of the Dardanians; (2) son of Eussorus, leader of the Thracians

Achaeans - the Greeks and their allies

Achelous - (1) a river or river god in Aetolia; (2) a river or river god in Phrygia

Achilles - son of Peleus and Thetis, greatest of Greek warriors, hero of the *Iliad*

Actor - (1) father of Echecles; (2) son of Azeus of Orchomenus; (3) father of Menoetius; (4) son of Phorbas, putative father of Cteatus and Eurytus

Adrastus - (1) father of Aegialeia, wife of Diomedes; (2) a leader of Trojan allies from Adrasteia; (3) Trojan slain by Menelaus; (4) Trojan slain by Patroclus

Aeacus - father of Peleus, grandfather of Achilles

Aegae - town in Aehaea loved by Poseidon

Aegeus - king of Athens, father of Theseus

Aegina - island off Attica, home of Ajax and Teucer

Aeneas - son of Anchises and Aphrodite, one of the great Trojan heroes, in later legend founder of the Latin race

Aesepus - (1) son of Bucolion and Abarbarea; (2) river on Mount Ida

Agamemnon - son of Atreus, brother of Menelaus, commander of the Greek forces

Agenor - Trojan, son of Antenor

Aias (Ajax) - (1) son of Telamon, half brother of Teucer, one of the chief Greek warriors; (2) son of Oileus, the lesser Aias, another Greek hero; together the *Aiantes*

Alastor - (1) Lycian slain by Odysseus; (2) leader of the Pylians; (3) father of Tros

Alcestis - wife of Admetus, mother of Eumelus

Alcimedon - a leader of the Myrmidons

Alcimus - charioteer of Achilles

Alcmenë - wife of Amphitryon, mother of Heracles

Alexander - another name of Paris, lover of Helen

Alpheus - a river or river god in Elis in the Peloponnesus

Amphimachus - (1) son of Cteatus, leader of the Epeians, slain by Hector; (2) son of Nomion, leader of the Carians

Amphitryon - husband of Alemenë

Anchises - father of Aeneas and Echepolus

Andromache - daughter of Eëtion, wife of Hector, mother of Astyanax

Antenor - Trojan leader, husband of Theano, father of Helicaon, Polybus, Agenor, Acamas, Iphidamas, and Coön

Antilochus - son of Nestor, a Greek hero

Antiphus - (1) Greek leader of islanders; (2) son of Talaemenes, Trojan ally, leader of the Maeonians; (3) son of Priam, captured and released by Achilles, slain by Agamemnon

Aphrodite - goddess of beauty; wife of Hephaestus, mistress of Ares; favors the Trojans

Apisaon - (1) son of Phausius, Trojan slain by Eurypylus; (2) son of Hippasus, Trojan slain by Lycomedes

Apollo - god of light, music, and medicine; son of Zeus and Leto, brother of Artemis; favors the Trojans

Arcadia - mountainous region in the Peloponnesus

Areithous - (1) father of the Boeotian Menestheus; (2) squire of the Thracian Rhigmus, slain by Achilles

Ares - god of war, son of Zeus and Hera, lover of Aphrodite, favors the Trojans

Argives - men of Argos (used as a general name for the Greeks)

Argos - (1) city in the Peloponnesus, ruled by Diomedes; (2) kingdom of Agamemnon, with capital at Mycenae in the Peloponnesus; (3) Pelasgic Argos, on the river Peneius in Thessaly, ruled by Achilles.

Arisbë- Trojan town

Artemis - goddess of the moon, the hunt, and childbirth; daughter of Zeus and Leto, sister of Apollo; favors the Trojans

Ascalaphus - son or Ares, leader of the Boeotians

Ascanius - (1) leader of the Phrygian allies of Troy; (2) son of Hippotion, a Bithynian ally of Troy

Asclepius - god of medicine; son of Apollo, father of the Greek physicians Machaon and Podaleirius

Asius - (1) son of Hyrtacus from Arisbë, a Trojan ally; (2) father of Adamas; (3) son of Dymas, brother of Hecabe, from Phrygia; (4) father of Phaenops from Abydus, a Trojan ally

Assaracus - son of Tros, an ancestor of Priam

Asteropaeus - son of Pelagon, leader of the Lycian allies of Troy

Astyanax - son of Hector and Andromache

Astynous - (1) Trojan slain by Diomedes; (2) son of Protiaon, a Trojan

Athena - goddess of wisdom, champion of the Greeks

Athos - a celebrated mountainous promontory in northern Greece

Atreus - father of Agamemnon and Menelaus, the "sons of Atreus"

Atymnius - (1) father of Mydon; (2) Trojan slain by Antilochus

Aulis - Boeotian harbor from which the Greeks sailed for Troy

Automedon - principal charioteer of Achilles

Autonous - (1) Greek slain by Hector; (2) Trojan slain by Patroclus

Axius - river in Paeonia in Thrace

Balius - one of the horses of Achilles

Bellerophon - slayer of the Chimaera

Boeotia - region in central Greece

Borus - (1) father of the Maeonian Phaestus; (2) husband of Peleus' daughter Polydora, putative father of Menesthius

Briareus - a hundred-handed sea giant

Briseis - mistress of Achilles, captured in war

Briseus - king and priest of Lyrnessus, father of Achilles' mistress Briseis

Bryseiae - town in Laconia, in the Peloponnesus

Cadmeians - Thebans, descendants of Cadmus, founder of the city

Calchas - Greek prophet and seer

Callicolonë - hill near Troy

Calydon - city in Aetolia, north of the Corinthian Gulf

Cassandra - daughter of Priam, a prophetess fated always to be disbelieved; taken captive by Agamemnon and slain with him by Clytemnestra

Castor - son of Zeus and Leda, brother of Polydeuces (Pollux) and Helen

Cebriones - bastard son of Priam, Hector's charioteer, slain by Patroclus

Centaurs - a wild Thessalian tribe, reputedly half man and half horse, famous for their battle with the Lapiths

Cheiron - the centaur who instructed Achilles. He was skilled in medicine and prophecy

Chimaera - mythical monster, part lion, part goat, part serpent, slain by Bellerophon

Chromius - (1) son of Priam, slain by Diomedes; (2) Lycian, slain by Odysseus; (3) Trojan, slain by Teucer; (4) Trojan ally, leader of the Mysians

Chrysë - harbor town in Troad, with a temple of Apollo

Chryseis - daughter of Chryses, priest of Apollo, given to Agamemnon as a prize of war

Chryses - father of Chryseis, priest of Apollo

Chrysothemis - daughter of Agamemnon and Clytemnestra, sister of Iphigenia, Electra, and Orestes

Cilla - Trojan town

Cleopatra - Halcyonë, wife of Meleager

Clytemnestra - wife and murderess of Agamemnon, mistress of Aegistheus

Corinth - wealthy commercial city on the isthmus connecting the Peloponnesus with the mainland of Greece

Cos - island in the Icarian Sea, off southern Asia Minor

Cronos - father of Zeus (called "son of Cronos")

Curetes - Aetolian tribe that beseiged Calydon

Daedalus - legendary craftsman, architect of the Labyrinth in Crete and the first man to fly

Danaans - the Greeks and their allies (the Achaeans)

Danaë - daughter of Acrisius, mother of Perseus

Dardania - city founded by Dardanus, at the foot of Mount Ida

Dardanians - inhabitants of Dardania; sometimes used for Trojans

Dardanus - ancestor of Priam (called "son of Dardanus") or "Dardanian"; also ancestor of Illus (similarly called)

Dares - Trojan priest of Hephaestus, father of Phegeus and Idaeus

Deiphobus - son of Priam, brother of Hector

Demeter - goddess of agriculture; sister of Hera, Zeus, and Poseidon, mother of Persephone

Deucalion - father of Idomeneus

Diomedë - woman from Lesbos, slave of Achilles

Diomedes - son of Tydeus, a Greek hero second only to Achilles in skill and valor

Dionë - mother of Aphrodite

Dionysus - god of wine and revelry; son of Zeus and Semele

Diores - (1) son of Amarynceus, leader of the Epeians, slain by Trojan ally Peiros; (2) father of Automedon

Dodona - oracle of Zeus in Eprius; on the western coast of Greece; its replies were supposed to be heard in the rustling of the leaves of an ancient oak

Dolon - Trojan spy slain by Odysseus and Diomedes

Dolopians - tribe from Thessaly

Dryas - (1) king of the Lapiths; (2) father of Lycurgus

Dymas - father of Hecuba and Asius

Echeclus - (1) Agenor's son, slain by Achilles; (2) Trojan slain by Patroclus

Echepolus - (1) descendant of Anchises, living in Sicyon in the Peloponnesus; (2) son of Thalysius, a Trojan slain by Antilochus

Echius - (1) father of Mecisteus; (2) Lycian slain by Patroclus; (3) Lycian slain by Polites

Eëtion - (1) father of Andromache; (2) of Imbros, friend of Priam; (3) Trojan, father of Podes

Eilithyia - goddess of childbirth

Eioneus - (1) father of Rhesus; (2) Greek slain by Hector

Elis - district in western Peloponnesus

Ennomus - (1) Trojan ally, chief of the Mysians, a seer, slain by Achilles; (2) Trojan slain by Odysseus

Enyo - personification of the tumult of battle

Eos - goddess of the dawn; mother of Memnon

Epeians - a Greek people in Elis, in northwestern Peloponnesus

Epeius - Greek boxer and athlete

Ephialtes - a giant

Ephyrë - (1) ancient name for Corinth; (2) city in Elis, in northwestern Peloponnesus; (3) town in Thessaly

Epidaurus - Argive town in northeastern Peloponnesus

Epistrophus - (1) leader of the Halizonians, Trojan allies; (2) son of Evenus, slain by Achilles; (3) Greek, son of Iphitus, leader of the Phocians

Erebus - the lower world

Erechtheus - legendary Athenian hero

Eretria - town in Euboea

Erichthonius - son of Dardanus

Eridanus - legendary river identified as the Po

Erinyes - the Furies

Eris - goddess of discord

Erymas - (1) Trojan slain by Idomeneus; (2) Trojan slain by Patroclus

Eteocles - son of Oedipus of Thebes, defender of the city against the Seven

Euboea - large island off the eastern coast of Attica and Boeotia

Eumelus - son of Admetus; charioteer in games at Patroclus' funeral

Euryalus - son of Mecisteus, comrade of Diomedes

Eurybates - Greek herald

Eurymedon - (1) squire of Agamemnon; (2) servant of Nestor

Eurypylus - (1) son of Euaemon of Thessaly, wounded by Paris; (2) a Greek from Cos, son of Poseidon

Eurystheus - king of Mycenae who imposed labors upon Heracles

Eurytus - (1) son of Actor, father of Thalpius; (2) an Oechalian from Thessaly

Evenus - (1) son of Selepius, father of Mynes and Epistrophus; (2) father of Marpessa

Ganymedes - son of Tros, so beautiful that Zeus bore him off to be his cup bearer

Gargarus - a peak of Mount Ida

Glaucus - (1) son of Hippolochus, leader of Lycians, ally of the Trojans; (2) father of Bellerophon

Grogon - one of three monstrous sisters whose heads were covered with serpents instead of hair. Medusa, slain by Perseus, is the best known. Her head adorned the Aegis

Granicus - river rising on Mount Ida

Hades - the god of the underworld; his abode

Halizones - Pontic allies of the Trojans from northern Asia Minor

Hebe - daughter of Zeus and Hera, wife of Heracles, a kind of maidservant among the gods

Hecabe (Hecuba) - wife of Priam, mother of Hector

Hector - son of Priam and Hecabe, husband of Andromache, father of Astyanax; the heroic leader of the Trojans

Helen - daughter of Zeus and Leda, sister of Castor and Polydeuces, wife of Menelaus, mistress of Paris

Helenus - (1) son of Priam, best of the Trojan seers; (2) Greek, slain by Hector and Ares

Helicë - town in Achaea, in the northern Peloponnesus, with a shrine of Poseidon

Hellas - originally a district in Thessaly, later a name for all Greece

Hellenes - inhabitants of Hellas, in Thessaly

Hellespont - narrow channel between Europe and Asia, through which the Black Sea empties into the Mediterranean

Hephaestus - god of smiths; son of Zeus and Hera, husband of Aphrodite

Hera - queen of the gods; sister and wife of Zeus, sister of Poseidon; favors the Greeks

Heracles - son of Zeus and Alcmena, performer of the famous labors, father of Tlepolemus and Thessalus

Hermes - god of commerce and travel, escort of the dead, escort of Priam to Achilles

Hippolochus - (1) son of Bellerophon, father of Glaucus; (2) Trojan slain by Agamemnon

Hyades - seven stars in Taurus, whose rising marks the beginning of the rainy season

Hypereia - a spring in Pelasgian Argos, in northern Greece

Hypsenor - (1) Trojan slain by Eurypylus; (2) Greek slain by Deiphobus

Iapetus - a Titan

Iardanus - (1) river in Crete; (2) river in Elis, in the Peloponnesus

Iasus - Athenian slain by Aeneas

Icarian Sea - part of Mediterranean southwest of Asia Minor

Ida - mountian range near Troy

Idaeus - (1) son of Dares, a Trojan; (2) Trojan herald, charioteer of Priam

Idomeneus - leader of the Cretans, a Greek hero

Ilios - Troy

Illus - son of Tros, father of Laomedon, an ancestor of Priam

Imbros - island off the coast of Thrace

Iris - goddess of the rainbow, messenger of the gods

Ithaca - island home of Odysseus, off western Greece

Jason - leader of the Argonauts, father of Euneus

Lacedaemon - district in the Peloponnesus; its capital was Sparta

Laertes - father of Odysseus (called "son of Laertes")

Lampus - (1) son of Laomedon, father of Dolops; (2) horse of Hector

Laodicë - (1) daughter of Agamemnon; (2) daughter of Priam, wife of Helicaon

Laodocus - (1) Antenor's son, a Trojan; (2) Greek, comrade of Antilochus

Laomedon - father of Priam

Lapiths - a tribe in Thessaly famous for their battle with the centaurs

Lectus - promontory on the Trojan coast opposite Lesbos

Lelegians - piratical tribe in southern Asia Minor

Lemnos - island west of Troad

Lesbos - island off Troad, home of Sappho and Alcaeus

Leto - mistress of Zeus, mother of Apollo and Artemis

Lycaon - (1) father of Pandarus; (2) son of Priam, slain by Achilles

Lycia - (1) region in the southwest corner of Asia Minor; (2) district on river Aesepus on Mount Ida

Lycurgus - (1) son of Dryas, who banished the worship of Dionysus from his country; (2) Arcadian warrior

Machaon - son of Asclepius, a Greek physician, wounded by Hector

Maeander - a river in Asia Minor famous for its winding course (hence "meander")

Maeonia - another name for Lydia, in Asia Minor

Mecisteus - (1) son of Talaus, brother of Adrastus, father of Euryalus; (2) companion of Antilochus, slain by Polydamas

Medon - (1) son of Oileus, stepbrother of Aias, leader of Methonians, slain by Aeneas; (2) Lycian warrior

Meges - great-nephew of Odysseus, leader of the men of Dulichium

Meleager - son of Oeneus and Althaea, husband of Cleopatra, slayer of the Calydonian boar

Menelaus - son of Atreus, brother of Agamemnon, husband of Helen, king of Sparta

Menoetius - father of Patroclus (called "son of Menoetius")

Meriones - son of Molus, squire of Idomeneus

Miletus - city in Crete

Minos - famous king of Crete, son of Zeus and Europa, father of Deucalion, Ariadne, and Phaedra, judge of the dead

Mycenae - city in Peloponnesus, home of Agamemnon

Myrmidons - people living in Phthia in Thessaly, ruled over by Achilles; hence, his followers at Troy

Mysians - (1) a tribe on the Danube; (2) their kindred living in Asia Minor, allies of the Trojans

Neleus - father of Nestor (called "son of Neleus")

Neoptolemus - son of Achilles

Nereids - the fifty daughters of Nereus

Nereus - a minor sea divinity, father of Thetis and of forty-nine other daughters

Nestor - son of Neleus, king of Pylos, father of Antilochus and Thrasymedes; his counsel was much respected by the Greeks

Niobe - daughter of Tantalus, wife of Amphion, king of Thebes, whose twelve children were slain by Apollo and Artemis; in her grief, she was changed to stone

Oceanus - a Titan, god of the sea; husband of Tethys

Odius - (1) Trojan ally slain by Agamemnon; (2) Greek herald

Odysseus - son of Laertes and Ctimene, husband of Penelope, father of Telemachus, king of the Cephallenians, living in Ithaca; the wiliest of the Greek leaders, hero of the *Odyssey*

Oeneus - father of Tydeus, grandfather of Diomedes

Oileus - (1) king of Locris, father of Aias and Medon; (2) Trojan charioteer slain by Agamemnon

Olympus - mountain in Thessaly, supposedly the home of the gods

Ophelestes - (1) Trojan slain by Teucer; (2) Paeonian slain by Achilles

Opheltius - (1) Greek slain by Hector; (2) Trojan slain by Euryalus

Orchomenus - (1) city in Boeotia; (2) city in Arcadia

Orestes - (1) Trojan slain by Leonteus; (2) Greek slain by Hector; (3) son of Agamemnon and Clytemnestra, who avenged his mother's murder of his father by slaying her and her lover, Aegistheus

Orion - mythical mighty hunter; the constellation named for him

Orsilochus - (1) variant name for Ortilochus, a Thessalian; (2) grandson of (1); (3) Trojan slain by Teucer

Otus - (1) a giant, son of Poseidon and Iphidameia; (2) Greek slain by Polydamas

Paeëon - (1) physician of the gods; (2) father of Agastrophus

Paeones or *Paeonians* - Trojan allies from Thrace and Macedonia

Pandarus - son of Lycaon, Trojan ally, leader of Lycians; a faithless archer slain by Diomedes

Panopeus - (1) father of Greek Epeius; (2) city in Phocis, in northern Greece

Panthous - father of Euphorbus and Polydamas, Trojan counselor and priest of Apollo

Paphlagonia - region in northern Asia Minor, south of the Black Sea

Paris - son of Priam, paramour of Helen, also called Alexander

Patroclus - son of Menoetius, foster brother and close friend of Achilles, slain by Hector

Pedasus - (1) town in Troad destroyed by Achilles; (2) town subject to Agamemnon; (3) Trojan slain by Euryalus; (4) horse of Achilles

Peirithous - king of Lapiths, friend of Theseus

Peisander - (1) son of Amtimachus, slain by Agamemnon; (2) Trojan slain by Menelaus; (3) a leader of the Myrmidons

Pelagon - (1) leader of the Pylians; (2) squire of Sarpedon

Pelasgians - (1) early inhabitants of Greece; (2) Trojan allies from Cyme; (3) Cretan tribe

Peleus - son of Aeacus, husband of Thetis, father of Achilles (called "son of Peleus")

Pelion - mountain in Thessaly

Pelops - son of Tantalus, father of Atreus and Thyestes, grandfather of Agamemnon, Menelaus, and Aegistheus

Peneleos - leader of the Boeotians

Percotë - town in Troad

Pergamon - citadel of Troy

Periphas - (1) Aetolian slain by Ares; (2) Trojan herald

Periphetes - (1) Mysian slain by Teucer; (2) Mycenaean slain by Hector

Persephone - daughter of Demeter, carried off and wedded by Hades or Pluto, with whom she ruled the underworld

Perseus - son of Zeus and Danaë, slayer of the Gorgon Medusa, father of Sthenelus

Phaestus - (1) Trojan ally slain by Idomeneus; (2) city in Crete

Pherae - (1) town in Thessaly; (2) town in the Peloponnesus

Pheres - grandfather of Eumelus (called "son of Pheres")

Philoctetus - possessor of the bow and arrows of Heracles, he was abondoned by the Greeks on Lemnos because of a noisome wound; he had to be brought to Troy to ensure its capture

Phoenix - (1) tutor and companion of Achilles; (2) father of Europa

Phrygia - region in Asia Minor, on the south shore of the Hellespont

Phthia - city and region where Peleus and Achilles ruled in Thessaly

Phyleus - father of Meges

Podaleirus - son of Asclepius, brother of Machaon, Greek physician

Podargus - (1) horse of Hector; (2) horse of Menelaus

Polites - son of Priam

Polydeuces - Pollux, son of Zeus and Leda, brother of Castor and Helen

Polydorus - (1) son of Priam, slain by Achilles; (2) a Greek

Polyneices - son of Oedipus and Jocasta of Thebes, brother of Eteocles and Antigone, mover of the expedition of the Seven Against Thebes

Polypoetes - son of Peirithous, one of the Lapiths

Poseidon - god of the sea; brother of Zeus and Hera; favors the Greeks

Priam - king of Troy, son of Laomedon, father of Hector

Protesilaus - husband of Laodameia; the first Greek to step on Trojan soil and the first to fall

Pygmy - member of a fabulous race of dwarfs

Pylaemenes - Paphlagonian ally of Trojans; slain by Menelaus in Book 5, he appears again in Book 13

Pylos - city and region in western Peloponnesus ruled by Nestor

Pytho - Apollo's oracle on Mount Parnassus; later Delphi

Rhadamanthus - son of Zeus, brother of Minos, judge of the dead

Rhea - daughter of Uranus and Gaea, sister and wife of Cronus, mother of Zeus, Poseidon, Hades, Hera, Demeter, and Hestia

Rhesus - Thracian ally of Trojans slain by Diomedes

Rhodes - island southwest of Asia Minor

Salamis - island near Athens, home of Ajax, son of Telamon

Samos - (1) island near Ithaca; (2) island off the coast of Asia Minor

Sarpedon - son of Zeus, leader of the Lycian allies of Troy, slain by Patroclus

Scaean Gates - gates of Troy facing the Greek camp

Scamander - river rising on Mount Ida and flowing past Troy

Scamandrius - (1) real name of Astyanax, Hector's son; (2) Trojan slain by Menelaus

Schedius - (1) son of Iphitus, leader of the Phocians; (2) son of Perimedes, Greek slain by Hector

Selleis - (1) river in Elis in Peloponnesus; (2) river in Troad

Selli - priests of Zeus at Dodona

Semelë - daughter of Cadmus, mistress of Zeus, mother of Dionysus

Sestos - town on north shore of Hellespont, opposite Abydus

Sicyon - city on south shore of Corinthian Gulf

Sidon - great Phoenician city

Simois - (1) small stream rising on Mount Ida and flowing across the plain of Troy into the Scamander; (2) god of the Scamander

Sparta - capital of Lacedaemon, home of Menelaus

Spercheius - river in Thessaly

Stentor - Greek with a voice of tremendous strength (hence, "stentorian")

Sthenelus - (1) son of Capaneus, Nestor's squire; (2) son of Perseus and Andromeda

Styx - river in the underworld, in whose name the gods swore their most sacred oaths

Talthybius - herald of Agamemnon

Tartarus - place of confinement in the underworld

Telamon - king of Salamis, son of Aeacus, brother of Peleus, father of Aias and Teucer

Telemachus - son of Odysseus and Penelope

Tenedos - small island just off the coast of Troad

Teucer - bastard son of Telamon, brother of Aias; best archer among the Greeks

Thamyris - a Thracian bard blinded by the Muses for his presumption in challenging them

Theano - Trojan priestess of Athena

Thebes - (1) city in Boeotia; (2) city in Troad; (3) city in Egypt

Themis - personification of Right

Thersites - buffoon and rabble-rouser in the Greek army

Theseus - Augeus' son, king of Athens, slayer of the Minotaur

Thessaly - region in northeastern Greece

Thestor - (1) father of Calchas; (2) father of Alcmaon; (3) son of Enops, slain by Patroclus

Thetis - daughter of Nereus, wife of Peleus, mother of Achilles

Thoas - (1) son of Andraemon, an Aetolian; (2) son of Dionysus and Ariadne; (3) Trojan slain by Menelaus

Thoön - (1) son of Phoenops, slain by Diomedes; (2) Trojan slain by Odysseus; (3) Trojan, comrade of Asius, slain by Antilochus

Thrace - region directly north of the Aegean Sea

Thrasymedes - son of Nestor

Thyestes - brother of Arteus, father of Aegistheus

Titans - children of Uranus and Gaea, confined in Tartarus by Zeus

Tlepolemus - (1) son of Heracles and Astyochia, king in Rhodes; (2) Trojan slain by Patroclus

Troad - region about Troy

Troilus - son of Priam and Hecabe

Trojans - people of Troy

Tros - (1) ancestor of Priam; (2) Trojan slain by Achilles

Troy - scene of the *Iliad*; city in northwestern Asia Minor, enriched by tolls of the Hellespont; also called Ilios

Tydeus - son of Oeneus, father of Diomedes, slain by Melanippus in expedition of the Seven Against Thebes

Xanthus - (1) Trojan slain by Diomedes; (2) one of Achilles' horses; (3) river in Lycia in Asia Minor; (4) another name for the Trojan river Scamander; (5) one of Hector's horses

Zeus - king of the gods; son of Cronos; husband of Hera; father of gods and men

STORY AND PLOT SUMMARY

The *Iliad* is a poem of nearly 16,000 lines, divided into twenty-four books, about Ilios or Troy. It was written in the late eighth or early seventh century B.C. (about 2,700 years ago) by an Ionian poet called Homer, whose life is virtually unknown. The story begins in the tenth year of a war between the Greeks and the Trojans, around 1200 B.C. (see the Historical Outline), and takes place before the city of Troy, which dominated the entrance to the narrow straits between present-day Europe and Asiatic Turkey, known as the Hellespont or Dardanelles. The narrative action lasts several weeks.

The Greeks (Achaeans) are camped before the walls of Troy. The king, Agememnon, refuses to return his captive Chryseis to her father, a priest of Apollo. The Greeks insist, and Agamemnon reluctantly complies, but he takes the maid Briseis from Achilles in her place. Enraged, Achilles withdraws himself and his men from the battle against the Trojans. The fighting continues with the participation of the gods, who aid and favor both sides, individually and collectively. Though Zeus has ordered the other gods not to become involved in the war, they frequently defy his wishes and aid their favored individuals. Athena, Hera, Poseidon, Hephaestus, and Hermes side with the Greeks; Apollo, Ares, Artemis, Aphrodite, and Leto with the Trojans. There are inconclusive duels between Menelaus and Paris, and later between Hector and Aias. When a truce is called to bury the dead, the Greeks build a wall to protect their camp, and their ships are drawn up on the shore.

The fighting resumes and the Trojans gain the upper hand. Agamemnon and the Greeks are discouraged, and he admits his mistake in quarreling with Achilles, offering to return Briseis with other gifts and tributes in the hope that Achilles and his men will rejoin the battle. Achilles is still angry and refuses, but he does agree not to leave the next day as he'd planned.

Odysseus and Diomedes go on a spying expedition to determine the strength of the Trojan forces, and, the next day, the battle continues with increased intensity. Agamemnon, Odysseus, and Diomedes are wounded, and the Trojans, under Hector, drive the Greeks back. Achilles sends Patroclus to inquire about the battle, and Nestor pleads with him to get Achilles to fight. The Trojan assault continues; Hector breaks through the Greek wall, threatens the Greek ships, and sets one on fire. Patroclus, distressed by the plight of the Greeks, persuades Achilles to give him his armor and his men so he can battle the Trojans. Achilles agrees, and Patroclus and the Greeks drive back the Trojans to their walls, where Hector kills Patroclus and strips Achilles' armor from the body. Menelaus and the Greeks, in a desperate fight, recover Patroclus' body and fall back to the ships.

Agonized and grief-stricken by the death of Patroclus, Achilles vows revenge and prepares for battle. At the request of Thetis, mother of Achilles, Hephaestus (god of smiths) makes a brilliant new set of armor for Achilles, who, though warned by Thetis and his own immortal horses, Aanthus and Balius, that he is soon fated to die, goes into battle, kills many, and drives the Trojans back inside their walls. They fight; Hector is killed and Achilles drags his body behind his chariot to the ships. Achilles gives Patroclus a magnificent funeral with games and ceremonies. Hector's body is protected from harm and decay by the gods, and Hermes, escort of the dead, brings Priam, Hector's father, to Achilles to ask for his son's body. Achilles pities the old man; they grieve together and Priam returns to Troy with Hector's body. A truce is arranged and Hector is properly buried, which ends the *Iliad*.

As had been foretold, Achilles meets his own death soon after, killed by Paris. Troy is captured and destroyed by the ruse of the Trojan Horse. Most of the defenders are killed or forced into slavery. Aeneas and his clan and the Greeks leave in their ships. Their stories are told by Homer in the *Odyssey* and Virgil in the *Aeneid*.

The Trojan War was verified as historical fact by the archaeological discoveries in the late nineteenth century of Heinrich Schliemann and his successors, though it was not the legendary battle described in the *Iliad*. The many myths and legends of the Trojan War were told and retold by bards over the centuries and, probably about four hundred years after the event, were collected and shaped into the form known as the *Iliad*. It is still not certain whether Homer was one poet or several. Many details of the Trojan War were imperfectly remembered or altered, such as the kind of shields used and the omission of brutal customs.

HISTORICAL OUTLINE

By about 2700 B.C. Cretan or Minoan civilization became a part of the Bronze Age, which had developed earlier in Asia Minor and Egypt. Probably monarchical, Minoan civilization was characterized by its elegant palaces, advanced and imaginative arts, a love of sports rather than war, and a dominating maritime and trade presence in the Aegean. The Minoans' language was not very developed, and their religion was practiced in caves and open-air shrines rather than in formal temples. Sometime after 1700 B.C. the technology of bronze was adopted by the people of the Greek mainland, and villages became towns with palaces and fortresses. The Mycenaean Age had begun, lasting until sometime after 1200 B.C., when Dorians, with iron weapons, invaded from the north, destroying Mycenae and other cities by 1100 B.C. and ushering in the Dark Age, which lasted three centuries before the beginning of the classical age of Greek civilization.

The Mycenaean Age was one of a warrior society ruled by a warlord aristocracy whose power and wealth were based on military prowess and new implements of war—long bronze swords, large shields, and horse-drawn war chariots. Comparable to Viking society, it was a heroic age, whose energy and purpose was wealth, fame, and power, gained by war, plunder, and piracy. The common people were exploited or enslaved. Minoan civilization declined after 1400 B.C. and Knossos was destroyed by earthquakes and Mycenaean invaders. The power and prosperity of the Mycenaeans reached new heights after 1400 B.C. when they took control of the sea and the Aegean trade from the Minoans. Colonies were established in Asia Minor and Cyprus, and settlements throughout central Greece multiplied. Palaces and tombs in Mycenae and Tirynes became increasingly magnificent. The expedition against Troy was the last effort of the predatory Mycenaeans. Weakened by frequent wars, Mycenaean society could not sustain itself and was overwhelmed by the Iron Age Dorians from the north. The age of heroes had ended, but this final phase of the brilliant Aegean Bronze Age was remembered in the Homeric epics, and later Greeks looked back on the Mycenaean Age as their own heroic age, when their ancestors and the founders of their cities lived.

*   *   *

The ten-year war between the Greeks, or Achaeans, and the inhabitants of Troy, or Ilios, is supposed to have lasted from 1193 to 1184 B.C. Both Herodotus and Thucydides believed it to be historical fact, but later it was regarded as myth, until the excavations of Heinrich Schliemann in 1871 and 1890 confirmed the existence of ancient Troy and its destruction. The abduction of the beautiful Helen, wife of Menelaus, by Paris, the second son of King Priam of Troy, was the ostensible cause of the war, but more likely it was a battle for control of the Hellespont (Dardanelles) and the major trade routes it dominated.

In 1822, Charles MacLaren identified a mound in northwestern Turkey, known to have Hellenistic and Roman remains, as the site of Homeric Troy, but scholars paid little attention until Heinrich Schliemann's excavations proved otherwise. With his colleague and successor, William Dorpfield, Schliemann discovered the remains of nine cities, the seventh of which was identified as the Troy of Priam. It is thought that the Trojans, for the most part, came from Thrace to the north and Phrygia to the east. Troy was a large and prosperous city, probably because of its strategic location. It had been weakened and badly damaged by a major earthquake about one hundred years before the Greek invasion, but it was mostly repaired and rebuilt. Troy in its prime was a city of magnificent walls, gates and towers, terraces, and fine houses. Every house was provided with large storage jars sunk deep into the ground, which suggest preparations for a siege. The city was burned and completely destroyed by the Greeks. Remains of human skulls and bones imply violence. The date of destruction coincides quite closely to the estimated end of the Trojan War. The site was uninhabited for several hundred years, until resettled in the Hellenistic and Roman periods. Romans believed their ancestors were Aeneas and his followers, so Troy was an important historical site.

ABOUT THE TRANSLATOR

Michael Pierce Reck was born in Washington, D.C., in 1928 and went to school there. He graduated from Harvard in 1950 and, after serving in the army in Japan, took his M.A. in Far Eastern languages at Harvard, then worked for four years as an editor in New York book publishing. He later taught English, Greek, and Japanese at the University of Puerto Rico, and he continued his studies of classical and Far Eastern languages at Munich University, Germany, from which he received his doctorate.

Reck returned to the University of Puerto Rico in 1967 to teach, and his book *Ezra Pound: A Close-Up* was published in the same year. In 1983–84 he was Fulbright Professor of American Literature in Erlangen and Bamberg, Germany. He retired from the University of Puerto Rico after twenty years of teaching and lived in Germany and Austria until his death in 1993.

Michael Reck worked on the translation of *The Iliad* during the last thirty years of his life. His poetry has been published in James Laughlin's *New Directions* anthology and in a number of magazines.